W9-CEM-442

The **Princeton Review®**

Math and Science Prep for the SAT® & ACT®

Second Edition

Jonathan Chiu and the Staff of The Princeton Review

PrincetonReview.com

Penguin
Random
House

The Princeton Review
110 East 42nd St, 7th Floor
New York, NY 10017
Email: editorialsupport@review.com

Copyright © 2018 by TPR Education IP Holdings, LLC. All rights reserved.

Published in the United States by Penguin Random House LLC, New York, and in Canada by Random House of Canada, a division of Penguin Random House Ltd., Toronto.

The material in this book was previously published as *Math Workout for the SAT, 4th Edition*, a trade paperback published by Random House, an imprint and division of Penguin Random House LLC, in 2016, and *Math and Science Workout for the ACT, 3rd Edition*, a trade paperback published by Random House, an imprint and division of Penguin Random House LLC, in 2015.

Terms of Service: The Princeton Review Online Companion Tools ("Student Tools") for retail books are available for only the two most recent editions of that book. Student Tools may be activated only once per eligible book purchased for a total of 24 months of access. Activation of Student Tools more than twice per book is in direct violation of these Terms of Service and may result in discontinuation of access to Student Tools Services.

ISBN: 978-0-525-56753-0
ISSN: 2575-5153

SAT is a registered trademark of the College Board, which is not affiliated with The Princeton Review.

ACT is a registered trademark of ACT, Inc., which is not affiliated with The Princeton Review.

The Princeton Review is not affiliated with Princeton University.

Editor: Aaron Riccio
Production Editor: Liz Rutzel
Production Artist: Craig Patches

Printed in the United States of America on partially recycled paper.

10 9 8 7 6 5 4 3 2 1

Second Edition

Editorial

Rob Franek, Editor-in-Chief
Casey Cornelius, VP Content Development
Mary Beth Garrick, Director of Production
Selena Coppock, Managing Editor
Meave Shelton, Senior Editor
Colleen Day, Editor
Sarah Litt, Editor
Aaron Riccio, Editor
Orion McBean, Associate Editor

Penguin Random House Publishing Team

Tom Russell, VP, Publisher
Alison Stoltzfus, Publishing Director
Jake Eldred, Associate Managing Editor
Ellen Reed, Production Manager
Suzanne Lee, Designer

Acknowledgments

The Princeton Review would like to thank the following individuals for their help on this book: Christina Bonvicino, Chris Chimera, Amy Minster, Melissa Hendrix, Kathryn Menefee, Jonathan Edwards, Erik Kolb, Eliz Markowitz, and Steve Voigt, as well as Jonathan Chiu, the National ACT & SAT Content Director at The Princeton Review.

The Princeton Review would also like to thank our marvelous production team of Liz Rutzel and Craig Patches, for their attention to both small details and big pictures.

Special thanks to Adam Robinson, who conceived of and perfected the Joe Bloggs approach to standardized tests and many of the other successful techniques used by The Princeton Review.

Contents

Get More (Free) Content

1 Go to **PrincetonReview.com/cracking.**

2 Enter the following ISBN for your book: 9780525567530.

3 Answer a few simple questions to set up an exclusive Princeton Review account. (If you already have one, you can just log in.)

4 Click the "Student Tools" button, also found under "My Account" from the top toolbar. You're all set to access your bonus content!

Need to report a potential **content** issue?

Contact **EditorialSupport@review.com**.
Include:

- full title of the book
- ISBN number
- page number

Need to report a **technical** issue?

Contact **TPRStudentTech@review.com**
and provide:

- your full name
- email address used to register the book
- full book title and ISBN
- computer OS (Mac/PC) and browser (Firefox, Safari, etc.)

The Princeton Review®

Once you've registered, you can...

- Take a full-length practice PSAT, SAT, and/or ACT

- Get valuable advice about the college application process, including tips for writing a great essay and where to apply for financial aid

- If you're still choosing between colleges, use our searchable rankings of *The Best 382 Colleges* to find out more information about your dream school

- Check to see if there have been any corrections or updates to this edition

Look For These Icons Throughout The Book

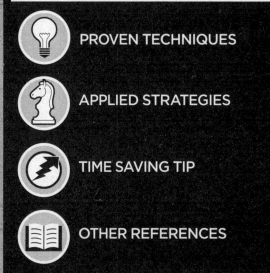

PROVEN TECHNIQUES

APPLIED STRATEGIES

TIME SAVING TIP

OTHER REFERENCES

Chapter 1
Introduction to the Math Sections of the ACT and SAT and the Science Section of the ACT

WELCOME

Standardized tests are an important part of college admissions. While many schools do not require applicants to submit either ACT or SAT scores, most require one of them. For a long time, different schools would accept only one or the other. If you wanted to apply to schools in the Midwest, you took the ACT; if you wanted to apply to schools on the East or West Coast, you took the SAT.

The good news is that these rules are obsolete. All schools that require a standardized test will take either the ACT or SAT.

This is good news indeed for test takers. While there are many similarities between the two tests, many students find they do better on one than the other. The expert advice of The Princeton Review is to take whichever test's practice version you do better on. While you can certainly take both, you should focus your efforts on one for substantive score improvement. True improvement takes hard work, and it can be tough to become an expert in both. And because schools will take either one, you won't win any brownie points for punishing yourself.

Because you bought this book, we assume you've already made the decision to boost your SAT or ACT score. This book provides a strategic and efficient way to improve your scores, specifically on the Math and Science sections. For a more thorough review of content and exhaustive practice, we recommend purchasing the latest editions of *Cracking the SAT* or *Cracking the ACT*.

FUN FACT ABOUT THE SAT AND ACT

The SAT and ACT are nothing like the math and science tests you take in school. All the content review and strategies we teach in the following lessons are based on the specific structure and format of these tests. This will help you develop an overall test-taking strategy. Then you need to learn some powerful test-taking skills, which will help you think your way through specific types of problems. Before you can beat a test, you have to know how it's built.

Structure of the SAT

The SAT is made up of 4 multiple-choice tests and an optional essay. The Math sections also have a handful of questions that are free-response. Like the ACT, the sections are always given in the same order.

Reading	Writing and Language	Math: No Calculator	Math: Calculator	Essay
65 minutes	35 minutes	25 minutes	55 minutes	50 minutes
52 questions	44 questions	20 questions	38 questions	1 Essay

Structure of the ACT

The ACT is also made up of four multiple-choice tests and an optional Writing test.

The five tests are always given in the same order.

English	Math	Reading	Science	Writing
45 minutes	60 minutes	35 minutes	35 minutes	40 minutes
75 questions	60 questions	40 questions	40 questions	1 Essay

If you feel like you need help with the English and Reading sections, please see our companion book, *Reading and Writing Prep for the SAT & ACT.*

Scoring on the SAT

When students and schools talk about SAT scores, they mean the composite score, a range from 400–1600. The composite is the total combined from the Evidence-based Reading and Writing and Language, or Verbal, sections, and from the Math sections. Both are scored from 200–800.

Your Math section score combines your raw scores from both the no calculator and calculator sections, so out of the 20 questions in Section 3 and 38 questions in Section 4, you can gain up to 58 raw points. This total raw score is then converted to a scaled score falling between 200 and 800 points. These scores are reported in 10-point increments, so you could score a 510 or a 520, but not a 515. This, in turn, makes up half of your total score. To get that total, simply add your Math score to your Evidence-Based Reading and Writing score, based on Sections 1 and 2.

When you receive your scores, you'll notice a number of other scores as well. These are your "test" scores, "cross-test" scores, and "subscores." Your "test" scores refer to the Reading, Writing and Language, and Math sections individually and are reported on a scale of 10–40. The two cross-test scores are also reported on a scale of 10–40 but cover questions that fall into the category of "Analysis in Science" or "Analysis of History/Social Studies." These questions can appear in any of the tests, including the Reading or Writing and Language tests. Lastly, the subscores tallied within the Math sections are Heart of Algebra, Problem Solving and Data Analysis, and Passport to Advanced Math. Each of these is reported on a scale of 1–15.

For information on how the SAT Essay is scored, see The Princeton Review's *Reading and Writing Prep for the SAT & ACT.*

Scoring on the ACT

When students and schools talk about ACT scores, they mean the composite score, a range of 1–36. The composite is an average of the four multiple-choice tests, each scored on the same 1–36 scale. Neither the Writing test score nor the combined English plus Writing score affects the composite.

Whether you look at your score online or wait to get it in the mail, the biggest number on the page is always the composite. While admissions offices will certainly see the individual scores of all five tests (and their subscores), schools will use the composite to evaluate your application, and that's why, in the end, it's the only one that matters.

The composite is an average: Let the full weight of that sink in. Do you need to bring up all four scores equally to raise your composite? Do you need to be a superstar in all four tests? Should you focus more on your weaknesses than your strengths? No, no, and absolutely not. The best way to improve your composite is to shore up your weaknesses but exploit your strengths as much as possible.

Since 2015, ACT score reports have included subscores in addition to the traditional (1–36) ACT score. These indicators are designed to measure student performance and predict career readiness, as well as competency in STEM (Science, Technology, Engineering, Mathematics) and English language arts. ACT believes that these additional scores will give students better insight into their strengths and how those strengths can be harnessed for success in college and beyond. In addition to the 1–36 score for each of the tests and their composite score, students will now see score breakdowns in the following categories:

- STEM score: This score represents students' overall performance on the math and science sections of the ACT. The goal of this score is to help students better understand their strengths in math and science and how they might use those strengths to guide their academic and career goals.

- Progress Toward Career Readiness Indicator: This is meant to help students understand the extent to which they are prepared for a future career. It can also help teachers guide their students towards numerous career pathways.

- English Language Arts Score: This score measures achievement in the English, reading, and writing portions of the exam (for students who take all three of those sections), and allows students to see how their performance compares with others.

- Text Complexity Progress Indicator: This is intended to help students determine how well they understand the kinds of complex texts that they will encounter in college and whether they need to improve. This score is based on a student's performance on all the writing passages.

As we said before, these changes to the test won't impact how students test or the types of questions they'll need to answer, but rather how their scores are reported and the kind of information they'll be able to gather from their results.

For more information on how the ACT Writing Test is scored, see The Princeton Review's *Reading and Writing Prep for the SAT & ACT.*

What's a Good Score?

Simply put, a good score is the one that gets you into the college of your dreams.

So, what's your first step to figuring out what's a good score for *you*? Start doing some research! Make a list of the schools you'd most like to attend and look into their average/median scores to get an idea of what you'll need to score to be considered for admission (we're a bit biased, but we've heard **www.princetonreview.com** and *The Best 382 Colleges* are both great resources for college research). From there, take a practice test and start putting a plan in place to hit your goal score. While colleges consider a LOT of factors when making admissions decisions, your SAT or ACT results are a big factor, and can be just what you need to get your foot in the door at the school of your dreams.

Timing on the SAT and ACT

Time is your enemy on the ACT. You have exactly one minute per question on the Math section and less than a minute on the Science section. The SAT Math sections are a bit more generous with time, but it's not as if there's extra time for reading wordy problems of doing tedious calculations in these sections. The Princeton Review's strategies are all based on this time crunch. We'll help you decide which questions to do, how to tackle them efficiently, and how to avoid making careless mistakes.

Math Content on the SAT and ACT

On the SAT Math test, there are two sections. The first one is shorter and calculator use is not allowed. The questions lean more toward conceptual ideas and algebraic manipulation problems. The second Math section is longer, allows for calculator use, and contains the statistical concepts that fall under the Problem Solving and Data Analysis subscore as well as some paired questions based on the same graph or set-up. The multiple-choice questions have 4 answers and are in a loose order of difficulty. Some questions won't have answers but are free-response, featuring grids into which the answers must be entered. The difficulty goes back to easy with the first of these "grin-ins" and gets a bit harder throughout this small subsection. The topics focus heavily on algebra, functions, and statistics, with only a few geometry questions appearing on the test.

The ACT Math section contains 60 multiple-choice questions in a rough order or difficulty. All the questions have 5 answer choices. Like the SAT, some of these questions will also be paired and based on the same introductory information. The topics tested range from algebra and geometry to trigonometry. There will only ever be 4 trig questions, but a few hard concepts like log, matrices, and vectors may show up. The main areas of focus on the ACT Math test are algebra and geometry.

Both tests include word problems and straightforward plug-and-chug calculation problems. The two main differences in the Math content of the tests are that the SAT has grid-ins and contains a handful of questions based on scientific studies, where few or no calculations are required.

Science Content on the ACT

The ACT Science section consists of 40 multiple-choice passage-based questions. There are typically 6 passages, but there may be 7, so check this out before starting the section to manage your time appropriately.

The passages, which are in no particular order, may feature charts and diagrams, multiple experiments, or differing viewpoints. The questions will require you to look up values, predict values, determine trends, and synthesize information. Though students tend to think of the Science test as similar to the Math test, it is really a lot like Reading—it is an open-book test and *most* of the answers are on the page. The one or two questions with answers that cannot be found on the page rely on some basic scientific knowledge that ACT assumes students should have.

Chapter 2
Strategies

You will raise your SAT or ACT score by working smarter, not harder, and a smart test taker is a strategic test taker. You will target specific content to review, you will apply an effective and efficient approach, and you will employ the common sense that frequently deserts many of us when we pick up a number 2 pencil. Each test on the SAT or ACT demands a different approach, and even the most universal strategies vary in their applications. In the chapters that follow, we'll discuss these terms in greater detail customized to Math and Science.

Math Order of Difficulty

In order to formulate a test-taking strategy, it can be helpful to understand the breakdown of the math sections. The questions are arranged in a rough order of difficulty, with most easier questions at the beginning of each section and most harder questions at the end. The majority of the test tends to be at a medium difficulty, somewhere between these two extremes. To better help you practice, we've included a variety of problems that give you exposure to questions of all types and categories, approximating the test-writers easy, medium, and hard categories. Your individual approach will likely differ in some areas, which is why we also suggest using the following section to craft an ideal approach.

Personal Order of Difficulty (POOD)

If time is going to run out, would you rather it run out on the most difficult questions or on the easiest questions? Of course you want it to run out on the points you are less likely to get right. The trick is to find all of the easiest questions and get them done first.

The Best Way to Bubble In

Work one page at a time, circling your answers right on the booklet. Transfer a page's worth of answers to the answer sheet. It's better to stay focused on working questions rather than disrupt your concentration to find where you left off on the answer sheet. You'll be more accurate at both tasks. Do not wait to the end, however, to transfer all the answers of that test on your answer sheet. Go one page at a time.

Now

Does a question look okay? Do you know how to do it? Do it *Now*.

Later

Does a question make you go, "hmm"? If you can't find a way to get your pencil moving right away, consider leaving it and coming back *Later*. Circle the question number for easy reference to return.

Never

Test taker, know thyself. Know the topics that are most difficult for you, and learn the signs that flash danger. Don't waste time on questions you should *Never* do. Instead, use more time to answer the Now and Later questions accurately.

Pacing

Almost everybody works too fast on the math sections of the SAT and ACT, losing a lot of points due to careless errors on easy question and spending way too much time on difficult questions. This isn't your usual math situation—you don't get *partial credit* for "having the right idea." The only thing that matters is what you bubble in on your answer sheet. Go slowly enough to avoid careless errors on Now questions, but go quickly enough to get to as many Later questions as you can.

Knowing the scale of the tests helps give you an idea of how many questions you need to attempt to get your goal score. On each test of the SAT, the number of correct answers converts to a scaled score of 200–800, and the ACT does the same on a scale of 1–36. The test writers work hard to adjust the scale of each test at each administration as necessary to make all scaled scores comparable, smoothing out any differences in level of difficulty across test dates. Thus, there is no truth to any one test date being "easier" than the others, but you can expect to see slight variations in the scale from test to test.

The following scales give you a general idea of the way raw scores convert to scaled scores on these tests.

SAT Math Pacing

Scale Score	Raw Score	Scale Score	Raw Score	Scale Score	Raw Score
200	0–1	440	19	620	41
210	2	450	20	630	42
230	3	460	21	640	43
240	4	470	22	650	44
260	5	480	23–24	660	45
280	6	490	25	670	46–47
290	7	500	26	680	48
310	8	510	27	690	49
320	9	520	28–29	700	50
330	10	530	30	710	51
340	11	540	31	730	52
360	12	550	32	740	53
370	13	560	33–34	750	54
380	14	570	35	760	55
390	15	580	36	780	56
410	16	590	37	790	57
420	17	600	38–39	800	58
430	18	610	40		

ACT Math Pacing

Scale Score	Raw Score	Scale Score	Raw Score	Scale Score	Raw Score
36	60	27	45–47	18	24–25
35	59	26	42–44	17	21–23
34	58	25	40–41	16	17–20
33	56–57	24	37–39	15	14–16
32	55	23	35–36	14	11–13
31	54	22	33–34	13	9–10
30	52–53	21	31–32	12	7–8
29	50–51	20	29–30	11	6
28	48–49	19	26–28	10	5

Our advice is to add about 5 questions to your targeted raw score. You have a cushion to get a few wrong—nobody's perfect—and you're likely to pick up at least a few points from your LOTDs. Track your progress on practice tests to pinpoint your target score.

Let's say your goal on ACT Math is a 24. Find 24 under the scale score column, and you'll see that you need 37–39 raw points. Take all 60 minutes and work 45 questions, using your Letter of the Day on 15 Never questions. With 60 minutes to work on just 45 questions, you'll raise your accuracy on the Now and Later questions. You may get a few wrong, but you're also likely to pick up a few points in your LOTDs, and you should hit your target score of 24. Spend more time to do fewer questions, and you'll raise your accuracy.

Here's another way to think about pacing. Let's say your goal is to move from an SAT Math score of 600 to a 650. How many more raw points do you need? As few as five. Do you think you could find five careless errors on your last practice test that you *should* have gotten right?

ACT Science Pacing

Scale Score	Raw Score	Scale Score	Raw Score	Scale Score	Raw Score
36	40	27	32	18	16–17
35	39	26	30–31	17	15
34	--	25	28–29	16	14
33	38	24	26–27	15	13
32	37	23	25	14	12
31	--	22	23–24	13	11
30	36	21	21–22	12	10
29	35	20	19–20	11	9
28	33–34	19	18	10	7–8

For the ACT Science test, pacing is less scientific, no pun intended, than it is for Math. There is no order of difficulty of the passages or their questions. In the Science lesson that follows, we'll teach you how to pick the best passages to do first. But even the easiest passages will have some tough questions.

Our advice is to be aggressive. Spend the time needed on the easiest passages first, but keep moving to get to your targeted raw score. Unless you are aiming for a score above 27, you are unlikely to work all the passages. Just don't forget to fill in a guess for those Never questions! Use the following chart to figure out how many raw points you need, then determine the number of passages to work from there.

Process of Elimination (POE)

In a perfect world, you'll know how to work all of your Now and Later questions, quickly and accurately circling the correct answer. The ACT is *not* a perfect world. But even with a ticking clock and a number 2 pencil in your sweaty hand, wrong answers can be obvious. POE can be a great alternative on Math when you're stuck, or it may be the best way to find the correct answer on Science. But even when you can't narrow the answers to only one, using POE to get rid of at least one or two wrong answers will substantially increase your odds of getting a question right.

The Power of POE
Very often, the quickest way to the correct answer is to eliminate the wrong answer choices rather than focusing on finding the right one.

Letter of the Day (LOTD)

Using the Process of Elimination on this test means that, even if you're not 100% sure your answer is the correct one, you're able to make an educated guess and earn a raw point you might not have otherwise earned. But what about those questions that you either aren't able to eliminate any answers on or that are too time-consuming? Since there's no penalty for getting a question wrong on the SAT or ACT, regardless of whether you're able to eliminate any answers or not, always have your **LOTD (Letter of the Day)** at the ready for questions you don't know how to do, don't want to do, or simply don't have time to do.

There is one thing to keep in mind: **Pick one letter for the SAT or a two-letter combo for the ACT and stick to it throughout the test!** For example, always choose (B) on the SAT or choose (B)/(G) or (C)/(H) on the ACT. (These are just arbitrary examples—choose whichever letter or letter pair you want!) Since both tests have a mostly even distribution of answers, by maintaining a consistent guessing pattern, you have a much better chance of picking up a few free raw points than if you were to guess at random. And, let's be honest: if you find yourself running out of time, scoring a few extra points without even reading a question is pretty awesome.

Use Your Pencil

There is no doubt about it: the Math and Science sections of these tests have their challenges. There is little time, a lot of information to process, and plenty of ways to make careless errors. With so much going on in so little time, you need every tool at your disposal to take down this test. That's why it's imperative that your pencil ALWAYS be moving. Whether it's doing Math calculations, crossing out bad answers, underlining key information in the Science passage, or bubbling in answers a passage at a time, it all comes down to keeping you actively engaged in what you are doing. Don't try to do too much in your head: That's what the test makers want you to do, and they right the trap answers with that in mind. Using that pencil to do the Math or to call out relevant details in Science is a key step for reaching your pacing goals. Every note helps to keep you focused and one step ahead of the test.

Take control of the test and use everything available to you to make this test a little easier. Remember the Ps and embrace your POE, pacing, POOD, and pencil.

A Change Will Do You Good

The practice in this workbook is designed to help you find the best way for you to take the test. But that means you need to be willing to give new methods a chance, especially if you want your score to change. As the saying goes, doing the same thing over and over again with the expectation of different results is the definition of insanity.

Throughout this book, we will introduce you to all of the question types you'll encounter on these tests and we'll show you how to strategically and systematically approach them to increase your score. Really give these strategies a try; if you don't get it the first time, don't just give up and go back to old habits. You've likely been taking tests for a long time, and it may be hard to approach some of these questions in a different way, but we won't steer you in the wrong direction. Think about learning a new skill to add to something you're already good at: for instance, if you're a golfer learning a new swing or a tennis player learning a new serve. It's not that your old swing or serve didn't serve you well, it got you where you are. But in order to get better, you sometimes need to try things that might seem a little odd. At first, you might not be used to shifting the weight in your hips or adjusting the angle at which your racquet hits the ball, but with practice your new swing or new serve can take you to the next level. It just takes practice.

Be Ruthless

The worst mistake a test taker can make is to throw good time after bad. You read a question and don't understand it, so you read it again. And again. If you stare at it really hard, you know you're going to just *see* it. And you can't move on, because really, after spending all that time, it would be a waste not to keep at it, right? Actually, that way of thinking couldn't be more wrong.

You can't let one tough question drag you down. Instead, the best way to improve your SAT or ACT score is to follow our advice.

1. Use the techniques and strategies in the lessons to work efficiently and accurately through all your Now and Later questions.
2. Know your Never questions, and use your LOTD.
3. Know when to move on. Use POE, and guess from what's left.

Now move on to the lessons, and learn the best way to approach the content.

Part I
Math on the SAT

Chapter 3
Test-Taking Techniques

We'll say it again: This isn't the kind of test you get in math class. You need some special techniques for handling SAT problems—techniques that will help you go faster and that take advantage of the format of the questions. Some of the things we suggest may seem awkward at first, so practice them. If you do the math questions on the SAT the way your math teacher taught you, you waste time and throw away points.

POE (PROCESS OF ELIMINATION)

Throughout this book, always look for opportunities to eliminate wrong answers. Each time you do so, you make it easier to pick out the right answer, especially if you have to guess. If you see something wrong, eliminate it.

Calcu-later

The first of the two math sections on the SAT does not permit the use of calculators. ETS and the College Board are specifically measuring how students will perform without electronic help. Don't panic! Many of the techniques in this book will make these questions more straightforward. To make sure you're practicing a mix of skills, only use the calculator when you see the calculator symbol.

CALCULATORS

Seems like a good deal, doesn't it? Well, maybe. It depends on the test section. Even for the portion of the test for which calculators are allowed, make sure you know how you're going to solve the problem before you just start running random calculations.

> Calculators can only calculate; they can't think. You need to figure out how to solve the problem before you can begin calculating.

Calculators are great for helping you avoid silly mistakes in your arithmetic, and you should use them when you can. They can help ensure that you make correct calculations, but they can't tell you which calculations are the right ones to make.

Tips to Calculator Happiness

- Get a calculator that follows the order of operations and has keys for x^2, y^x, and $\sqrt{\ }$.

- Use the same calculator every time you practice SAT problems.

- Check each number after you punch it in.

Practicing With a Calculator

Not every problem on the calculator section is best solved with the calculator. That said, you should try solving the questions indicated in this book with the calculator icon shown above so that you have a better sense of when it's more efficient for you not to use it.

CARELESS MISTAKES

If you are prone to careless mistakes—and most of us are—you probably make the same kinds of careless mistakes over and over. If you take the time to analyze the questions you get wrong, you will discover which kinds are your personal favorites. Then you can compensate for them when you take the SAT.

In the world, and in math class, it's most important for you to understand concepts and ways to solve problems. On the SAT, it's most important that you bubble in the correct answer. Students typically lose anywhere from 30 to 100 points simply by making careless, preventable mistakes.

Some common mistakes to watch for:

- misreading the question

- computation error

- punching in the wrong thing on the calculator

- on a medium or hard question, stopping after one or two steps, when the question requires three or four steps

- answering a different question from the one asked

If, for example, you find you keep missing questions because you multiply wrong, then do every multiplication twice. Do every step on paper, not in your head. If you make a lot of mistakes on positive/negative, write out each step, and be extra careful on those questions. Correcting careless mistakes is an easy way to pick up more points, so make sure you analyze your mistakes so you know what to look out for.

PLUGGING IN

One of the most powerful math techniques on the SAT is called Plugging In. The idea of Plugging In is to take all of the variables—things like x, y, z—in a problem and replace them with actual numbers. This turns your algebra problems into simple arithmetic and can make even the hardest problem an easy one.

How To Recognize a Plugging-In Question

- There are variables in the answer choices.

- The question says something like *in terms of x*.

- Your first thought is to write an equation.

- The question asks for a percentage or fractional part of something, but it doesn't give you any actual amounts.

How To Solve a Plugging-In Question

- Don't write an equation.

- Pick an easy number and substitute it for the variable.

- Work the problem through and get an answer. Circle it so you don't lose track of it.

- Plug in your number—the one you chose in the beginning—to the answer choices and see which choice produces your circled answer.

Here's an example:

> **4**
>
> Jill spent x dollars on pet toys and 12 dollars on socks. If the amount Jill spent was twice the amount she earns each week, how much does Jill earn each week in terms of x ?
>
> A) $2(x + 12)$
>
> B) $2x + 24$
>
> C) $\dfrac{x}{2} + 12$
>
> D) $\dfrac{x + 12}{2}$

Solution: Plug in 100 for x. That means Jill spent a total of 112 dollars. If that was twice her weekly salary, then she makes half of 112, or 56 dollars a week. Circle 56. Now plug 100 into the answers to see which one yields 56. Choice (A) is 2(100 + 12) = 224. No good. Choice (B) is 224, which is also too big. Choice (C) is 50 + 12 = 62. Choice (D) = 56! Yes! The answer is (D). Here's a more complicated example:

Kimberly and Elizabeth are having lunch at a diner. The price of Kimberly's meal is z dollars, and the price of Elizabeth's meal is $4 more than the price of Kimberly's meal. They decide to evenly share the cost of lunch, and a 10% tax is applied to the meal. Which of the following expressions represents the amount, in dollars, that each of them owes, without tip?

A) $0.1z + 4.0$

B) $1.1z + 2.2$

C) $2.2z + 4.4$

D) $4.2z + 0.1$

Solution: Start by picking a value for the variable z. Let's say Kimberly's meal was $10, so $z = 10$. Elizabeth's meal was $4 more, or $14, for a total of $24. The 10% tax would add another $2.40 for a grand total of $26.40. When they split that, each will owe $13.20. Circle that number: It is the target number that answers this question. Now go to the answer choices and plug in 10 for z. Whichever one matches the target is the correct answer. Choice (A) becomes $0.1(10) + 4 = 1 + 4 = 5$, so eliminate it. Choice (B) becomes $1.1(10) + 2.2 = 11 + 2.2 = 13.2$, which matches the target number. Don't stop there, though! Occasionally, more than one answer will match the target number, so always check all four just to be sure. If more than one matches, you can just pick new values for the variables and check the remaining answers. Choice (C) becomes $2.2(10) + 4.4 = 22 + 4.4 = 26.4$, and (D) becomes $4.2(10) + 0.1 = 42 + 0.1 = 42.1$. Neither of these matches the target, so (B) is the correct answer. Notice how the value of (C) was the grand total for the meal. You might have chosen this if you missed that Kimberly and Elizabeth were splitting the cost of the meal. Make sure to read carefully to avoid careless mistakes and trap answers.

Here's a different kind of example:

At his bake sale, Mr. Heftwhistle sold 30% of his pies to one friend. Mr. Heftwhistle then sold 60% of the remaining pies to another friend. What percent of his original number of pies did Mr. Heftwhistle have left?

A) 10%

B) 18%

C) 28%

D) 36%

Solution: If you don't plug in, you may make the sad mistake of picking (A) or of working with ugly fractions. Plugging in a number is much easier. Let's say Mr. Heftwhistle had 100 pies. 30% of 100 equals 30, so he's left with 70. 60% of 70 equals 42, so he's left with 28. Here's the great thing about plugging in 100 on percentage problems—28 (left) out of 100 (original number) is simply 28%. That's it. Choice (C) is the answer.

Tips for Plugging In Happiness

- Pick easy numbers like 2, 4, 10, and 100. The best number to choose depends on the question. For example, use 100 for percents.

- Avoid picking 0, 1, or any number that shows up in the answer choices.

- If the number you picked leads to ugly computations—fractions, negatives, or anything you need a calculator for—bail out and pick an easier number.

- Practice!

The following Quick Quiz allows you to practice Plugging In before you continue. Answers and explanations immediately follow every Quick Quiz.

QUICK QUIZ #1

Easy

5

If $\dfrac{c-d}{c} = \dfrac{5}{8}$, which of the following must also be true?

A) $\dfrac{c-d}{d} = \dfrac{8}{5}$

B) $\dfrac{d}{c} = \dfrac{13}{8}$

C) $\dfrac{c+d}{c} = \dfrac{13}{8}$

D) $\dfrac{c}{d} = \dfrac{8}{3}$

Medium

13

If $\dfrac{y}{3} = 6x$, then in terms of y, which of the following is equivalent to x?

A) $2y$

B) y

C) $\dfrac{y}{2}$

D) $\dfrac{y}{18}$

Hard

$$2x + p = 7x - 3$$

$$2y + q = 7y - 3$$

In the above equations, p and q are constants. If q is 5 less than p, which of the following statements is true?

A) x is 1 less than y.

B) x and y are equal.

C) x is 1 more than y.

D) x is 2 more than y.

Answers and Explanations: Quick Quiz #1

5. **D** Plugging in is all about making your life easier, so do the easiest thing here and make $c = 8$. Now figure out what value of d makes the equation true. The numerators must be equal, so $8 - d = 5$ and $d = 3$. Use these values to test the answer choices. Choice (A) becomes $\frac{8-3}{3} = \frac{8}{5}$, which is not true. Choice (B) becomes $\frac{3}{8} = \frac{13}{8}$, which can be eliminated. Choice (C) is also wrong, because $\frac{8+3}{8}$ is equal to $\frac{11}{8}$, not $\frac{13}{8}$. Choice (D) becomes $\frac{8}{3} = \frac{8}{3}$, which is true and so must be the correct answer.

13. **D** Plug in $y = 36$, which makes $x = 2$. Now plug in 36 for y in the answer choices and look for x, which is 2. Choice (A) is something huge. Choice (B) is 36. Choice (C) is 18, which is still too big. Choice (D) is 2, so (D) is correct.

29. **C** There is a lot more going on in this question, so write things down to avoid confusion. Start with q and p since their relationship is given. If $p = 7$, then $q = 2$. Plug these values into the equations and solve for x and y. The first equation becomes $2x + 7 = 7x - 3$ or $5x = 10$, so $x = 2$. The second equation becomes $2y + 2 = 7y - 3$ or $5y = 5$, so $y = 1$. Use POE to get rid of answers that aren't true. All but (C) are false, so (C) is the correct answer.

In Question 13, you may have had a hard time coming up with numbers that worked evenly. That's OK—it takes practice. You can plug in any numbers you want, as long as they satisfy the conditions of the problem, so you might as well plug in numbers that are easy to work with.

In Question 29, you could have solved this without plugging in, but then you'd be dealing with a whole lot of algebraic manipulation. It would be easy to get lost or make a mistake while solving and substituting. Plugging in real numbers lets you turn ugly algebra into simple arithmetic problems. Use it any time you are having trouble imagining how the numbers behave. Another example of a situation in which you will be better off with concrete numbers is when you are asked for some percent or fractional part of an unknown total. Making that total a real number will make it easier to deal with.

PLUGGING IN THE ANSWER CHOICES

Good news. Unlike the math tests you usually have in school, the SAT is primarily multiple choice. That means that on many problems, you don't have to generate your own answer to a problem. Instead, the answer will be one of the four answers sitting on the page right in front of you. All you have to figure out is which one is the answer.

How to Recognize Questions for Plugging In the Answer Choices

- The question will be straightforward—something like "How old is Bob?" or "How many potatoes are in the bag?" or "What was the original cost of the stereo?"

- The answer choices will be actual values.

How to Plug In the Answer Choices

Don't write an equation. Instead, pick an answer and work it through the steps of the problem, one at a time, and see if it works. In essence, you're asking *what if (C) is the answer? Does that solve the problem?*

Here's an example:

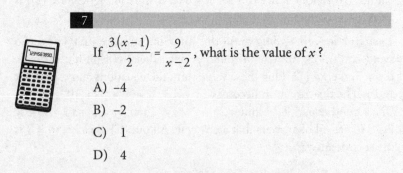

7

If $\dfrac{3(x-1)}{2} = \dfrac{9}{x-2}$, what is the value of x ?

A) −4

B) −2

C) 1

D) 4

Solution: Start with one of the answers in the middle. Let's try (C) first. Plug in 1 for x and see if the equation works:

$$\frac{3(1-1)}{2} = \frac{9}{1-2}$$

$$\frac{0}{2} = \frac{9}{-1}$$

Okay, so (C) isn't the answer. Cross it out. Try (D):

$$\frac{3(4-1)}{2} = \frac{9}{4-2}$$

$$\frac{9}{2} = \frac{9}{2}$$

The equation works, so (D) is the answer. Sure, you could have done the algebra, but wasn't plugging in easier? Once again, you've seen an algebra problem turned into an arithmetic problem, and all it required was managing simple operations like $4-1$. You're much more likely to make mistakes dealing with x than with $4-1$. Also, when you plug in, you're taking advantage of the fact that there are only four answer choices. One of them is correct. You might as well try them and find out which one it is—and you no longer have to face the horror of working out a problem algebraically and finding that your answer isn't one of the choices.

Here's a harder example:

20

A store sells shirts for \$7.50 each and hats for \$5.00 each. The store earns \$1,822.50 in one day from selling a total of 307 shirts and hats. How many shirts were sold on that day?

A) 37

B) 89

C) 115

D) 202

Solution: Start by labeling your answers and the other parts of the problem to keep your work organized in a chart, like this:

shirts	earnings from shirts	hats	earnings from hats	total earnings

A)   37

B)   89

C) 115

D) 202

Try (B) first and fill the numbers into the chart as you go. If the store sold 89 shirts, it would earn $89 \times \$7.50 = \$667.50$ from them. The store sold 307 shirts and hats, so in this case it sold $307 - 89 = 218$ hats. The earnings from the hats would be $218 \times \$5 = \$1,090$, for a total of \$1,757.50 from both shirts and hats. That's not enough money, so eliminate (B). Sometimes, you might not be sure if you need a larger number or a smaller one. In that case, just pick a direction and see if you get closer to what you want. In order to make more money in this question, the store would need to sell more of the expensive item and fewer of the cheaper item, so try a larger number of shirts. If the store sold 115 shirts, the earnings would be $862.50. The store would sell 192 hats and earn $960 for a total of $1,822.50. This matches the target earnings, so (C) is correct.

Tips for Happiness when Plugging In the Answer Choices

- Choices (B) and (C) are good answers to start with; use whichever one is easiest to work with.

- The answers will be in numerical order, so you will often be able to eliminate answers that are either too big or too small, based on the result of the first choice you plug in. If the answer to (B) or (C) was too small, you should try bigger answer choices. If the answer was too big, try smaller answer choices.

- Don't try to work out all the steps in advance—the nice thing about plugging in is that you do the steps one at a time.

- Plugging In questions may be long word problems or short arithmetic problems, and they can be easy, medium, or hard. The more difficult the question, the better off you'll be plugging in.

- Make a chart if you have a lot of stuff to keep track of.

QUICK QUIZ #2

Easy

6

If 4 less than the product of b and 6 is 44, what is the value of b ?

A) 4

B) 6

C) 8

D) 14

Medium

13

A store reduces the price of a CD player by 20% and then reduces that price by 15%. If the final price of the CD player is $170, what was its original price?

A) $140

B) $185

C) $200

D) $250

Hard

24

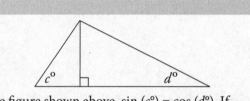

In the figure shown above, sin ($c°$) = cos ($d°$). If $c = 3y - 27$ and $d = 7y - 16$, what is the value of y ?

A)   3.3

B)   5.3

C)   10.3

D)   13.3

Answers and Explanations: Quick Quiz #2

6. **C**   Try (B) first, so $b = 6$. The product of 6 and 6 is 36, and 4 less than 36 is 32. 32 isn't 44, so cross out (B). Try a higher number, (C). If $b = 8$, the product of 8 and 6 is 48, and 4 less than 48 is 44.

13. **D**   Try (C) first. If the original price of the CD player was $200, then 20% of 200 is 40. That leaves us with a price of $160. Hey—the final price was $170, and you're already below that. You need a higher number. Try (D): If the original price was $250, take 20% of 250, which is 50. Now the price is $200. Take another 15% ($30) off and you get 200 − 30 = 170.

24. **D**   This is a hard one that expects you to know some things about trigonometry. You may not recognize the rule being tested, but you should see the opportunity to use PITA. The answers represent y, so plug them into the equations for c and d and get those values. Then it's just a matter of using your calculator's handy SIN and COS buttons to see if sin ($c°$) = cos ($d°$). Start with (C): if $y = 10.3$, $c = 3(10.3) - 27 = 3.9$ and $d = 7(10.3) - 16 = 56.1$. Use your calculator, in degree mode, to find that sin (3.9°) = 0.068 and cos (56.1°) = 0.557. These aren't equal,

so eliminate (C). It may be hard to tell which way to go, but at worst, you'll have to try three of the four answers, which should still be worth the time. In this case, a smaller number will make c negative, which probably won't work, so go bigger. Now try (D): if $y = 13.3$, $c = 12.9$ and $d = 77.1$. Since sin (12.9°) = 0.223 and cos (77.1°) = 0.223, (D) is correct. You may notice how 12.9° and 77.1° add up to 90°. This question is really testing if you know that for the complementary angles in a right triangle, the sine of one is equal to the cosine of the other, and vice versa. Using PITA, though, you could avoid that entirely.

Do a little analysis. See how the questions got harder as you went along? For the easy question, you had to read carefully, multiply, and subtract. For the medium question, you had to take percentages. For the hard question, you had to deal with geometry and were confronted with a trigonometry rule that you might not have known. For all the questions, plugging in allowed you to avoid writing an equation or getting confused. Less work is good.

ESTIMATING

A Rough Estimate May Be All That's Necessary

The less work the better. Maybe you'll only be able to eliminate a couple of answers. That's okay too.

For example:

> 8
>
> Chris can run 3.6 miles in 44 minutes. If he continues to run at this pace, which of the following is closest to the distance he will travel in 3 hours?
>
> A)   5 miles
>
> B)   10 miles
>
> C)   15 miles
>
> D)   20 miles

Solution: This question appears in the calculator section, so you could take the time to get an exact answer to it. However, the question asks for which answer is the "closest" to the actual value, and the choices are spread apart. These are clues that you can estimate. If Chris can run 3.6 miles in 44 minutes, he would go about another mile in another 15 minutes. So his speed is almost 5 miles per hour. In 3 hours, he would go about 15 miles, making (C) the most likely answer. (It's also the correct one!)

There are two advantages to solving the problem this way. First, you avoid having to do the last step of the problem and gain yourself some time. Second, you avoid even the possibility of making a careless mistake along the way.

We know you can probably find the "real" answer to this question. That's not the issue. On a timed test, with a lot of pressure on you, the fewer steps you have to do, the better off you are.

This is a fabulous piece of news—it means that you should use your eyes to estimate distances and angles, instead of jumping immediately to formulas and equations. You aren't allowed to bring a ruler or a protractor into the test. But you can often tell if one line is longer than another, or if the shaded part of a circle is larger than the unshaded part, just by estimating. That should allow you to eliminate at least a couple of answers, maybe more.

Is this a sketchy technique? Are we telling you to take the easy way out? No and yes. ETS and the College Board, the companies that write the SAT, don't mind if you use your common sense. Neither do we. And as for the easy way out…yes, that's exactly what you're training yourself to look for.

Estimating is not totally foreign to you. Think of geometry problems you encounter in real life—parking a car, packing a box, even shooting a basketball. We guess you don't take out a pad and pencil and start calculating to solve any of these problems. You estimate them, and see what happens.

Same deal on the SAT.

For example:

25

In the circle above with center *O*, the radius of the circle is equal to the length of a side of the square. If the shaded region represents two semicircles inscribed in the square, the ratio of the area of the shaded region to the area of the circle is

A) 1:16

B) 1:8

C) 1:4

D) 2:3

Solution: Look at the figure. How much of it looks shaded? Less than half? Sure. Cross out (D). If you're good at estimating, maybe you can cross out (A) as well. (Try drawing more semi-circles in the big circle and see how many will fit.) Now let's figure it out, using our good friend Plugging In: Let the radius = 2. So the area is 4π. If the radius = 2, the side of the square is 2. The shaded part consists of 2 semi-circles, each with a diameter that's the side of the square, so the radius of the small circle is 1, and the area is π. Put the small area over the big area and you get $\frac{\pi}{4\pi}$, which is a ratio of 1:4.

QUICK QUIZ #3

Easy

4

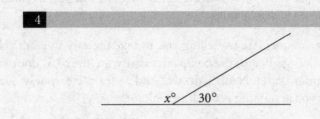

Which of the following is equal to $3x$?

A) 50

B) 150

C) 360

D) 450

Medium

13

Dan, Laura, and Jane went grocery shopping. Dan spent three times as much as Laura and half as much as Jane. If they spent a total of $50 on groceries, how much did Jane spend?

A) $15

B) $25

C) $30

D) $45

Hard

21

Three numbers, a, b, and c, have a sum of 672. The value of a is 25% less than the sum of b and c. What is the value of a ?

A) 97

B) 135

C) 288

D) 372

Answers and Explanations: Quick Quiz #3

4. **D** Angle x is pretty big, isn't it? So $3x$ is really, really big. Cross out (A). Now work it out: $x + 30 = 180$, so $x = 150$. And $3x = 450$. If you fail to estimate, you might forget to multiply by 3 and pick (B). You might fall asleep for a split second and divide by 3 and pick (A). Estimating protects you against such disasters.

13. **C** You might start by asking yourself, "Who spent the most money?" Since Jane spent twice as much as Dan, and Dan spent three times as much as Laura, Jane spent the most. You can definitely eliminate (A); it's too small an amount for Jane to have spent. Now Plug In the Answers. Begin with (B) or (C), since (A) is out. Which is the easier number to cut in half?

	J	D	L
(C)	30	15	5

    $30 + $15 + $5 = $50, so (C) is the answer.

21. **C** Start by estimating. The value of a can't be too small, if it is close to the sum of b and c. Choice (A) is probably too small, so eliminate it. The value of a also can't be more than half the total, since it is less than the sum of the other two numbers. Therefore, (D) is too big. With only (B) and (C) left, you could just guess and go, but using PITA will get you the right answer. For (C), if $a = 288$, there is $672 - 288 = 384$ left for the sum of b and c. Is $288 = 384 - \dfrac{25}{100}(384)$? Yes, it is, so (C) is the correct answer.

Tips for Estimating Happiness

- With geometry, especially on hard questions, the answer choices need to be translated into numbers that you can work with.

- Translate π to a bit more than 3; $\sqrt{2}$ is 1.4; $\sqrt{3}$ is 1.7.

- Practice estimating *a lot*, even if you're going to work out the problem—and notice how your estimates improve.

- The farther apart the answer choices, the bigger the opportunity for eliminating answers by estimating.

- If the figure is NOT drawn to scale, redraw it if you can, using whatever measurements are provided. Then go ahead and estimate. If you can't redraw it, don't estimate.

- If two things look about equal, you can't assume that they're *exactly* equal.

- Trust what your eyes tell you.

How to Apply These Techniques

To study efficiently for the SAT, you must:

- Practice plugging in. Plug in whenever and wherever you can.

- Analyze your work so that you can avoid making the same mistakes over and over.

- Do the problems in this book as though you are taking the real thing—practice with the same focus and intensity you will need on the actual SAT.

Chapter 4
Arithmetic

Much of this chapter will be review, but study it well. Even though the SAT tests many basic mathematical concepts, these concepts are tested in very particular ways. To do well on the SAT requires that you know these definitions backward and forward.

After each section of review is a Quick Quiz with a variety of questions: easy, medium, and hard. If you get *all* of them right, you're in very good shape. And keep in mind: You could leave all the hard questions blank and still get a good score. So make sure you're getting the easy and medium ones right first.

DEFINITIONS

consecutive	numbers in order (1, 2, 3, etc.)
denominator	the bottom number of a fraction
difference	what you get when you subtract one number from another
digit	a number from 0 to 9. For example, 376 is a three-digit number.
distinct	different (i.e., the distinct factors of 4 are 1, 4, and 2—not 1, 4, 2, and 2)
even	a number evenly divisible by 2 (0 is even)
factor	same meaning as "division": a smaller number that goes into your number (example: 2 is a factor of 8)
multiple	a bigger number that your number goes into (example: 8 is a multiple of 2)
numerator	the top number of a fraction
odd	a number not evenly divisible by 2
PEMDAS	you won't see that written on the test—it's a handy acronym for the order of operations: Parentheses, Exponents, Multiplication, Division, Addition, Subtraction. Learn it, live it.
places	in 234.167, 2 is the hundreds place, 3 is the tens place, 4 is the ones or units digit, 1 is the tenths place, 6 is the hundredths place, and 7 is the thousandths place.
prime	a number divisible evenly only by itself and 1. The first five primes are 2, 3, 5, 7, and 11. (Note: 1 is not prime.)
product	what you get when you multiply two numbers together
quotient	what you get after dividing one number into another
reciprocal	whatever you multiply a number by to get 1 (i.e., the reciprocal of $\frac{1}{2}$ is $\frac{2}{1}$. The reciprocal of 6 is $\frac{1}{6}$.)
remainder	what's left over if a division problem doesn't work out evenly
sum	what you get when you add together two numbers

DIVISIBILITY

On the SAT, **divisible** means dividing evenly, with no remainder. This means that 16 is divisible by 4, but 18 is not divisible by 4. To figure out whether one number is divisible by another, one option may be to use your calculator. However, if you're working in the section in which there is no calculator allowed, you may have to rely on long division.

Long division may be something you haven't done in a while and may seem a little intimidating. However, if your younger self was able to master it, you can too! Let's look at an example. Is 120 divisible by 8? Try to divide.

$$8\overline{)120}$$

Divide one digit at a time. Does 8 go into 1? No, because 8 is greater than 1. Does 8 go into 12? Not evenly, but it does go in one time.

$$\begin{array}{r} 1 \\ 8\overline{)120} \end{array}$$

Multiply 8 by 1 and subtract it from 12.

$$\begin{array}{r} 1 \\ 8\overline{)120} \\ -8 \\ \hline 4 \end{array}$$

Now go to the next digit. Carry down the 0 in 120 to the bottom to make 40.

$$\begin{array}{r} 1 \\ 8\overline{)120} \\ -8 \\ \hline 40 \end{array}$$

Does 8 go into 40? Yes, it goes in 5 times. Put a 5 above the 0 and multiply 5 by 8 to get 40.

$$\begin{array}{r} 15 \\ 8\overline{)120} \\ -8 \\ \hline 40 \\ -40 \end{array}$$

Subtract 40 from 40 to get 0. Because there is no remainder, 8 divides evenly into 120 and thus 120 is divisible by 8.

Let's look at another example. Is 124 divisible by 8? The long division will work similarly.

$$\begin{array}{r} 15 \\ 8\overline{)124} \\ -8 \\ \hline 44 \\ -40 \\ \hline 4 \end{array}$$

One difference, however, is that the 4 from 124 is carried down rather than the 0 from 120. As a result, 40 is subtracted from 44 rather than from 40, so the remainder is no longer 0. Because the remainder isn't 0, 124 is not divisible by 8.

A possible alternative to long division is reducing fractions. Remember that the fraction bar is the same as the division sign, so $120 \div 8 = \frac{120}{8}$ and $124 \div 8 = \frac{124}{8}$. To determine whether 120 is divisible by 8, reduce the fraction $\frac{120}{8}$. Because both the numerator and the denominator are even, divide both by 2 to get $\frac{60}{4}$. Both the numerator and denominator are still even, so divide by 2 again to get $\frac{30}{2}$. This can be repeated yet again, to get $\frac{15}{1} = 15$. Because this fraction reduces to a whole number, $120 \div 8 = 15$ and 120 is divisible by 8. Similarly, reduce the fraction $\frac{124}{8}$ by 2 to get $\frac{62}{4}$ and by 2 again to get $\frac{31}{2}$. This cannot reduce further. Because $\frac{124}{8}$ does not reduce to a whole number, 124 is not divisible by 8.

Factoring shows up on the SAT all over the place. That's okay; it's easy.

To find all of the factors of a number, factor in pairs. Start with 1 and make a list of all the pairs that multiply together to equal the original number:

What are the factors of 36?

1, 36

2, 18

3, 12

4, 9

6, 6

To find the prime factors of a number, simply find all the factors as shown above, and then select only those that are also prime numbers.

QUICK QUIZ #1

Easy

2

Which of the following could be a factor of $n(n + 1)$, if n is a positive integer less than 3 ?

A) 3

B) 4

C) 5

D) 9

Medium

23

An art teacher has a jar containing b buttons to distribute to her class for a project. In order to give each child in the class 6 buttons, she will need 18 more buttons. If she gives each child 5 buttons, she will have 4 left over. How many children are in the class?

A) 17

B) 19

C) 22

D) 24

Answers and Explanations: Quick Quiz #1

2. **A**   Plug In. If $n = 1$, $1(1 + 1) = 2$. None of the answers are factors of 2. If $n = 2$, $2(2 + 1) = 6$. 3 is a factor of 6, so the answer is (A).

23. **C**   Plug In the Answers, starting with one of the middle ones. If there are 22 students in the class, the teacher will need $22 \times 6 = 132$ buttons in order to give each child 6 buttons. The question says she is 18 buttons short, so subtract 18 from 132 to find that $b = 114$ buttons. In the second scenario, she has 4 buttons left over, so subtract 4 to get 110. Is that divisible by 5 to give 5 buttons to each child? Yes! 110 divided by 5 is 22, the number of children in the class. So (C) works and is the correct answer.

FRACTIONS

To add fractions, get a common denominator and then add across the top:

$$\frac{1}{2} + \frac{2}{3} = \frac{3}{6} + \frac{4}{6} = \frac{7}{6} \qquad \frac{1}{x} + \frac{2}{x+2} = \frac{(x+2)}{x(x+2)} + \frac{(x \cdot 2)}{x(x+2)} = \frac{3x+2}{x^2+2x}$$

To subtract fractions, it's the same deal, but subtract across the top:

$$\frac{3}{4} - \frac{1}{3} = \frac{9}{12} - \frac{4}{12} = \frac{5}{12} \qquad \frac{2}{x^2} - \frac{1}{xy} = \frac{2 \cdot y}{x^2 \cdot y} - \frac{x}{x \cdot xy} = \frac{2y - x}{x^2 y}$$

To multiply fractions, cancel if you can, then multiply across, top and bottom:

$$\frac{1}{2} \cdot \frac{3}{5} = \frac{3}{10} \qquad \frac{2}{7} \cdot \frac{14}{9} = \frac{4}{9} \qquad \frac{x}{x-1} \cdot \frac{x(x-1)}{x^2+2} = \frac{x^2}{x^2+2}$$

To divide fractions, flip the second one, then multiply across, top and bottom:

$$\frac{2}{3} \div \frac{1}{2} = \frac{2}{3} \cdot \frac{2}{1} = \frac{4}{3} \qquad \frac{3x}{1-x} \div \frac{1+x}{x} = \frac{3x}{1-x} \cdot \frac{x}{1+x} = \frac{3x^2}{1-x^2}$$

To see which of the two fractions is bigger, cross-multiply from bottom to top. The side with the bigger product is the bigger fraction.

$$55 \nwarrow \frac{5}{7} \times \frac{8}{11} \nearrow 56$$

56 is bigger than 55, so $\frac{8}{11}$ is bigger.

QUICK QUIZ #2

Easy

18

If $\dfrac{9}{10}y - \dfrac{7}{10}y = \dfrac{4}{3} - \dfrac{8}{15}$, what is the value of y ?

Medium

21

In a jar of cookies, there is a $\dfrac{1}{6}$ probability of randomly selecting an oatmeal-raisin cookie and a $\dfrac{1}{8}$ probability of selecting a sugar cookie. If the remaining cookies are all chocolate chip cookies, then which one of the following could be the number of cookies in the jar?

A) 16

B) 20

C) 24

D) 32

Hard

At a track meet, $\frac{2}{5}$ of the first-place finishers attended Southport High School, and $\frac{1}{2}$ of them were girls. If $\frac{2}{9}$ of the first-place finishers who did NOT attend Southport High School were girls, what fractional part of the total number of first-place finishers were boys?

A) $\frac{1}{9}$

B) $\frac{2}{15}$

C) $\frac{3}{5}$

D) $\frac{2}{3}$

Answers and Explanations: Quick Quiz #2

18. **4**   Since the fractions on the left have a common denominator, start there. Subtract across the top to get $\frac{2}{10}y$, which can be reduced to $\frac{1}{5}y$. Now get a common denominator on the right by multiplying $\frac{4}{3}$ by $\frac{5}{5}$. This becomes $\frac{20}{15}$, and now you can subtract across the top on the right to get $\frac{12}{15}$. The full equation is now $\frac{1}{5}y = \frac{12}{15}$. Multiply both sides by 5 to get $y = \frac{12}{15} \cdot 5 = \frac{12}{3} = 4$. Grid that into the box.

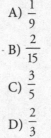

21. **C**   Plug In the Answers. Start with one of the middle choices, such as (B). If there are 20 cookies in the jar, how many oatmeal-raisin cookies are there? Not a whole number, so this can't be correct. While it is not clear whether you need a bigger or smaller number, you now see that you need a number that is divisible by both six and eight, so both fractions will yield a whole number. Choice (A) is 16, which is divisible by 8 but not by 6. Eliminate (A). Choice (C) is 24, which is divisible by both 6 and 8. Keep (C). Choice (D) is 32, which is divisible by 8 but not by 6. Eliminate (D). The correct answer is (C).

28. **D** Plug In. The total number of first-place finishers was 30. You can find the number who were from Southport by taking $\frac{2}{5}$ of 30 = 12. That leaves 18 who did not go to Southport High School. If half the 12 Southport runners were girls, that means 6 were girls and 6 were boys. If $\frac{2}{9}$ of the non-Southport runners were girls, then $\frac{2}{9}$ of 18 = 4 girls, which leaves 14 boys. That means a total of 14 + 6 = 20 boys, out of a total of 30, or $\frac{20}{30} = \frac{2}{3}$. You will be happier if you make a tree chart:

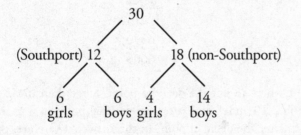

DECIMALS

To add, subtract, multiply, or divide decimals, the easiest way is use your calculator. Remember to check each number as you punch it in, and be extra careful with the decimal point. However, on the non-calculator section, you'll need to know how to do it by hand.

Addition and subtraction use the same method. Stack the two numbers with the decimal points lined up. Then add or subtract as you normally would. For example, to add 12.2 + 5.91, line it up like this:

$$\begin{array}{r} 12.20 \\ +\ 5.91 \\ \hline \end{array}$$

Notice that a 0 is added to the end of 12.2 to help the number align properly. Now carry down the decimal point and add the numbers to get

$$\begin{array}{r} \overset{1}{12.20} \\ +\ 5.91 \\ \hline 18.11 \end{array}$$

Subtraction works the same way. For example, to subtract 4.8 from 7.94, line it up to get

$$\begin{array}{r} 7.94 \\ -\ 4.80 \\ \hline \end{array}$$

Then bring down the decimal and subtract to get

$$\begin{array}{r} 7.94 \\ -\ 4.80 \\ \hline 3.14 \end{array}$$

To multiply, start by ignoring the decimals and multiplying as if the terms were whole numbers. Then count the total number of decimal places in the two numbers combined. That is the number of places that should be after the decimal point in the answer. For example, to multiply 2.13 by 3.1, set up

$$\begin{array}{r} 2.13 \\ \times\ 3.1 \\ \hline \end{array}$$

There is no need to line up the decimal points in the case of multiplication, because the decimal points are ignored in the first step. Proceed as if you're multiplying 213 by 31 to get

$$\begin{array}{r} 2.13 \\ \times\ 3.1 \\ \hline 213 \\ +\ 6390 \\ \hline 6603 \end{array}$$

Now determine where to put the decimal point. Since there are 2 digits after the decimal point in 2.13 and 1 digit after the decimal point in 3.1, there have to be 2 + 1 = 3 digits after the decimal point in the answer. Therefore, the final answer is 6.603.

$$\begin{array}{r} 2.13 \\ \times\ 3.1 \\ \hline 213 \\ +\ 6390 \\ \hline 6.603 \end{array}$$

To divide decimals, use long division. For example, let's do 7.15 ÷ 2.2 Begin by setting up normal long division.

$$2.2\overline{)7.15}$$

You don't want to deal with a decimal on the outside, so move the decimal to the right by 1. To compensate for this, do the same to the number on the inside to get

$$22\overline{)71.5}$$

Now, carry up the decimal to get

$$22\overline{)71.5}\,{}^{\textstyle .}$$

Now proceed with long division as if the decimal is not there. 22 goes into 71 three times, so

$$22\overline{)71.5}\,{}^{\textstyle 3.}$$

Multiply 22 by 3 to get 66. Subtract 66 from 71 to get 5. Carry down the 5 to get

$$\begin{array}{r} 3. \\ 22\overline{)71.5} \\ -\ 66 \\ \hline 55 \end{array}$$

22 goes into 55 twice. Multiply 22 by 2 to get 44. Subtract 44 from 55 to get 11.

$$
\begin{array}{r}
3.2 \\
22\overline{\smash)71.5} \\
-\ 66 \\
\hline
55 \\
-\ 44 \\
\hline
11
\end{array}
$$

There is 11 left over. To handle this, add a 0 to the end of 71.5 and carry down the 0.

$$
\begin{array}{r}
3.2 \\
22\overline{\smash)71.50} \\
-\ 66 \\
\hline
55 \\
-\ 44 \\
\hline
110
\end{array}
$$

Now, 22 goes into 110 five times. Multiply 22 by 5 to get 110. Subtract 110 from 110 to get 0.

$$
\begin{array}{r}
3.25 \\
22\overline{\smash)71.50} \\
-\ 66 \\
\hline
55 \\
-\ 44 \\
\hline
110 \\
-\ 110 \\
\hline
0
\end{array}
$$

Since the remainder is 0, the division is complete and 7.15 ÷ 2.2 = 3.25.

To convert a fraction to a decimal, divide the numerator by the denominator:

$$\frac{1}{2} = 1 \div 2 = 0.5 \qquad \frac{5}{8} = 5 \div 8 = 0.625 \qquad \frac{4}{3} = 4 \div 3 = 1.3\overline{33}$$

To convert a decimal to a fraction, count up the number of digits to the right of the decimal point and put that many zeros in your denominator:

$$0.2 = \frac{2}{10} \qquad 0.314 = \frac{314}{1,000} \qquad 2.23 = \frac{223}{100}$$

QUICK QUIZ #3

Easy

If $0.2p = 4$, what is the value of $4p$?

A) 2

B) 8

C) 40

D) 80

Medium

For positive integers y and z, if $z^2 = y^3$ and $y^2 = 16$, what is the value of $\dfrac{y}{z}$?

A) 0.2

B) 0.4

C) 0.5

D) 2

Hard

For all values of a, b, c, and d, which of the following

is equivalent to $\dfrac{\frac{ad}{bc}}{\frac{ac}{bd}}$?

A) $a^2 c^2$

B) $\dfrac{a^2}{b^2}$

C) $\dfrac{d^2}{c^2}$

D) $b^2 d^2$

Answers and Explanations: Quick Quiz #3

1. **D**   If $0.2p = 4$, then divide both sides by 0.2 to get $p = 20$. Then, multiply both sides by 4 to get $4p = 80$.

15. **C**   If $y^2 = 16$, then $y = 4$. If $z^2 = y^3$, then $z^2 = 64$ and $z = 8$.

    So $\dfrac{y}{z} = \dfrac{4}{8} = \dfrac{1}{2} = 0.5$.

29. **C**   Remember that to divide fractions, you flip the denominator and multiply. (Dividing is the same as multiplying by the reciprocal.)

    So $\dfrac{\dfrac{ad}{bc}}{\dfrac{ac}{bd}} = \dfrac{ad}{bc} \cdot \dfrac{bd}{ac} = \dfrac{a\,bd^2}{abc^2} = \dfrac{d^2}{c^2}$.

PERCENTAGES

For some reason, many people get hung up on percents, probably because they are trying to remember a series of operations rather than using their common sense.

A percentage is simply a fractional part—50% of something is one-half of something, and 47% is a little less than half. It is very helpful to approximate percents in this way, and not to think of them as abstract, meaningless numbers. 3.34% is very little of something, 0.0012% a tiny part of something, and 105% a little more than the whole.

Keep in mind that since percents are an expression of the fractional part, they do not represent actual numbers. If, for example, you're a salesperson, and you earn a 15% commission on what you sell, you'll get a lot richer selling Rolls-Royces than you will selling doughnuts. Even thousands of doughnuts. All examples of 15% are not created equal, unless they are 15% of the same number.

Now for the nitty-gritty:

To convert a percent to a decimal, move the decimal point two spaces to the left:

$\qquad$ 50% = 0.5 $\qquad$ 4% = 0.04 $\qquad$ 0.03% = 0.0003 $\qquad$ 112% = 1.12

To convert a decimal to a percent, move the decimal point two spaces to the right:

$\qquad$ 0.5 = 50% $\qquad$ 0.66 = 66% $\qquad$ 0.01 = 1% $\qquad$ 4 = 400%

To convert a percent to a fraction, put the number over 100:

$\qquad$ $50\% = \dfrac{50}{100}$ $\qquad$ $4\% = \dfrac{4}{100}$ $\qquad$ $106\% = \dfrac{106}{100}$ $\qquad$ $x = \dfrac{x}{100}$

To get a percent of a number, multiply by the decimal. For example, to get 22% of 50, first change the percentage to a decimal by moving the decimal point two places to the left = 0.22. Then multiply on your calculator.

If no calculator is allowed, it may be easier to use fractions. In this case, to get 22% of 50,

$$\frac{22}{100} \cdot 50 = \frac{22}{100} \cdot \frac{50}{1} = \frac{22}{\underset{2}{\cancel{100}}} \cdot \frac{\overset{1}{\cancel{50}}}{1} = \frac{22}{2} = 11$$

The second way to get a percent of a number is to translate your sentence into an equation. This is easier than it sounds. Convert the percent to a fraction and substitute × for *of*, = for *is*, and x for *what*.

What is 50% of 16?

This question translates to $x = \frac{50}{100} \times 16$.

This method is particularly useful for complicated percents:

What is 10% of 40% of 22?

This question translates to $x = \frac{10}{100} \times \frac{40}{100} \times 22$.

To calculate what percent one number is of another number, use the translation method, substituting $\frac{x}{100}$ for what percent.

What percent of 16 is 8?

This question translates to $\frac{x}{100} \times 16 = 8$.

8 is what percent of 16?

This question translates to $8 = \frac{x}{100} \times 16$.

Notice that even though these equations look a little different, they will produce the same answer.

QUICK QUIZ #4

Easy

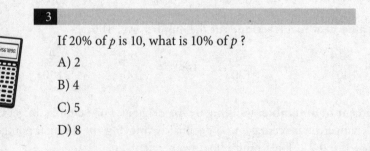

3

If 20% of p is 10, what is 10% of p ?

A) 2

B) 4

C) 5

D) 8

Medium

11

Mabel agreed to pay the tax and tip for dinner at a restaurant with her four friends. Each of the friends paid an equal part of the cost of the dinner, which was $96. If the tax and tip together were 20% of the cost of the meal, Mabel paid how much less than any one of her friends?

A) $2.40

B) $4.80

C) $19.20

D) $24.00

Hard

28

If 200% of 40% of x is equal to 40% of y, then x is what percent of y ?

A) 10%

B) 20%

C) 50%

D) 80%

Answers and Explanations: Quick Quiz #4

3.   **C**   The question asks for 10% of p and gives 20% of p. Because 10% is half of 20%, cut the value of 20% of p (10) by half (5). You could also have solved this problem by solving for p. To do so, translate the sentence: $\frac{20}{100} \times p = 10$. $\frac{p}{5} = 10$, and $p = 50$. Now do the next step: $0.1 \times 50 = 5$.

11.   **B**   First, calculate what each friend paid: $96 \div 4 = \$24$. Now do the percentage: $0.20 \times 96 = \$19.20$. Subtract the second number from the first. If you noticed that each of the four friends paid 25%, and Mabel paid 20%, you could take a fast shortcut by taking the difference, or 5% of 96. [If you picked (C) or (D), you should reread the question before picking your final answer.]

28. **C** Plug in 100 = *x*. 40% of 100 is 40, and 200% of 40 is 2 × 40 = 80.

Now the question says that 80 is 40% of *y*, so *y* = 200, and (80 = 0.4*y*).

The question asks "*x* is what percent of *y*?," which you can write out as $100 = \dfrac{p}{100} \times 200$. Or you can simply realize that 100 is half of 200, which is 50%.

More on Percentages

To calculate percent increase or decrease, use the following formula:

$$\text{percent increase or decrease} = \frac{\text{difference}}{\text{original amount}} \times 100$$

For instance, if a $40 book was reduced to $35, the difference in price is $5. Therefore, the percent decrease is equal to $\dfrac{5}{40} \times 100$, which is the same as 0.125 × 100, or 12.5%.

CHARTS AND GRAPHS

Many questions about percents and other arithmetic topics will involve charts and graphs. The key to these questions is to take a moment to size up the data before you attack the question. Pay particular attention to what units are used.

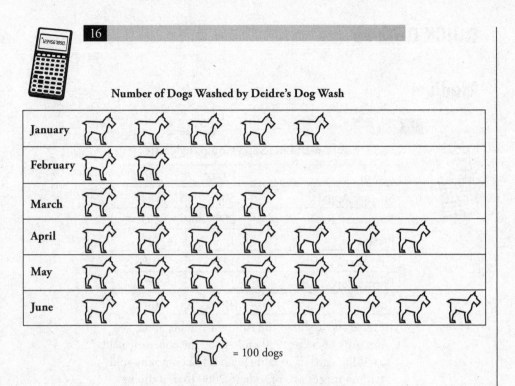

Number of Dogs Washed by Deidre's Dog Wash

January	🐕	🐕	🐕	🐕	🐕		
February	🐕	🐕					
March	🐕	🐕	🐕	🐕			
April	🐕	🐕	🐕	🐕	🐕	🐕	🐕
May	🐕	🐕	🐕	🐕	🐕		
June	🐕	🐕	🐕	🐕	🐕	🐕	🐕 🐕

🐕 = 100 dogs

Above is a chart representing how many dogs were washed by Deirdre's Dog Wash in the first half of 2004. Which month features the greatest percent increase of the number of dogs washed over the previous month?

A) February

B) March

C) April

D) June

First, note the units. Each dog shape represents 100 dogs. Now, attack the question. You need to find the percent increase, which you'll recall is the difference between two numbers divided by the original number. Choice (A) shows a decrease in the number of dogs, so eliminate it. In March, 400 dogs were washed, while 200 dogs were washed in the previous month. Using the percent increase formula, we get

$$\frac{\text{difference}}{\text{original}} \times 100 =$$

$$\frac{(400 - 200)}{200} \times 100 =$$

$$\frac{200}{200} \times 100 =$$

$$1 \times 100 = 100\%$$

None of the other choices is even close, so (B) is our answer.

QUICK QUIZ #5

Medium

Adore-a-Bubble Soda Company's Sales

Flavor	1980	2000
Snappy Apple	50%	50%
Raspberry Rush	25%	25%
Fresh Fizz	10%	12%
Cranberry Crackle	12%	10%
Purple Pop	3%	3%
Total	100%	100%

The table above shows the Adore-a-Bubble Soda Company's sales for 1980 and 2000. The company sold 200 trillion cans of soda in 1980. If the company sold 40 trillion more cans of soda in 2000 than it did in 1980, then for which flavor did the <u>number</u> of cans of soda sold increase by 20% from 1980 to 2000 ?

A) Snappy Apple

B) Raspberry Rush

C) Fresh Fizz

D) Cranberry Crackle

14

A store owner buys a pound of grapes for 80 cents and sells it for a dollar. What percent of the selling price of grapes is the store owner's profit?

A) 20%

B) 25%

C) 40%

D) 80%

Hard

27

On the first test of the semester, Barbara scored a 60. On the last test of the semester, Barbara scored a 75. By what percent did Barbara's score improve?

A) 15%

B) 18%

C) 20%

D) 25%

Answers and Explanations: Quick Quiz #5

6. **A** Use percent translation and the percent increase/decrease formula. For example, the number of cans of Snappy Apple sold in 1980 is 50% of 200 trillion. Using translation, you get $\frac{50}{100} \times 200$ trillion $= \frac{1}{2} \times 200$ trillion $= 100$ trillion. In 2000, the company sold 50% of 240 trillion. Using translation again gives you 120 trillion. Now you need to find the percent increase using the formula:

$$\text{percent increase} = \frac{\text{difference}}{\text{original}} \times 100$$

Plugging in the values you found above gives you

$\frac{120 \text{ trillion} - 100 \text{ trillion}}{100 \text{ trillion}} \times 100 = \frac{1}{5} \times 100 = 20$. This means that sales of Snappy Apple increased by 20%, so (A) is the correct answer.

14. **A** First, determine the store owner's profit. Change everything to cents so that you're only working with one unit: $100 - 80 = 20$. Now translate the question into math terms: $\frac{x}{100} \cdot 100 = 20$.

27. **D** Find the difference: $75 - 60 = 15$. Put this difference (15) over the lower number: $\frac{15}{60}$. Reduce the fraction to $\frac{1}{4}$, which is 25%. Or divide it on your calculator, which will give you 0.25. Convert it to a percentage by moving the decimal two places to the right.

> Estimating is always a good idea when you're doing a percentage question—often there are silly answers that you can cross out before you do any math at all.

RATIOS

A ratio is like a percentage—it tells you how much you have of one thing compared to how much you have of another thing. For example, if you have hats and T-shirts in a ratio of 2:3, then for every two hats, you have three T-shirts. What we don't know is the actual number of each. It could be two hats and three T-shirts. Or it could be four hats and six T-shirts. Or 20 hats and 30 T-shirts.

A ratio describes a relationship, not a total number.

Whenever you need to convert from a ratio in its most reduced form to real-life numbers, there are two key steps:

- Always add the ratio numbers to get a whole.

- Find the factor that connects a ratio number to its real-life counterpart. All of the ratio numbers get multiplied by this factor to convert to real-life numbers.

A great way to see those two steps in action is to use a Ratio Box.

In Mr. Peterson's class of 48 students, the ratio of boys to girls is 3:5.

Boys	Girls	Whole
3 +	5 =	8 ← Ratio
×	×	×
=	=	6 ← Multiply by
=	=	=
+	=	48 ← Actual number

i. How many girls are in the class? _____

ii. How many boys are in the class? _____

iii. Boys make up what fractional part of the class? _____

iv. If you answered $\frac{18}{48}$ above, what does that reduce to? _____

Don't get the order of the ratio mixed up—if the problem says red marbles and blue marbles in a ratio of 1:2, the first number represents the red marbles and the second number represents the blue marbles.

QUICK QUIZ #6

Medium

12

If $\dfrac{x}{y} = \dfrac{4}{3}$ and $\dfrac{x}{k} = \dfrac{1}{2}$, what is the value of $\dfrac{k}{y}$?

A) $\dfrac{3}{8}$

B) $\dfrac{2}{3}$

C) $\dfrac{3}{2}$

D) $\dfrac{8}{3}$

16

The junior class at Mooreland High is composed of boys and girls in a ratio of 5:1. All of the following could be the number of students in the junior class EXCEPT

A) 24

B) 42

C) 54

D) 62

Hard

20

In a certain ocean region, the ratio of sharks to tuna to damselfish to guppies is 1 to 3 to 5 to 6. If there are 1,500 total fish in that region, how many of the fish are sharks?

A) 15

B) 100

C) 150

D) 450

Answers and Explanations: Quick Quiz #6

12. **D**   Since $x = 4$ in one ratio and $x = 1$ in the other, you can't compare them. First, make them equal. If you multiply the second ratio by $\frac{4}{4}$, you get $\frac{4}{8}$. (Notice that if you multiply all parts of the ratio by the same number, it doesn't change. It just takes an unreduced form.) Now the x's are the same in both ratios, so you can compare them, and $\frac{k}{y} = \frac{8}{3}$. You could also plug in, which would work at least as well.

16. **D**   If the ratio is 5:1, you can add the parts and get 6 students. Therefore, the number of students in the class must be a multiple of 6. All of the choices are multiples of 6 except (D).

20. **B**   Make the Ratio Box. There are always three rows: ratio, multiply by, and actual. Here, the columns are: sharks, tuna, damselfish, guppies, and Total. In the first row, enter the ratio numbers: 1, 3, 5, and 6. Add them up, and put the sum (15) under Total. As the actual total is 1,500, enter that number in the lower, right cell. What times 15 is 1,500? 100. So, enter 100 in all of the multiply by cells. You can solve for all four fish types by multiplying the ratio number by 100, or just solve for sharks, as that is the question.

PROPORTIONS

To set up a proportion, match categories on top and bottom. For example:

If 10 nails cost 4 cents, how much do 50 nails cost?

$$\begin{array}{cc}(\text{nails}) & \dfrac{10}{4} = \dfrac{50}{x} \\ (\text{cents}) & \end{array}$$

$10x = 200$, so $x = 20$ cents

The great thing about proportions is that it doesn't matter which is on top—if you match nails to nails and cents to cents (or whatever), you'll get the right answer. Be consistent.

To solve an **inverse variation** problem, use the following set-up.

$$x_1 y_1 = x_2 y_2$$

If the value of x is inversely proportional to the value of y and $y = 4$ when $x = 15$, what is the value of x when y is 12?

$$x(12) = (15)(4)$$

$$x = 5$$

To solve rate problems, set up a proportion:

If Bonzo rode his unicycle 30 miles in 5 hours, how long would it take him to ride 12 miles at the same rate?

$$\text{(miles)} \quad \frac{30}{5} = \frac{12}{x} \quad \text{(hours)}$$

$$30x = 60$$

$$x = 2 \text{ hours}$$

Harder questions may require extra work by requiring unit conversions: hours to minutes, miles to feet, etc. Be on the lookout for shifts in units within the problem.

If Bonzo rode his unicycle 2,640 feet in 5 minutes, what is his speed in miles per hour? (1 mile = 5,280 feet)

$$\text{(feet)} \quad \frac{2,640}{5} = \frac{x}{60} \quad \text{(minutes)}$$

$$5x = 158,400$$

$$x = 31,680 \text{ feet per hour}$$

$$\text{(feet)} \quad \frac{5,280}{1} = \frac{31,680}{x} \quad \text{(miles)}$$

$$5,280x = 31,680$$

$$x = 6 \text{ miles per hour}$$

Easy

2

Laura can solve 6 math questions in 12 minutes. Working at the same rate, how many minutes would it take Laura to solve 5 math questions?

A) 6

B) 9

C) 10

D) 11

Medium

12

The length of time in hours that a certain battery will last is inversely proportional to the length of time in years that the battery spends in storage. If the battery spends 3 years in storage, it will last 25 hours, so how long must the battery have been in storage if it will last 15 hours?

A) 1.75 years

B)   5 years

C) $41\dfrac{2}{3}$ years

D)   75 years

Hard

26

A factory produced 15 trucks of the same model. If the trucks had a combined weight of $34\dfrac{1}{2}$ tons, how much, in pounds, did one of the trucks weigh?

(One ton = 2,000 pounds)

A) 2,200

B) 4,500

C) 4,600

D) 5,400

Answers and Explanation: Quick Quiz #7

2. **C** $\frac{6}{12} = \frac{5}{x}$. Cross-multiply to get $6x = 60$ and $x = 10$.

12. **B**   To do this problem, it is important to know the formula for inverse variation: $x_1y_1 = x_2y_2$. In this case, the x_1 is 3 years, y_1 is 25 hours, and y_2 is 15 hours. So set up the equation as follows: $3 \times 25 = x_2 \times 15$. $\frac{75}{15} = x_2 = 5$ years.

26. **C**   You can do this two ways: You can convert from tons to pounds first or do it later. If you do it first, multiply $34.5 \times 2{,}000$. That gives you 69,000. Your proportion should look like this: $\frac{15}{69{,}000} = \frac{1}{x}$. So $15x_1 = 69{,}000$ and $x = 4{,}600$. Or you can divide 15 into 34.5, which gives you 2.3 tons per truck. Then multiply 2.3 times 2,000.

AVERAGES

You already know how to figure out an average. You can figure out your GPA, right?

To get the average (arithmetic mean) of a set of numbers, add them up, then divide by the number of things in the set:

What's the average of 3, 5, and 10? $3 + 5 + 10 = 18$ and $18 \div 3 = 6$.

Most of the time on the SAT you are not given a set of numbers and asked for the average—they want to make their questions a little harder than that. There are three elements at work here: the sum of the numbers, the number of things in the set, and the average. To get any of these elements, you need to know the other two.

The easy way to remember these relationships is by memorizing the "Average Pie."

Here's a glimpse of what that looks like:

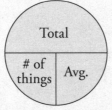

The *total* is the sum of all the numbers you're averaging, and the *number of things* is the number of elements you're averaging. Here's what the Average Pie looks like using the simple average example we just gave you.

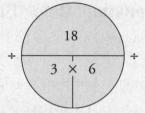

Here's how the Average Pie works mathematically. The horizontal line in the middle means *divide*. If you know the total and the number of things, just divide to get the average (18 ÷ 3 = 6). The vertical line means *multiply*. Thus, if you know the total and the average, just divide to get the number of things (18 ÷ 6 = 3). If you know the average and the number of things, simply multiply to get the total (6 × 3 = 18). The key to most average questions is finding the total.

Here's another simple example:

Problem: If the average of three test scores is 70, what is the total of all three test scores?

Solution: Just put the number of things (3 tests) and the average (70) in the pie. Then multiply to find the total, which is 210.

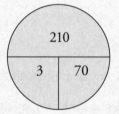

QUICK QUIZ #8

Easy

6

The average of 3 numbers is 22, and the smallest of these numbers is 2. What is the value of the other two numbers if they are equal?

A) 22

B) 30

C) 32

D) 64

Medium

17

Caroline scored 85, 88, and 89 on three of her four history tests. If her average score for all tests was 90, what did she score on her fourth test?

A) 90

B) 93

C) 96

D) 98

Hard

24

The average of 8, 13, x, and y is 6. The average of 15, 9, x, and x is 8. What is the value of y ?

A) −1

B) 0

C) 4

D) 6

6.   **C**   If the average of 3 numbers is 22, then their sum is 3 × 22 or 66. Take away the 2 and you've got 64 left. If the other two numbers are equal, divide 64 by 2 = 32.

17.   **D**   Caroline's final average was 90 on 4 tests. Therefore, you can use the Average Pie to figure out the total number of points she had on those four tests, by multiplying 90 × 4 = 360. You also know her scores on the first three tests, so if you subtract 360 − 85 − 88 − 89, you get 98 points, which is the total score she must have gotten on her fourth test.

24.   **A**   Since the average of 8, 13, x, and y is 6, you know that their total must be equal to 6 × 4 or 24. This means that 8 + 13 + x + y = 24. If you subtract the 8 and the 13, you find that x + y = 3. You also know that the average of 15, 9, x, and x is 8, so their total must be equal to 32. 15 + 9 + x + x = 32, so x + x must equal 8, and x = 4. Since you know from earlier that x + y = 3, y = −1.

MEDIAN, MODE, SET, AND RANGE

Each of these terms involves finding a value or values in sets of numbers. A **set** is just a fancy term for a list of numbers.

One common type of set question involves median.

To find the median, first put the group of numbers in ascending order. If the group has an odd number of elements, the median is the middle number.

> set: 1, 4, 9, 18, 54   median: 9

> set: 2, 4, 4, 4, 5   median: 4

If the group has an even number of elements, the median is *the average (arithmetic mean)* of the two middle numbers.

> set: 3, 15, 17, 74   median: 16

> set: 1, 6, 7, 8   median: 6.5

The remaining types of set questions are quite rare:

To find the mode, just look to see which number in the group appears the most often.

> set: 1, 1, 3, 5, 3, 4, 22, 3, 6   mode: 3

> set: 2, 5, 9, 11, 11, 15, 22   mode: 11

To find the range, subtract the smallest number from the largest.

> set: 3, 15, 28, 33, 33, 33, 42   range: 39

QUICK QUIZ #9

Easy

6

Set Q: {10, 2, 3, 5, 1, 7, 5, 2}

If the smallest and largest numbers in Set Q are removed, what is the median of Set Q?

A) 3.5

B) 4

C) 5

D) 6

Medium

12

High Temperatures

Temperature	Number of days
22	2
25	2
28	3
31	0
34	4
37	1
40	2

Janet recorded the number of days certain high temperatures were reached over a 14-day period. She later decided to add data for one more day. If the high temperature on that day was 37, what is the median temperature for the set of days?

A) 26.5

B) 28

C) 31

D) 34

Hard

28

If a set of 9 randomly selected numbers is generated, which one of the following changes CANNOT affect the value of the median?

A) Subtracting 2 from each number

B) Decreasing the largest number only

C) Decreasing the smallest number only

D) Increasing the largest and smallest numbers only

Answers and Explanations: Quick Quiz #9

6. **B** Take out 10 and 1. Now write down the numbers in order: 2, 2, 3, 5, 5, 7. The middle of the list falls between 3 and 5, so the median is 4.

12. **D** On a median question, it is essential to list out all of the numbers in order, including all of the repeated numbers. The original list of numbers, in order, is:

22, 22, 25, 25, 28, 28, 28, 34, 34, 34, 34, 37, 40, 40

Once the new number is added, the set of numbers is:

22, 22, 25, 25, 28, 28, 28, 34, 34, 34, 34, 37, 37, 40, 40

The middle number of the new list is 34. If you picked (C), you chose the original median.

28. **C** Write out any set of nine numbers, such as 1 through 9. The median is 5. If you subtract 2 from each number, the median changes to 3, so (A) is wrong. If you decrease the largest number to 4 or less, the median will change to 4, so (B) is wrong. On the other hand, no matter how much you decrease the smallest number, the median will remain the same, so (C) is correct. Choice (D) is wrong because increasing the smallest number to 6 or more will change the median.

EXPONENTS AND ROOTS

An exponent tells you how many times to multiply a number by itself. So x^3 is really shorthand for $x \cdot x \cdot x$. If you have a momentary lapse and can't remember the following rules, it may help to write out your problem the long way and work from there.

For exponents with the same base, remember MADSPM:

To Multiply, Add the exponents: $x^2 \cdot x^5 = x^{2+5} = x^7$.

To Divide, Subtract the exponents: $x^6 \div x^3 = x^{6-3} = x^3$.

To raise the Power, Multiply: $(x^4)^3 = x^{4 \times 3} = x^{12}$.

You cannot add or subtract different exponents, so $x^6 + x^3$ is just $x^6 + x^3$. You can't simplify it.

For exponents with different bases:

The trick is to try to rewrite the numbers in terms of the same base. For example:

$$6^2 \times 12^4$$

becomes

$$6^2 \times (6 \times 2)^4 = 6^2 \times 6^4 \times 2^4$$

Now you can combine terms with the same base as above.

To deal with exponents and parentheses, remember that the exponent carries over to all parts within the parentheses:

$$2(3a^3)^2 = 2[(3^2)(a^6)] = 2(9a^6) = 18a^6$$

Keep in mind that 1 raised to any power is still just 1. ($1^{357} = 1$.)

Negative numbers with even exponents are positive; negative numbers with odd exponents are negative. Fractions between 0 and 1 with exponents get smaller, not bigger.

A **square root** is just a backward exponent; in other words, the number under the $\sqrt{\ }$ is what you get when you raise a number to a power of 2.

$$\sqrt{4} = 2 \qquad \sqrt{36} = 6 \qquad \sqrt{1} = 1$$

To multiply or divide square roots, combine the numbers under one root sign and then multiply or divide as usual.

$$\sqrt{7} \cdot \sqrt{3} = \sqrt{21} \qquad \sqrt{15} \div \sqrt{3} = \sqrt{5}$$

To add or subtract square roots, first make sure you have the same number under the $\sqrt{\ }$. Then add or subtract the number outside of the $\sqrt{\ }$.

$$5\sqrt{3} + 2\sqrt{3} = 7\sqrt{3} \qquad 6\sqrt{2} - \sqrt{2} = 5\sqrt{2}$$

Note that:

- A square root multiplied by itself is just that number without the $\sqrt{}$.
  $$\sqrt{3} \cdot \sqrt{3} = 3$$

- The square root of a fraction between 0 and 1 gets bigger. For example,
  $$\sqrt{\frac{1}{4}} = \frac{\sqrt{1}}{\sqrt{4}} = \frac{1}{2}.$$

- The square root of a number, when the radical is shown, is always positive (on the SAT, anyway).

- The square root of 1 is 1.

Rational exponents combine powers with roots. To simplify the following expression:

$$8^{\frac{2}{3}}$$

First, we raise the base to the power of the numerator of the fraction. In this case, the numerator is two, so we'll square the base and get the following:

$$8^2 = 64$$

Now we'll deal with the denominator of the fraction. The denominator tells us what root to take the number to. In this case, the denominator is three, so we'll find the third root and end up with the following:

$$\sqrt[3]{64} = 4$$

QUICK QUIZ #10

Easy

Exponentially Easier
When tackling fractional exponents without a calculator, it can be helpful to take the root first before applying the power. Look at how much simpler the numbers from this example are to work with: $8^{\left(\frac{2}{3}\right)} = (\sqrt[3]{8})^2 = (2)^2 = 4$.

1

If $(3x)^2 = 81$, which of the following is a possible value of x?

A) 2

B) 3

C) 6

D) 9

Medium

If $2a + b = 8$, what is the value of 9^a3^b ?

A) The value cannot be determined from the information given.

B) 3^8

C) 9^3

D) 27^4

Hard

Which one of the following must be greater than x, if x is a real number?

A) $\dfrac{x}{4}$

B) $4x$

C) $x^2 + 1$

D) $x^3 + 1$

Answers and Explanations: Quick Quiz #10

1. **B**   Square everything within the parentheses, so you get $3^2x^2 = 81$, or $9x^2 = 81$. Divide by 9 and you get $x^2 = 9$, and x could equal 3.

13. **B**   Start by trying to get a common base. This is the key to many exponent questions. Rewrite the 9 as 3^2, so the expression in question becomes $(3^2)^a3^b$ or $3^{2a}3^b$. Now use MADSPM rules to combine the two parts of the expression. When you multiply, you add the exponents, so the expression becomes 3^{2a+b}. Now the equation comes into play. Just substitute the value of $2a + b$ as the exponent to get 3^8.

18. **C**   Because there are variables in the answer choices, plug in. Start with an easy number, such as $x = 2$. Choice (A) is less than x, so eliminate it. Choice (B) is greater than x, so keep it. Choices (C) and (D) are greater than x, so keep them as well. Now try a different type of number. If you try 0 or a fraction, you'll get rid of (B), but not (C) or (D). Try a negative number, such as -3. While (C) is still greater than x, (D) is not.

PROBABILITY AND ARRANGEMENTS

Probability measures the likelihood something will happen:

$$\text{Probability} = \frac{\text{What You Want}}{\text{What You Have}}$$

Here's an example:

> In a small garden of flowers, 3 are daisies, 4 are sunflowers, 2 are gardenias, and 3 are carnations. If a flower is selected at random, what is the probability that it will be a gardenia?

Solution: As there are 2 gardenias, the numerator of the fraction is 2. As there are 12 flowers in all, the denominator of the fraction is 12. Thus, the probability of selecting a gardenia is $\frac{2}{12}$, or $\frac{1}{6}$.

Questions about **arrangements** ask such questions as how many ways there are to order something or how many outfits are possible. These are easy to solve if you follow the steps shown for this example:

> A restaurant offers a three-course dinner menu from which a person can select 1 of 4 appetizers, 1 of 5 main courses, and 1 of 3 desserts. How many different combinations of appetizer, main course, and dessert are possible?

As we are selecting three different items, first draw three slots as place-holders:

_____ _____ _____

Let's use the first slot for appetizers. How many appetizers are there, any one of which might be selected? 4, so write 4 above the slot. The next slot is for main course. How many main courses are there, any one of which can be selected? 5, so write 5 above the slot. The final slot is for dessert. As there are 3 desserts from which the selection can be made, write 3 in that slot. Your slots now look like this:

_4_ _5_ _3_

The final step is to multiply: $4 \times 5 \times 3 = 60$. That's it!

QUICK QUIZ #11

Easy

3

Language	Gender		Total
	Boys	Girls	
French	5	11	16
Spanish	8	6	14
Total	13	17	30

The table above shows the distribution of the gender and the language studied of the 30 students in an after-school language program. If a student is chosen at random, what is the probability that the student will be either a boy studying French or a girl studying Spanish?

A) $\dfrac{3}{30}$

B) $\dfrac{10}{30}$

C) $\dfrac{11}{30}$

D) $\dfrac{13}{30}$

Medium

11

In a drawer that contains only black, blue, and brown socks, the probability of selecting a black pair of socks is $\dfrac{3}{8}$, and there are $\dfrac{1}{3}$ as many blue pairs of socks as there are black pairs of socks. If there are 12 brown pairs of socks, how many pairs of socks are there in the drawer?

A) 16

B) 24

C) 32

D) 48

Hard

25

Janice has 3 belts (one blue, one red, and one green), 3 bracelets (one blue, one red, and one green), and 3 scarves (one blue, one red, and one green). If Janice wants to create an outfit containing a belt, a bracelet, and a scarf such that each item is a different color, how many possible outfits can she create?

A) 6

B) 9

C) 21

D) 27

Answers and Explanations: Quick Quiz #11

3. **C** Remember that probability is defined as "what you want" over "what you have." Find the necessary applicable numbers from the chart. In this case, you have 30 total students, so that's the denominator. You can also tell this by looking at the answer choices. Now look for what you want: the number of boys studying French or the number of girls studying Spanish. Since you don't care if you have one or the other, you'll add these numbers. There are 5 boys studying French and 6 girls studying Spanish, so you have 11 possible candidates. Therefore, (C) is the correct answer.

11. **B** You can Plug In the Answers. Start with (C). If $\frac{3}{8}$ of the pairs of socks are black, there are 12 pairs of black socks ($\frac{3}{8} \times 32$). As there are $\frac{1}{3}$ as many pairs of blue socks as pairs of black socks, there are 4 pairs of blue socks ($\frac{1}{3} \times 12$). Add the 12 pairs of brown socks to the pairs of black and blue socks to get 28 socks—not 32. At this point, it may not be clear whether to pick a bigger number or a smaller number, so just pick a direction. If the answer is even further off, then switch directions. Try a smaller number. If $\frac{3}{8}$ of the pairs of socks are black, there are 9 pairs of black socks ($\frac{3}{8} \times 24$). As there are $\frac{1}{3}$ as many pairs of blue socks as pairs of black socks, there are 3 pairs of blue socks ($\frac{1}{3} \times 9$). Add the 12 pairs of brown socks to the pairs of black and blue socks to get 24 socks—exactly what you wanted.

25. **A** Set up a slot for each of the three items. Start with the belt. How many belts are there, any one of which Janice might select? 3, so write 3 in the first slot. Move on to the bracelet. This time, there are only 2 bracelets she might choose, as she has already chosen a belt in a particular color—that color cannot be repeated. So, write 2 in the second slot. From the scarves, Janice may select only 1, as the other two colors are already chosen, so write 1 in the last slot. Multiply to get 6. If you picked (D), you did not account for the restriction on colors; there are 27 possible combinations, but only 6 involving all three colors.

SEQUENCES

Sequence questions may show up in a couple of ways on the SAT. The first way involves a repeating pattern in a set of numbers. To attack questions like this, write out the pattern until it repeats itself. Then extend the pattern until you can answer the question.

If imaginary number $i = \sqrt{-1}$, which of the following is equivalent to i^{85} ?

Start by writing out powers of i.

$$i = \sqrt{-1}$$

$$i^2 = -1$$

$$i^3 = i^2 \times i = -i$$

$$i^4 = i^2 \times i^2 = 1$$

$$i^5 = i^2 \times i^3 = i$$

$$i^6 = (i^2)^3 = -1$$

$$i^7 = i^3 \times i^4 = -i$$

$$i^8 = (i^2)^4 = 1$$

As you can see, the pattern repeats every 4 numbers, so look for a multiple of 4 that's near 85. One that's close is 84, so i^{84} equals 1, then i^{85} goes back to i again.

If all this stuff about strange patterns of i is making you nervous, don't worry. Most of the SAT sticks to real numbers and to more predictable sequences. The main two are called arithmetic and geometric sequences.

An **arithmetic sequence** is one in which each new term is obtained by adding or subtracting the same number. Examples include {1, 4, 7, 10, 13} and {10, 5, 0, –5, –10}. The question may refer to the "common difference" between terms in the sequence. In our examples, it's +3 in the first one and –5 in the second one. You may also see words like "linear increase" or "linear decrease" in the question. These refer to the fact that graphs of arithmetic sequences are straight lines in the xy-plane.

A **geometric sequence** is one in which each new term is obtained by multiplying or dividing by the same number. Examples include {1, 4, 16, 64, 256} and {100, 50, 25, 12.5, 6.25}. The question may refer to the "common ratio" between terms in the sequence. In our examples, it's 4 in the first one and $\frac{1}{2}$ in the second one. You may also see words like "exponential increase," "growth," "exponential decrease," or "decay" in the question. These refer to the fact that there is an exponent in the equation. The graphs of these in the xy-plane will be curved, not straight, lines.

There are actually some handy formulas for **growth and decay**. When the growth is a **multiple** of the total population, as we had with our geometric sequences, the formula for exponential growth or decay is

$$\textit{final amount} = \textit{original amount} \, (\textit{multiplier})^{\textit{number of changes}}$$

Sometimes, the population changes by a constant **percent** of the total population over time, and the formula for that is

$$\textit{final amount} = \textit{original amount} \, (1 \pm \textit{rate})^{\textit{number of changes}}$$

Knowing these formulas can help you save time and make tricky questions a bit easier.

QUICK QUIZ #12

Medium

11

The first three numbers of a sequence are 1, 3, and 5, respectively. Every number in the sequence beyond the first three numbers can be found by taking the three preceding numbers, subtracting the second from the first, and adding the third. Which of the following is the sum of the first 40 numbers of the above sequence?

A) 6

B) 12

C) 24

D) 120

12

The number of bacteria in a colony is estimated over the course of 9 days, as shown in the table below.

Time (days)	Number of Bacteria
0	50
3	500
6	5,000
9	50,000

Which of the following best describes the relationship between time and the estimated number of bacteria over these 9 days?

A) Linear decrease

B) Linear increase

C) Exponential decay

D) Exponential growth

Hard

37

The balance of a savings account at a certain bank is $280 today. The customer knows that the balance will gain 4 percent interest each year for the next 2 years. The customer uses the equation $B = 280(x)^y$ to model the balance, B, of the account after y years. To the nearest dollar, what does the customer estimate the value of the account will be at the end of two years if no money is deposited or withdrawn? (Note: Disregard the $ sign when gridding your answer.)

Answers and Explanations: Quick Quiz #12

11. **D**   If you follow the sequence out, the next number is 3, and then if you keep following the instructions, the sequence repeats itself (1,3,5,3 1,3,5,3 1,3,5,3 1,3,5,3) in sets of 4. So, take the first four numbers and find the sum (12) and multiply by 10 since you actually want the first 40 numbers.

12. **D**   Start with POE. The numbers are clearly increasing, so eliminate (A) and (C), which indicate a decrease. Now figure out what kind of sequence these numbers represent. Is the same number added each time? No, the numbers increase very quickly, which means this is not a linear relationship. Eliminate (B). You could calculate that the number of bacteria is multiplied by 10 every 3 days, indicating exponential growth, but (D) is the only answer left anyway.

37. **303**   If you remember the parts of the growth formula, you can plug them into the function to make your calculations easier. The value in the parentheses is (1 + rate), and the rate is 4% or 0.04, so the number in parentheses is (1.04). The exponent is the number of changes, which is 2 years in this case. So the equation becomes $B = 280(1.04)^2 = 302.848$. To the nearest dollar, that's $303. If you forget the formula, you can still do this problem on your calculator. Just take it one year at a time. After the first year, the value of the original $280 will increase by 4% of 280, or by 0.04(280) = 11.2. So the total after one year is 280 + 11.2 = 291.2. For the second year, it will increase by 4% of this new total, or by 11.648. The total now will be $302.848, or $303.

Chapter 5
Algebra

In the section on strategy, we gave you some ways to avoid algebra altogether—but you still need to be able to work with simple equations and review some other algebraic principles that don't exactly crop up in everyday life.

SIMPLE EQUATIONS

Sometimes you can plug in with these, sometimes not. You will definitely need to be comfortable manipulating equations to do well on the SAT.

To solve a simple equation, get the variable on one side of the equals sign and the numbers on the other.

$$9x - 4 = 12 + x$$

$$8x - 4 = 12$$

$$8x = 16$$

$$x = 2$$

We just added 4 to both sides and subtracted x from both sides. Then we divided both sides by 8. You can add, subtract, multiply, or divide either side of an equation, but remember that what you do to one side you have to do to the other.

Polynomial equations look tricky but follow all the same rules of simple equations. You can add and subtract like terms—terms that have the same variables raised to the same powers.

What is the value of z if $3z + 4z + 7z = -42$?

In this case, the terms all have the same variable and are all to the same power. Thus, we can combine them to get $14z = -42$.

Now we'll divide each side by 14 and get $z = -3$.

Many times, however, it won't be that simple. Look at this example.

$$4x^2 - 3x + 5$$

$$2x^2 - 9x + 1$$

Which of the following is the sum of the two polynomials shown above?

A) $6x^2 + 12x + 6$

B) $6x^2 - 12x + 6$

C) $6x^4 + 12x^2 + 6$

D) $6x^4 - 12x^2 + 6$

Add one pair of terms at a time. The $4x^2$ and the $2x^2$ have the same variable and base, so they can be added to get $6x^2$. The answer choices have a couple of options that start this way and a couple that start with $6x^4$. As soon as you add the first pair of terms, look to the answer choices to eliminate any that don't match. Eliminate (C) and (D). The next pair of terms, $-3x$ and $-9x$, can also be added to get $-12x$. Again eliminate answers that don't match, like (A). The complete answer is seen in (B), but you likely won't have to add all the terms together if you wisely use POE.

To solve a proportion, cross-multiply:

$$\frac{3}{x} = \frac{1}{2}$$

$$x = 6$$

Remember that you can't cancel across an equals sign!

QUICK QUIZ #1

Easy

3

If $\frac{3x}{5} = \frac{x+2}{3}$, what is the value of x ?

A) $\frac{1}{2}$

B) 1

C) 2

D) $2\frac{1}{2}$

Medium

6

If $\frac{5}{x} = \frac{y}{10}$ and $x - y = y$, what is the value of $y + x$?

A) 5
B) 10
C) 15
D) 25

Hard

25

If 40 percent of x is equal to 160 percent of y, what is the value of $\frac{x}{y}$?

A) $\frac{1}{12}$

B) $\frac{1}{4}$

C) 4

D) 20

3.   **D**   Cross-multiply, and you get $9x = 5(x + 2)$. Solve for x:

$$9x = 5x + 10$$

$$4x = 10$$

$$x = 2\frac{1}{2}$$

6.   **C**   Plug in 10 for x and 5 for y. Both equations are satisfied by those numbers. So $y + x = 15$.

Just to show you the kind of algebra that you'd be forced to do if you didn't plug in—first, cross-multiply to get $xy = 50$. Your other equation is $x - y = y$, so $x = 2y$. Substitute that x into the first equation, and you get $2y^2 = 50$, or $y^2 = 25$. So $y = 5$. Substitute $y = 5$ into either equation and solve for x. You get $x = 10$. Now add them up and you get $x + y = 15$. A lot more work, huh? If you don't plug in when you can, it's really going to slow you down. And that's the least of it. You're also more likely to get the question wrong because the algebra takes so many steps.

25.   **C**   Although you can plug in for one of the variables and solve for the other, you may find it easier to translate English into Math, and then isolate the two variables. As *percent* means "over 100," *of* means "times," and *is equal to* means "equals," the expression can be rewritten as follows:

$$\frac{40}{100} \cdot x = \frac{160}{100} \cdot y$$

Reduce the two fractions:

$$\frac{2}{5} \cdot x = \frac{8}{5} \cdot y$$

Now, isolate the variables on one side of the equation and the numbers on the other side. So, divide both sides by y, and multiply both sides by $\frac{5}{2}$:

$$\frac{x}{y} = \frac{8}{5} \times \frac{5}{2} = \frac{8}{2} = 4$$

QUADRATIC EQUATIONS

Even the name is scary. What does it mean, anyway? No matter. All you need to know are a few simple things: factoring and recognizing perfect squares.

To factor, first draw a pair of empty parentheses. Deal with the first term, then the signs, then the last term. For example:

$$x^2 + x - 12$$

$$(\quad)(\quad)$$
$$(x\quad)(x\quad) \ldots \text{first term}$$
$$(x + \quad)(x - \quad) \ldots \text{signs}$$
$$(x + 4)(x - 3) \ldots \text{last term}$$

Check your factoring by multiplying the terms:

$$\text{first term} = x \bullet x = x^2$$

$$\text{inner term} = 4x$$

$$\text{outer term} = -3x$$

$$\text{last term} = 4 \times -3 = -12$$

Then add them up:

$$x^2 + 4x + -3x + -12 = x^2 + x - 12$$

Some guidelines:

If the last term is positive, your signs will be either +, + or −, −.

If the last term is negative, your signs will be +, −.

Your first try may not be right—don't be afraid to mess around with it a little.

To recognize the difference of two squares, memorize the following:

$$(x + y)(x - y) = x^2 - y^2$$

This format works whether you have variables, as above, or numbers:

$$57^2 - 43^2 = (57 + 43)(57 - 43) = 100 \times 14 = 1,400$$

One more thing—memorize the following:

$$(x + y)^2 = (x + y)(x + y) = x^2 + 2xy + y^2$$

$$(x - y)^2 = (x - y)(x - y) = x^2 - 2xy + y^2$$

> When you see anything that looks like one form of these expressions, try converting to its other form. That should lead you straight to the correct answer.

QUICK QUIZ #2

Easy

7

If $\dfrac{x^2 + 5x + 6}{x + 2} = 12$, what is the value of x?

A) −2

B) 2

C) 3

D) 9

Medium

15

If $a - b = 3$ and $a^2 - b^2 = 21$, what is the value of a?

A) −3

B) −2

C) 2

D) 5

Hard

29

If $x < 0$ and $(2x - 1)^2 = 25$, what is the value of x^2?

A) −2

B) 3

C) 4

D) 9

Answers and Explanations: Quick Quiz #2

7. **D**   First, factor the expression to $(x + 3)(x + 2)$. Now you have $\dfrac{(x + 3)(x + 2)}{x + 2} = 12$. The $(x + 2)$ cancels, and you have $x + 3 = 12$, so $x = 9$. Or you could Plug In the Answers: If $x = 9$, $\dfrac{9^2 + 5(9) + 6}{9 + 2} = 12$, or $\dfrac{132}{11} = 12$. It looks funny, but it works.

15. **D**   Factor $a^2 - b^2$ to equal $(a + b)(a - b) = 21$. If $a - b = 3$, then $a + b = 7$. Here you could do one of two things. You can try some different numbers and see what satisfies both simple equations, or you could add the two equations together and get $2a = 10$ and $a = 5$.

29. **C**   Lots of algebra:

$$(2x - 1)^2 = 25$$

$$(2x - 1)(2x - 1) = 25$$

$$4x^2 - 4x + 1 = 25$$

$$4x^2 - 4x - 24 = 0$$

$$x^2 - x - 6 = 0$$

$$(x - 3)(x + 2) = 0$$

So x can be 3 or –2. If x is negative, it has to be –2, and $(-2)^2 = 4$. You could also Plug In the Answers, but you have to remember that the question asks for x^2, not x. That means (C) and (D) are good answers to try, since they're squares.

Don't forget that one of your main jobs on the SAT is following directions. If you picked (A) or (B), we suspect you did most of the problem correctly but forgot that x is negative, or failed to square x. Don't let carelessness rob you of your hard-earned points!

SIMULTANEOUS EQUATIONS

Two different equations, two different variables. You will not usually have to solve for both variables.

To solve simultaneous equations, stack 'em up, and either add or subtract:

If $2x + 3y = 12$ and $3x - 3y = -2$, what is the value of x ?

$$
\begin{array}{r}
2x + 3y = 12 \\
+\ 3x - 3y = -2 \\
\hline
5x = 10 \\
x = 2
\end{array}
$$

If we had subtracted, we'd have gotten $-x + 6y = 14$, which wouldn't get us anywhere. If you choose the wrong operation, no big deal, just try the other one.

> Don't automatically start solving for x and y—you may not need to.
> Focus on what the question is specifically asking.

Sometimes, you won't have to solve for either of the variables. One situation involves slopes of lines, which we'll cover in the next chapter. In another situation, you'll have to determine the equations that could be used to solve for the variables in the context of a long word problem. These aren't too bad if you translate one piece of information at a time and use Process of Elimination.

8

A ferry is used to transport vehicles that weigh either 2 tons or 2.5 tons each. Let a be the number of 2-ton vehicles and b be the number of 2.5-ton vehicles. The ferry can transport up to either 34 vehicles or a weight of 74 tons. Which of the following systems of inequalities represents this relationship?

A) $\begin{cases} \dfrac{a}{2} + \dfrac{b}{2.5} \le 74 \\ a + b \le 34 \end{cases}$

B) $\begin{cases} a + b \le 74 \\ 2a + 2.5b \le 74 \end{cases}$

C) $\begin{cases} 2a + 2.5b \le 34 \\ a + b \le 74 \end{cases}$

D) $\begin{cases} 2a + 2.5b \le 74 \\ a + b \le 34 \end{cases}$

Solution: First, translate the one piece of information that seems most straightforward. You may decide that the upper limit on the total number of vehicles, 34, is the best place to start. The total number of vehicles includes both 2-ton vehicles (*a*) and 2.5-ton vehicles (*b*), so $a + b \leq 34$. Now eliminate any answer choices that do not include this inequality: (B) and (C). The difference between the remaining answers is what is less than or equal to 74. That number refers to the total weight the ferry can hold, which will again be made up of 2-ton and 2.5-ton vehicles. To get the total weight, you'd multiply the weight of each vehicle category by the number of vehicles in that category and then add up all the category weights. For 2-ton vehicles, it would be 2 times the number of 2-ton vehicles, (*a*), so the correct answer must have $2a$ in it. Add in the weight of the 2.5-ton vehicles, $2.5b$, and you get (D) as the correct answer.

QUICK QUIZ #3

Easy

5

If $3x + 5y = 15$ and $x - 2y = 10$, what is the value of $2x + 7y$?

A) 5

B) 10

C) 15

D) 25

Medium

7

$$3c - 4d = -11$$
$$4c - 3d = -3$$

If (c, d) is a solution to the system of equations above, what is the value of $c - d$?

A) 8

B) −2

C) −8

D) −14

Hard

33

At a conference, 94 salespeople are discussing effective strategies to expand a customer base. The discussion has been divided into 20 subtopics, and each subtopic will be discussed by a group of either 4 or 6 salespeople. How many of the subtopics will be discussed by a group of 6 salespeople?

Answers and Explanations: Quick Quiz #3

5. **A** Stack 'em and subtract:

$$3x + 5y = 15 \qquad 3x + 5y = 15$$
$$\underline{-(x - 2y = 10)} \qquad \underline{-x + 2y = -10}$$
$$ 2x + 7y = 5$$

That's it. You don't have to solve for x or y individually. Less work is good. (Be careful with the signs when you subtract one equation from another.)

7. **B** Start with the easiest option: Add the equations together to see if you get what you want.

$$3c - 4d = -11$$

$$\underline{+\, 4c - 3d = -3}$$

$$7c - 7d = -14$$

That's not exactly $c - d$, but if you divide the whole equation by 7, you'll get $c - d$ on the left and -2 on the right. So the answer is (B).

33. **7** This one will take some translation before you can solve anything. Let's call the groups with four people f and those with 6 people s. There are going to be 20 groups altogether, so $f + s = 20$. The number of people in 4-person groups can be found by multiplying 4 by f, and the number of people in 6-person groups is $6s$. Add those together to get the total number of people, which is 94. So the second equation is $4f + 6s = 94$. With two equations and two variables, you can solve for s, which is the value the question asks for. Start by stacking and adding the equations.

$$4f + 6s = 94$$

$$f + s = 20$$

As you can see, just adding or subtracting them won't isolate s, and solving and substituting could take a while. You need to manipulate the equations so that when you add them together, the f's disappear. To do this, multiply the second equation by -4 to get $-4f - 4s = -80$. Now stack and add.

$$4f + 6s = 94$$

$$\underline{-4f - 4s = -80}$$

$$2s = 14$$

Divide both sides by 2 to find that $s = 7$, and you're done!

INEQUALITIES

Treat these just like equations, but remember one rule: **If you multiply or divide by a negative number, the sign changes direction.**

$$x + 6 > 10 \qquad\qquad 2x > 16 \qquad\qquad -2x > 16$$

$$x > 4 \qquad\qquad\qquad x > 8 \qquad\qquad\quad x < -8$$

> It's very easy to mix up the direction of the > or < sign. Be extra careful.

QUICK QUIZ #4

Easy

3

If $3x + 7 < 5x - 4$, which of the following is true?

A) $\dfrac{11}{2} < x$

B) $x < \dfrac{3}{2}$

C) $x < \dfrac{11}{8}$

D) $\dfrac{11}{2} > x$

Medium

11

If $3b + 8 > 6 + 2b$, and b is a negative integer, what is the value of b?

A) 0

B) −1

C) −2

D) −3

Hard

22

A mail clerk estimates that a package will cost f dollars to ship, where $f > 20$. His goal is for the estimate to be within 2 dollars of the actual cost to ship the package. If the mail clerk meets his goal and it costs g dollars to ship the package, which of the following inequalities represents the relationship between the estimated cost and the actual shipping cost?

A) $-2 < g - f < 2$

B) $g > f + 2$

C) $g < f - 2$

D) $f + g < 2$

Answers and Explanations: Quick Quiz #4

3. **A**   Treat the inequality just like an equation—subtract $3x$ from both sides, and you get $7 < 2x - 4$. Add 4 to both sides to get $11 < 2x$. Divide through by 2, which leaves you with $\frac{11}{2} < x$.

11. **B**   Move the bs to one side and the integers to the other, and you get $b > -2$. If b is a negative integer, the only possibility is -1.

22. **A**   The question already states that $f > 20$, so (D) wouldn't make sense. Eliminate (D). Now use Plugging In to see what would happen. Say $f = 25$. One value of g that works is 26, since it is within 2 dollars of 25. Choice (A) becomes $-2 < 26 - 25 < 2$. This is true, so keep it. Choice (B) becomes $26 > 25 + 2$, which is not true and can be eliminated. Choice (C) becomes $26 < 25 - 2$, which is also false, so (A) is the correct answer.

FUNCTIONS

Functions will be tested in many ways on the SAT, and the test will use the standard mathematic notation $f(x)$ for a function named f.

If $f(x) = 2x^2 + 4x + 12$, what is the value of $f(4)$?

Don't be distracted by the fancy symbols; just pop the number into the function and crank out the answer. We want the $f(4)$, so wherever there is an x in the function, we'll replace it with a 4.

$$f(4) = 2(4)^2 + 4(4) + 12$$
$$= 2(16) + 16 + 12$$
$$= 60$$

Of course, the SAT will deal with concepts beyond testing which values of $f(x)$ will result from putting in a certain value of x or which values of x will yield a specific result for $f(x)$ or y. One advanced concept is related to the factors of a function, which can give you the roots or zeroes of that function.

8

x	$g(x)$
-1	6
0	4
3	1
5	0

The function g is defined by a polynomial. Some of the values of x and $g(x)$ are shown in the table above. Which of the following must be a factor of g ?

A) $x - 6$

B) $x - 5$

C) $x - 4$

D) $x - 3$

Solution: When you factor a polynomial, you can set each factor equal to zero to find the roots. These are the places where the function crosses the x-axis, or the x-values for which $f(x)$ or y equal zero. In this question, you can work backwards from y or $g(x) = 0$. This happens when $x = 5$. For the factor to equal zero, you solve for zero by subtracting 5 from both sides to get $x - 5 = 0$. Therefore, $x - 5$ is a factor of the polynomial, and (B) is the answer.

QUICK QUIZ #5

Easy

4

If $f(x) = 2x^2 + 3$, for which of the following values of x does $f(x) = 21$?

A) -9

B) -3

C) 0

D) 1

Medium

9

$$h(x) = cx^2 + 18$$

For the function h defined above, c is a constant and $h(2) = 10$. What is the value of $h(-2)$?

A) -10

B) -2

C) 10

D) 18

Hard

23

The height of the steam burst of a certain geyser varies with the length of time since the previous steam burst. The longer the time since the last burst, the greater the height of the steam burst. If t is the time in hours since the previous steam burst and H is the height in meters of the steam burst, which of the following could express the relationship of t and H ?

A) $H(t) = \dfrac{1}{2}(t - 7)$

B) $H(t) = \dfrac{2}{t - 7}$

C) $H(t) = 2 - (t - 7)$

D) $H(t) = 7 - 2t$

Answers and Explanations: Quick Quiz #5

4. **B**   In this case, Plug In the Answers for the value of x, starting with (C). Plugging in 0 for x gives you $f(0) = 2(0)^2 + 3 = 3$. But you want $f(x) = 21$, so eliminate (C). Now try (B): $f(-3) = 21$, so this is the right answer. Alternatively, set $f(x) = 21$, and solve $21 = 2x^2 + 3$.

9. **C**   If you are a Zen master of algebra, you may recognize that this function is a parabola. Parabolas are symmetrical about a center line, and since there is no number added or subtracted in parentheses [such as $(x - 2)^2$], this parabola is symmetrical about the y-axis. As such, any value of x will give the same y-value as $-x$ will, so $h(2) = h(-2) = 10$.

If you are thinking, "Wait, what?" right now—never fear! Your old friend Plugging In can come to the rescue here. Plug $x = 2$ into the function to get $h(2) = c(2)^2 + 18 = 4c + 18$. The question says this is 10, so you have $4c + 18 = 10$. Subtract 18 from both sides to get $4c = -8$, so $c = -2$. Now you have the full function, $-2x^2 + 18$, and can easily Plug In (-2). You get $h(-2) = -2(-2)^2 + 18 = -2(4) + 18 = -8 + 18 = 10$. Either way, the answer is (C).

23. **A**   The relationship is the greater the time, the greater the height. So the correct function is one that yields a greater H as you increase t. Try plugging in for t in the functions to see which one increases as t increases. Try $t = 10$ and $t = 20$. Only (A) has a greater H for $t = 20$ than it does for $t = 10$. That is $\frac{1}{2}(10 - 7) < \frac{1}{2}(20 - 7)$. The answer is (A).

Chapter 6
Additional Topics

This chapter will cover some topics that may not be tested as often. Tackle these once you've mastered the strategies and content in the previous chapters.

GEOMETRY

You're not going to believe how simple this is. Just a few rules, a couple of formulas, and your common sense. And don't forget about estimating.

Definitions

arc	part of a circumference
area	the space inside a two-dimensional figure
bisect	cut in two equal parts
chord	a straight line joining two points on a circle's circumference
circumference	the distance around a circle
diagonal	a line from one corner of a square to its opposite corner
diameter	the longest chord in a circle, which passes through the center of the circle
equidistant	exactly in the middle
equilateral	a triangle with three equal sides, therefore three equal angles (60° each)
hypotenuse	the longest leg of a right triangle, opposite the right angle
isosceles	a triangle with two equal sides and two equal angles
parallel	lines that will never intersect (think railroad tracks)
perimeter	the distance around a figure
perpendicular	meeting at a 90° angle
quadrilateral	any four-sided figure
radius	a line from the center of a circle to the edge of the circle (half the diameter)
volume	the space inside a three-dimensional figure

LINES AND ANGLES

A line has 180°, so the angles formed by any cut to your line will add up to 180°:

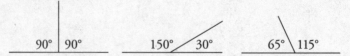

Two intersecting lines form a pair of **vertical angles,** which are equal:

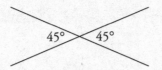

Parallel lines cut by a third line will form two kinds of angles: big ones and little ones. All the big ones are equal to each other; all the little ones are equal to each other. Any big angle plus any little angle will equal 180°:

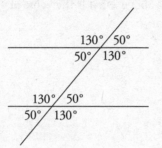

QUICK QUIZ #1

Easy

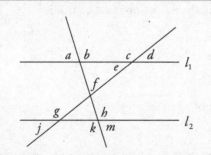

In the figure above, l_1 is parallel to l_2. Which of the following angles are NOT equal?

A) c and g

B) b and h

C) a and m

D) a and k

Medium

10

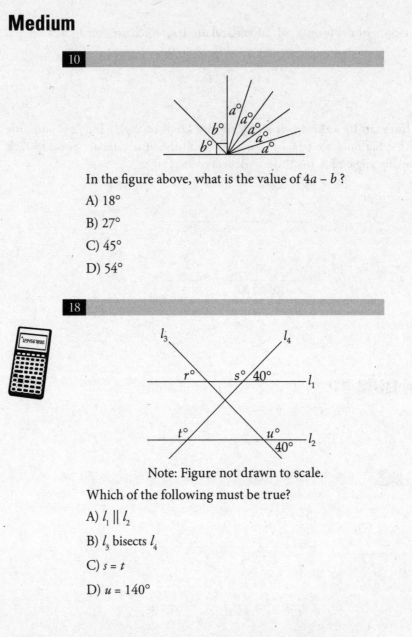

In the figure above, what is the value of $4a - b$?

A) 18°

B) 27°

C) 45°

D) 54°

18

Note: Figure not drawn to scale.

Which of the following must be true?

A) $l_1 \parallel l_2$

B) l_3 bisects l_4

C) $s = t$

D) $u = 140°$

Answers and Explanations: Quick Quiz #1

4. **D** Start with (A) and cross off as you go along. In (D), $a = m$, not k. Keep in mind that the two lines cutting through l_1 and l_2 aren't parallel, and so the angles made by one line have no relationship to the angles made by the other line.

10. **B** Estimate first. Outline the measurement of four of the a's. That's about 60. Now pretend you are subtracting b, about 45. How much is left? Not so much, right? Cross out (D). Now do the math: $2b = 90°$, so $b = 45°$. $5a = 90$, so $a = 18°$. Now plug those numbers into the equation: $4(18) - 45 = 27$.

18.   **D**   This question is actually very easy, as long as you don't pick the first answer that looks halfway decent before reading (D). Angle *u* has to be 140° because it's on a straight line with the angle marked 40°. All the other answers look like they're true, but you can't know for certain. The only thing you know for sure is that angles on the same line add up to 180°, and vertical angles are equal. None of these lines are necessarily parallel, so you can't assume anything else.

TRIANGLES

Triangles have 180°.

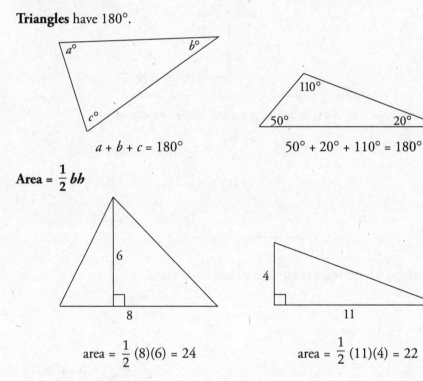

$a + b + c = 180°$ $50° + 20° + 110° = 180°$

Area = $\dfrac{1}{2} bh$

area = $\dfrac{1}{2}$ (8)(6) = 24   area = $\dfrac{1}{2}$ (11)(4) = 22

Perimeter: Add up the sides.

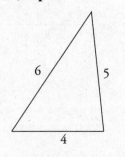

Perimeter = 15

Right triangles have a right, or 90°, angle:

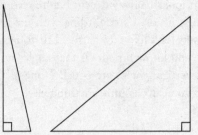

Isosceles triangles have two equal sides and two equal angles:

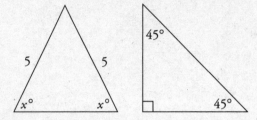

Equilateral triangles have three equal sides and three equal angles:

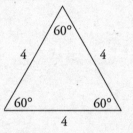

Similar triangles have equal angles and proportional sides:

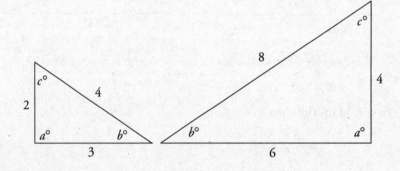

The Wonderful World of Right Triangles

For any right triangle, if you know the lengths of two of the sides, you can figure out the length of the third side by using the Pythagorean Theorem:

$$a^2 + b^2 = c^2$$

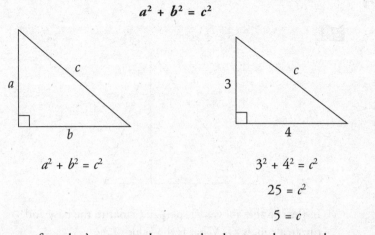

$$a^2 + b^2 = c^2$$

$$3^2 + 4^2 = c^2$$

$$25 = c^2$$

$$5 = c$$

However, you often don't even need to use the theorem, because the test-writers sometimes create right triangles that feature these common Pythagorean triples.

$$3{:}4{:}5 \qquad\qquad 6{:}8{:}10 \qquad\qquad 5{:}12{:}13$$

In two special cases, you only have to know one side to figure out the other two, because the sides are in a constant ratio.

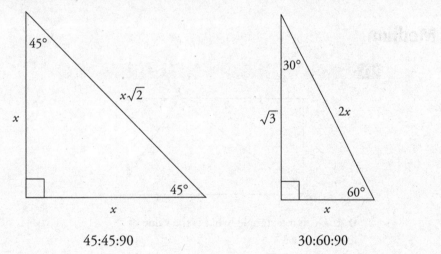

45:45:90   30:60:90

Easy

5

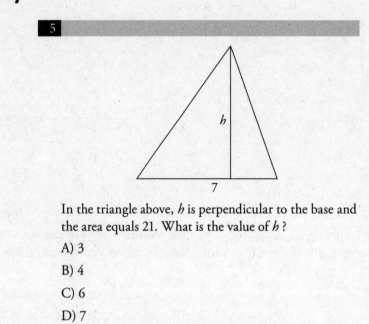

In the triangle above, h is perpendicular to the base and the area equals 21. What is the value of h?

A) 3

B) 4

C) 6

D) 7

Medium

14

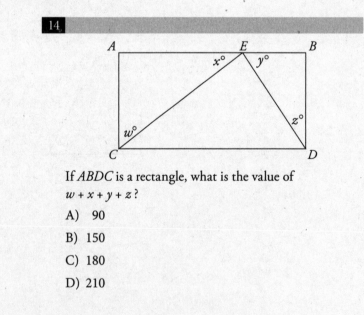

If $ABDC$ is a rectangle, what is the value of $w + x + y + z$?

A) 90

B) 150

C) 180

D) 210

Hard

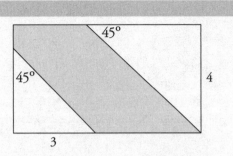

Note: Figure not drawn to scale.

If the rectangle above has an area of 32, and the unshaded triangles are isosceles, what is the perimeter of the shaded area?

A) 16

B) $10 + 7\sqrt{2}$

C) $10 + 12\sqrt{2}$

D) 32

Answers and Explanations: Quick Quiz #2

5. **C**   Estimate first—it's drawn to scale. If the base is 7, how long does the height look? About the same? Cross out at least (A), as well as (B) if you're feeling confident. Now do the math: area = $\frac{1}{2}$ bh, so $\frac{1}{2}(7h) = 21$, and $h = 6$. It would be easy to pick (A) if you weren't paying attention, because $7 \times 3 = 21$, and so it seems appealing.

14. **C**   If you picked (A) or (D), you didn't estimate. See how the rectangle is cut up into three triangles? Each of those triangles has 180°. Both of the triangles with marked angles also have right angles because they're corners of a rectangle. So $\triangle ACE + \triangle EBD = 360°$. Subtract the two right angles, and you're left with 180°.

20. **B**   First, write in everything you know: If the area is 32, the length is 8. That means the base is 3 + 5 and the left side is 1 + 3. The triangles in opposing corners are both 45-45-90 triangles: The one on the base has a hypotenuse of $3\sqrt{2}$, and the one with sides of 4 has a hypotenuse of $4\sqrt{2}$. Add up all the sides of the shaded part, and you get $10 + 7\sqrt{2}$.

Here's how it should look:

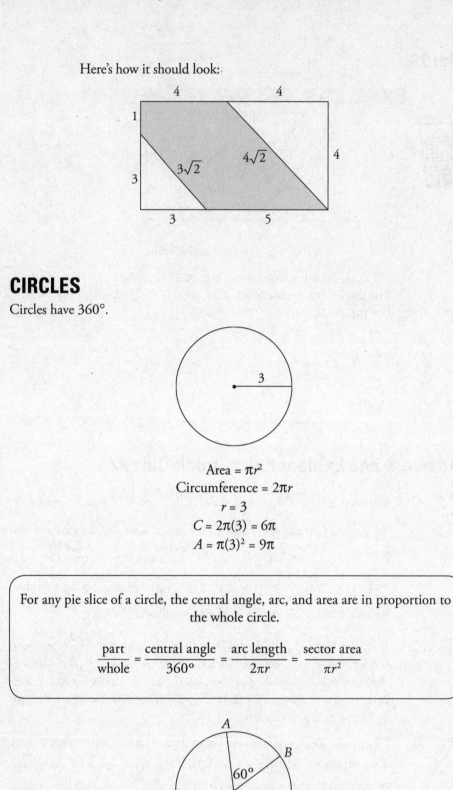

CIRCLES

Circles have 360°.

$$\text{Area} = \pi r^2$$
$$\text{Circumference} = 2\pi r$$
$$r = 3$$
$$C = 2\pi(3) = 6\pi$$
$$A = \pi(3)^2 = 9\pi$$

> For any pie slice of a circle, the central angle, arc, and area are in proportion to the whole circle.
>
> $$\frac{\text{part}}{\text{whole}} = \frac{\text{central angle}}{360°} = \frac{\text{arc length}}{2\pi r} = \frac{\text{sector area}}{\pi r^2}$$

$\dfrac{60°}{360°} = \dfrac{1}{6}$, so arc AB is $\dfrac{1}{6}$ of the circumference, and pie slice AOB is $\dfrac{1}{6}$ of the total area.

QUICK QUIZ #3

Easy

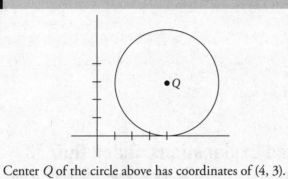

Center Q of the circle above has coordinates of (4, 3). What is the circumference of the circle?

A) π

B) 2π

C) 6π

D) 9π

Medium

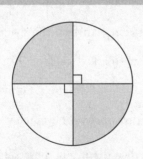

If the circumference of the circle above is 16π, what is the total area of the shaded regions?

A) 64π

B) 32π

C) 12π

D) 8π

Hard

One circle has a radius of r, and another circle has a radius of $2r$. The area of the larger circle is how many times the area of the smaller circle?

A) 1.5

B) 2

C) 3

D) 4

Answers and Explanations: Quick Quiz #3

4. **C**   The easiest way to solve this is simply to count the number of units in the radius, which is 3. Make sure you draw a radius on the diagram—if you draw it perpendicular to the y-axis, you'll be able to count the units with no problem. If you picked (D), you found the area. Read the question carefully and give 'em what they ask for.

13. **B**   The circumference is 16π, so use the circumference formula to get the radius: $2\pi r = 16\pi$, and $r = 8$. The area of the whole circle is $\pi r^2 = \pi(8)^2 = 64\pi$. Hold on—don't pick (A). At this point, you could happily estimate the shaded area as half the circle and pick (B). (Nothing else is close.) In fact, the shaded area is exactly half of the circle because each marked angle is 90°, which makes each of those pie slices $\frac{90°}{360°}$, or $\frac{1}{4}$ of the circle. So two of them make up $\frac{1}{2}$ of the circle, or 32π. Trust what your eyes tell you.

20. **D**   Plug In. If $r = 2$, then the area of the small circle is 4π. The radius of the second circle is $2(2)$, or 4, so the area is 16π. The larger circle is 4 times as big as the smaller circle. (Don't you just love to plug in?)

> Notice how the hard question doesn't give you a picture or any real numbers to use. So draw the picture and make up your own numbers. Try to visualize the problem. Plugging In works just as well on geometry problems as it does on algebra problems.

Note: A very common careless error on circle problems is getting the area and circumference mixed up. Don't worry! The formulas are printed on the first page of each math section in case you forgot them.

CIRCLE EQUATIONS

You may also need to know the equation of a circle, which will tell you the center of the circle (h, k) and the radius r.

$$(x - h)^2 + (y - k)^2 = r^2$$

Use it when working with circles in the xy-plane to eliminate those with the wrong radius or center.

VOLUME

The most common shapes you'll have to find the volume of on the SAT are rectangular solids (boxes), cubes (square boxes), and possibly cylinders (cans).

For these shapes, the volume equals the area of one face × the third dimension (the depth or the height). Here are the formulas you need to know:

Rectangular Box

Volume = $l \times w \times h$

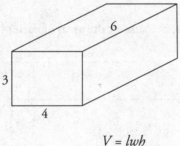

$$V = lwh$$
$$V = 6(3)(4)$$
$$V = 72$$

Cube

Volume = s^3

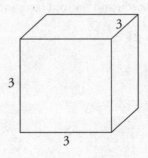

$$V = s^3$$
$$V = 3^3$$
$$V = 27$$

Think Inside the Box

The formulas for the volume of rectangular solids, cylinders, spheres, cones, and even pyramids will be provided in the box at the start of the math sections.

Cylinder

Volume = $\pi r^2 h$

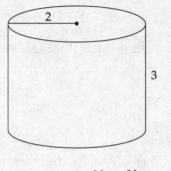

$V = \pi r^2 h$

$V = \pi 2^2(3)$

$V = 12\pi$

SURFACE AREA

The surface area of a box is the sum of the areas of each of the faces.

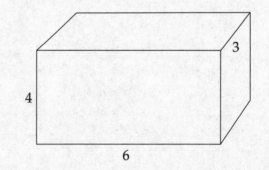

In the figure above, the front and back faces each measure 6 by 4; the side faces each measure 4 by 3; and the top and bottom faces each measure 6 by 3.

Front face $(6 \times 4) = 24$

Back face $(6 \times 4) = 24$

Left face $(4 \times 3) = 12$

Right face $(4 \times 3) = 12$

Top face $(6 \times 3) = 18$

Bottom face $(6 \times 3) = 18$

The surface area is the sum of these faces: $24 + 24 + 12 + 12 + 18 + 18 = 108$.

QUICK QUIZ #4

Easy

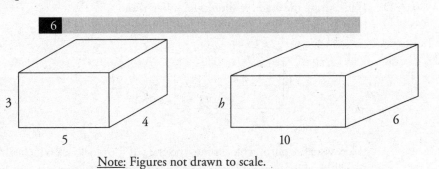

Note: Figures not drawn to scale.

If the volumes of the two boxes above are equal, what is the value of h ?

A) 1

B) 2

C) 4

D) 5

Medium

9

Sam is packing toy blocks into a crate. If each block is a cube with a side of 6 inches, and the crate is 1 foot high, 2 feet long, and 2 feet wide, how many blocks can Sam fit into the crate?

A) 6

B) 12

C) 24

D) 32

Hard

19

The surface area of a rectangular solid measuring $5 \times 6 \times 8$ is how much greater than the surface area of a rectangular solid measuring $3 \times 6 \times 8$?

A) 12

B) 24

C) 48

D) 56

Answers and Explanations: Quick Quiz #4

6. **A**   The box on the left has volume = $3 \times 4 \times 5 = 60$. The box on the right is then $10 \times 6 \times h = 60$. So $h = 1$. Don't forget to estimate!

9. **D**   First, draw the crate. It should look like this:

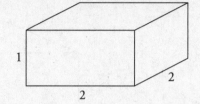

Now visualize putting blocks into the crate. If the blocks are 6 inches high, you'll be able to stack 2 rows in the crate since the crate is a foot high. Now mark off 6-inch intervals along the side of the crate. (You're dividing 2 feet, or 24 inches, by 6 inches.) You can fit 4 blocks along each side. Now multiply everything together and you get $2 \times 4 \times 4 = 32$ blocks.

You can also divide the volume of the crate by the volume of each block, as long as your units are consistent:

$$\frac{1 \text{ ft} \times 2 \text{ ft} \times 2 \text{ ft}}{\frac{1}{2}\text{ft} \times \frac{1}{2}\text{ft} \times \frac{1}{2}\text{ft}} \text{ or } \frac{12 \text{ in.} \times 24 \text{ in.} \times 24 \text{ in.}}{6 \text{ in.} \times 6 \text{ in.} \times 6 \text{ in.}}$$

19. **D**   Find the surface area of the first figure. It has two sides 5×6, two sides 6×8, and two sides 5×8. Therefore, its surface area is $30 + 30 + 48 + 48 + 40 + 40$, which makes 236. The second figure has two sides 3×6, two sides 6×8, and two sides 3×8. Its surface area is $18 + 18 + 48 + 48 + 24 + 24$, or 180. The difference between these two surface areas is 56.

TRIGONOMETRY

The SAT may include trig questions. Understanding the basic definitions of sine, cosine, and tangent will help you answer these questions.

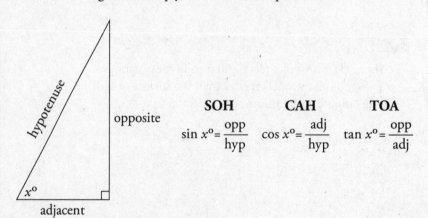

SOH	CAH	TOA
$\sin x° = \dfrac{\text{opp}}{\text{hyp}}$	$\cos x° = \dfrac{\text{adj}}{\text{hyp}}$	$\tan x° = \dfrac{\text{opp}}{\text{adj}}$

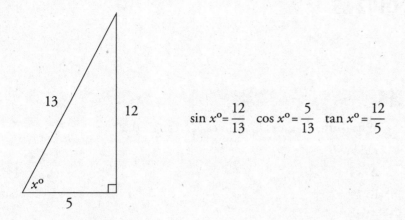

$$\sin x^\circ = \frac{12}{13} \quad \cos x^\circ = \frac{5}{13} \quad \tan x^\circ = \frac{12}{5}$$

Radians and Degrees

Radians and degrees are just different units used to measure angles. Your calculator has both modes, so make sure you are using the correct mode when answering these questions.

Here is how to convert between degrees and radians (or vice versa):

$$\frac{\pi}{180} = \frac{\text{degrees}}{\text{radians}}$$

COMPLEX NUMBERS

Occasionally, a mathematical operation will require taking a square root of a negative number. With real numbers, that isn't possible—no real number can be squared to get a negative number. This is where i comes in. The i stands for "imaginary," to distinguish it from "real" numbers, and it equals $\sqrt{-1}$. When i is squared, the result is −1.

$$i = \sqrt{-1}$$
$$i^2 = -1$$
$$i^3 = -i$$
$$i^4 = 1$$

"Complex numbers" combine real and imaginary numbers in the form $a + bi$, where a is real and bi is imaginary.

QUICK QUIZ #5

Easy

8

What is the measure in degrees of an angle that is $\dfrac{\pi}{4}$ radians?

A) 4°

B) 25°

C) 45°

D) 90°

Medium

14

A 25-foot ladder is placed against the side of a building at an angle of 70° from the ground. How far away is the base of the ladder from the building?

A) 25 cos 70°

B) 8.5 sin 70°

C) 25 tan 70°

D) 8.5 cos 70°

Hard

15

Which of the following is equivalent to the expression $\left(\dfrac{6 + 3i}{2} - \dfrac{7 + 4i}{3} \right)^2$?

A) $\dfrac{13 + 7i}{6}$

B) $\dfrac{14 + 8i}{6}$

C) $\dfrac{4 - i}{36}$

D) $\dfrac{15 + 8i}{36}$

Answers and Explanations: Quick Quiz #5

8. **C**   Use the conversion $\dfrac{\pi}{180} = \dfrac{\text{radians}}{\text{degrees}}$.

$$\frac{\pi}{180} = \frac{\frac{\pi}{4}}{x}$$

Cross-multiply:

$$180 \cdot \frac{\pi}{4} = \pi \cdot x$$
$$45 \cdot \pi = \pi \cdot x$$
$$x = 45°$$

14. **A**   Remember SOHCAHTOA and draw a picture.

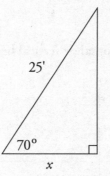

You will need to use cosine to find the answer, so eliminate (B) and (C).

$$\cos 70° = \frac{x}{25'}$$

$$x = 25 \cos 70°$$

15. **D**   Find a common denominator with which to subtract the fractions by multiplying the top and bottom of the first fraction by 3 and the top and bottom of the second fraction by 2.

$$\left(\frac{18 + 9i}{6} - \frac{14 + 8i}{6} \right)^2$$

Combine.

$$\left(\frac{18 + 9i - 14 - 8i}{6} \right)^2 = \left(\frac{4 + i}{6} \right)^2 =$$

$$\frac{16 + 4i + 4i + i^2}{36} = \frac{16 + 8i + i^2}{36}$$

Remember that $i^2 = -1$, so the expression becomes $\dfrac{15 + 8i}{36}$.

COORDINATE GEOMETRY

Remember how to plot points? The first number is *x* and the second is *y*.

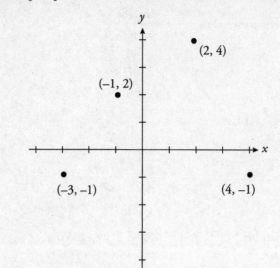

To find the length of a horizontal or vertical line, count the units:

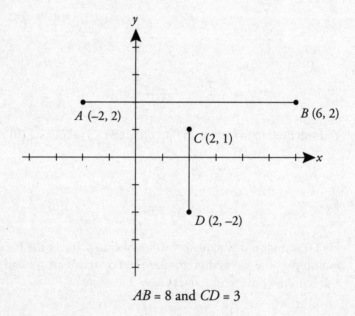

$AB = 8$ and $CD = 3$

To find the length of any other line, draw in a right triangle and use the Pythagorean Theorem:

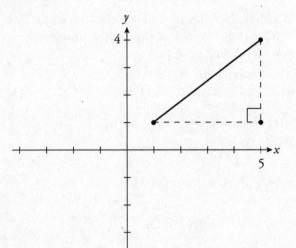

The triangle has legs of 3 and 4, so $3^2 + 4^2 = c^2$, and $c = 5$. (It's a Pythagorean triple again.)

To find the slope, put the rise over the run. The formula is

$$\textbf{slope} = \frac{y_1 - y_2}{x_1 - x_2}$$

It doesn't matter which point you begin with, just be consistent.

What is the slope of the line containing points $(2, -3)$ and $(4, 3)$?

$$\text{slope} = \frac{-3 - 3}{2 - 4} = \frac{-6}{-2} = 3 \text{ or } \frac{3 - (-3)}{4 - 2} = \frac{6}{2} = 3$$

A slope that goes from low to high is positive.

A slope that goes from high to low is negative.

A slope that goes straight across is 0.

---

positive slope   negative slope   0 slope

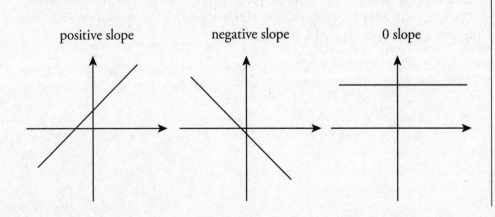

Parallel lines have equal slopes. **Perpendicular lines** have slopes that are negative reciprocals of each other. For example:

> Which of the following sets of points lies on the line that is parallel to the line that passes through the points (1, 3) and (5, 8) ?
>
> A) (–5, –8), (1, 3)
>
> B) (12, 2), (8, –3)
>
> C) (5, 3), (1,8)
>
> D) (15, 3), (6, 2)

First, find the slope of the first set of points.

$$\text{slope} = \frac{3-8}{1-5} = \frac{-5}{-4} = \frac{5}{4}$$

Then, check the answer choices and look for the set of points that has an equal slope. The correct answer is (B).

Try the same thing with perpendicular lines.

> Which of the following sets of points lies on the line that is perpendicular to the line that passes through the points (1, 3) and (5, 8) ?
>
> A) (16, 7), (11, 11)
>
> B) (8, 5), (3, 1)
>
> C) (2, 5), (3, 13)
>
> D) (7, 8), (5, 11)

We already found the slope. Now we need its negative reciprocal, which is $-\frac{4}{5}$. Check the answers. Choice (A) gives us:

$$\text{slope} = \frac{7-11}{16-11} = -\frac{4}{5}$$

Bingo!

Sometimes, a question will be about parallel lines, even if it doesn't seem like it. Questions that refer to two equations with "no solution" are actually testing your knowledge of slopes of parallel lines.

$$cx - 5y = 6$$
$$2x - 3y = 8$$

In the system of equations above, c is a constant and x and y are variables. For what value of c will the system have no solution?

A) $-\dfrac{10}{3}$

B) $-\dfrac{13}{11}$

C) $\dfrac{13}{11}$

D) $\dfrac{10}{3}$

Solution: The two equations represent two lines. If these lines have no solution, that means they never intersect and are parallel. Parallel lines have the same slope, so you need to figure out what value of c will make that happen. Start by finding the slope of the second line. In the form $Ax + By = C$, the slope is $-\dfrac{A}{B}$, or you could get it into $y = mx + b$ form, where m is the slope. Either way, the slope is $\dfrac{-2}{-3} = \dfrac{2}{3}$. For the first line, the slope is $\dfrac{-c}{-5} = \dfrac{c}{5}$. Now set the two slopes equal and cross-multiply.

$$\frac{2}{3} = \frac{c}{5}$$
$$3c = 10$$
$$c = \frac{10}{3}$$

Finally, if the question asks about two lines with "infinitely many solutions," the equations actually represent the same exact line. Of course, the equations will also have the same slope in that situation.

QUICK QUIZ #6

Easy

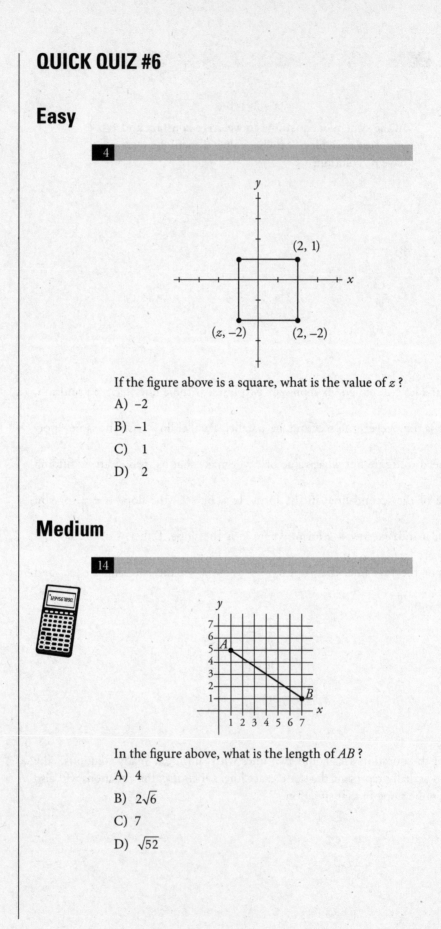

4

If the figure above is a square, what is the value of z ?

A) −2

B) −1

C) 1

D) 2

Medium

14

In the figure above, what is the length of AB ?

A) 4

B) $2\sqrt{6}$

C) 7

D) $\sqrt{52}$

Hard

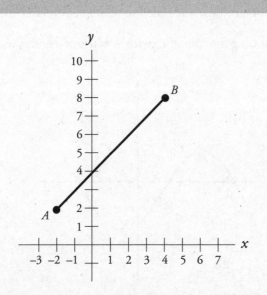

In the figure above, the coordinates for point A are $(-2, 2)$ and the coordinates for point B are $(4, 8)$. If line CD, not shown, is parallel to the line AB, what is the slope of line CD ?

A) -1

B) 0

C) 1

D) 2

Answers and Explanations: Quick Quiz #6

4. **B**   Just count the units. Remember that coordinates in the lower left quadrant will always be negative.

14. **D**   Use the units to measure each leg. You should get one leg = 4 and the other = 6. Now use the Pythagorean Theorem: $4^2 + 6^2 = c^2$.

$$16 + 36 = c^2$$
$$52 = c^2$$
$$\sqrt{52} = c$$

24. **C**   Write in the coordinates of A and B. $A = (-2, 2)$ and $B = (4, 8)$. So the slope of $AB = \dfrac{2 - 8}{-2 - 4} = \dfrac{-6}{-6} = 1$. If CD is parallel to AB, it has the same slope. (You could draw in a parallel line and recalculate the slope, but you'd be doing extra work.)

GRAPHS OF FUNCTIONS

For graphs involving functions, you will sometimes be asked to provide info on a portion of a function or how one function was translated into another function.

Consider the following function $f(x)$, with x values of a and b, as indicated:

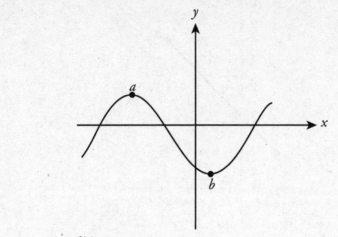

At $x < a$, $f(x)$ is rising.

At $a < x < b$, $f(x)$ is falling.

At $b < x$, $f(x)$ is rising again.

If a new function, $g(x)$, is formed by moving our original function $f(x)$, $g(x)$ would be defined as follows:

If $f(x)$ is moved 4 units up the y-axis, then $g(x) = f(x) + 4$.

If $f(x)$ is moved 5 units down the y-axis, then $g(x) = f(x) - 5$.

If $f(x)$ is moved 2 units to the right along the x-axis, then $g(x) = f(x - 2)$.

If $f(x)$ is moved 3 units to the left along the x-axis, then $g(x) = f(x + 3)$.

Another aspect of functions that may be tested is the form in which they are written. For parabolas, you are probably used to the standard form, which is $ax^2 + bx + c = 0$. We've also factored quadratics, such as $(x - 2)(x + 5) = 0$ to find the roots of the parabola, or the places where it crosses the x-axis. Now let's talk about the vertex form of a parabola, which reveals the maximum or minimum value of a quadratic.

In the vertex form, $f(x) = a(x - h)^2 + k$, the vertex is (h, k).

Knowing this form can make short work of a question that would be tough without it.

$$g(x) = (x - 5)(x + 3)$$

Which of the following is an equivalent form of the function g above in which the minimum value of g appears as a constant or coefficient?

A) $g(x) = x^2 - 15$

B) $g(x) = x^2 - 2x - 15$

C) $g(x) = (x - 1)^2 - 16$

D) $g(x) = (x + 1)^2 - 12$

Solution: There are a few opportunities to use POE here. The question asks for the minimum value, which is the vertex of the parabola. Only (C) and (D) are in vertex form, so (A) and (B) can be eliminated. To find out which one is correct, start by multiplying out the factors in the function using FOIL to get $g(x) = x^2 + 3x - 5x - 15 = x^2 - 2x - 15$. If you hadn't already eliminated (B), it would be a tempting choice at this point, since it is equivalent, but it's out of the running. From here, you could FOIL out (C) and (D) to see which is equivalent to the given function, or you could graph g and the remaining answers on your calculator to find a match. Knowing how to complete the square to convert a function to the vertex form will be necessary on some questions, though, so let's try that here. First, move the constants over to the other side to get $15 = x^2 - 2x$. Take half the coefficient on the x term, square it, and add it to both sides to get $15 + 1 = x^2 - 2x + 1$. The left side can be simplified and the right side written in square form, so the function becomes. $16 = (x - 1)^2$. Move the constant on the left back over to the other side to get $0 = (x - 1)^2 - 16$, which is (C).

QUICK QUIZ #7

Easy

t	-1	0	1	2
$g(t)$	0	-2	0	6

The table above provides values for the function g for selected values of t. Which of the following defines the function g ?

A) $g(t) = t^2 - 2$

B) $g(t) = t^2 + 2$

C) $g(t) = 2t^2 - 2$

D) $g(t) = 2t^2 + 2$

Medium

18

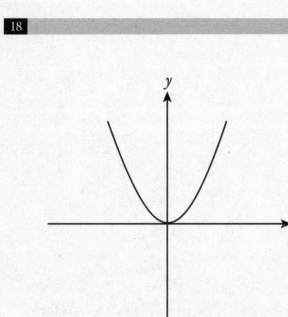

The quadratic function $y = f(x)$ is shown above.
Which of the following graphs represents the function
$y = f(x + 3) - 4$?

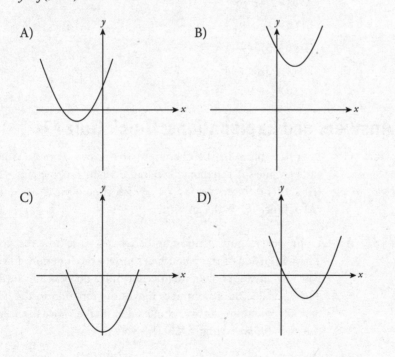

A)

B)

C)

D)

Hard

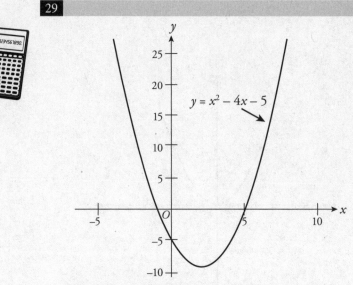

Which of the following is an equivalent form of the equation of the graph shown in the xy-plane above, from which the coordinates of vertex Z can be identified as constants in the equation?

A) $x(x - 4) - 5$

B) $(x - 2)^2 - 9$

C) $(x + 5)(x - 1)$

D) $(x - 5)(x + 1)$

Answers and Explanations: Quick Quiz #7

6. **C**   Plug the values in the chart into the answer choices. Start with the easiest value for t, namely 0. Because when t is 0, $g(t)$ is –2, eliminate (B) and (D). Now check $t = 1$, which should yield $g(t) = 0$. Eliminate (A). Choice (C) is the answer.

18. **A**   Don't worry about actual numbers here—just how the graph moves. The –4 outside of the parentheses moves the function down, so eliminate any answer choices that do not move down. Choice (B) is wrong. The +3 inside the parentheses moves the function to the left, so eliminate any remaining answer choices that do not move to the left. Choices (C) and (D) are wrong. Only (A) works.

29. **B**   There are many chances to eliminate answers here, depending on what you see first. You may see there is a root at $x = 5$, so $(x - 5)$ must be one of the factors, eliminating (C). You may see that the equation must be in vertex form, and only (B) is in that form. You may also see from the graph that the vertex looks to be about $(2, –9)$, and only (B) has 2 and 9 in it. You could even graph the function on your calculator and see exactly what the vertex is. No matter how you get there, (B) is correct.

GEOMETRY: FINAL TIPS AND REMINDERS

- Always estimate first when the figure is drawn to scale.

- Always write the information given on the diagram, including any information you figure out along the way.

- If you don't know how to start, just look and see what shapes are involved. The solution to the problem will come through using the information we've gone over that pertains to that shape.

Chapter 7
Grid-In Questions

GRID-INS

We've seen a few grid-in questions in the Quick Quizzes, so let's now take this time to focus on them. There will be 5 grid-ins at the end of Section 3 and 8 at the end of Section 4. The last two questions in Section 4 may be a pair of grid-ins based on the same information. Grid-in questions have no answer choices. You must solve the question, write your answer on a grid, and bubble it in. This isn't as bad as it sounds. Just as with the rest of the questions, there's a loosely ordered group of easy, medium, and hard grid-ins. Take your time on the easy and medium ones, as always.

Tips for Grid-In Happiness

- Don't bother to reduce fractions if they fit in the grid: $\frac{3}{6}$ is as good as $\frac{1}{2}$.

- Don't round off decimals. If your answer has more than four digits, just start to the left of the decimal point and fit in as many as you can.

- Don't grid in mixed fractions. Either convert to a mixed number or a decimal. (Use 4.25 or $\frac{17}{4}$, not $4\frac{1}{4}$.)

- If the question asks for "one possible value," any answer that works is okay.

- Forget about negatives, variables, and π. You can't grid them.

- You can still Plug In if the question has an implied variable.

QUICK QUIZ #1

Easy

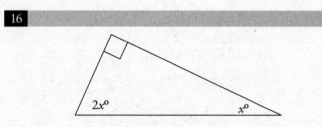

16

What is the value of x ?

Medium

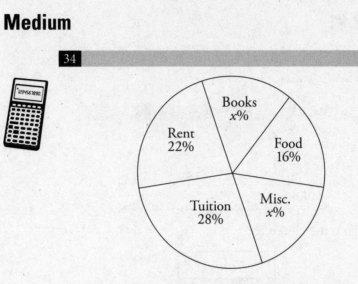

The chart above shows Orwell's projected expenditures for his freshman year at River State University. If he plans to spend a total of $10,000 for the year, how many dollars will Orwell spend on books?

Hard

If the function $r(s)$ is defined as $2s + 3$ for all values of s and $r(4) = x$, what is the value of $r(x)$?

Answers and Explanations: Quick Quiz #1

16. **30** Since this is a right triangle, the other 2 angles add up to 90. So $3x = 90$ and $x = 30$.

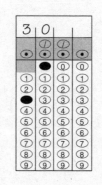

34. **1700** There are two steps: First, figure out the percentage of the budget spent on books. Then calculate the actual amount. All the pie slices add up to 100%, so $28 + 16 + 22 + 2x = 100$. $2x = 34$ and $x = 17\%$. Take 17% of 10,000, which is 1,700.

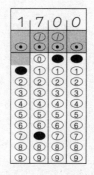

19. **25** When a number is inside the parentheses, plug it into the equation. Thus, $r(4) = 2(4) + 3 = 11$, so $x = 11$. The question is not asking for $r(4)$, but $r(x)$. As you know $x = 11$, the question is asking for $r(11)$, so plug 11 into the formula: $r(11) = 2(11) + 3 = 25$.

Chapter 8
Problem Sets

The following groups of questions were designed for quick, concentrated study. The problems come in groups of ten and have a full range of difficulty. Answers and explanations follow immediately. The idea is for you to check your answers right after working the problems so that you can learn from your mistakes before you continue.

Don't simply count up how many you got wrong and then breeze on to the next thing—take a careful look at *how* you got the question wrong. Did you use the wrong strategy? Not remember the necessary basic math? Make a goofy computation error? Write an equation and Plug In at the same time?

> You need to know the cause of your mistakes before you can stop making them.

Here are sets of plugging in, geometry, exponent, and other typical problem types to help you learn how to recognize those types of questions when they come up—so pay attention to the look and feel of them.

One last thing—the question numbers here do not reflect the exact place the questions might appear on a real test. They are simply numbered 1 through 10. Since there's a loose order of difficulty on the test, you cannot count on the first third of a given section to be easy or the last third to be hard. You need to use your Personal Order of Difficulty to decide how to best spend your time.

PROBLEM SET 1: PLUGGING IN

Easy

1

Sinéad has 4 more than three times the number of hats that Maria has. If Maria has x hats, then in terms of x, how many hats does Sinéad have?

A) $3x + 4$

B) $3(x + 4)$

C) $4(x + 3)$

D) $4(3x)$

2

When 6 is subtracted from 10p, the result is t. Which of the following equations represents the statement above?

A) $t = 6(p - 10)$

B) $t = 6p - 10$

C) $t = 10(6 - p)$

D) $10p - 6 = t$

3

Sally scored a total of $4b + 12$ points in a certain basketball game. She scored the same number of points in each of the game's 4 periods. In terms of b, how many points did she score in each period?

A) $b + 3$

B) $b + 12$

C) $4b + 3$

D) $16b + 48$

Medium

4

$$v = \frac{1}{2}at^2$$

The velocity, v, of an object t seconds after beginning to accelerate from rest at a constant acceleration, a, can be found using the equation above. According to the formula, what is the ratio of the velocity of the object t seconds after the object begins to accelerate to the velocity of the object $2.5t$ seconds after the object begins to accelerate?

A) $\dfrac{4}{25}$

B) $\dfrac{2}{5}$

C) $\dfrac{5}{2}$

D) $\dfrac{25}{4}$

5

Roseanne is 6 years younger than Tom will be in 2 years. Roseanne is now x years old. In terms of x, how old was Tom 3 years ago?

A) $x - 7$

B) $x - 1$

C) $x + 1$

D) $x + 3$

6

A phone company charges 10 cents per minute for the first 3 minutes of a call and $10 - c$ cents for each minute thereafter. What is the cost, in cents, of a 10-minute phone call?

A) $100c + 70$

B) $30 + 7c$

C) $100 - 7c$

D) $100 - 70c$

7

If $0 < pt < 1$ and p is a negative integer, which of the following must be less than -1 ?

A) p

B) $p - t$

C) $t + p$

D) $2t$

Hard

8

If x and y are positive integers and $\sqrt{x} = y + 3$, then what is the value of y^2 ?

A) $x - 9$

B) $x + 9$

C) $x - 6\sqrt{x} + 9$

D) $x^2 - 6\sqrt{x} + 9$

9

If cupcakes are on sale at 8 for c cents, and gingerbread squares are on sale at 6 for g cents, what is the cost, in cents, of 2 cupcakes and 1 gingerbread square?

A) $8c + 3g$

B) $\dfrac{8c + 6g}{3}$

C) $\dfrac{8c + 3g}{14}$

D) $\dfrac{3c + 2g}{12}$

10

If the side of a square is $x + 1$, which of the following is the value of the diagonal of the square?

A) $x^2 + 1$

B) $x\sqrt{2} + \sqrt{2}$

C) $x^2 + 2$

D) $\sqrt{2x} + \sqrt{2}$

ANSWERS AND EXPLANATIONS: PROBLEM SET 1

Easy

1. **A** Forget the algebra. Plug in 2 for x, so Maria has 2 hats. Triple that number is 6. Sinéad has 4 more than triple, so Sinéad has $4 + 6 = 10$. You should put a circle around 10, so you can remember it's the answer to the question, the target number. Now plug 2 into the answer choices. Choice (A) gives you $3(2) + 4 = 10$, which matches the target, so keep (A). Choice (B) gives you $3(2 + 4) = 18$, which doesn't match the target, so eliminate (B). Choice (C) gives you $4(2 + 3)$, which doesn't match the target, so eliminate (C). Choice (D) is $4(3(2))$, which doesn't match the target, so eliminate (D). The answer is (A).

2. **D** Plug in 2 for p: $2 \times 10 = 20$ and $20 - 6 = 14$. So $t = 14$. (Since this is an equation, when you pick one number, the other number is auto-matically produced by the equation.) If $p = 2$ and $t = 14$, (A) is $14 = 6(2 - 10)$. Does $14 = 12 - 60$? Not on this planet. Choice (B) is $14 = 6(2) - 10$. This is false, so eliminate (B). Choice (C) is $14 = 10(6 - 2)$. This is false, so eliminate (C). Choice (D) is $10(2) - 6 = 14$, or $20 - 6 = 14$. The equation works, so that's your answer.

3. **A**   Make $b = 2$. That means she scored $4(2) + 12 = 20$ points total. If she scored the same number of points in each of the 4 periods, you have to divide the total by 4, so she scored $20 \div 4 = 5$ points per period. Put a circle around 5. Now on to the answer choices. Choice (A) is $2 + 3 = 5$, which is the target number. Choice (B) is $2 + 12 = 14$, so eliminate (B). Choice (C) is $4(2) + 3 = 11$, so eliminate (C). Choice (D) is $16(2) + 48 = 80$, so eliminate (D). The answer is (A).

Notice how we keep plugging in 2? That's because we're trying to make things as easy as possible. To get these questions right, you didn't have to pick 2; on some questions, 2 might not work so well. You can pick whatever you want. Just make sure your number doesn't require you to make ugly, unpleasant calculations. Avoiding hard work is the name of the game. If the number you pick turns bad on you, pick another one.

Always check all four answers when you plug in, just in case you get two correct answers. In that case, quickly plug in a new number to find out which one was wrong.

Medium

4. **A**   There are variables in the answer choices, so Plug In. Make $t = 2$. The question asks for the ratio of the velocity t (or 2) seconds after the object begins to accelerate to the velocity of the object $2.5t$ (or $2.5 \times 2 = 5$) seconds after it begins to accelerate. The velocity 2 seconds after the object begins to accelerate is $\frac{1}{2}a(2)^2 = 2a$. The velocity 5 seconds after the object begins to accelerate is $\frac{1}{2}a(5)^2 = \frac{25a}{2}$. Therefore, the ratio is $\frac{2a}{\frac{25a}{2}}$. Dividing by a fraction is the same as multiplying by its reciprocal, so the ratio becomes $2a \cdot \frac{2}{25a} = \frac{4a}{25a} = \frac{4}{25}$. The answer is (A).

5. **C**   Let $x = 10$, so Roseanne is now 10 years old. That's 6 years younger than 16, so Tom must be 16 in 2 years, which makes him 14 now. The question asks for Tom's age 3 years ago; if he's 14 now, 3 years ago he was 11. Circle 11. In the answer choices, plug 10 in for x. Choice (A) is $10 - 3$. Nope. Choice (B) is $10 - 1$. Nope. Choice (C) is $10 + 1$. Yeah! Just to be sure, let's check (D): $10 + 3 = 13$. Nope. The answer is (C).

6. **C** Let $c = 8$. The first 3 minutes of the call would be 3(10), or 30 cents. The remaining minutes would be charged at $10 - 8$ cents, or 2 cents a minute. There are 7 minutes remaining, so $2 \times 7 = 14$. The total cost is $30 + 14 = 44$ cents. On to the answer choices: (A) is way too big. Choice (B) is $30 + 7(8) = 86$. Choice (C) is $100 - 56 = 44$. Choice (D) becomes $100 - 70(8)$, which is way too small and can be safely eliminated. The answer is (C).

7. **C** First, take a good look at $0 < pt < 1$. You know that pt is a positive fraction. If p is a negative integer, then t must be a negative fraction. Now Plug In. (Or you can just try numbers until you find some that satisfy the inequality.) Let $p = -1$ and $t = -\frac{1}{2}$. Try them in the answer choices, crossing out any answer that's -1 or higher. Choice (A) is -1, so cross it out. Choice (B) is $-\frac{1}{2}$, so cross it out. Choice (C) is $-1\frac{1}{2}$, so leave it in. Choice (D) is -1, so cross it out. The trouble with *must be* questions is that you can only *eliminate* answers by plugging in, you can't simply choose the first answer that works. That's because the answer may work with certain numbers but not with others—and you're looking for an answer that *must be true*, no matter what numbers you pick. These questions can be time-consuming, so if you're running low on time, you may want to skip them.

Hard

8. **C** Let $x = 25$. That makes $y = 2$. The question asks for y^2, and $2^2 = 4$. Circle it. Now try the answer choices. Choice (A) is $25 - 9$. Choice (B) is $25 + 9$. Choice (C) is $25 - 30 + 9 = 4$. Choice (D) is also huge. The answer is (C).

9. **D** Let $c = 16$ and $g = 12$. That means the cupcakes and the gingerbread squares sell for 2 cents apiece. One gingerbread square and two cupcakes will cost 6 cents. Circle 6. On to the answer choices, plugging in 16 for c and 12 for g. Choice (A) is $8(16) + 3(12)$, which is a lot bigger than 6. Choice (B) is $\frac{8(16) + 6(12)}{3} = \frac{200}{3}$, which is

not 6. Choice (C) is $\dfrac{8(16) + 3(12)}{14} = \dfrac{164}{14}$, which is not 6. Choice (D)

gives you $\dfrac{3(16) + 2(12)}{12} = 6$. Use your calculator for that last part. Get it

right? Then go to a bakery and celebrate.

10. **B**   Draw yourself a little square and label the sides $x + 1$. Draw in a diagonal. Let $x = 2$. The side of the square is then 3, and the diagonal is $3\sqrt{2}$. (The diagonal is the hypotenuse of a 45-45-90 triangle.) Plug 2 into the answer choices. Choice (A) gives you $2^2 + 1 = 5$. Eliminate (A). Choice (B) gives you $2\sqrt{2} + \sqrt{2} = 3\sqrt{2}$, so keep it and check the remaining answers. Choice (C) gives you $2^2 + 2 = 4 + 2 = 6$, so eliminate it. Choice (D) gives you $\sqrt{2(2)} + \sqrt{2} = 2 + \sqrt{2}$, so eliminate (D). The answer is (B).

PROBLEM SET 2: MORE PLUGGING IN

Easy

1

Jim and Pam bought x quarts of ice cream for a party. If 10 people attended the party, including Jim and Pam, ate all the ice cream, and each person ate the same amount of ice cream, which of the following represents the amount of ice cream, in quarts, eaten by each person at the party?

A) $10x$

B) $5x$

C) $\dfrac{x}{5}$

D) $\dfrac{x}{10}$

2

Addison has a reading assignment to complete. The number of pages he has left to read d days after being given the assignment can be modeled by the equation $n = 252 - 47d$, where n is the number of pages left to read. What is the meaning of 252 in the equation?

A) Addison reads 252 pages per day.

B) Addison reads 252 pages per hour.

C) Addison's book contains 252 pages.

D) Addison will complete the book in 252 days.

If $3x - y = 12$, which of the following is equivalent to $\frac{y}{3}$?

A) $x - 4$

B) $3x - 4$

C) $9x - 12$

D) $3x + 4$

Medium

When x is divided by 3, the remainder is z. In terms of z, which of the following could be equal to x?

A) $z - 3$

B) $3 - z$

C) $3z$

D) $6 + z$

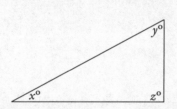

In the figure above, $2x = y$. Which of the following is equivalent to z?

A) $180 + 2x$

B) $180 + x$

C) $180 - 3x$

D) $180 - 4x$

The 2005 to 2015 population density of a certain town can be modeled by the equation $d = 21.3y + 1,927.3$, where y represents the number of years since 2005 and d represents the population density. Which of the following best describes the meaning of the number 21.3 in the equation?

A) The estimated difference between the population density in 2005 and 2015

B) The estimated increase in the population density each year

C) The population density in 2005

D) The total population in 2005

The volume of a certain rectangular solid is $12x$. If the dimensions of the solid are the integers x, y, and z, what is the greatest possible value of z?

A) 24

B) 12

C) 6

D) 4

Hard

If $r = \dfrac{6}{3s + 2}$ and $tr = \dfrac{2}{3s + 2}$, what is the value of t?

A) $\dfrac{1}{4}$

B) $\dfrac{1}{3}$

C) 3

D) 4

When a is divided by 7, the remainder is 4. When b is divided by 3, the remainder is 2. If $0 < a < 24$ and $2 < b < 8$, which of the following could have a remainder of 0 when divided by 8 ?

A) $\dfrac{a}{b}$

B) $\dfrac{b}{a}$

C) $a + b$

D) ab

If $3x$, $\dfrac{3}{x}$, and $\dfrac{15}{x}$ are integers, which of the following must also be an integer?

    I. $\dfrac{x}{3}$

    II. x

    III. $6x$

A) II only

B) III only

C) I and III only

D) I, II, and III

ANSWERS AND EXPLANATIONS: PROBLEM SET 2

Easy

1.   **D**   Plug in 20 for x. If 10 people eat 20 quarts, and they all eat the same amount, then each person eats 2 quarts. Put a circle around 2. Go to the answers and remember that $x = 20$. Choice (A) = $10 \times 20 = 200$. Nope. Choice (B) = $5 \times 20 = 100$. Nope. Choice (C) = $\dfrac{20}{5} = 4$. Nope. Choice (D) = $\dfrac{20}{10} = 2$. Yep.

2. **C** The question asks for the meaning of 252 in the equation. Go through each choice one at a time. Choice (A) says that Addison reads 252 pages per day. To determine the number of pages he reads per day, plug in $d = 1$ and $d = 2$ and look at the difference in n. If $d = 1$, then $n = 252 - 47(1) = 205$. If $d = 2$, then $n = 252 - 47(2) = 252 - 94 = 158$. The difference is $205 - 158 = 47$, so Addison reads 47 pages per day. Eliminate (A). Choice (B) says that Addison reads 252 pages per hour. No information is given about hours. Furthermore, the work done on (A) reveals that he reads fewer than 252 pages per day, so he must read less than that per hour. Eliminate (B). Choice (C) says that the book Addison is reading contains 252 pages. The number of pages in the book is the total number of pages that Addison has to read. Therefore, this is the number of pages that Addison has left to read after $d = 0$ days. Plug in $d = 0$ and see if $n = 252$. If $d = 0$, then $n = 252 - 47(0) = 252$. This is consistent with (C), so keep it. Choice (D) says that Addison will complete the book in 252 days. If that is the case, then when $d = 252$, n should be 0. Plug in $d = 252$ to get $n = 252 - 47(252)$. This is clearly less than 0, so eliminate (D). The answer is (C).

3. **A** Plug in 5 for x, which makes $y = 3$. So $\frac{y}{3} = \frac{3}{3} = 1$. Circle 1. On to the answers, and plug in $x = 5$. Choice (A) $= 5 - 4 = 1$. Keep (A). Choice (B) $= 3(5) - 4 = 11$. Eliminate (B). Choice (C) $= 9(5) - 12 = 33$. Eliminate (C). Choice (D) $= 3(5) + 4 = 19$. Eliminate (D). The answer is (A).

Why do we keep saying "circle it" in the explanations? Because that's the arithmetic answer to the question. All that's left to do is plug in for the variables in the answer choices, and look for your circled number. We tell you to circle that number so that it won't get lost in the shuffle and you can keep track of what you're doing.

Notice how sometimes, as in Question 2, you may have to plug in more than one set of numbers. That doesn't mean you're doing anything wrong, it's just the nature of the question. It also tends to happen on *must be* questions.

Also remember that you are trying to find numbers to plug in that make getting an answer to the question easy—so in Question 3, if we'd plugged in $x = 2$, that would've made y negative. Who wants to deal with negatives if they don't have to? If some kind of nastiness happens, bail out and *pick new numbers.*

Medium

4. **D**   Let $x = 7$ so $z = 1$. Try the answers. Choice (A) is $z - 3$, or $1 - 3 = -2$. Nope. Choice (B) is $3 - z$ or $3 - 1 = 2$. Nope. Choice (C) is $3z$, or $3(1) = 3$. Nope. Choice (D) is $6 + z$, or $6 + 1 = 7$. Yep, that's correct!

5. **C**   Plug in 10 for x, which makes $y = 20$. Remember that a triangle has 180°, so the third angle, z, must equal $180 - 30 = 150$. Circle 150. Try the answers, with $x = 10$. Choice (A) gives you $180 + 2(10) = 200$. No. Choice (B) gives you $180 + 10 = 190$. No. Choice (C) gives you $180 - 30 = 150$, which is what you're looking for. Choice (D) gives you $180 - 4(10) = 140$. No. The answer is (C).

6. **B**   The question asks for the meaning of 21.3 in the equation. Go through each choice and determine whether each is 21.3. Choice (A) is the estimated difference between the population density in 2005 and 2015. Since y represents the years since 2005, $y = 0$ for 2005 and $y = 10$ for 2015. To determine the difference in population density between 2005 and 2015, plug in $y = 0$ and $y = 10$. If $y = 0$, then $d = 21.3(0) + 1,927.3 = 1,927.3$ If $y = 10$, then $d = 21.3(10) + 1,927.3 = 2,140.3$. The difference is $2,140.3 - 1927.3 = 213$. The difference is not 21.3, so eliminate (A). Choice (B) is the estimated increase in population density each year. To determine whether this is 21.3, plug in $y = 0$ and $y = 1$ and look at the increase in d. If $y = 0$, then $d = 21.3(0) + 1,927.3 = 1,927.3$. If $y = 1$, then $d = 21.3(1) + 1,927.3 = 1,948.6$. The increase is $1948.6 - 1927.3 = 21.3$. This is consistent with the target, so keep (B). Choice (C) is the population density in 2005. This is represented by the value of d, when $y = 0$, which is 1,927.3, so eliminate (C). Choice (D) is the total population. The equation only models population density, not total population. In order to determine total population, the area of the town would be needed. This information is not given, so total population cannot be determined. Eliminate (D). The answer is (B).

7. **B**   First, draw yourself a picture. (Think shoebox.) Plug in 2 for x. The formula for volume of a rectangular solid is length × width × height—in this case, xyz. The volume is $12x = 12(2) = 24$. Now come up with 3 different numbers—2 is one of them—that result in a total of 24 when multiplied together.

A chart is never a bad idea. It keeps you organized.

x	y	z
2	1	12

Since y is as low as possible, z is as big as possible. Go with it. If you're not convinced, try other combinations—but don't forget, the question asks for the greatest possible value of z.

Hard

8. **B** Both equations have s in them, so plug in a value for s, such as 2. If

$s = 2$, $r = \dfrac{6}{3(2) + 2} = \dfrac{6}{8}$. Now plug the values for s and r into the second

equation to get $t\left(\dfrac{6}{8}\right) = \dfrac{2}{3(2) + 2}$ or $\dfrac{6t}{8} = \dfrac{2}{8}$. Therefore, $6t = 2$ and $t = \dfrac{1}{3}$.

The answer is (B).

9. **C** Plug in 11 for a and 5 for b. Those two choices satisfy all the conditions of the problem. Check the answers: (A) is a fraction; forget about it. Choice (B) is $11 - 5 = 6$, which isn't divisible by 8. Choice (C) gives you $11 + 5 = 16$. If you divide 16 by 8, you get a quotient of 2 and a remainder of 0. Choice (D) gives you $(11)(5) = 55$, which is not divisible by 8 and can be eliminated. End of story.

10. **B** How about plugging in 3 for x? Try the answers—you're looking for integers, so if the answer isn't an integer, you can cross it out.

   I. $\dfrac{x}{3} = \dfrac{3}{3} = 1$ OK so far.

   II. $x = 3$ OK so far.

   III. $6x = 6 \bullet 3 = 18$.   OK so far.

At this point, your average test taker figures the question is pretty easy and picks (D). Not you, my friend. *This is a hard question.* You must go an extra step. Plug in a new number. Since the question concerns integers, what if you plug in something that isn't an integer, like $x = \dfrac{1}{3}$?

   I. $\dfrac{\frac{1}{3}}{3} = \dfrac{1}{9}$.   That's no integer. Cross it out.

   II. $\dfrac{1}{3}$.   No good either.

   III. $6\left(\dfrac{1}{3}\right) = 2$.   Okay.

Since you have eliminated I and II, only III remains.

PROBLEM SET 3: PLUGGING IN THE ANSWER CHOICES

Easy

1

If x is a positive integer, and $x + 12 = x^2$, what is the value of x?

A) 2

B) 4

C) 6

D) 12

2

If twice the sum of three consecutive numbers is 12, and the two lowest numbers add up to 3, what is the highest number?

A) 2

B) 3

C) 6

D) 9

3

If $2^x = 8^{(x-4)}$, what is the value of x?

A) 4

B) 6

C) 8

D) 64

Medium

4

If Jane bought 3 equally priced shirts on sale, she would have 2 dollars left over. If instead she bought 10 equally priced pairs of socks, she would have 7 dollars left over. If the prices of both shirts and socks are integers, which of the following, in dollars, could be the amount that Jane has to spend?

A) 28

B) 32

C) 47

D) 57

During a vacation together, Bob spent twice as much as Josh, who spent four times as much as Ralph. If Bob and Ralph together spent $180, how much did Josh spend?

A) $20

B) $80

C) $120

D) $160

Tina has half as many marbles as Louise. If Louise gave away 3 of her marbles and lost 2 more, she would have 1 more marble than Tina. How many marbles does Tina have?

A) 3

B) 5

C) 6

D) 7

In a bag of jellybeans, $\frac{1}{3}$ are cherry and $\frac{1}{4}$ are licorice. If the remaining 20 jellybeans are orange, how many jellybeans are in the bag?

A) 16

B) 32

C) 36

D) 48

Hard

If the circumference of a circle is equal to twice its area, which of the following is equal to the area of this circle?

A) π

B) 2π

C) 4π

D) 16π

9

If $12y = x^3$, and x and y are positive integers, what is the least possible value for y?

A) 6

B) 18

C) 144

D) 216

10

If x^2 is added to $\dfrac{5}{4y}$, the sum is $\dfrac{5+y}{4y}$. If y is a positive integer, which of the following is the value of x?

A) $\dfrac{1}{4}$

B) $\dfrac{1}{2}$

C) $\dfrac{4}{5}$

D) 1

ANSWERS AND EXPLANATIONS: PROBLEM SET 3

Easy

1. **B**   Start with (C), $6 = x$. That gives you $6 + 12 = 36$. No good. At this point, don't stare at the other choices, waiting for divine inspiration—just pick another one and try it. It's okay if the next answer you try isn't right either. If you plug in 4 for x, you get $4 + 12 = 16$. The equation is true, so that's that.

2. **B**   Start with (C). If the highest number is 6, the other two are 5 and 4. 5 and 4 don't add up to 3—cross out (C). Try (B). If the highest number is 3, the other two numbers are 1 and 2. (They have to be consecutive.) The sum of $3 + 2 + 1 = 6$, and twice the sum of $6 = 12$. If you picked (A), you didn't pay attention to what the question asked for. Be sure to reread the question so you know which number they want.

3. **B**   Try (C) first. Does $2^8 = 8^4$? Nope. (Use your calculator.) Try something lower, like (B). Does $2^6 = 8^2$? Yes.

Medium

4. **C** Try (C) first. If Jane has $47 to spend, 47 ÷ 3 = 15 with 2 left over. (The shirts cost $15 apiece.) Now try 47 ÷ 10 = 4, with 7 left over. (Socks are $4 a pair.) It works.

5. **B** Try (C) first. If Josh spent $120, Bob spent $240 and Ralph spent $40. That means Bob and Ralph together spent $280, not $180 as the problem states. Choice (C) is no good. Since (C) was way too big, try something smaller. If Josh spent $80, Bob spent $160 and Ralph spent $20. So Bob and Ralph together spent $180. That's more like it.

6. **C** Start with (B). If Tina has 5 marbles, then Louise has 10. If Louise gives away 3, then she has 7. If she loses 2 more, she's down to 5. You're supposed to end up with Louise having 1 more than Tina, but they both have 5. Cross out (B)—and you know you're close to the right answer. Try (C). If Tina has 6, Louise has 12. If Louise gives away and loses 5, she's got 7, which is 1 more than Tina has.

7. **D** Try (B) first. Oops—$\frac{1}{3}$ of 32 is a fraction. Forget (B). Try (C): $\frac{1}{3}$ of 36 = 12 and $\frac{1}{4}$ of 36 = 9. Does 12 + 9 + 20 = 36? No. Try (D). $\frac{1}{3}$ of 48 = 16 and $\frac{1}{4}$ of 48 = 12. Does 16 + 12 + 20 = 48? Yes!

Making a simple chart will help you keep track of your work:

	C	D
cherry	12	16
licorice	9	12
orange	20	20
TOTAL	41	48

Hard

8. **A**   Try (B) first. If the area is 2π, then the radius becomes a fraction. That's probably not going to be the answer, so you should move on. Try (A). If the area is π, then the radius is 1 ($\pi r^2 = \pi$, $r^2 = 1$, $r = 1$). If $r = 1$, the circumference is $2\pi(1) = 2\pi$. So the circumference is twice the area. Beautiful.

9. **B**   Solve this problem with a combination of factoring and Plugging In. The question looks like this: $2 \times 2 \times 3y = x^3$. Now factor the answer choices, starting with the smallest one, as the question asks for the least possible value of y. Choice (A) is $3 \cdot 2$. If you plug that in for y, does it give you a cube? Nope. Choice (B) is $2 \times 3 \times 3$—now you have $(2 \times 3)(2 \times 3)(2 \times 3) = x^3$. It works.

10. **B**   Choice (C) is particularly nasty here, so try (B) first. This gives you

   $\dfrac{1}{4} + \dfrac{5}{4y}$. When these fractions are added together, the sum is $\dfrac{5+y}{4y}$,

   which matches what the question is looking for. You could also solve by

   plugging in—choose a positive integer for y, plug it into the equation,

   and see what happens. You end up with $x = \dfrac{1}{2}$.

When you Plug In, start with the easier of the two middle choices, as you hopefully did for Question 10. Don't worry if you have to try a couple of answer choices before you hit the right one—the first one you do is always the slowest, because you're still finding your way. Subsequent tries should be easier, and in most cases, it's still likely to be easier than writing out equations.

PROBLEM SET 4: MORE PLUGGING IN THE ANSWER CHOICES

Easy

1

If $\dfrac{a-4}{28} = \dfrac{1}{4}$, what is the value of a ?

A) 11

B) 10

C) 7

D) 6

2

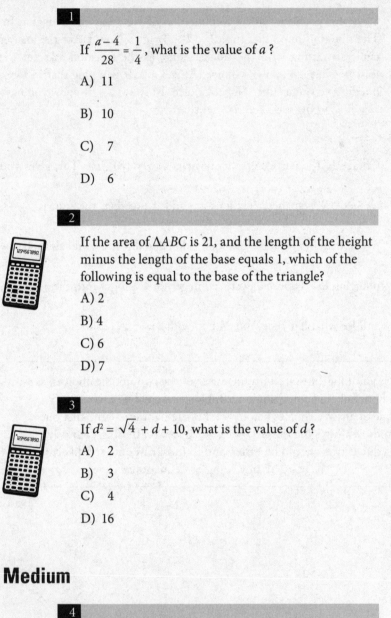

If the area of $\triangle ABC$ is 21, and the length of the height minus the length of the base equals 1, which of the following is equal to the base of the triangle?

A) 2

B) 4

C) 6

D) 7

3

If $d^2 = \sqrt{4} + d + 10$, what is the value of d ?

A) 2

B) 3

C) 4

D) 16

Medium

4

If $\dfrac{4}{x-1} = \dfrac{x+1}{2}$, which of the following is a possible value of x ?

A) −1

B) 1

C) 2

D) 3

$$f(x) = \frac{1}{(x-3)^2 - 6(x-3) + 9}$$

For what value of x is the function f defined above undefined?

A) –6

B) –3

C) 3

D) 6

If $16{,}000 = 400(x + 9)$, what is the value of x ?

A) 391

B) 310

C) 40

D) 31

What is the radius of a circle with an area of $\frac{\pi}{4}$?

A) 0.2

B) 0.4

C) 0.5

D) 2.0

Hard

If 20 percent of x is 36 less than x percent of $x - 70$, what is the value of x ?

A) 140

B) 120

C) 100

D) 50

If $x^2 = y^3$ and $(x - y)^2 = 2x$, then which of the following is a possible value of y ?

A) 64

B) 16

C) 8

D) 4

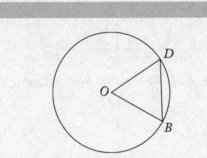

In the circle with center O, $OD = DB$ and arc $DB = 2\pi$.
What is the area of the circle?

A) 36π

B) 16π

C) 12π

D) 4π

ANSWERS AND EXPLANATIONS: PROBLEM SET 4

Easy

1. **A** Try (C) first. Does $\dfrac{3}{28} = \dfrac{1}{4}$? Nope. Look for a bigger number—(B) gives you $\dfrac{6}{28}$, which is closer, but still no cigar. Choice (A) gives you $\dfrac{7}{28} = \dfrac{1}{4}$.

2. **C** Try (B) first. If the base = 4, then $h - 4 = 1$ and $h = 5$. The formula for area of a triangle is $\dfrac{1}{2}\,bh$, so the area would be 10. Too small. Try (C). If the base is 6, then $h - 6 = 1$ and $h = 7$. The area is $\dfrac{42}{2} = 21$.

3. **C** Yes, it looks nasty, but it's a breeze with the miracle of Plugging In the Answers. Try (B) first: $3^2 = \sqrt{4} + 3 + 10$; $9 = 2 + 13$. Forget it. Try (C): $4^2 = 2 + 4 + 10$; $16 = 16$. That's it.

> If you try one of the middle choices and it doesn't work, take a second to see if you need a bigger or smaller number. But if you can't tell quickly, don't spend too much time thinking about it—just try one direction and keep going.

Medium

4. **D**   Try (B) first. If $x = 1$, does $\frac{4}{0}$ ...forget it. You can't divide by 0. Try (C). If $x = 2$, does $\frac{4}{1} = \frac{3}{2}$? No way. Try (D). If $x = 3$, does $\frac{4}{2} = \frac{4}{2}$? Yes. Remember to avoid trying negatives [such as (A)] unless they're all you have left or you have some reason to think they'll be right.

5. **D**   The question asks for a specific value, and there are numbers in the answer choices. A fraction is undefined when the denominator is zero, so plug in the values to see which one makes $(x-3)^2 - 6(x-3) + 9 = 0$. Start with (C). When $x = 3$, the denominator becomes $(3-3)^2 - 6(3-3) + 9 = 0^2 - 6(0) + 9 = 9$. Eliminate (C). It may be hard to tell if you need a bigger number or a smaller one, so just pick a direction. For (D), if $x = 6$, the denominator becomes $(6-3)^2 - 6(6-3) + 9 = 3^2 - 6(3) + 9 = 9 - 18 + 9 = 0$. The answer is (D).

6. **D**   Try (C) first. Does $400 \cdot 49 = 16,000$? No, and hopefully you just estimate that and don't bother doing it, with or without your calculator. How about (D)? $400(40) = 16,000$. Yep. If you picked (A), you miscounted the zeros. Try checking your answers on your calculator.

7. **C**   This is a fabulous Plugging In question. Try (C) first. Convert 0.5 to a fraction, because fractions are better than decimals and because the question has a fraction in it. If the radius is $\frac{1}{2}$, the area is $\pi \left(\frac{1}{2} \right)^2 = \pi \left(\frac{1}{4} \right) = \frac{\pi}{4}$.

> ### Why do we like fractions better than decimals?
>
> Mostly because that irritating little decimal point is so easily misplaced. Also because decimals can get very tiny and hard to estimate. You don't want to convert decimals to fractions automatically—only when the question would be easier to do that way. If the question is in decimals and the answers are in decimals, then don't bother converting.

Hard

8. **B**   Try (C) first because the question is about percents and 100 is easy to do. 20% of 100 is 20. 100% of $100 - 70$ is 30. Does $30 - 20 = 46$? Nah. Try (B). 20% of 120 is 24. 120% of 50 is 60. Does $60 - 24 = 36$? Yes.

9. **D**   Try (C) first. If $y = 8$, then $x^2 = 8^3$. $8^3 = 512$. If $x^2 = 512$, x isn't an integer. Forget (C). Try (D). If $y = 4$, then $x^2 = 4^3$, $x^2 = 64$, and $x = 8$. Now try them in the second equation: $(8-4)^2 = 2(8)$. $4^2 = 16$. It works. Notice that when (C) didn't work, you went with a smaller number because it was easier.

10.   **A**   First, write in 2π beside arc *DB*. Now try (B). If the area is 16π, the radius is 4. Write in 4 beside the two radii, and also *DB*, because *OD* = *DB*. Aha! That makes triangle *DOB* equilateral! Since angle *DOB* is 60°, and $\dfrac{60}{360} = \dfrac{1}{6}$, that makes arc *DB* $\dfrac{1}{6}$ of the circumference. Remember our radius is 4, so the circumference is 8π. Uh oh—2π is not $\dfrac{1}{6}$ of 8π. So cross off (B). But at least now you know what to do. Try (A). If the area is 36π, the radius is 6 and the circumference is 12π. Is $\dfrac{1}{6}$ of 12π equal to 2π? Yeah! Did that seem really painful? It was a lot of work, but then, it was a hard question. The reason Plugging In is a good technique for this problem is that if you Plug In the Answers, you get to move through the question like a robot, one step after the other, and you don't have to depend on a flash of insight.

PROBLEM SET 5: ESTIMATING

Easy

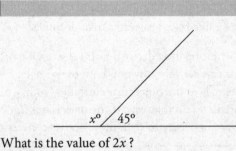

What is the value of 2x ?

A)   270

B)   135

C)   90

D)   67.5

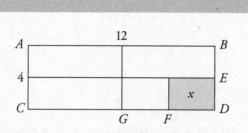

If *F* is equidistant from *G* and *D*, and *E* is equidistant from *B* and *D*, what fractional part of rectangle *ABDC* is area *x* ?

A) $\dfrac{1}{16}$

B) $\dfrac{1}{8}$

C) $\dfrac{1}{4}$

D) $\dfrac{1}{2}$

If Sarah bought 12 pies for $30, how many pies could she have bought for $37.50 at the same rate?

A) 9

B) 12

C) 15

D) 24

Medium

If a runner completes one lap of a track in 64 seconds, approximately how many minutes will it take her to run 40 laps at the same speed?

A) 30

B) 43

C) 52

D) 128

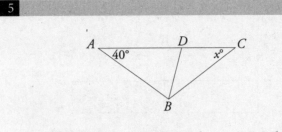

In the figure above, $BD = DC$ and $AB = AD$. What is the value of x ?

A) 110

B) 70

C) 55

D) 35

Martina wants to buy as many felt-tip pens as possible for $10. If the pens cost between $1.75 and $2.30, what is the greatest number of pens Martina can buy?

A) 4

B) 5

C) 6

D) 7

If 1.2 is p percent of 600, what is the value of p ?

A) 0.2%

B) 5%

C) 20%

D) 500%

Hard

8

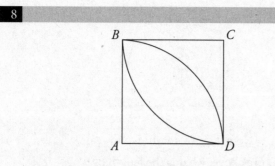

In the figure above, *ABCD* is a square with sides of 4. What is the length of arc *BD* ?

A) 8π

B) 4π

C) 2π

D) π

9

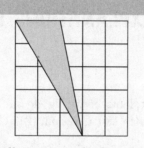

Each of the small squares in the figure above has an area of 4. If the shortest side of the triangle is equal in length to 2 sides of a small square, what is the area of the shaded triangle?

A) 40

B) 24

C) 20

D) 16

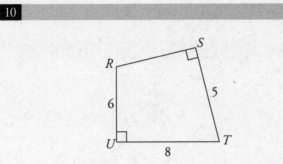

Note: Figure not drawn to scale.

In the figure above, what is the length of *RS* ?

A)   10

B) $5\sqrt{3}$

C)   8

D) $2\sqrt{3}$

ANSWERS AND EXPLANATIONS: PROBLEM SET 5

Easy

1. **A**   Estimate first: x looks pretty big, doesn't it? Bigger than 90? Yes. So $2x$ will be bigger than 180. Cross out (B), (C), and (D). Only (A) remains.

2. **B**   Use your eyeballs and compare against the answer choices. The horizontal line and the longer vertical line appear to divide the rectangle into four equal pieces. Since the shaded region is only part of one of those pieces, the answer is less than $\frac{1}{4}$. Eliminate (C) and (D). The shaded region appears to be about half of the piece. Therefore, the shaded region should be about half of a quarter, which is $\frac{1}{2} \cdot \frac{1}{4} = \frac{1}{8}$. It's also helpful to draw more boxes in the figure, and then you could count them up:

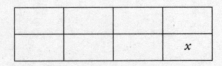

3. **C** $37.50 is going to buy more pies than $30, right? So cross out anything less than or equal to 12. Say goodbye to (A) and (B). Now, any chance an extra 7.50 will buy nearly another 12 pies? No. Eliminate (D).

Medium

4. **B**   This is a great question for estimating. Don't like 64 seconds? Call it 60, or 1 minute. If the runner completes a lap in just over a minute, she'll complete 40 laps in just over 40 minutes. Only (B) is close.

5. **D**   First, just eyeball the angle. It's smaller than 90°. It's close to angle *BAD*, which is marked 40. You're down to (C) and (D). Is it a little smaller than *BAD* or 15° bigger than *BAD*? Go for it! You can always come back and check your answer the long way if you have time.

   The long way: *BAD* is isosceles, since $AB = AD$. The two base angles of *BAD* = 140, so each is 70°. If $\angle BDA = 70°$, then $\angle BDC$ is 110°. Triangle *BDC* is isosceles too, with $\angle DCB$ and $\angle CBD = x°$. $2x = 70$, so $x = 35°$. Now admit it—isn't estimating easier?

6. **B**   If Martina wants to buy as many pens as possible, she'll want to buy the cheaper pens, which cost a little less than $2. If the pens cost exactly $2, she can buy 5 pens for $10. Therefore, she can buy more than 4, so eliminate (A). Because the pens cost a little bit less than $2, it is possible that she can buy a little more than 5 pens. It won't be a lot more than 5, so eliminate (D). On medium questions, estimating may only get rid of one or two answers, so try the remaining ones. Test (C). If she buys 6 pens for $1.75, she will have to pay $6 \times \$1.75 = \$10.50$. Since this is more than $10, eliminate (C).

7. **A**   Start by finding 10% of 600, which is 60. Since 1.2 is less than 60, the answer must be less than 10%. Eliminate (C) and (D). Now, 1% of 600 is 6. Since 1.2 is less than 6, the value of p must be less than 1%. Eliminate (B).

Hard

8. **C**   First, mark the sides of the square with 4. Now estimate the length of *BD*, based on the side of the square. Think of the side of the square as a piece of spaghetti that you are going to drape over *BD*. So *BD* is longer than 4. *BD* is also shorter than the distance from *B* to *C* to *D*, which would be 8. Now go to the answers, and substitute 3 for π. (You know, $\pi = 3.14$, but you don't have to be so exact. You're just estimating.) Choice (A) is around 24. Way too big. Choice (B) is around 12, and (C) is around 6. Choice (D) is too small. Pick (C) and move on.

9. **C**   When you estimate, remember that each shaded square has an area of 4. It's tricky to do this exactly, because mostly only slivers of squares are shaded. So estimate it. Almost 2 full squares at the top, another square on the next row (that's 3 so far) and then slivers on the next 3 rows that make up about 2 full squares. So you've got 5 squares each with area 4; the area of the triangle is around 20, so pick (C).

As an alternative, you can work out an exact answer. If each square has an area of 4, then the side of a little square is 2. Write that on the figure, in a couple of places. Now use the top of the triangle as the base. It equals 4. The other thing you need is the height, or altitude, of the triangle—and in this case, the height is equal to a side of the big square, or 10. Using the formula for the area of a triangle, plug 4 in for the base and 10 in for the height and you get 20 for the area.

10. **B**   Hey, wake up! You can't estimate anything if the figure isn't drawn to scale! But you may want to redraw the figure to make it look more like it's supposed to look. Now for the solution: Draw a line from R to T, slicing the figure into 2 triangles. Now all you have to do is use the Pythagorean Theorem to calculate the lengths. Triangle RUT is a 6:8:10 triangle, a Pythagorean triple. Now for RST: $a^2 + 5^2 = 10^2$. So $a^2 = 75$ and $a = 5\sqrt{3}$.

PROBLEM SET 6: FRACTIONS, DECIMALS, AND PERCENTS

Easy

1

A big-screen TV is on sale at 15% off the regular price. If the regular price of the TV is $420, what is the sale price?

A) $63

B) $357

C) $405

D) $483

2

Which of the following is the decimal form of

$$70 + \frac{7}{10} + \frac{3}{1,000}?$$

A) 70.0703

B) 70.7003

C) 70.703

D) 70.73

3

If n is six more than two-thirds of twelve, what is the value of n?

A) 10

B) 12

C) 14

D) 18

Medium

4

Walking at a constant rate, Stuart takes 24 minutes to walk to the nearest bus stop and $\frac{1}{3}$ of that time to walk to the movie theater. It takes him half the time to walk to school than it does for him to walk to the movie theater. How many minutes does it take Stuart to walk to school?

A) 36

B) 24

C)   8

D)   4

5

What is the value of x if $\dfrac{\frac{1}{2}}{x} = 4$?

A) 8

B) 2

C) $\dfrac{1}{4}$

D) $\dfrac{1}{8}$

6

If $x\%$ of y is 10, which of the following is equal to $y\%$ of x?

A)   1

B)   5

C) 10

D) 90

7

A certain drink is made by adding 4 parts water to 1 part drink mix. If the amount of water is doubled, and the amount of drink mix is quadrupled, what percent of the new mixture is drink mix?

A) $33\frac{1}{3}\%$

B) 50%

C) $66\frac{2}{3}\%$

D) 80%

Hard

8

Set A consists only of fractions with a numerator of 1 and a denominator d such that $1 < d < 8$, where d is an integer. If Set B consists of the reciprocals of the fractions with odd denominators in Set A, then what is the product of all the numbers that are elements of either Set A or Set B?

A) $\dfrac{1}{96}$

B) $\dfrac{1}{48}$

C) $\dfrac{1}{24}$

D) 1

9

The function g is defined as $g(x) = \dfrac{x^2}{3 - |x - 4|}$.

For which values of x is $g(x)$ NOT defined?

A) $x = 4$ and $x = 7$

B) $x = 3$ and $x = 4$

C) $x = 3$ and $x = 7$

D) $x = 1$ and $x = 7$

If a, b, and c are distinct positive integers, and 10% of abc is 5, then which of the following is a possible value of $a + b$?

A) 3

B) 5

C) 8

D) 25

ANSWERS AND EXPLANATIONS: PROBLEM SET 6

Easy

1. **B**   The numbers are too awkward to plug in, so do it the old-fashioned way: 15% of $420 is $0.15 \times 420 = 63$. $420 - 63 = 357$. Use your calculator.

2. **C**   Take the pieces one at a time and eliminate. The first piece is 70. The second piece is $\frac{7}{10}$, or 0.7. Eliminate (A). The last piece is $\frac{3}{1,000}$, or 0.003. Eliminate (B) and (D).

3. **C**   Translate the problem into math language: $n = 6 + \frac{2}{3} \times 12$. Then, don't forget PEMDAS: Multiply before you add. $n = 6 + \frac{2}{3}(12) = 6 + 8 = 14$.

Medium

4. **D**   Start working from the 24 minutes it takes poor Stuart to walk to the bus stop. (Won't anybody give the guy a ride?) If it takes $\frac{1}{3}$ of 24 to walk to the movies, that's 8 minutes. If it takes him half of that time to walk to school, $\frac{1}{2}$ of 8 is 4. This question requires close reading more than anything else.

5. **D**   Plugging In the Answers wouldn't be a bad idea here—you can eliminate (A) and (B) pretty quickly that way. Choice (C) is $\dfrac{\frac{1}{2}}{\frac{1}{4}} = 2$. Choice (D) is $\dfrac{\frac{1}{2}}{\frac{1}{8}} = 4$.

6. **C** Plug in 10 for y, which makes $x = 100$. Plug those numbers into the second part: 100% of 10 = 10.

Alternatively, translate. The sentence x% of y is 10 translates to $\frac{x}{100} \cdot y = 10$. This simplifies to $\frac{xy}{100} = 10$. The expression y% of x translates to $\frac{y}{100} \cdot x$. This simplifies to $\frac{yx}{100} = \frac{xy}{100}$, which equals 10.

7. **A** First, make a little chart: If you double the water and quadruple the mix, you get

water		mix
4	:	1
8	:	4

Reread the question. It asks for the percentage of the new mixture that's drink mix. You've got $\frac{4 \text{ (mix)}}{12 \text{ (total)}}$, which equals $\frac{1}{3}$, or $33\frac{1}{3}$%.

If you made it almost to the end but picked (B), don't forget that you have to express the mix as a percentage of the total, not a percentage of the water.

Hard

8. **B** Read this carefully. Set A has different fractions, each with a numerator of 1. (You might as well write them down like that and fill in the denominators when you get there.) The denominators are between 1 and 8. That gives you Set A: $\frac{1}{2}, \frac{1}{3}, \frac{1}{4}, \frac{1}{5}, \frac{1}{6}, \frac{1}{7}$. Set B has the reciprocals of the members of Set A with odd denominators, so Set B: $\frac{3}{1}, \frac{5}{1}, \frac{7}{1}$. Now multiply all the elements together—see how the fractions that have reciprocals cancel each other out? You're left with $\frac{1}{2} \times \frac{1}{4} \times \frac{1}{6}$, which is $\frac{1}{48}$.

9. **D** The function will not be defined when the denominator is equal to 0. If you don't want to analyze the denominator to determine when it would equal 0, you can Plug In the Answers. Even though the answers are not in ascending or descending order, you can still start with (C). If you plug 3 into the denominator, you do not get zero, so eliminate anything with a 3: (B) and (C). Notice that both of the remaining answers have 7, so there's no need to test it. Try 1 in (D). You get 0, so eliminate (A) and then pick (D).

10. **A** First, translate the middle part of the problem into an equation. 10% of abc is 5 translates to $\frac{10}{100} \cdot abc = 5$. Now solve for abc and get $abc = 50$. Reread the question. Each variable is different, each is positive, and multiplied together they produce 50. Now Plug In the Answers, remembering that the answers represent $a + b$. In (A), $a + b$ would have to be 1 + 2. If $a = 1$ and $b = 2$ and $abc = 50$, what is c? $c = 25$, so it works.

A couple of reminders: If you are making mistakes on the easy and medium problems, don't spend a lot of time—if any—working on the hard problems. You need to hone your skills first; you may want to go back to the review section and do some work before continuing. And don't forget, you probably want to leave some questions blank on the real thing.

PROBLEM SET 7: AVERAGES, RATIOS, PROPORTIONS, AND PROBABILITIES

1

Three consecutive integers add up to 258. What is the smallest integer?

A) 58

B) 85

C) 86

D) 89

2

A factory produces 6,000 plates per day. If one out of 15 plates is broken, how many unbroken plates does the factory produce each day?

A) 5,800

B) 5,600

C) 800

D) 400

3

It takes 4 friends 24 minutes to wash all the windows in Maria's house. The friends all work at the same rate. How long would it take 8 friends, working at the same rate, to wash all the windows in Maria's house?

A) 48

B) 20

C) 12

D) 8

Medium

4

The value of t is inversely proportional to the value of w. If value of w increases by a factor of 5, what happens to the value of t ?

A) t increases by a factor of 5.

B) t increases by a factor of 2.

C) t decreases by a factor of 2.

D) t decreases by a factor of 5.

5

A drawer holds only blue socks and white socks. If the ratio of blue socks to white socks is 4:3, which of the following could be the total number of socks in the drawer?

A) 4

B) 7

C) 12

D) 24

6

The probability of choosing a caramel from a certain bag of candy is $\frac{1}{5}$, and the probability of choosing a butterscotch is $\frac{5}{8}$. If the bag contains 40 pieces of candy, and the only types of candy in the bag are caramel, butterscotch, and fudge, how many pieces of fudge are in the bag?

A) 5

B) 7

C) 8

D) 25

7

Dixie spent an average of x dollars on each of 5 shirts and an average of y dollars on each of 3 hats. In terms of x and y, how many dollars did she spend on shirts and hats?

A) $5x + 3y$

B) $15(x + y)$

C) $8xy$

D) $15xy$

Hard

If the ratio of $\frac{1}{6} : \frac{1}{5}$ is equal to the ratio of 35 to x, what

is the value of x ?

A) 24

B) 30

C) 36

D) 42

An artist makes a certain shade of green paint by mixing blue and yellow in a ratio of 3:4. She makes orange by mixing red and yellow in a ratio of 2:3. If on one day she mixes both green and orange and uses equal amounts of blue and red paint, what fractional part of the paint that she uses is yellow?

A) $\frac{7}{12}$

B) $\frac{17}{29}$

C) $\frac{7}{5}$

D) $\frac{12}{17}$

The areas of two circles are in a ratio of 4:9. If both radii are integers, and $r_1 - r_2 = 2$, which of the following is the radius of the larger circle?

A) 4

B) 6

C) 8

D) 9

ANSWERS AND EXPLANATIONS: PROBLEM SET 7

Easy

1. **B** If the three integers add up to 258, then their average is 258 ÷ 3, or 86. Since the integers are consecutive, they must be 85, 86, and 87. Check it on your calculator. If you picked (C), what did you do wrong? Forget what the question asked for? Divide 258 by 3 and then quit? Even easy problems may have more than one step. This would also be a good question in which to Plug In the Answers.

2. **B** First, estimate. You're looking for the number of unbroken plates—if only one broke out of 15, there should be a lot of unbroken plates, right? Cross out (C) and (D). Now set up a proportion:

$$\frac{\text{broken}}{\text{total}} = \frac{1}{15} = \frac{x}{6,000}$$

   Now cross-multiply. You get 6,000 = 15x, so using your calculator, x = 400. That's the number of broken plates, so subtract 400 from 6,000 and you've got the answer. If you picked (D), you could have gotten the problem right if you had either estimated first or reread the question right before you answered it.

3. **C** There are twice as many people, so the work will go twice as fast. You can't set up a normal proportion because it's an inverse proportion—the more people you have, the less time the work takes. So if you multiply the number of people by 2, you divide the work time by 2.

Medium

4. **D** Since no values were given, try plugging in values of your own to test what happens. If t starts out as 10 and w starts out as 5, you can set up the formula for inverse variation as follows: $t_1 w_1 = t_2 w_2$. In this case, the t_1 is 10, w_1 is 5, and w_2 is 25 (since you multiply it by 5). So set up the equation as: $10 \times 5 = t_2 \times 25$. $\frac{50}{25} = t_2 = 2$. So what happened to the value of t? It decreased by a factor of 5.

5. **B** The total must be the sum of the numbers in a ratio, or a multiple of that sum. In this case, 4 + 3 = 7, so the number of socks could be 7 or any multiple of 7. (You can have fractions in a ratio, it's true, but not when you're dealing with socks or people or anything that you can't chop into pieces.)

6. **B** Here's what to do: Take $\frac{1}{5}$ of 40, which is 8 caramels. Take $\frac{5}{8}$ of 40, which is 25 butterscotches. The caramels and the butterscotches are 8 + 25 = 33. Subtract that from 40 and you've got the fudge.

7. **A** Plug In. Let $x = 2$. If Dixie spent an average of $2 a shirt, then she spent a total of $10 on shirts. Let $y = 4$, and she spent an average of $4 a hat, for a total of $12. Our total is $10 + 12 = $22. Circle that. Now on to the answer choices, plugging in $x = 2$ and $y = 4$. Choice (A) is $5(2) + 3(4) = 22$. Keep (A) and check the remaining answers. Choice (B) gives you $15(2 + 4) = 90$, so no good. Choice (C) gives you $8(2)(4) = 64$ and can be eliminated for not matching the target. Choice (D) can be estimated as too big and safely eliminated. If checking, it's $15(2)(4) = 120$.

Hard

8. **D** First, multiply the ratio by something big to get rid of the fraction. Any multiple of 6 and 5 will do. So $30\left(\dfrac{1}{6}\right) : 30\left(\dfrac{1}{5}\right) = 5{:}6$. Now you've got $5{:}6 = 35{:}x$. Since 35 is 5×7, x is 6×7, or 42. The new ratio is 35:42, which is the same as 5:6.

9. **B** Write down your ratios and label them neatly. You have

$$\frac{b{:}y}{3{:}4} \qquad \frac{r{:}y}{2{:}3}$$

If the artist uses equal amounts of blue and red, you have to multiply each ratio so that the numbers under b and r are the same:

$$\frac{b{:}y}{(2)(3:4)} \qquad \frac{r{:}y}{(2:3)(3)}$$

The result is

$$\frac{b{:}y}{6:8} \qquad \frac{r{:}y}{6:9}$$

The yellow is 8 parts + 9 parts = 17 parts, and the total is $6 + 8 + 6 + 9 = 29$ parts. On complicated ratio problems, it's important to organize the information legibly and label everything as you go along, or else you'll find yourself looking at a bunch of meaningless numbers.

10. **B** Plug In the Answers. Start with (B). If the larger radius is 6, the smaller radius is 2 less than that, or 4. The area of the smaller circle is 16π, and the area of the larger circle is 36π. $16\pi{:}36\pi$ is a ratio of 4:9. (Just divide the whole ratio by 4π.) If you picked (D), you must've had a momentary blackout—that answer is way too appealing to be right on a hard question. If you're going to guess, guess something that is not too good to be true.

A shortcut for averages: If the list of numbers is consecutive, consecutive odd, or consecutive even, then the average will be the middle number. (If the list has an even number of elements, you have to average the two middle numbers.) The average will also be the middle number (or average of the two middle numbers) of any list that goes up in consistent increments. For example, the average of 6, 15, 24, 33, and 42 is 24, since the numbers go up in increments of 9.

PROBLEM SET 8: CHARTS AND DATA

Easy

1

	Original Price	Sale Price
Store A	$25	$20
Store B	$20	$15
Store C	$30	$25
Store D	$35	$30

The chart above shows the original and sale prices of a certain item at each of four different stores. Which of the following stores provides a discount of 20% or more on this item?

    I. Store A

   II. Store B

  III. Store C

A) I only

B) III only

C) I and II only

D) I and III only

2

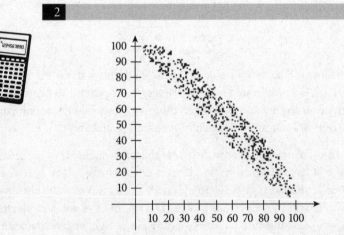

Which of the following is most likely the slope of the line of best fit for the scatterplot above?

A) −10

B) −1

C) 1

D) 10

Questions 3 and 4 refer to the following information.

Favorite Ice Cream Flavors

	Men	Women	Total
Chocolate	74	63	137
Vanilla	68	22	90
Strawberry	17	39	56
Cookie Dough	51	87	138
Mint Chip	65	14	79
Total	275	225	500

The table above shows the results of a random survey of 500 men and women. Each individual chose a flavor of ice cream that was his or her favorite.

3

Approximately what percent of the men chose mint chip as their favorite ice cream flavor?

A) 25%

B) 50%

C) 65%

D) 80%

4

If a woman is chosen at random, what is the probability that her favorite ice cream flavor is strawberry?

A) 0.06

B) 0.09

C) 0.11

D) 0.17

Medium

Bacteria Reproduction

Time (in seconds) t	Population (in thousands) p
1	2
2	6
3	18
4	54

The table above shows the population growth of a certain bacteria over four seconds. Which one of the following equations shows the relationship between t and p, according to the table?

A) $p = 3t$

B) $p = 2t^2$

C) $p = 2 \times 3t$

D) $p = 2 \times 3^{(t-1)}$

Questions 6-8 refer to the following information.

A coffee distributor randomly polled 200 employees from each of two companies and asked each employee how many cups of coffee he or she drinks per day. The data is shown in the table below.

Employee Coffee Survey

Number of Cups of Coffee	0	1	2	3	4
Company X	5	25	30	40	100
Company Y	20	25	35	45	75

There are 4,000 employees at Company X and 3,000 employees at Company Y.

6

Of the employees polled at Company X, approximately what is the average number of cups of coffee consumed per employee on a given day?

A) 1

B) 2

C) 3

D) 4

7

Based on the poll, the number of employees at Company Y who drank 0 cups of coffee was what percent greater than the number of employees at Company X who drank 0 cups of coffee?

A) 75%

B) 100%

C) 300%

D) 400%

8

What is the difference between the expected total number of employees who drink 1 cup of coffee at Company X and the expected total number of employees who drink 1 cup of coffee at Company Y?

A) 0

B) 25

C) 125

D) 1,000

Hard

Questions 9 and 10 refer to the following information.

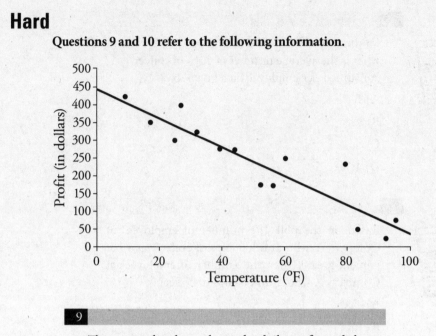

9

The scatterplot above shows the daily profit made by a school store from selling sweatshirts and the average daily temperature for several days in the year 2004. The line of best fit is also shown and has equation $y = -4.1x + 446$. Which of the following best explains how the number −4.1 in the equation relates to the scatterplot?

A) For every 1° increase in average daily temperature, the school store's profit fell by approximately $4.10.

B) For every 1° increase in average daily temperature, the school store's profit increased by approximately $4.10.

C) For every 4.1° increase in average daily temperature, the school store's profit fell by approximately $1.00.

D) For every 4.1° increase in average daily temperature, the school store's profit increased by approximately $1.00.

10

In a given school week, the average daily temperature is 20°F on Monday, Tuesday, and Wednesday and 30°F on Thursday and Friday. Based on the line of best fit, what was the school store's approximate profit during this school week?

A) $325

B) $650

C) $1,475

D) $1,700

ANSWERS AND EXPLANATIONS: PROBLEM SET 8

Easy

1. **C** Remember that the formula for percent change is $\frac{\text{difference}}{\text{original}} \times 100$. The discount at Store A is $\frac{5}{25} \times 100 = 20\%$, and the discount at Store B is $\frac{5}{20} \times 100 = 25\%$. On the other hand, the discount at Store C is $\frac{5}{30} \times 100 = 16.67\%$. Thus, only Stores A and B have discounts of 20% or greater.

2. **B** Draw a line that connects most of the points. It is a straight line that goes down from left to right, which means it has a negative slope. Only (A) and (B) are negative slopes. Eyeball the line to see that it is not very steep. So, the slope is closer to 1 than 10. Alternatively, you could find points and ballpark the slope. The line roughly includes (50, 50), so the rise and run are the same. Therefore, the slope is –1.

3. **A** Percent is defined as $\frac{\text{part}}{\text{whole}} \times 100$. On the chart, the number of men who chose mint chip is 65, so that's the *part*. The *whole* is the total number of men, which is 275. So the percent is $\frac{65}{275} \times 100 = 23.6\%$. This is approximately 25%, so the answer is (A). Once you get the numbers, you can also estimate. Definitely less than half the men chose mint chip, so only (A) would work.

4. **D** Probability is defined as $\frac{\text{what you want}}{\text{total}}$, and in this case, you want the number of women who prefer strawberry out of the number of all the women polled. So the probability is $\frac{39}{225}$. Some questions will stop there and leave the probability as a fraction, but the answers here are decimals. Divide 39 by 225 to get about 0.17, which is (D).

Medium

5. **D** Don't try to figure this one out by deriving an equation. Plug In by testing the numbers in the table against the functions in the answer choices. Plug in $t = 1$ and $p = 2$. Choice (A) is $2 = 3(1)$. This is incorrect, so eliminate (A). Choice (B) is $2 = 2(1)^2$. This is correct, so keep (B). Choice (C) is $2 = 2 \times 3^1$. This is incorrect, so eliminate (C). Choice (D) is $2 = 2 \times 3^{(1-1)}$. This is correct, so keep (D). Now plug $t = 2$ and $p = 6$ into the remaining choices. Choice (B) is $6 = 2(2)^2$. This is incorrect, so eliminate (B). Choice (D) is $6 = 2 \times 3^{(2-1)}$. This is correct and is the only remaining choice, so the answer is (D).

6. **C** Average is defined as $\dfrac{\text{total}}{\text{\# of things}}$. There are 200 employees at Company X, so that's the number of things. The total is a bit harder to get from the chart. You need to find all the cups of coffee consumed by these 200 employees. Some people drank 0 cups, so you don't need to worry about that. The chart says that 25 people drank 1 cup each, for 25 cups, and 30 people drank 2 cups each, for 60 more cups. There were 40 employees who drank 3 cups each, adding 120 cups, and 100 people drank 4 cups each, adding 400 more cups to the total. Add up all the cups to get $25 + 60 + 120 + 400 = 605$ total cups of coffee. Plug the numbers into the average formula to get $\dfrac{605}{200} = 3.025$. This is approximately 3, so the answer is (C).

7. **C** Percent change is defined as $\dfrac{\text{difference}}{\text{original}} \times 100$. The chart says that 5 employees at Company X and 20 employees at Company Y drank 0 cups of coffee. The difference is $20 - 5 = 15$. The original is the number of employees from Company X who drank 0 cups. You can tell this because it asks for the "percent greater than," which means that the original must be the smaller one. Therefore, the percent increase is $\dfrac{15}{5} \times 100 = 300\%$, which is (C).

8. **C**   In order to extrapolate poll results to a larger population, find the percent that fit the requirement in the poll and apply it to the general population. In this case, both companies had 25 employees out of the 200 polled that drank 1 cup of coffee. Therefore, $\frac{25}{200} \times 100 = 12.5\%$ of the employees at both companies can be expected to drink one cup of coffee per day. At Company X, there are 4,000 employees, and 12.5% of 4,000 = 500. At Company Y, there are 3,000 employees, and 12.5% of 3,000 = 375. The difference is 500 − 375 = 125, which is (C).

Hard

9. **A**   On tricky questions, look for opportunities to use POE. As the temperature increases, the profits of the store decrease. Look for any answer choices that say otherwise and eliminate them. Both (B) and (D) say that profits will increase with an increase in temperature, so those are incorrect. Test out the remaining answer choices by plugging in some numbers into the equation for the line of best fit. Since this is in the No Calculator section, pick easy numbers. Start with (A) and plug in $x = 0$ and $x = 1$. At $x = 0$, $y = -4.1(0) + 446 = 446$, and at $x = 1$, $y = -4.1(1) + 446 = 441.9$. The difference between these values is $446 - 441.9 = 4.1$, so (A) is true. There is no need to check out (C): (A) is the correct answer.

10. **D**   You could take these values and plug them into the formula to get an exact answer, but that's a lot of work, especially without the use of a calculator. Instead, use the line of best fit to estimate the profit at these temperatures. Since the answers are spread apart and you are only asked for the "approximate profit," this will get you close enough. When the temperature is 20°F, the line of best fit predicts a profit of about $360. Use your scantron sheet as a straightedge if you have a hard time reading the graph. There are three days in the week with a temperature of 20°, so the profit for those three days is approximately $360 × 3 = $1,080. For the two days with a temperature of 30°, the profit is about $325, so the store earns $325 × 2 = $650 in those two days. In total, the store earns about $1,080 + $650 = $1,730 for the week. This is closest to (D), so that's the answer.

PROBLEM SET 9: EXPONENTS, ROOTS, AND EQUATIONS

Easy

1

If $t^3 = -8$, what is the value of t^2 ?

A) -4

B) -2

C) 2

D) 4

2

If $60 = (7 + 8)(x - 2)$, what is the value of x ?

A) 10

B) 9

C) 7

D) 6

3

If $4x - 2y = 10$ and $7x + 2y = 23$, what is the value of x ?

A) $\dfrac{1}{3}$

B) 1

C) 3

D) 13

Medium

4

Which of the following equations is equal to $6y + 6x = 66$?

A) $33 = x + y$

B) $11 - x = y$

C) $11 - 2x = y$

D) $4y - 4x = 44$

5

For their science homework, Brenda and Dylan calculated the volume of air that filled a spherical basketball. If the diameter of the basketball was 6, what was the volume of the air inside the basketball, to the nearest integer?

A) 44

B) 100

C) 113

D) 226

6

Which of the following is equivalent to $\dfrac{\sqrt{a} \times \sqrt{b}}{3\sqrt{a} - 2\sqrt{a}}$?

A) $\dfrac{\sqrt{b}}{\sqrt{a}}$

B) $\sqrt{b}$

C) $\dfrac{2\sqrt{a}}{b}$

D) $\sqrt{ab}$

7

On a certain test, Radeesh earned 2 points for every correct answer and lost 1 point for every incorrect answer. If he answered all 30 questions on the test and received a score of 51, how many questions did Radeesh answer incorrectly?

A) 3

B) 7

C) 15

D) 21

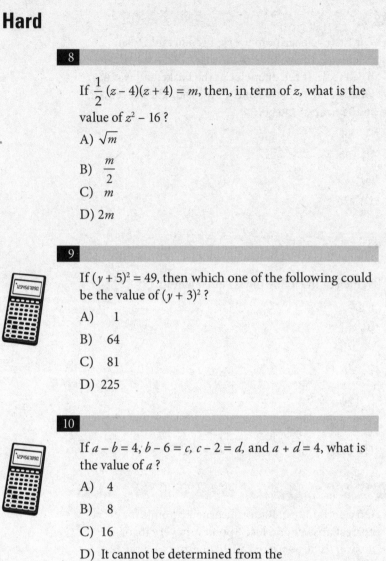

8

If $\dfrac{1}{2}(z-4)(z+4) = m$, then, in term of z, what is the value of $z^2 - 16$?

A) $\sqrt{m}$

B) $\dfrac{m}{2}$

C) m

D) $2m$

9

If $(y+5)^2 = 49$, then which one of the following could be the value of $(y+3)^2$?

A)   1

B)   64

C)   81

D)   225

10

If $a - b = 4$, $b - 6 = c$, $c - 2 = d$, and $a + d = 4$, what is the value of a?

A)   4

B)   8

C)   16

D)   It cannot be determined from the information given.

ANSWERS AND EXPLANATIONS: PROBLEM SET 9

Easy

1. **D**   Take the cube root of both sides to get $t = -2$, and $t^2 = (-2)^2 = 4$.

2. **D**   Plug In the Answers. Try (B) first: $(15)(9 - 2) = (15)(7) = 105$. It should equal 60, so you need a much smaller number. Try (D): $(15)(6 - 2) = (15)(4) = 60$. It works. Or you could solve the equation algebraically:

$$60 = 15(x - 2)$$
$$60 = 15x - 30$$
$$90 = 15x$$
$$6 = x$$

3. **C**   Stack 'em and add:

$$
\begin{array}{rcl}
4x - 2y &=& 10 \\
\underline{7x + 2y} &=& \underline{23} \\
11x &=& 33 \\
x &=& 3
\end{array}
$$

Medium

4. **B**   Try reducing the equation in the question first, by dividing the whole thing by 6. That leaves you with $x + y = 11$. That's the same as (B), if you just move the x to the other side.

5. **C**   Don't worry—you weren't supposed to know this formula. It's provided at the start of each math section, so don't get freaked out. Just use the information in the question to solve for V, using your calculator. If the diameter of the basketball was 6, the radius was 3:

$$
V = \frac{4}{3}\pi r^3, \text{ so } V = \frac{4}{3}\pi(3^3) = \frac{4}{3}\pi(27) = 36\pi = 113
$$

You may see some totally unfamiliar formula on the test—physics, for instance—but you don't have to understand the formula or know anything about it. All you have to do is substitute in any value they give you and solve for the variable they ask for.

6. **B**   Remember that you can multiply or divide what's under a square root sign and add or subtract when what's under the square root sign is the same. Begin by simplifying the denominator.

$$
\frac{\sqrt{a} \cdot \sqrt{b}}{3\sqrt{a} - 2\sqrt{a}} = \frac{\sqrt{a} \cdot \sqrt{b}}{\sqrt{a}} = \sqrt{b}.
$$

7. **A**   Plug In the Answers. If Radeesh got 2 points for every right answer, and the test had 30 questions, the top score was 60. If he got a 51, he did pretty well, so start with (A). (Remember, the answer choices represent the number of questions he answered incorrectly.) If he missed 3, then he got 27 right. $27 \times 2 = 54$. Subtract 3 for 3 wrong answers, and you get 51.

[Don't worry if you didn't see which answer to start with. If you started with (C), it gave you way too many wrong answers, didn't it? So cross off (C) and (D) and you've only got two left to try.]

Hard

8. **D** The easiest way to solve this question is to recognize that $(z - 4)$ $(z + 4) = (z - 16)^2$. Thus, you can rewrite the initial equation as $\frac{1}{2}$ $(z - 16)^2 = m$. Thus, $z - 16^2 = 2m$. Otherwise, Plug In. Try $z = 6$, which means $m = 10$. The value of $z^2 - 16$ is 20, which is twice as much as m, or $2m$.

9. **C** Since $(y + 5)^2 = 49$, take the square root of both sides. Don't forget that the result could be positive or negative, so $y + 5 = \pm 7$. Consider both cases. If $y + 5 = 7$, then $y = 2$. In this case, $(y + 3)^2 = (2 + 3)^2 = 5^2 = 25$. This is not a choice, so consider the other case. If $y + 5 = -7$, then $y = -12$. In this case, $(y + 3)^2 = (-12 + 3)^2 = (-9)^2 = 81$, which is (C).

10. **B** Start off by eliminating (D), as that would be too easy for a complicated looking question toward the end. Before you start the lengthy process of substitution, try stack-and-add. You need to bring all of the variables to the left and all of the numbers to the right, so your stack will look like this:

$$a - b = 4$$
$$b - c = 6$$
$$c - d = 2$$
$$a + d = 4$$

Add everything up. It turns out that b, c, and d disappear, leaving $2a = 16$, or $a = 8$.

PROBLEM SET 10: LINES, ANGLES, AND COORDINATES

Easy

1

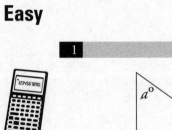

In the figure above, what is the value of $3a - a$?

A) 55°

B) 90°

C) 110°

D) 165°

2

In the figure above, what is the value of b ?

A) 20°

B) 30°

C) 40°

D) 45°

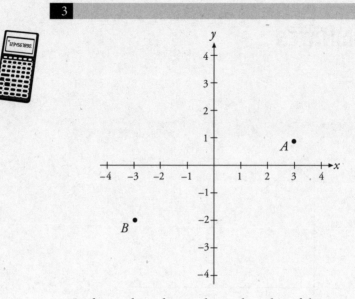

In the *xy*-plane above, what is the value of the *x*-coordinate of Point *A* minus the *y*-coordinate of Point *B* ?

A) –2

B) –1

C) 3

D) 5

Medium

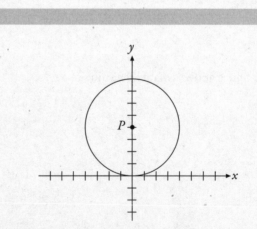

Point *P* is the center of the circle shown above, which has a radius of 4. Which of the following points lies on circle *P* ?

A) (4, 0)

B) (0, 4)

C) (–4, 4)

D) (4, 3)

5

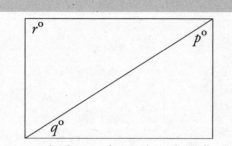

In the rectangle above, what is the value of $p + q - r$?

A) 0°

B) 15°

C) 35°

D) 50°

6

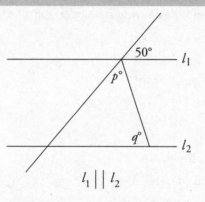

$l_1 \parallel l_2$

Note: Figure not drawn to scale.

In the figure above, what is the value of $p + q$?

A) 150°

B) 130°

C) 90°

D) 70°

7

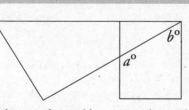

The figure above is formed by a triangle overlapping a rectangle. What is the value of $a + b$?

A) 90°

B) 150°

C) 180°

D) 270°

Hard

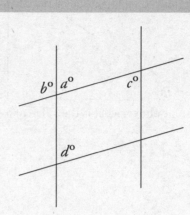

Note: Figure not drawn to scale.

Which of the following statements must be true?

I. $a + b < 180$

II. $a + d = 180$

III. $a + d > 180$

A) None

B) II only

C) I and II only

D) II and III only

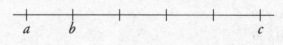

The tick marks on the number line above are equally spaced. If 2 is halfway between b and c, and the value of $c - a$ is 10, what is the value of b ?

A) −4

B) −2

C) 0

D) 6

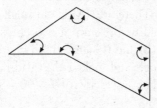

What is the total number of degrees of the marked angles?

A) 180

B) 360

C) 540

D) 720

ANSWERS AND EXPLANATIONS: PROBLEM SET 10

Easy

1. **C**   A triangle has 180°. So $90 + 35 + a = 180$, and $a = 55$. Plug that into the equation and get $3(55) - 55 = 110$.

2. **B** $5b$ and b lie on a straight line, so $5b + b = 180$ and $b = 30$.

3. **D**   The x-coordinate of Point A is 3, and the y-coordinate of Point B is -2. So $3 - (-2) = 5$.

Medium

4. **C**   The coordinates are given, so don't worry about trying to make an equation or manipulating the radius or anything like that. Just plot the points and see which one falls on the circle. Remember that on the circle means on the circumference rather than inside the circumference. Choices (A), (B), and (D) are all inside the circle. Only (C) is on the circumference.

5. **A**   As always, mark whatever info you can on your diagram: $r = 90$, and the angle on the bottom right is also 90, because this is a rectangle. $p + q = 90$, because they are the two remaining angles in a right triangle. That means $p + q - r = 90 - 90 = 0$.

6. **B**   Again, mark info on the diagram. The unmarked angle of the triangle is 50° because l_1 and l_2 are parallel, and the unmarked angle and the 50° angle are both small, so $50 + p + q = 180$ and $p + q = 130°$. (You can't figure out what p and q are individually, but the question doesn't ask you to anyway.)

7. **C** Estimate first. The angle marked *a* is greater than 90, and you are adding *b* to it. Therefore, (A) is too small. Choice (D) looks too big, since that would be the sum of two obtuse angles, and *b* is less than 90. Now only (B) and (C) are left. To figure out the sum of the angles, ignore the triangle and look at the quadrilateral in the bottom half of the rectangle. The angles are $a + b + 90 + 90$. Since a quadrilateral has 360°, $a + b = 180$.

Hard

8. **A** It's important to realize what you *don't* know: Are any of these lines parallel? *You don't know.* So you can't draw any conclusions at all other than the rule that a line contains 180°. Keep this simple and imagine that all the intersecting lines are perpendicular. In this case, $a + b = 180$, so I is false. Also, $a + d = 180$, so II is true but III is false. Eliminate any choice that includes I or III: Choices (C) and (D) are out. Because the lines do not have to be parallel, there is no necessary relationship between *a* and *d*. It could be the case that *a* is a right angle and *d* is acute. For example, *a* could be 90 and *d* could be 60. In this case, $a + d = 150$, so II is false. Eliminate (B). Only (A) remains.

9. **B** The best way to approach this question is to Plug In the Answers. Try (B) and suppose *b* is –2. Because the midpoint between *b* and *c* is 2, you can see that each tick mark represents a value of 2 more than the previous tick mark. Thus, *a* is –4 and *c* is 6. Now, you have to check this against the remaining information in the question. So $c - a$ must be 10. Is it? Yes, so (B) is the answer!

10. **C** Estimate first and see what you can cross out. Since you have two angles that are bigger than 90 and one angle that's bigger than 180, you should be able at least to cross out (A) and (B). To figure out the exact number of degrees, divide the figure into three triangles:

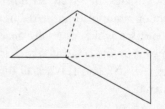

The total degrees will be $180 \times 3 = 540$. Alternatively, know that each side added to a figure adds 180°. A three-sided figure (i.e., a triangle) has 180°, so a four-sided figure has 360°, and a five-sided figure has 540°.

PROBLEM SET 11: TRIANGLES

Easy

1

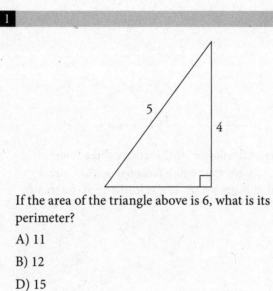

If the area of the triangle above is 6, what is its perimeter?

A) 11

B) 12

D) 15

D) 16

2

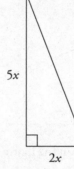

If $x = 3$, what is the area of the triangle above?

A) 10

B) 21

C) 30

D) 45

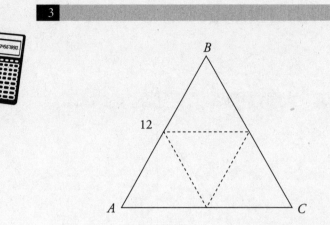

If equilateral triangle *ABC* is cut by three lines, as shown, to form four equilateral triangles of equal area, what is the length of a side of one of the smaller triangles?

A) 3

B) 4

C) 5

D) 6

Medium

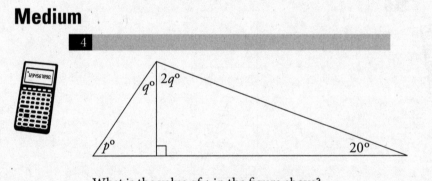

What is the value of *p* in the figure above?

A) 50

B) 55

C) 60

D) 70

5

A movie theater is 3 blocks due north of a supermarket, and a beauty parlor is 4 blocks due east of the movie theater. How many blocks long is the street that runs directly from the supermarket to the beauty parlor?

A) 2.5

B) 3

C) 5

D) 7

6

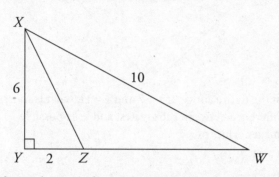

What is the area of triangle *WXZ* in the figure above?

A) 6

B) 12

C) 18

D) 24

Hard

7

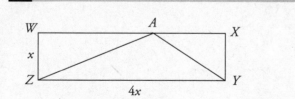

In the figure above, what is the area of triangle *YAZ*?

A) $3x$

B) $5x$

C) $2x^2$

D) $4x^2$

8

A square is inscribed in a circle with area 9π. What is the area of the square?

A) $3\sqrt{2}$

B) $9\sqrt{2}$

C) 18

D) 36

9

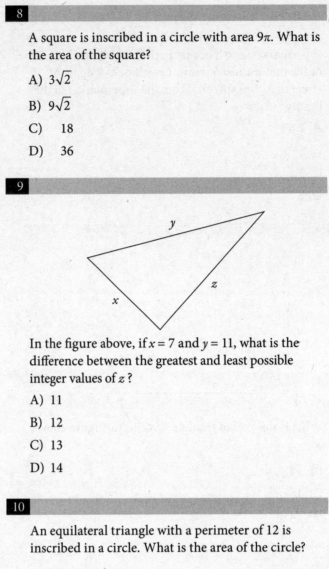

In the figure above, if $x = 7$ and $y = 11$, what is the difference between the greatest and least possible integer values of z ?

A) 11

B) 12

C) 13

D) 14

10

An equilateral triangle with a perimeter of 12 is inscribed in a circle. What is the area of the circle?

A) $\dfrac{16\pi}{9}$

B) $\dfrac{4\pi\sqrt{3}}{3}$

C) 3π

D) $\dfrac{16\pi}{3}$

ANSWERS AND EXPLANATIONS: PROBLEM SET 11

Easy

1. **B** There are several ways to get this question: You could recognize that it's a Pythagorean triple (3:4:5), which would give you the length of the unmarked leg. Or you could set up the following equation:

$$a = \frac{1}{2}bh$$

$\frac{1}{2}b(4) = 6$ so $2b = 6$ and $b = 3$. All that did was substitute the height and the area, both of which are given in the problem, into the formula for the area of a triangle. Either way, the perimeter is the sum of the sides, which is $3 + 4 + 5 = 12$.

2. **D** If $x = 3$, then the base of the triangle is 6 and the height is 15. That would mean the area is $\frac{1}{2}(6)(15) = 45$.

3. **D** Because all the small triangles and the big triangle are equilateral, each vertex of the small triangles bisects a side of the big triangle, which means that each side is 6. (Don't forget to estimate.)

Medium

4. **B** Start with the triangle to the right of the height line. As the height forms an angle of 90 and the given angle is 20, the third angle is 70 (180 − 110). Thus, $2q = 70$, and $q = 35$. Now go to the triangle to the left of the height line. As the height forms an angle of 90 and q is 35, p is 55.

5. **C** Draw a little map, which should look like this:

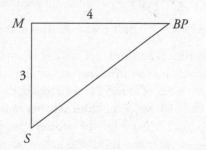

Now you have a 3:4:5 right triangle, so the street from the supermarket to the beauty parlor is 5 blocks long.

6. **C** Use the Pythagorean Theorem to find the base of triangle WYZ: $6^2 + b^2 = 10^2$. The base is 8. (This is the 6-8-10 triple, so you didn't really need to use the Pythagorean Theorem.) As $YZ = 2$, the base of triangle WXZ is 6. Even though segment XY lies outside triangle WXZ, segment XY is still perpendicular to an extension of the base, thus representing the height. Since its length is 6, the height of the triangle is 6. Thus, the area ($\frac{1}{2} bh$) is 18.

Hard

7. **C** Plug In. If $x = 2$, then ZY is 8 and WZ is 2. (Write that on your diagram.) To get the area of YAZ, notice that WZ is the height of the triangle, so $\frac{1}{2}(8)(2) = 8$. Plug 2 back into the answers. Choice (A) is $3(2) = 6$, so eliminate (A). Choice (B) is $5(2) = 10$, so eliminate (B). Choice (C) is $2(2^2) = 8$, so keep (C). Choice (D) is $4(2^2) = 16$, so eliminate (D). The answer is (C).

8. **C** As there is no diagram, first draw a square in a circle. As the area of the circle is 9π, the radius is 3 (Area = πr^2). How does this help? Often on the SAT, questions involving squares are really about the diagonal of the square, so draw in the diagonal. The diagonal is the diameter of the circle, so the diagonal is 6. You can use the Pythagorean Theorem or your knowledge of 45-45-90 triangles to figure out the sides. Label the sides of the square x. If you use the Pythagorean Theorem, you will solve $x^2 + x^2 = 6^2$ and $x = \sqrt{18}$. If you use the 45-45-90 relationships, you will get $x = \frac{6}{\sqrt{2}}$. Either way, the area of the square is 18.

9. **B** Here's the rule: The third side of any triangle must be greater than the difference and less than the sum of the other two sides. So if you already have sides of 7 and 11, the longest the third side could be is a little less than 18. Since the third side has to be an integer, the longest it could be is 17. Now for the shortest possible length of the third side: $11 - 7 = 4$, so the third side has to be an integer bigger than 4, which is 5. So the difference between the greatest possible and the least possible is $17 - 5 = 12$.

10. **D**   There is no figure provided, so draw your own.

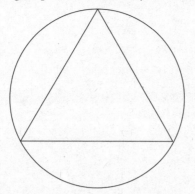

The perimeter of the equilateral triangle is 12, so each side is 12 ÷ 3 = 4. The question asks for the area of the circle, so find a radius. A radius can be drawn from each vertex of the triangle to the center of the circle. Each radius bisects the angle in each corner of the triangle. Since all the angles in an equilateral triangle are 60°, each newly formed angle is 30°. Take one of the new triangles, say the one on the bottom. Because it has two 30° angles, the third angle must be 180° − 30° − 30° = 120°. Because two sides of this triangle are radii, it is isosceles and thus has a perpendicular bisector. Drawing the perpendicular bisector of the base breaks this triangle into two 30-60-90 triangles, like below.

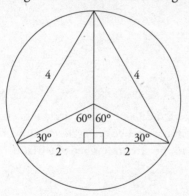

In a 30-60-90 right triangle, the side opposite the 30° is x, the side opposite the 60° angle is $x\sqrt{3}$, and the side opposite the 90° angle is $2x$.

Since the side opposite the 60° angle is 2, $x\sqrt{3} = 2$. Thus, $x = \dfrac{2}{\sqrt{3}}$ and $2x = \dfrac{4}{\sqrt{3}}$. Because the radius is the side opposite the 90°, the radius is $\dfrac{4}{\sqrt{3}}$. Thus, the area of the circle is $A = \pi r^2 = \pi \left(\dfrac{4}{\sqrt{3}}\right)^2 = \dfrac{16\pi}{3}$.

PROBLEM SET 12: CIRCLES, QUADRILATERALS, AND VOLUME

Easy

1

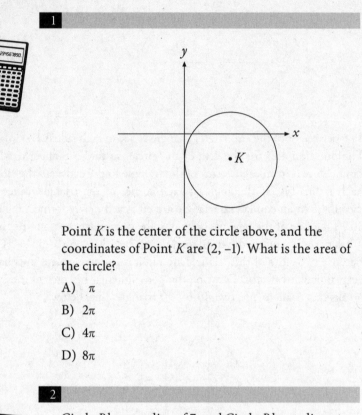

Point K is the center of the circle above, and the coordinates of Point K are (2, –1). What is the area of the circle?

A) π

B) 2π

C) 4π

D) 8π

2

Circle P has a radius of 7, and Circle R has a diameter of 8. The circumference of Circle P is how much greater than the circumference of Circle R?

A) π

B) 6π

C) 16π

D) 33π

6

2

How many squares with sides of 1 could fit into the rectangle above?

A) 3

B) 4

C) 6

D) 12

Medium

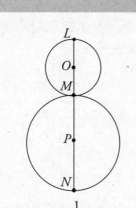

In the figure above, *LM* is $\frac{1}{3}$ of *LN*. If the radius of the circle with center *P* is 6, what is the area of the circle with center *O* ?

A) 4π

B) 9π

C) 12π

D) 18π

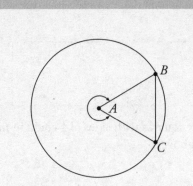

In the figure above, the circle has center *A*, and *BC* = *AB*. What is the degree measure of the marked angle?

A) 60°

B) 270°

C) 300°

D) 340°

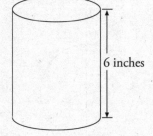

6 inches

In the figure above, the radius of the base of the cylinder is half its height. What is the approximate volume of the cylinder in cubic inches?

A)   28

B)   57

C) 117

D) 170

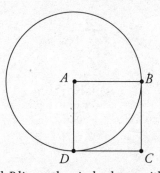

Points *D* and *B* lie on the circle above with center *A*.
If square *ABCD* has an area of 16, what is the length of
arc *BD* ?

A) 4

B) 2π

C) 8

D) 4π

Hard

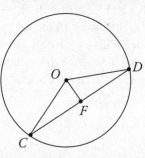

In the figure above, what is the circumference of the
circle with center *O*, if *COD* is 120° and *OF* bisects *CD*
and has a length of 1.5 ?

A) $\dfrac{2\pi}{3}$

B) $\dfrac{3\pi}{2}$

C) 6π

D) 9π

9

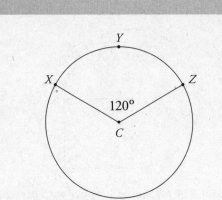

In the figure above, C is the center of a circle. If the length of the arc XYZ is 4π, what is the radius of the circle?

A) 4

B) $2\sqrt{3}$

C) 6

D) 12

10

Jeremy will fill a rectangular crate that has inside dimensions of 18 inches by 15 inches by 9 inches with cubical tiles, each with edge lengths of 3 inches. If the tiles are packaged in sets of 8, how many packages will Jeremy need to completely fill the crate?

A) 11

B) 12

C) 90

D) 101

ANSWERS AND EXPLANATIONS: PROBLEM SET 12

Easy

1. **C** Because the circle is tangent to the y-axis, the radius that intersects the y-axis is perpendicular to the y-axis, and thus parallel to the x-axis. Since the radius is parallel to the x-axis, the y-coordinate is constant. To find the length of the radius, find the difference between the x-coordinates of the end points. On the y-axis, the x-coordinate is 0. Since the center at K has an x-coordinate of 2, the length of the radius is $2 - 0 = 2$. Then use the formula for area of a circle: $\pi r^2 = \pi(2^2) = 4\pi$.

2. **B** Circumference can be found with either the formula $2\pi r$ or πd. You have the radius of one circle and the diameter of the other, so use both. The circumference of Circle P is $2\pi r = 2\pi(7) = 14\pi$. The circumference of Circle R is $\pi d = 8\pi$. Now just subtract. If you picked (D), you calculated area instead of circumference.

3. **D** Drawing on the diagram could help. How many sides of 1 can fit along the long edge of the rectangle? 6. And how many rows will fit along the short edge? 2. Now just multiply $6 \times 2 = 12$. Or draw them in and count them up.

Medium

4. **B** Write in 6 by the radius of the bigger circle. That makes the diameter of the bigger circle 12. If LM (the diameter of the smaller circle) is $\frac{1}{3}$ the length of LN, the equation is $\left(\frac{1}{3}\right)(12 + x) = x$. $4 = x - \frac{x}{3}$, and $x = 6$. (You don't have to write an equation. You could estimate and try some numbers. Doesn't LM look like it's about half of MN? It is.) If the diameter of the smaller circle is 6, then its radius is 3 and its area is 9π.

5. **C** Estimate first. The marked angle is way more than 180—in fact, it's not that far from 360. Cross out (A). You know $AC = AB$ because they're both radii. That means $BC = AB = AC$, and the triangle is equilateral. So angle BAC is 60°. Subtract that from 360 and you're in business. (Even if all you could do was estimate, go ahead and take a guess.)

6. **D** If the radius is half the height, then the radius is 3. To get the volume of a cylinder, multiply the area of the base times the height—in this case, $\pi(3^2) \times 6 = 54\pi$, which is approximately 170.

7. **B** If the square has an area of 16, then the side of the square is 4. Write that on your diagram. Now you know the radius of the circle is also 4, so the circumference is 8π. Angle BAD has 90°, since it's a corner of the square. And since 90 is $\frac{1}{4}$ of 360, arc BD is $\frac{1}{4}$ of the circumference. So arc BD is $\left(\frac{1}{4}\right)(8\pi)$, or 2π. If you estimated first, you could have crossed out (D), and maybe even (C).

Hard

8. **C** Write the info on your diagram. If *OF* bisects *CD*, it also bisects angle *COD*, making two 60° angles. Now there are two 30-60-90 triangles. If the shortest leg of one of those triangles is 1.5, then the hypotenuse is 2 × 1.5, or 3. Aha! That distance is also the radius of the circle, so the circumference is 6π.

9. **C** The ratio of the length of an arc to the circumference of the circle is the same as the ratio of the degree measure of the arc to the 360 degrees of the circle. As 120° is one-third of the circle, the length of the arc is one-third of the circumference. Thus, the circumference of the circle is 12π. As Circumference = $2\pi r$, the radius is 6.

10. **B** To find the number of tiles that will fit in the crate, you must divide the dimensions of the crate by all three dimensions of the tiles:

$$\frac{18 \times 15 \times 9}{3 \times 3 \times 3} = 90$$

But don't select 90 as your answer! The question asks how many packages of 8 tiles are needed. So, divide 90 by 8, which equals 11 plus a remainder. As 11 packages will contain only 88 of the 90 tiles needed, Jeremy must buy a 12th package.

> One more thing: Circle questions tend to appear most often in the later medium and hard questions.

PROBLEM SET 13: ADVANCED GEOMETRY

Easy

1

The density of an object is equal to the mass of the object divided by the volume of the object. What is the volume, in square feet, of an object with a mass of 2,000 pounds and a density of 500 pounds per square foot?

A) 1,000,000

B) 1,500

C) 4

D) 0.25

2

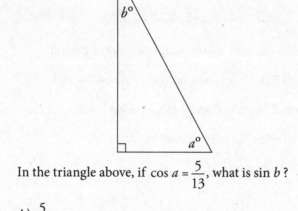

In the triangle above, if $\cos a = \dfrac{5}{13}$, what is $\sin b$?

A) $\dfrac{5}{13}$

B) $\dfrac{5}{12}$

C) $\dfrac{12}{13}$

D) $\dfrac{12}{5}$

3

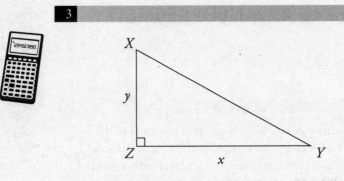

Given the right triangle above, which of the following is equivalent to $\frac{y}{x}$?

A) tan X

B) tan Y

C) cos X

D) cos Y

Medium

4

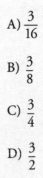

In a circle with center O, the measure of central angle POQ is $\frac{3\pi}{2}$ radians. The length of the arc formed by central angle POQ is what fraction of the circumference of the circle?

A) $\frac{3}{16}$

B) $\frac{3}{8}$

C) $\frac{3}{4}$

D) $\frac{3}{2}$

5

In a right triangle, one angle measures $y°$, where $\cos y = \dfrac{3}{5}$. What is $\sin(90° - y°)$?

A) $\dfrac{3}{5}$

B) $\dfrac{3}{4}$

C) $\dfrac{4}{5}$

D) $\dfrac{4}{3}$

6

In a right triangle, $\sin x° = \cos y°$. If $x = 3c + 14$ and $y = 7c + 11$, what is the value of c ?

A) 3.5

B) 6.5

C) 11.5

D) 22.5

7

In triangle PQR, $\angle Q$ is a right angle, $QR = 24$, and $PR = 26$. Triangle XYZ is similar to triangle PQR, where vertices X, Y, and Z correspond to vertices P, Q, and R, respectively, and each side of triangle XYZ is $\dfrac{1}{2}$ the length of the corresponding side of triangle PQR. What is the value of $\sin Z$?

A) $\dfrac{5}{13}$

B) $\dfrac{5}{12}$

C) $\dfrac{12}{13}$

D) $\dfrac{12}{5}$

8

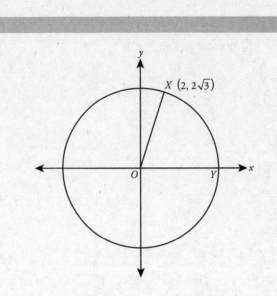

In the *xy*-plane above, the circle has center *O*, and the measure of $\angle XOY$ is $\dfrac{\pi}{n}$ radians. What is the value of *n* ?

A) 1

B) 3

C) 6

D) 12

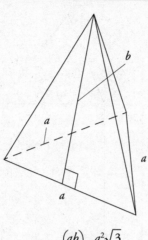

$$SA = 3\left(\frac{ab}{2}\right) + \frac{a^2\sqrt{3}}{4}$$

The formula above can be used to find the surface area of the right pyramid with equilateral triangular base shown, where a is the length of each side of the triangular base and b is the slant height of the lateral face. What must the expression $1.5ab$ represent?

A) The area of the base

B) The area of a lateral face

C) The area of the base and one lateral face

D) The sum of the areas of the lateral faces

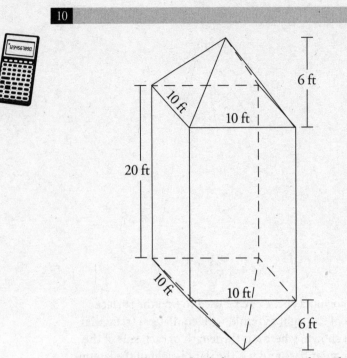

An art installation is built from a rectangular solid and two pyramids with dimensions as indicated by the figure above. Which is the volume of the art installation in square feet?

A) 2,400

B) 2,000

C) 400

D) 200

ANSWERS AND EXPLANATIONS: PROBLEM SET 13

Easy

1. **C** Translate the first sentence into an equation. If *the density of an object is equal to the mass of the object divided by the volume of the object*, then $d = \frac{m}{V}$. Since the density is 500 pounds per square foot and the mass is 2,000 pounds, plug $d = 500$ and $m = 2,000$ into the equation to get $500 = \frac{2,000}{V}$. Multiply both sides by V to get $500V = 2,000$. Divide both sides by 500 to get $V = 4$. The answer is (C).

2. **A** The question says that $\cos a = \dfrac{5}{13}$, and $\cos = \dfrac{\text{adj}}{\text{hyp}}$, so place 5 adjacent to a and 13 as the hypotenuse. The question asks for $\sin b$, which is $\dfrac{\text{opp}}{\text{hyp}}$. You just labeled the side opposite of b as 5 and you know the hypotenuse is 13, so $\sin b = \dfrac{\text{opp}}{\text{hyp}} = \dfrac{5}{13}$. The answer is (A).

3. **B** The question asks for which choice is equivalent to $\dfrac{y}{x}$. The answer choices include trig functions, so use SOHCAHTOA. The functions included in the choices are cos, which is equal to $\dfrac{\text{adj}}{\text{hyp}}$, and tan, which is equal to $\dfrac{\text{opp}}{\text{adj}}$. To find cosine, the length of the hypotenuse is needed, but it is not given. Eliminate the two choices that include cosine: (C) and (D). Therefore, the answer will be either tan X or tan Y. Since $\tan = \dfrac{\text{opp}}{\text{adj}}$, determine which angle y is opposite and x is adjacent to. Look at the figure to see that this is Y, which is (B). In the case of tan X, x is opposite the angle and y is adjacent to the angle, so $\dfrac{\text{opp}}{\text{adj}} = \dfrac{x}{y}$. This is not what the question asks for, so eliminate (A). The answer is (B).

Medium

4. **C** When a question asks about the arc, use the formula $\dfrac{\text{arc}}{\text{circumference}} = \dfrac{\text{central angle}}{2\pi}$ with the measure of the central angle in radians. Since you're literally looking for the fraction of the arc's length to the circumference of the circle, all that is needed to solve this problem is $\dfrac{\text{central angle}}{2\pi}$. Substitute the central angle of $\dfrac{3\pi}{2}$ into the formula to get $\dfrac{\text{central angle}}{2\pi} = \dfrac{\frac{3\pi}{2}}{2\pi}$. To solve $\dfrac{\frac{3\pi}{2}}{2\pi}$, put the denominator over 1 and multiply the numerator by the reciprocal of the denominator

$\dfrac{\dfrac{3\pi}{2}}{\dfrac{2\pi}{1}} = \dfrac{3\pi}{2} \times \dfrac{1}{2\pi} = \dfrac{3\pi}{4\pi} = \dfrac{3}{4}$. The answer is (C).

5. **A** The question asks for $\sin(90° - y°)$. To answer this, use the formula $\cos x = \sin(90° - x°)$. Since $\cos y = \dfrac{3}{5}$, $\sin(90° - y°) = \dfrac{3}{5}$. The answer is (A). If you forget the formula, draw a right triangle and label y and the sides you know given $\cos y$. The side that measures 3 will be adjacent to y, and 5 is the hypotenuse.

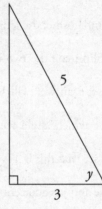

Whatever y is, the top angle will be $90 - y$, since there are $180°$ in a triangle. Therefore, the sine of the top angle is $\sin(90° - y°) = \dfrac{3}{5}$.

6. **B** The question says that $\sin x = \cos y$. Use the fact that $\sin x = \cos(90 - x)$. Therefore, $y = 90 - x$. The question also says that $x = 3c + 14$ and $y = 7c + 11$. Substitute these into $y = 90 - x$ to get $7c + 11 = 90 - (3c + 14)$. Distribute the negative to get $7c + 11 = 90 - 3c - 14$. Simplify the right side to get $7c + 11 = 76 - 3c$. Add $3c$ to both sides to get $10c + 11 = 76$. Subtract 11 from both sides to get $10c = 65$. Divide both sides by 10 to get $c = 6.5$. The answer is (B). If you forget this rule about the complimentary angles in a right triangle, you can always use PITA. Starting with (B), plug in 6.5 for c. The value of $x = 3(6.5) + 14 = 19.5 + 14 = 33.5$, and the value of $y = 7(6.5) + 11 = 45.5 + 11 = 56.5$. Now, with your calculator in degree mode, see if $\sin(33.5°) = \cos(56.5°)$. It does, so (B) is correct.

7. **A** The question asks for the value of $\sin Z$. According to the question, triangles PQR and XYZ are similar. Similar triangles, by definition, have congruent corresponding angles. Since $\angle Z$ corresponds to $\angle R$, $\angle Z \cong \angle R$. Therefore, $\sin Z = \sin R$. Since there is more information directly provided about triangle PQR than about triangle XYZ, use this information to determine $\sin R$, which will be equal to the answer. Start by sketching triangle PQR.

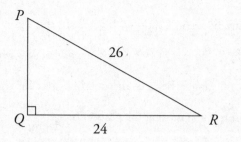

The value of $\sin R$ is $\dfrac{\text{opposite}}{\text{hypotenuse}}$. The hypotenuse is 26. Determine the opposite side. There are two ways to do this. One is to use the Pythagorean Theorem. However, since a calculator is not allowed on this question, it may be difficult to do this with large numbers. The other way is to notice that 24:26 = 12:13. Therefore, this is a 5:12:13 right triangle with the sides multiplied by 2. PQ represents the 5 side, so $PQ = 2 \times 5 = 10$. Therefore, the opposite side is 10. Plug this in to get $\cos R = \dfrac{10}{26}$. Reduce the fraction by 2 to get $\cos R = \dfrac{5}{13}$. The answer is (A).

Hard

8. **B**   The question asks about the measure of $\angle XOY$. Notice that point X has a y-coordinate of $2\sqrt{3}$. An instance of $\sqrt{3}$ in a geometry question will often be an indicator of a 30-60-90 right triangle. In the figure, draw a segment from point X that is perpendicular to segment OY to form a right triangle. For reference, we'll call the point of intersection Z.

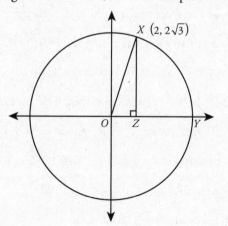

In the figure, $OZ = 2$ and $XZ = 2\sqrt{3}$. In a 30-60-90 right triangle, the sides opposite the 30° angle, the 60° angle, and the 90° angle, respectively, are in a ratio of $1:\sqrt{3}:2$. In this triangle, that ratio is multiplied by 2. Since $\angle XOY$ is opposite segment XZ, which has measure $2\sqrt{3}$, it is a 60° angle. Because the question asks for the measure in radians, convert to radians using the proportion $\dfrac{\text{radians}}{\text{degrees}} = \dfrac{\pi}{180}$. Substitute 60° to get $\dfrac{r}{60} = \dfrac{\pi}{180}$. Cross-multiply to get $180r = 60\pi$. Divide both sides by 180 to get $r = \dfrac{60\pi}{180} = \dfrac{\pi}{3}$. The question says that the measure of $\angle XOY$ is $\dfrac{\pi}{n}$, so $\dfrac{\pi}{n} = \dfrac{\pi}{3}$ and $n = 3$. The answer is (B).

9. **D** The question asks for what $1.5ab$ represents, but $1.5ab$ doesn't actually appear directly in the equation. The expression ab, however, does appear as part of the term $3\left(\dfrac{ab}{2}\right)$. Notice that $3\left(\dfrac{ab}{2}\right) = \dfrac{3ab}{2} = 1.5ab$. Therefore, the question is really asking for what the first term represents. Why would the expression $\dfrac{ab}{2}$ be multiplied by 3? The definition of surface area is the sum of the areas of each face. Since there are 3 lateral faces, determine whether $\dfrac{ab}{2}$ represents the area of each face. The area of a triangle is $A = \dfrac{1}{2}bh$. The base of the lateral side is a and the height is b, so the area is $A = \dfrac{1}{2}bh = \dfrac{ab}{2}$. Since the area of one lateral face is $\dfrac{ab}{2}$, the area of all three must add up to $3\left(\dfrac{ab}{2}\right) = 1.5\,ab$. The answer is (D).

10. **A** In order to determine the volume of the art installation, find the volume of the rectangular solid and each pyramid and get the sum. The rectangular solid has dimensions 10 feet, 10 feet, and 20 feet. Therefore, the volume is $V = lwh = (10)(10)(20) = 2{,}000 \text{ ft}^3$. Now determine the area of each pyramid. The base of the pyramid is a 10 feet by 10 feet square. The height is 6 feet. Therefore, the volume of each pyramid is $V = \dfrac{1}{3}lwh = \dfrac{1}{3}(10)(10)(6) = 200 \text{ ft}^3$. Therefore, the total volume of the art installation is $2{,}000 \text{ ft}^3 + 200 \text{ ft}^3 + 200 \text{ ft}^3 = 2{,}400 \text{ ft}^3$. The answer is (A).

PROBLEM SET 14: FUNCTIONS

Easy

1

If the function *f* has three distinct zeros, which of the following represents the graph of *f* in the *xy*-plane?

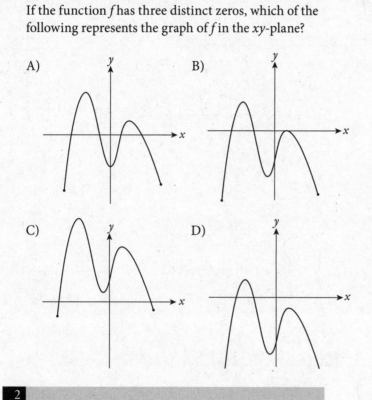

A)

B)

C)

D)

2

In the *xy*-plane, the graph of the function *g* has zeroes at –4, 2, and 4. Which of the following could define *g* ?

A) $g(x) = (x - 4)(x - 2)(x + 4)$

B) $g(x) = (x - 4)^2(x - 2)$

C) $g(x) = (x - 4)(x + 2)(x + 4)$

D) $g(x) = (x + 2)(x + 4)^2$

3

If $f(x) = 2x + 1$ and $f(a) = 2$, what is the value of *a* ?

A) $-\dfrac{1}{2}$

B) $\dfrac{1}{2}$

C) 2

D) 5

Medium

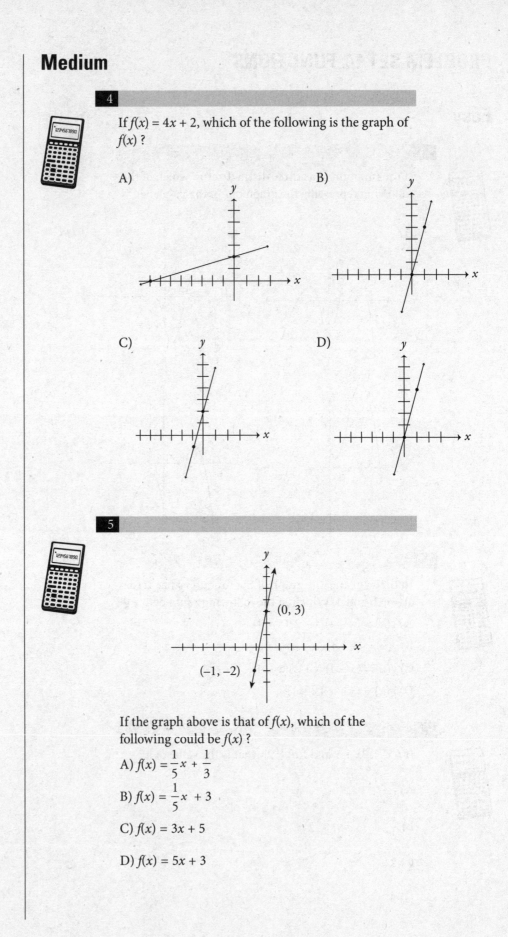

4

If $f(x) = 4x + 2$, which of the following is the graph of $f(x)$?

A)

B)

C)

D)

5

If the graph above is that of $f(x)$, which of the following could be $f(x)$?

A) $f(x) = \dfrac{1}{5}x + \dfrac{1}{3}$

B) $f(x) = \dfrac{1}{5}x + 3$

C) $f(x) = 3x + 5$

D) $f(x) = 5x + 3$

6

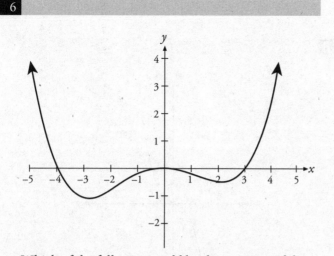

Which of the following could be the equation of the graph in the *xy*-plane shown above?

A) $f(x) = x(x + 3)(x - 4)$

B) $f(x) = x(x + 4)(x - 3)$

C) $f(x) = x^2(x + 3)(x - 4)$

D) $f(x) = x^2(x + 4)(x - 3)$

7

If $f(x) = 2x^2 + 8x + 2$, for what values of x does $f(x) = 0$?

A) $x = -8 \pm 4\sqrt{3}$

B) $x = -8 \pm \sqrt{3}$

C) $x = -2 \pm \sqrt{3}$

D) $x = -8 \pm \dfrac{\sqrt{40}}{2}$

Hard

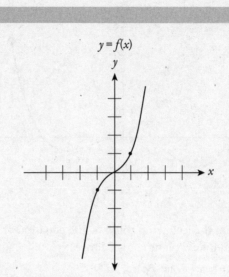

$$y = f(x)$$

If the graph above shows the function $f(x) = x^3$, which one of the following graphs shows $f(x) = (x + 2)^3 - 3$?

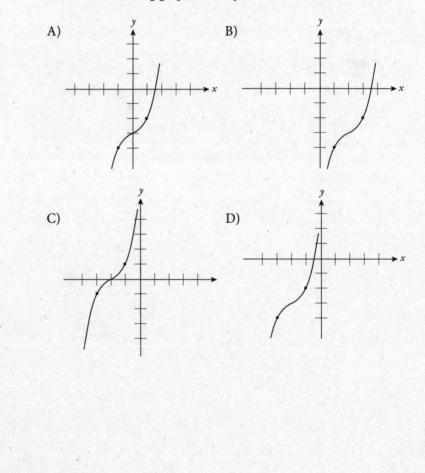

A)

B)

C)

D)

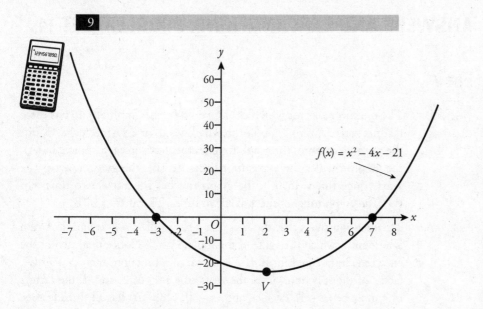

$$f(x) = x^2 - 4x - 21$$

Which of the following is an equivalent form of the equation of the function graphed above from which the coordinates of the vertex V can be identified as constants in the equation?

A) $f(x) = (x - 3)(x + 7)$

B) $f(x) = (x + 3)(x - 7)$

C) $f(x) = (x - 2)^2 - 25$

D) $f(x) = x(x - 4) - 21$

$$p(x) = 3x^3 + 15x^2 + 18x$$

$$q(x) = x^2 + 5x + 6$$

The polynomials $p(x)$ and $q(x)$ are defined above. Which of the following polynomials is divisible by $3x - 2$?

A) $f(x) = p(x) - 2q(x)$

B) $g(x) = 2p(x) - 3q(x)$

C) $h(x) = 3p(x) - 2q(x)$

D) $j(x) = 4p(x) - 3q(x)$

ANSWERS AND EXPLANATIONS: PROBLEM SET 14

Easy

1. **B** The question asks for which choice could be the graph of f if f has three distinct zeros. A zero is a point in which $y = 0$, or an x-intercept. Count the number of times the graph touches the x-axis in each choice. In (A), the graph touches the x-axis four times. In (B), the graph touches the x-axis three times. In (C), the graph touches the x-axis two times. In (D), the graph touches the x-axis two times. The answer is (B).

2. **A** The question states that the function g has zeros at -4, 2, and 4. A zero is a point in which the value of the function is 0. Notice that each of the choices is in factored form. If k is a zero of a function, then $(x - k)$ is a factor of the function. Since the zeros of g are -4, 2, and 4, the factors of g must be $(x + 4)$, $(x - 2)$, and $(x - 4)$. Only (A) has all three factors. Alternatively, since -4, 2, and 4, are zeros, then $g(-4) = 0$, $g(2) = 0$, and $g(4) = 0$. Plug these points into each of the answer choices, crossing off any for which g is not 0. First, $g(4) = 0$ in (A), (B), and (C) but not (D), so eliminate (D). Then, $g(2) = 0$ in (A) and (B) but not (C), so eliminate (C). Finally, $g(-4) = 0$ in (A) but not (B), so eliminate (B). The answer is (A).

3. **B** The question asks for the value of a. Since a is inside the parentheses, it is an x-value. When a function question asks for an x-value, Plug In the Answers. Start with (C). If $a = 2$, then $f(a) = f(2) = 2(2) + 1 = 5$. Since $f(a)$ should be 2, this is incorrect, so eliminate (C). Since the correct answer must be smaller, eliminate (D) as well. Now try (B). If $a = \frac{1}{2}$, then $f(a) = f\left(\frac{1}{2}\right) = 2\left(\frac{1}{2}\right) + 1 = 2$. Since this is what the question says $f(a)$ is, the answer is (B).

Medium

4. **C** Don't do a lot of formula work. Think about how graphs work. In the equation, 2 represents the y-intercept, so eliminate any graphs that do not cross the y-axis at 2. You are down to (A) and (C). A slope of greater than 1 is relatively steep as compared with a 45-degree angle, while a fractional slope is relatively shallow. The slope here is 4, so you need a steep graph. Eliminate (A), and the answer is (C).

5. **D** Don't do a lot of formula work. Think about how graphs work. The y-intercept on the graph is 3, so you need a formula that ends in +3. Eliminate (A) and (C). A slope of greater than 1 is relatively steep as compared with a 45-degree angle, while a fractional slope is relatively shallow. The slope of the lines on the graph is relatively steep, so eliminate (B), and the answer is (D).

6. **D** To determine a possible equation of the graph function, identify the zeroes, or the x-intercepts. The x-intercepts occur at $x = -4$, $x = 0$, and $x = 3$. If b is an x-intercept, then $(x - b)$ is a factor. Therefore, the factors of the equation of this function must be $(x + 4)$, (x), and $(x - 3)$. Eliminate the choices that do not have these three factors: (A) and (C). Look at the difference between (B) and (D). Both have factors of $(x + 4)$ and $(x - 3)$, but (B) has x, while (D) has x^2. There are two possible ways to determine which one it should be. One is to notice that at $x = 0$, the graph doesn't cross the x-axis but is tangent to it. This indicates a double root, or a root that is squared. Therefore, the equation must have x^2. The other way is to notice that the graph has three turning points. A graph must be of a degree that is at least one higher than the number of turning points. Therefore, this equation must be at least fourth degree. When an equation is in factored form, determine the degree by adding the degree of each factor. Choice (B) has three first degree factors, so it has a degree of $1 + 1 + 1 = 3$. Choice (D) has a second degree factor and two first degree factors, so it has a degree of $2 + 1 + 1 = 4$. Either way, the answer is (D).

7. **C** The question asks for where $f(x) = 0$, or where $2x^2 + 8x + 2 = 0$. To solve a quadratic in the form $ax^2 + bx + c = 0$, either factor or use the quadratic formula: $x = \dfrac{-b \pm \sqrt{b^2 - 4ac}}{2a}$. For a hint as to which to use, look at the answer choices. Since the answers more closely resemble the quadratic formula, use the quadratic formula. In this case, $a = 2$, $b = 8$, and $c = 2$. Plug these values into the quadratic formula to get $x = \dfrac{-8 \pm \sqrt{8^2 - 4(2)(2)}}{2(2)}$. Simplify to get $x = \dfrac{-8 \pm \sqrt{64 - 16}}{4}$ and $x = \dfrac{-8 \pm \sqrt{48}}{4}$. None of the choices include $\sqrt{48}$, so simplify the square root by finding a perfect square factor. List out the factors of 48: 1 and 48, 2 and 24, 3 and 16, 4 and 12, and 6 and 8. Of those factors, the greatest perfect square is 16. Therefore, $\sqrt{48} = \sqrt{16 \times 3} = \sqrt{16} \times \sqrt{3} = 4\sqrt{3}$. Substitute this to get $x = \dfrac{-8 \pm 4\sqrt{3}}{4}$. None of the answers have a

denominator of 4, so find a way to cancel the 4. To do so, factor a 4 from both terms in the numerator to get $x = \dfrac{4(-2 \pm \sqrt{3})}{4}$. Cancel the 4's to get $x = -2 \pm \sqrt{3}$. The answer is (C).

Hard

8. **D**   The easiest way to handle this is to understand how functions move. The –3 outside the parentheses shifts the original graph down by 3 units. Eliminate (C) because it is not shifted down. The +2 inside the parentheses shifts the original graph to the left by 2 units. Eliminate (A) and (B) because they are not shifted to the left. You can also Plug In, testing one of the points indicated by a dot against the function you are looking for.

9. **C**   The question asks for an equivalent form of the equation of the function in which the coordinates of the vertex can be found as constants. Therefore, the question is asking for the vertex form of the equation: $f(x) = a(x - h)^2 + k$, where (h, k) represents the vertex of the parabola. Eliminate any choice that is not in this form. Choices (A), (B), and (D) are not in vertex form, so eliminate them. Only one choice remains. Alternatively, find the vertex in the graph. The vertex is the minimum (or maximum) point on the graph and the point at which at parabola turns on the axis of symmetry. On the graph, this point appears to be at (2, –25). Eliminate any choices that do not have 2 and 25 as constants. Once again, this eliminates (A), (B), and (D). The answer is (C).

10. **A**   You could do a lot of algebraic manipulation and factoring to solve this, but there are variables everywhere, so Plug In. Pick a value for x such as $x = 3$. Find the values of p and q when $x = 3$. $p(3) = 3(3)^3 + 15(3)^2 + 18(3) = 81 + 135 + 54 = 270$. $q(3) = (3)^2 + 5(3) + 6 = 9 + 15 + 6 = 30$. The question asks for which of the given functions is divisible by $3x - 2$, so see which answer choices are divisible by $3(3) - 2 = 7$. In (A), $f(x) = p(x) - 2q(x)$, so when $x = 3$, $f(3) = 270 - 2(30) = 210$. This is divisible by 7, so keep (A). In (B), $g(3) = 2p(x) - 3q(x) = 2(270) - 3(30) = 450$. This is not divisible by 7, so eliminate it. In (C), $h(x) = 3p(x) - 2q(x) = 3(270) - 2(30) = 750$, and in (D), $j(x) = 4p(x) - 3q(x) = 4(270) - 3(30) = 990$. Neither of these are divisible by 7, so the answer is (A).

PROBLEM SET 15: GRID-INS

Easy

1

If $x - y = -6$, then y is how much greater than x ?

2

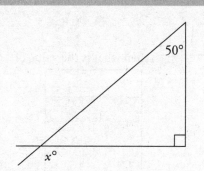

In the figure above, what is the value of x ?

A certain solution requires $3\frac{1}{2}$ grams of additive for each 7 liters of water. At this rate, how many grams of additive should be used with 11 liters of water?

Medium

If $\left(\dfrac{x+2}{y+2}\right) = \dfrac{3}{4}$, then what is the value of $\left(\dfrac{2+y}{2+x}\right)^2$?

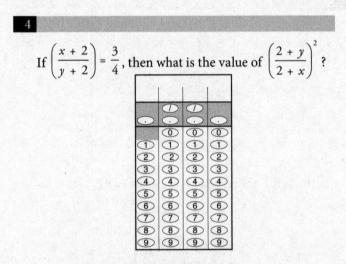

5

The speed, in miles per hour, of a particular experimental spacecraft t minutes after it is launched is modeled by the function M, which is defined as $M(t) = 200(3)^{\frac{t}{3}}$. According to this model, what is the speed, in miles per hour, 9 minutes after the spacecraft is launched?

6

Climate Preferences

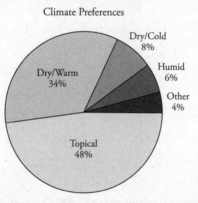

Dry/Cold
8%

Humid
6%

Other
4%

Dry/Warm
34%

Topical
48%

The graph above shows the results of a survey in which adults were asked to name their first preference among various types of climates. Of the adults surveyed, a total of 280 answered "Humid" or "Other." How many answered "Other" in the survey?

7

−4, 0, 2, 3

A sequence of numbers is formed by repeating the set of numbers until 80 numbers have been listed. What is the sum of the first 31 terms of the sequence?

8

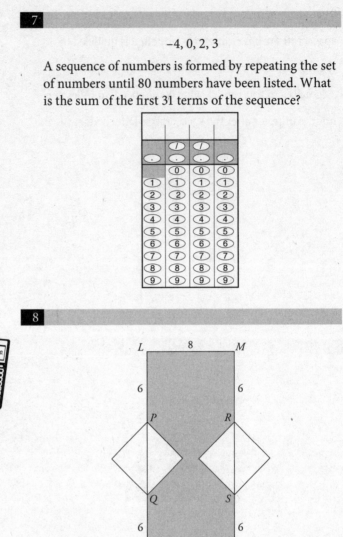

In the figure below, rectangle *LMNO* has dimensions of 18 by 8. Segments *PQ* and *RS* are diagonals of the squares shown. What is the area of the shaded region?

Questions 9 and 10 refer to the information below.

A scientist studies Bacteria Culture A, which grows ten percent every hour. Bacteria Culture A initially contained 200 microbes, and she models the growth using the equation $n = 200(m)^h$, where n is the number of microbes and h is the number of hours.

9

What is the value of m in the equation?

10

The same scientist also studies another culture, Bacteria Culture B, which grows 15% every hour. The two cultures began at the same time with the same number of microbes. After 20 hours, how many more microbes will Bacteria Culture B contain than Bacteria Culture A? (Round your answer to the nearest whole number.)

ANSWERS AND EXPLANATIONS: PROBLEM SET 15

Easy

1. **6** Set the equation equal to y, since that's what the question asks for. You get $-y = -6 - x$. Multiply through by -1 and you get $y = 6 + x$, so the answer is 6. For an easier solution, you could also Plug In here: Say $x = 2$ and $y = 8$, which satisfies the equation. Then y is equal to x plus 6.

2. **140** The unmarked angle in the triangle is $40°$, since triangles have $180°$ and the other angles are $50°$ and $90°$. The $40°$ angle and x lie on a straight line, so $40 + x = 180$, and $x = 140$.

3. **5.5** You can set up the proportions as follows and cross-multiply:

$$\frac{3.5\text{ g}}{7} = \frac{x}{11}$$

Cross-multiply to get $7x = 38.5$. Divide both sides by 7 to get $x = 5.5$. However, if you noticed that the number of grams is one-half the number of liters (not accounting for units), then all you need to do is divide 11 by 2.

Medium

4. $\dfrac{16}{9}$ This is a good example of plugging in on a grid-in question. If you make $x = 1$ and $y = 2$, the equation will work:

$$\left(\frac{1 + 2}{2 + 2}\right) = \frac{3}{4}$$

Now it is easy to solve the problem. By the way, if you noticed that $\left(\dfrac{2 + y}{2 + x}\right)$ is the reciprocal of $\left(\dfrac{x + 2}{y + 2}\right)$, you didn't need to Plug In. Just square $\dfrac{4}{3}$!

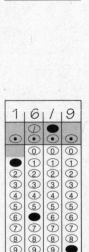

5. **5400** This question asks you to plug $t = 9$ into the given formula:

$$M(t) = 200(3)^{\frac{9}{3}} = 200(3)^3 = 200(27) = 5,400.$$

6. **112** Make sure you understand the information you are given and the information you need to find before trying to answer the question. There are 280 people who answered "Humid" or "Other," not 280 total people, so don't take 10 percent of 280. Also, there is no need to calculate the total number of people surveyed. Of the people who answered "Humid" and "Other," 4 out of 10 answered "Other." Thus, the number of people who answer "Other" is $\frac{4}{10}$ of 280, or 112.

Hard

7. **5** If you are stumped here, you can always type the pattern into your calculator and find the answer. However, on pattern questions, once you understand how the pattern operates, you can arrive at the answer faster. Here, add up the first four numbers of the repeating sequence. They add up to 1. Thus, every time you add another set of the sequence, the total sum will increase by 1. Because you are interested in the first 31 terms of the sequence, there will be 7 complete sets (the first 28 terms) added together and then part of a set (the remaining 3 terms). Those 7 complete sets will add up to 7. So now add in – 4, 0, and 2 to get $7 - 4 + 0 + 2 = 5$.

8. **126** Without answer choices, you can't Ballpark, so you need to slog through! The area of the entire rectangle is 144(18 × 8). Now you need to find the area of the triangles inside of the rectangle. You can see that the measurements on either side of the squares are all 6 and the entire length of the rectangle is 18, so the portion of the rectangle inside each square is also 6. When a square is cut in half along its diagonal, two 45-45-90 triangles are created. If you don't know how 45-45-90 triangles work, you can look up the ratio in the formula box at the beginning of the section. If each side of the triangle (here, the sides of the square) is x, the hypotenuse (here, the diagonal) is $x\sqrt{2}$. Thus, here $6 = x\sqrt{2}$, so $x = \dfrac{6}{\sqrt{2}}$. Now that you have the sides of the squares, you can find the areas of the squares: $\dfrac{6}{\sqrt{2}} \times \dfrac{6}{\sqrt{2}} = \dfrac{36}{2} = 18$. Because the two triangles inside the rectangle add up to one square, you can subtract 18 from 144 to find the area of the shaded region.

9. **1.1** The equation $n = 200(m)^h$ is in the form of the standard equation for exponential growth: *final amount = original amount*$(1 + rate)^{number\ of\ changes}$, where *rate* is the percent in decimal form. The *final amount* is n, the *original amount* is 200, and the *number of changes* is h. Therefore, m from the original equation represents $1 + rate$ from the standard equation. Since the increase per hour is 10%, $m = 1 + 0.10 = 1.1$. The answer is 1.1.

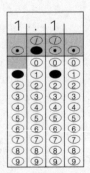

10. **1928** The question asks for how many more microbes Bacteria Culture B contains than Bacteria Culture A after 20 hours. As we just saw in the previous question, m, the rate of increase, is equal to 1.1 for Bacteria Culture A and 1.15 for Bacteria Culture B. After h = 20 hours, Bacteria Culture A has n = $200(1.1)^{20} \approx 1,345.5$ microbes, and Bacteria Culture B has $n = 200(1.15)^{20} \approx 3,273.3$ microbes. Therefore, after 20 hours, Bacteria Culture B has $3,273.3 - 1,345.5 = 1,927.8$ more microbes than Bacteria Culture A. The question asks for this to be rounded to the nearest whole number, so the answer is 1,928.

PROBLEM SET 16: MORE GRID-INS

Easy

1

If $2x - 3y = 7$ and $y = 3$, then what is the value of x?

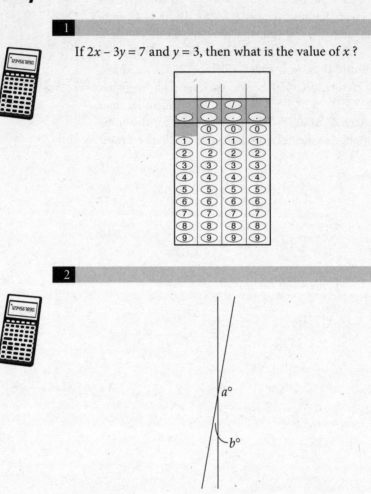

2

In the figure above, if $a = 170$, what is the value of b?

3

At a certain beach, the cost of renting a beach umbrella is $4.25 per day or $28.00 per week. If Kelly and Brandon rent a beach umbrella for 2 weeks instead of renting one each day for 14 days, how much money, in dollars, will they save? (Leave off the dollar sign when gridding in your answer.)

Medium

4

The average (arithmetic mean) of 8 numbers is 65. If one of the numbers, 65, is removed, what is the average of the remaining 7 numbers?

The face of a wall measures 30 yards by 24 yards. If the wall is to be completely covered with square bricks measuring 3 yards on each side, how many bricks will be needed to cover the wall?

In a recent marathon, 70 percent of those who entered the race reached the finish line. If 720 did not reach the finish line, how many people entered the race?

Hard

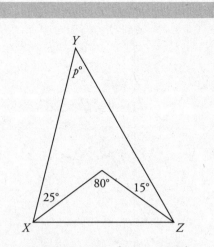

Note: Figure not drawn to scale.

In triangle XYZ above, what is the value of p ?

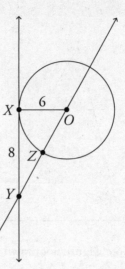

In the figure above, *O* is the center of the circle,
the length of segment *XY* is 8, and the line passing
through points *X* and *Y* is tangent to the circle at point
X. What is the length of segment *ZY* ?

Let the function *g* be defined as $g(x) = -3x + 6$.
If $g(6) = r$, what is the value of $g(r)$?

When a number is subtracted from 8 less than three times the number, the result is 142. What is the number?

ANSWERS AND EXPLANATIONS: PROBLEM SET 16

Easy

1. **8** The problem tells you that $y = 3$, so plug that into the equation and you get $2x - 9 = 7$. So $2x = 16$ and $x = 8$.

2. **10** Write 170° next to a. There are 180° in a line, so $b = 10$.

3.   **3.50**   Kelly and Brandon spent $28 per week for 2 weeks for a total of $56. If they had rented the umbrella by the day, they would've spent 14 × $4.25 for a total of $59.50. That means they saved 59.50 − 56 = 3.50.

Medium

4.   **65**   You can use the Average Pie: 8 (the number of items) times 65 (the average) gives you a sum of 520. If you subtract 65, the new sum is 455. Divide 455 by 7 (the new number of items) to get the new average: 65. You can also think about this logically: If all 8 numbers were 65, and one of those numbers were removed, the remaining 7 numbers would still average 65.

5.   **80**   To find out how many bricks will fit on the wall, you need to divide the dimensions of the wall by the dimensions of the bricks:

$$\frac{30 \times 24}{3 \times 3} = \frac{720}{9} = 80$$

6.   **2400**   Translate the question to create an equation that you can solve. If 70% of the runners finished, then 30% did not. So the question is asking, "720 is 30% of what number?" As an equation, that translates to 720 = 0.3x. Divide both sides by 0.3 to find that x = 2,400.

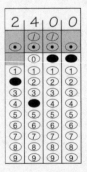

Hard

7. 40 This figure is not drawn to scale, so be careful as you fill in the information you need. In order to find the value of *p*, you need to find the sum of angles *YXZ* and *YZX*. You are given some information about those angles: the measurements 25 and 15 above the smaller triangle. However, because the figure is not drawn to scale, there is no way to determine the missing measurements. That said, it doesn't matter what angles *YXZ* and *YZX* actually are. Only their sum is important. So, let's look at the smaller triangle. The top vertex is 80, which means that the sum of the bottom vertices is 100. Plug in some numbers, such as 50 and 50. Now you have measures for *YXZ* and *YZX*: 75 and 65, for a sum of 140. Subtract that from 180 to find angle *p* : 180 − 140 = 40.

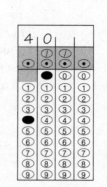

8. 4 To get this question right, you need to know that a line tangent to a circle forms a right angle with the radius at the point of tangency. Thus, triangle *XOY* is a right triangle. You can use the Pythagorean Theorem or recognize the 6-8-10 triangle to find that the hypotenuse is 10. You're not done yet, though. To find *YZ*, you need to subtract the length of *OZ* from 10. *OZ* is a radius, just as is *OX*. As *OX* is 6, so is *OZ*, leaving 4 for *ZY*.

9. 42 When you are given a function, always take the number inside the parentheses and plug it into the function. Here, you must plug 6 into the function:

$$g(6) = -3(6) + 6 = -18 + 6 = -12$$

Thus, *r* = −12. Are you worried that there is no way to grid in a negative number? Actually, you are not done. The question asks for *g(r)*, not *g(6)*. Knowing that *r* = −12, you can plug that number into the function:

$$g(-12) = -3(-12) + 6 = 36 + 6 = 42$$

10. **75** You need to translate English into Math. Let's call "a number" x. You need to subtract x from 8 less than 3 times x. Three times x is $3x$. To find the number 8 less than $3x$, you need to subtract 8. Thus, putting it all together, you get:

$$(3x - 8) - x$$

You are told that the result of this operation is 142, so:

$$(3x - 8) - x = 142$$

Now, you can solve for x:

$$2x - 8 = 142$$
$$2x = 150$$
$$x = 75$$

PROBLEM SET 17: MIXED BAG

Easy

1

If $x = 14 - y$, what is $3x$ when $y = 11$?

A) −9

B) −3

C) 3

D) 9

2

At Rose's Flower Shop, the cost of purchasing a bundle of 8 ferns is $57. The cost of each fern, when purchased separately, is $9. How much money would be saved by purchasing a bundle of 8 ferns, rather than purchasing 8 ferns separately?

A) 12

B) 13

C) 14

D) 15

3

In isosceles triangle *ABC*, one angle measures 55° and another angle measures 70°. Which one of the following is the measure of the third angle?

A) 40

B) 55

C) 70

D) It cannot be determined from the information given.

Medium

4

If $24b^2 - 4x = 32$, what is the value of $6b^2 - x$?

A) 6

B) 8

C) 12

D) 16

5

Sasha has a collection of 60 vinyl records, some of which are classic jazz and the rest of which are hip hop. If Sasha has $\frac{1}{4}$ as many classic jazz records as she has hip hop records, how many classic jazz records does she have?

A) 12

B) 15

C) 45

D) 48

6

If p is an integer such that $-5 < p < 5$ and $q = 3p - p^3$, what is the least possible value of q ?

A) -76

B) -52

C) -4

D) 0

Hard

7

In terms of x, what is the difference between $6x + 9$ and $2x - 4$, if $x > 2$?

A) $3x + 5$

B) $4x - 5$

C) $4x + 5$

D) $4x + 13$

8

In triangle ABC, the measures of angles a, b, and c, respectively, are in the ratio 2:3:4. What is the measure of angle b ?

A) 20

B) 40

C) 60

D) 80

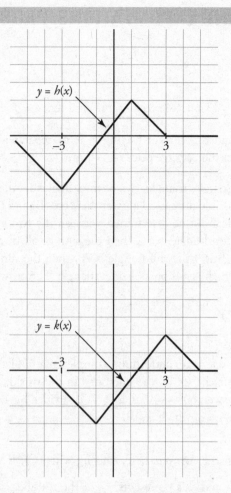

The graphs above show the complete functions h and k. Which one of the following expresses $k(x)$ in terms of $h(x)$?

A) $k(x) = h(x) + 2$

B) $k(x) = h(x) - 2$

C) $k(x) = h(x + 2)$

D) $k(x) = h(x - 2)$

If $h^{\frac{2}{3}} = k^2$, then in terms of k, what is the value of h^2 ?

A) $k^{\frac{2}{3}}$

B) $k^{\frac{4}{9}}$

C) k^3

D) k^6

ANSWERS AND EXPLANATIONS: PROBLEM SET 17

Easy

1. **D**   Plug $y = 11$ into the equation to find that $x = 3$. Therefore, $3x = 9$.

2. **D**   Calculate the cost of buying 8 ferns separately: $8 \times 9 = 72$. Now, subtract the package price of 57 from 72.

3. **B**   In an isosceles triangle, two of three angles are the same. Thus, the only two possible numerical answers here are (B) and (C). Before you decide that it cannot be determined between the two answers, try them out. If the third angle is 55, then the sum of all three angles is 180. That works. But if the third angle is 70, then the sum of all three angles is 195, which is not possible in a triangle. The answer is therefore (B).

Medium

4. **B**   Before you start performing complex manipulations and calculations, ask yourself "Of all the questions in the world, why ask for $6b^2 - x$?" The answer: $6b^2 - x$ is just $24b^2 - 4x$ divided by 4! Therefore, the answer is $32 \div 4 = 8$, which is (B).

5. **A**   Plug In the Answers here, starting with (C). If she has 45 classic jazz albums and this represents $\frac{1}{4}$ of the number of hip hop albums she has, she would have 180 hip hop albums. This is way too big. The answer must be smaller, so eliminate (C) and (D). Try (B). If she has 15 classic jazz albums, she has 60 hip hop albums. 60 should be the total, not just the number of hip hop albums, so eliminate (B). For (A), she would have 48 hip hop albums—for a total of 60.

6. **B**   There are only 9 possible values of p between –5 and 5. Since there are relatively few values, it may be easiest to plug in all possible values of p. If $p = -4$, then $3p - p^3 = 52$. If $p = -3$, then $3p - p^3 = 18$. If $p = -2$, then $3p - p^3 = 2$. If $p = -1$, then $3p - p^3 = -2$. If $p = 0$, then $3p - p^3 = 0$. If $p = 1$, then $3p - p^3 = 2$. If $p = 2$, then $3p - p^3 = -2$. If $p = 3$, then $3p - p^3 = -18$. If $p = 4$, then $3p - p^3 = -52$. The least possible value is –52, so the answer is (B).

Hard

7. D   Plug In. If $x = 3$, then $6x + 9 = 27$ and $2x - 4 = 2$. The difference is 25. Plug 3 into the answer choices, eliminating any choice that doesn't give you 25. Choice (A) is $3(3) + 5 = 14$, so eliminate (A). Choice (B) is $4(3) - 5 = 7$, so eliminate (B). Choice (C) is $4(3) + 5 = 17$, so eliminate (C). Choice (D) is $4(3) + 13 = 25$. Since (D) is the only choice that resulted in 25, it is the answer.

8. C   Create a Ratio Box. For the actual total, use 180, as there are 180° in a triangle. Your completed Ratio Box will look like this:

	a	b	c	Total
Ratio	2	3	4	9
Multiplier	20	20	20	20
Actual Numbers	40	60	80	180

The question asks for the measure of angle b, which is 60, so the answer is (C).

9. D   The easiest way to answer this question is to understand transformation of graphs. Just count how many units the graph moved. It moved 2 units to the right but did not move up or down. When a graph moves to the right, you need to subtract the number of units from x *inside* the parentheses.

10. D   If you are comfortable manipulating equations with exponents, first isolate h by raising $h^{\frac{2}{3}}$ to the power of $\frac{3}{2}$. Having done so on the left side of the equation, you must do the same on the right side. Thus, you get: $h = k^3$. The question, however, asks for h^2, not x, so square both sides, using the Power-Multiply Rule to get $h^2 = (k^3)^2 = k^6$. As an alternative, understand that $h^{\frac{2}{3}} = \sqrt[3]{h^2}$, so you can cube both sides to get $h^2 = (k^2)^3$, which leads you down the same steps of then using the Power-Multiply Rule to get $h^2 = k^6$.

PROBLEM SET 18: MORE MIXED BAG

Easy

1

For $i = \sqrt{-1}$, what is the sum of $(5 + 2i) + (-7 + 3i)$?

A) $-2 - i$

B) $-2 + 5i$

C) $12 - i$

D) $12 + 5i$

2

If n and s are integers, and $n + 5 < 7$, and $s - 6 < -4$, which of the following could be a value of $n + s$?

A) 2

B) 3

C) 4

D) 6

3

A home designer will carpet n rooms with the same dimensions in a house using a specific type of carpeting. The designer charges using the expression $nClw$, where n is the number of rooms, C is a constant with units of dollars per square meter, l is the length of each room in meters, and w is the width of each room in meters. If a customer asks the designer to use a less expensive type of carpeting, which of the following factors in the expression would change?

A) n

B) C

C) l

D) w

Medium

Which of the following lines is perpendicular to $y = 2x + 7$?

A) $y = 3x + \dfrac{1}{7}$

B) $y = 3x - \dfrac{1}{7}$

C) $y = -\dfrac{1}{2}x + 3$

D) $y = \dfrac{1}{2}x + 3$

5

Which of the following complex numbers is equivalent to $\dfrac{7 - 3i}{2 + 4i}$?

(Note: $i = \sqrt{-1}$)

A) $\dfrac{1}{10} - \dfrac{17i}{10}$

B) $\dfrac{1}{10} + \dfrac{17i}{10}$

C) $\dfrac{7}{2} - \dfrac{3i}{4}$

D) $\dfrac{7}{2} + \dfrac{3i}{4}$

6

The total cost, y, for Rosa to go on vacation for x days is given by the equation $y = A + (H + M)x$, where A represents the airfare, H represents the cost per day for the hotel, and M represents the cost of meals. If the relationship between the total cost of the vacation and the number of days of the vacation is graphed on the xy-plane, what does the slope of the line represent?

A) The total cost daily cost of the hotel and meals

B) The total daily cost of the vacation

C) The total cost of the hotel and meals

D) The total cost of the vacation

7

A bank account pays interest at an annual rate of 4%. If the initial deposit on the account is $1,250 and no other deposits or withdrawals are made to the account, which of the following functions A models the amount of money in the bank account after y years?

A) $A(y) = 0.04(1,250)^y$

B) $A(y) = 1.04(1,250)^y$

C) $A(y) = 1,250(0.04)^y$

D) $A(y) = 1,250(1.04)^y$

HARD

8

$$x^2 + y^2 - 6x + 8y = -9$$

The equation of a circle in the xy-plane is shown above. What is the radius of the circle?

A) 3

B) 4

C) 9

D) 16

Questions 9 and 10 refer to the following information.

In a certain company, 55% of the employees are male. 64% of the female employees and 58% of the male employees receive year-end raises.

9

What percent of the employees at the company receive year-end raises?

(Ignore the percent symbol when entering your answer. For example, if the answer is 42.1%, enter 42.1.)

10

What percent of the employees who receive raises are female? (Ignore the percent symbol when entering your answer. For example, if the answer is 42.1%, enter 42.1.)

ANSWERS AND EXPLANATIONS: PROBLEM SET 18

Easy

1. **B**   To add complex numbers, just treat i like a variable and combine like terms: $5 + (-7) = 5 - 7 = -2$ and $2i + 3i = 5i$. Therefore, $(5 + 2i) + (-7 + 3i) = -2 + 5i$. The answer is (B).

2. **A**   First, fix the ranges. You can see $n < 2$ and $s < 2$. Since they both must be integers, the greatest either n or s could be is 1. $1 + 1$ is 2, so that is the only answer that works.

3. **B**   To determine which factor would change with a less expensive type of carpeting, determine the meaning of each variable in the expression. Choice (A) is n, which represents the number of rooms. This does not change when the type of carpeting changes, so eliminate (A). Choice (B) is C, which is a constant, with units of dollars per square meter. Since this seems to be related to the cost of the carpet, keep (B). Choice (C) is l, which represents the length of each room. The length would not change with a different type of carpet, so eliminate (C). Choice (D) is w, which represents the width of each room. The width would not change with a different type of carpet, so eliminate (D). Only one choice remains. The answer is (B).

Medium

4. **C**   In the form $y = mx + b$, m is the slope, which means that the line given by the equation $y = 2x + 7$ has a slope of 2. A line perpendicular to $y = 2x + 7$ will have a slope that is the negative reciprocal to 2. Choice (C) has a slope of $-\dfrac{1}{2}$.

5. **A**   To simplify a fraction of complex numbers, multiply the numerator and denominator by the conjugate of the denominator. The conjugate is the same expression, but with the opposite sign between terms. In this case, the denominator is $2 + 4i$, so the conjugate of the denominator is $2 - 4i$. Multiply the numerator and denominator by this conjugate to get $\frac{7 - 3i}{2 + 4i} \times \frac{2 - 4i}{2 - 4i}$. FOIL both the numerator and denominator to get $\frac{14 - 28i - 6i + 12i^2}{4 - 8i + 8i - 16i^2}$. Combine like terms to get $\frac{14 - 34i + 12i^2}{4 - 16i^2}$. By definition, $i^2 = -1$, so substitute this to get $\frac{14 - 34i + 12(-1)}{4 - 16(-1)} = \frac{14 - 34i - 12}{4 + 16}$. Combine like terms again to get $\frac{2 - 34i}{20}$. Since each of the answer choices is in the form of two fractions, break up the fraction to get $\frac{2}{20} - \frac{34i}{20}$. Reduce both fractions by 2 to get $\frac{1}{10} - \frac{17i}{10}$. The answer is (A).

6. **A**   Rewrite the equation $y = A + (H + M)x$ in $y = mx + b$ form, where m represents the slope of the line and b represents the y-intercept. To do this, simply reverse the order of the terms to get $y = (H + M)x + A$. When the question asks what the slope represents, it's really asking for the meaning of $(H + M)$. Since H represents the daily cost of the hotel and M represents the daily cost of meals, $H + M$ represents the total daily cost of these two things together. The answer is (A).

7. **D**   Interest is an example of exponential growth, which uses the formula *final amount = original amount*$(1 + rate)^{number\ of\ changes}$. The *original amount* is the initial deposit, which is 1,250. The *rate* is 4% written in decimal form, which is 0.04. Because the account pays annual interest, the *number of changes* is the number of years, which is y. Therefore, the amount of money in the account after y years is $1{,}250(1 + 0.04)^y = 1{,}250(1.04)^y$. The answer is (D).

Hard

8. **B** To find the radius of the circle from the equation, get the equation in the standard form for a circle: $(x - h)^2 + (y - k)^2 = r^2$, where (h, k) represents the center of the circle and r represents the radius. To do this, complete the square. Start by grouping the terms with x and grouping the terms with y to get $(x^2 - 6x) + (y^2 + 8y) = -9$. Now take half of the coefficient on x and square it. In this case, the coefficient on x is -6. Half of the coefficient is -3, and the square is 9. Add 9 to both sides to get $(x^2 - 6x + 9) + (y^2 + 8y) = -9 + 9$. Do the same for the coefficient on y. The coefficient on y is 8. Half of 8 is 4, and the square of 4 is 16. Add 16 to both sides to get $(x^2 - 6x + 9) + (y^2 + 8y + 16) = -9 + 9 + 16$. Simplify the right side to get $(x^2 - 6x + 9) + (y^2 + 8y + 16) = 16$. Factor the x terms to get $(x - 3)^2 + (y^2 + 8y + 16) = 16$. Factor the y terms to get $(x - 3)^2 + (y + 4)^2 = 16$. Note that completing the square is a deliberate effort to get a quadratic that is the square of a binomial, so there will always be a way to get the equation in this form. The question asks for the radius. The question is in the form $(x - h)^2 + (y - k)^2 = r^2$, so $r^2 = 16$. Take the square root of both sides to get $r = 4$. The answer is (B).

9. **60.7** The question asks for percents, so plug in 100 for the total number of employees. The question says that 55% of the employees are male, so there are 55 male employees and 45 female employees. If 64% of the female employees receive a raise, then $\frac{64}{100} \times 45 = 28.8$ female employees receive a raise. This is a decimal but that's fine. While you can't have fractions of people in the real world, the math will work out fine for this problem and you won't have to stress about finding a perfect number to plug in. If 58% of male employees receive a raise, then $\frac{58}{100} \times 55 = 31.9$ male employees receive a raise. Therefore, a total of $28.8 + 31.9 = 60.7$ employees receive a raise. Since the total number of employees is 100, 60.7 employees represents 60.7%. The answer is 60.7.

10. **47.4** The question asks what percent of the employees who receive raises are female, so determine $\frac{\text{female raises}}{\text{total raises}} \times 100$. If you did the work for the previous question, you already have some numbers to work with. According to our previous calculations, there are 28.8 females who get raises out of 60.7 total employees who get raises. Therefore, $\frac{\text{female raises}}{\text{total raises}} \times 100 = \frac{28.8}{60.7} \times 100 = 47.446$. Unless otherwise specified, always enter as many digits as you can into the grid-in box: The answer is 47.4.

Part II
Science on the ACT

Chapter 9
All About the
Science Test

THE ACT SCIENCE TEST

For many students, the Science test is the most difficult. Whether the subject matter alone intimidates or the time crunch stresses, the Science test can be difficult to finish. In this chapter, you'll learn how to order the passages and apply a basic approach that makes the most of the time you have.

FUN FACTS ABOUT THE SCIENCE TEST

The Science test consists of 40 questions and up to 7 passages that you must answer in 35 minutes.

This is not a test of science content, but of science reasoning. ACT describes the necessary skills required for the natural sciences as "interpretation, analysis, evaluation, reasoning, and problem solving."

Trends and Relationships

We think all those skills are best understood as identifying trends and relationships. Whether you are asked to look up a value or synthesize information, it all comes down to the patterns and connections shown by variables, figures, experiments, and scientists. Look for trends *within* a figure, and look for relationships *between* figures.

Outside Knowledge

For the topics of the passages, ACT will pull from biology, chemistry, physics, and the Earth/space sciences, such as geology, astronomy, and meteorology. Most of the questions are answered by the passages and figures provided, but you should also expect two to three questions on outside knowledge.

The Passages

On each ACT, the order of the passages will vary, but the distribution of passage types is always the same.

Charts and Graphs

ACT calls these "Data Representations." We call them "Charts and Graphs" because that's what they're all about. They *always* come with figures. There are three Charts and Graphs passages, each with five questions.

Experiments

ACT calls these "Research Summaries." They look a lot like the Charts and Graphs passages because they *usually* come with figures. However, they come with more reading because they include the descriptions of the experiment set up. There are three Experiments passages, each with six questions.

Fighting Scientists

ACT calls these "Conflicting Viewpoints," but admit it: Our name is way more fun. There is only one Fighting Scientists passage, featuring seven questions, on each ACT. It is inherently different from the other six, even if it *sometimes* comes with figures. The fundamental task of the Fighting Scientists passage is to compare and contrast opposing views of an issue.

PERSONAL ORDER OF DIFFICULTY (POOD)

There are many factors about the structure of this test that make it difficult. It's last, which doesn't help at all. But even if it were first, many would find it the most challenging. Science phobes are intimidated by the subject matter. Science geeks are thwarted by the time crunch. Pick your poison; no one benefits from following ACT's order. On every ACT, you need to work the passages in an order that makes sense for you.

NOW PASSAGES

Every time you take the ACT, for practice and for real, pick the order of the passages that makes sense for you. The best passages to do Now are those with the most transparent relationships. When you pick your Now passages, choose exclusively among the Charts and Graphs and Experiments passages. By nature, the Fighting Scientists passage is different, and even superior readers find it takes longer to work than the best of the Now passages. So what makes a good Now passage? There are five signs to abide by.

1. Small Tables and Graphs

A good Now passage can have only tables, only graphs, or both. Tables should be no more than 3–4 rows or columns, and graphs should have no more than 3–4 curves.

2. Easy-to-Spot Consistent Trends

Look for graphs with all the curves heading in the same direction: all up, all down, or all flat. Look for tables with numbers in a consistent direction: up, down, or flat.

3. Numbers, not Words or Symbols

To show a consistent trend, the figure has to feature numbers, not words or symbols.

4. Short Answers

Look for as many questions as possible with short answers, specifically answers with values and short relationship words like "increase" or "decrease."

5. Your Science POOD

Don't forget to factor in your familiarity and comfort with the topic when spotting good Now passages. For example, if you've just studied DNA, a passage on DNA will strike you as easier, regardless of how the figures look.

Now Versus Easy

We are deliberately calling these Now passages rather than Easy passages. Even a passage with great figures will have one or two tough questions, but even the toughest questions are easier to crack when you get the central trends and relationships. On passages with incomprehensible figures, even the easiest questions will take you longer because you will keep asking yourself, "What is this saying again?" You'll always work good Now passages more quickly, and good time management is what the ACT is all about.

PACING

With just 35 minutes to read as many as 7 passages and answer 40 questions, you have an average of five minutes for every passage. But should you spend 5 minutes on every passage? Of course not. If you make smart choices of good Now passages, you should be able to work them in less time, leaving yourself more time for the tougher passages. Think about the pacing chart we discussed in Chapter 2. Think about how many points you need to hit your goal.

Be Ruthless and Flexible

Every Now passage will have one or two tough questions, just as every Later passage will have at least one or two easy questions. Use Chapters 10 and 11 to practice, but even on the Now passages, know when to guess on a tough question and move onto the next passage. Don't let one tough question drag you down.

Need More Practice?

1,471 ACT Practice Questions provides 6 tests' worth of Science passages. That's 42 passages and 240 questions.

POE

The most direct Science questions will ask you to look up a value or a relationship. But the most complex will ask you to synthesize information or draw a conclusion. The more difficult the question, the less it will help to just stare at the figure waiting for divine guidance to help you magically *see* the answer. As is often the case on the ACT, spotting the wrong answers can be much easier than magically divining the right answers. In our 3-step Basic Approach, we'll discuss in greater detail how to use POE.

THE BASIC APPROACH

The most efficient way to boost your Science score is to pick your order and apply our 3-step Basic Approach to passages with figures. Follow our smart, effective strategy to earn as many points as you can.

> **Fighting Scientists**
> The Fighting Scientists passage is fundamentally different from the Charts and Graphs and Experiments passages and requires a different approach.

Step 1: Work the Figures

Take 10–30 seconds to review your figures. What are the variables? What are the units? In what direction do the variables move?

Graphs present trends visually. For tables, you need to make it visual. Mark the trends for each variable with an arrow. Here are three tables from a good Now passage with the trends marked.

Passage II

Table 1	
Angle between axis of first and second filters (degrees)	Intensity of emerging beam (W/m^2)
0	4.00
15	3.73
30	2.99
45	2.01
60	1.00
75	0.27
90	0.00

↑   ↓

Table 2	
Angle between axis of first and second filters (degrees)	Intensity of emerging beam (W/m^2)
0	8.00
15	7.46
30	6.01
45	3.99
60	2.00
75	0.54
90	0.00

↑   ↓

Table 3	
Angle between axis of first and second filters (degrees)	Intensity of emerging beam (W/m²)
0	6.01
15	5.60
30	4.49
45	2.99
60	1.50
75	0.41
90	0.00

↑   ↓

Step 2: Work the Questions

For each question, look up the value or relationship on the figures as directed. Use your POOD to leave for Later tougher questions. Read *if and only* when you can't answer a question from the figures.

———————○———————

Try an example.

12. According to Table 3, if the angle between the axes of polarization increases by 15°, the intensity of the resulting beam:

    F. halves.
    G. doubles.
    H. increases, but not by any constant factor.
    J. decreases, but not by any constant factor.

Here's how you might use the POOD strategy on ACT Science questions.

Here's How to Crack It

Because you've already marked the trends, you know that as the angle increases, the intensity decreases. Eliminate (G) and (H). Look closely at the trend, and choose (J).

Both the Charts and Graphs and Experiments passages will include actual text. Read the passage intros and experiment descriptions *only* when you can't answer a question from a figure.

———————○———————

Try another example.

───────────────────○───────────────────

10. How does the setup of Experiment 1 differ from that of Experiment 2 ?

   F. In Experiment 1, the original beam was polarized, but in Experiment 2, it was unpolarized.

   G. In Experiment 1, the original beam was unpolarized, but in Experiment 2, it was polarized.

   H. In Experiment 1, the scientists tested a wider range of angles than they did in Experiment 2.

   J. In Experiment 1, the original beam of light was more intense than the one in Experiment 2.

Here's How to Crack It

The variables are the same in Tables 1 and 2. To answer this question, you have to read the experiment descriptions.

Experiment 1

The scientists used a laser emitting unpolarized light. The light was directed toward a polarization filter with an axis of polarization pointing straight up, and then through another whose axis of polarization varied. The scientists chose to describe the axis of the second filter by examining the angle between its axis and the axis of the first filter. The intensity of the original beam was 8 W/m^2 (watts per square meter). Their results are shown in Table 1.

Experiment 2

The scientists repeated the experimental setup of Experiment 1 but used a laser emitting polarized light with an axis of polarization pointing straight up. The intensity of the original beam was still 8 W/m^2. The results are shown in Table 2.

The light in Experiment 1 was unpolarized, while the light in Experiment 2 was polarized. Choice (G) provides this information correctly.

───────────────────○───────────────────

Step 3: Work the Answers

In question 12, the central task involved looking up a relationship you've already marked. You used POE to eliminate two answers, but from the beginning you were in command of the question. On question 10, the difference between the two experiments was addressed in the first line of the experiment descriptions. However, if you didn't spot that, good POE would have eliminated (F), and you'd have been able to eliminate (H) and (J) as well.

On more difficult questions, POE will always be the best bet. You'll be asked to synthesize information from several figures, evaluate a hypothesis, or draw a conclusion, and it will always be easier to eliminate what the figures and passage disprove.

———————○———————

Try another example.

11. The scientists hypothesize that the color of the original beam of light will affect the intensity of the emerging beam. The frequency of a beam of light determines its color. Which of the following would be the best way to test this hypothesis?

   A. Repeating the experiments using more than two polarizing filters
   B. Repeating the experiments on different planets
   C. Repeating the experiments using beams of both high and low frequencies
   D. Repeating the experiments using different intensities for the original beam

Here's How to Crack It

Use POE. Whenever a question asks about how to test something, eliminate answers that have nothing to do with the goal. The question identifies color as an important variable on intensity and identifies frequency as the determinant of color. Eliminate any choice that doesn't address color or frequency. Only (C) is left standing.

———————○———————

Remember POE
If you're stuck, don't forget about POE. It can get you out of a tight spot!

Repeat

Steps 3 and 4 repeat: Make your way through the rest of the questions. Look up your answers on the figures, and read only when you can't answer a question from the figures. The less the questions involve a value or relationship, the more you should rely on POE to find the answers.

LATER PASSAGES

The Basic Approach works on all passages with figures, not just the Now passages featuring consistent trends in tables and graphs.

Step 1: Work the Figures

Some ACT passages will feature an illustration, a diagram, or tables and graphs with no consistent trends. Take 10–15 seconds to review the figure. When there are no consistent trends, a figure doesn't reveal the main point as readily. You'll learn the main point as you work the questions and answers. Spend the limited time devoted to Step 1 looking for any patterns or terms.

Step 2: Work the Questions

Even on Later passages, several questions will ask you to look something up on the figure. The more confusing the figure, however, the more likely you are to waste valuable time trying to figure everything out from staring at the figure, waiting for a flash of inspiration to hit. Use your POOD to seek out the most straightforward questions in a passage to tackle first. As we wrote above, most questions will ask you to look something up on the figure. For more complicated questions, move to Step 3 and use POE.

Step 3: Work the Answers

The wordier the answers, the more you should use POE. Read each answer, then review the figure and ask yourself: does the answer choice accurately describe the figure?

FIGHTING SCIENTISTS

Fighting Scientists passages sometimes come with figures, but Fighting Scientists utilizes different skills and thus requires a different basic approach.

Step 1: Preview

Go straight to the questions and identify which theory you'll need to read in order to answer the question. For example, if the passage features "Hypothesis 1" and "Hypothesis 2," then label any question that just covers the first "1" and any passage that just covers the second "2." Label questions on both with "1 & 2." For passages with multiple theories, label the questions as needed.

Step 2: One Side at a Time

Read Hypothesis 1 and do all the questions labeled "1." Reading and working the questions for one scientist at a time will give you the firm grasp of each theory you need.

Step 3: The Other Side

Read Hypothesis 2 and do all the questions labeled "2." On passages with multiple hypotheses, read each theory one at a time and work its stand-alone questions before moving on to the next theory.

Step 4: Compare and Contrast

Save for last all the questions on multiple theories. You'll have a much easier time keeping track of who said what, how they agree, how they disagree, and so on. Use POE as much as possible.

PRACTICE

Try the Basic Approach on your own. Start with the Now passages in Chapter 10 before moving on to the Later Passages in Chapter 11. Then try a complete Science practice test in Chapter 12.

Summary

o   The Science test is not a test of science content but of science reasoning skills.

o   Pick your order of the passages.

o   Now passages feature small tables and graphs with easy-to-spot consistent trends made up of numbers, not words or symbols, and feature short answers.

o   Use the 3-step Basic Approach.
1. Work the Figures. Note the variables and mark the trends.
2. Work the Questions. Look up answers on your figures. Read if and only when you can't answer a question from a figure.
3. Work the Answers. On tougher questions, lean heavily on POE to eliminate wrong answers.

Chapter 10
Now Passages

Passage I

Reduction by carbon process, thermite process, and reduction by heating alone are different ways of converting a metal oxide to pure metal. Reactions 1–3 are examples of these processes using zinc oxide, manganese dioxide, and mercuric oxide, respectively.

Reaction 1: $ZnO + C \rightarrow Zn + CO$

Reaction 2: $3MnO_2 + 4Al \rightarrow 3Mn + 2Al_2O_3$

Reaction 3: $2HgO \xrightarrow{\text{heating}} 2Hg + O_2$

In each case, the resulting sample is composed of the metal and another product, which is filtered out to leave only the pure metal.

Figures 1–3 below show how *percent pure metal* (% PM) varied as a function of time in each of the reactions in the presence of a magnetic field and without a magnetic field.

$$\% \text{ PM} = \frac{\text{mass of pure metal}}{\text{mass of metal oxide} + \text{mass of pure metal}} \times 100$$

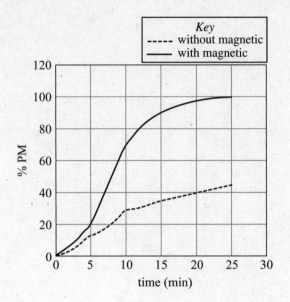

Figure 2

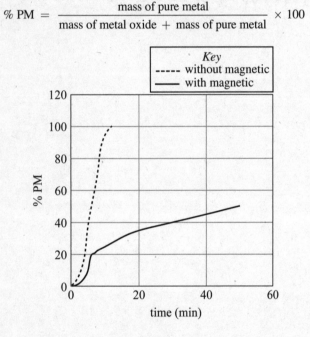

Figure 1

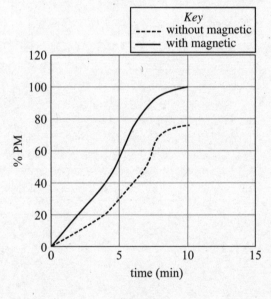

Figure 3

1. According to Figure 1, during Reaction 1 with a magnetic field, the % PM observed at 20 mins was approximately:

   A. 40%.
   B. 35%.
   C. 25%.
   D. 20%.

2. Suppose that during Reaction 3 with a magnetic field, the magnetic field had been removed at time = 5 min. Three minutes later, at time = 8 min, the % PM would most likely have been:

F. greater than 60%.
G. between 40% and 60%.
H. between 20% and 40%.
J. less than 20%.

3. According to Figure 2, in Reaction 2, how did the removal of the magnetic field affect the yield of pure metal at time = 20 min? The yield obtained without a magnetic field was about:

A. $\frac{2}{5}$ the yield obtained with a magnetic field.

B. $\frac{4}{5}$ the yield obtained with a magnetic field.

C. $2\frac{1}{2}$ times that of the yield obtained with a magnetic field.

D. 3 times the yield obtained with a magnetic field.

4. A chemist claimed that separating pure metal using a magnetic field is always faster than without a magnetic field. Do Figures 1–3 support this claim?

F. No; in Reaction 1 the % PM reached 0% sooner without a magnetic field than with a magnetic field.
G. No; in Reaction 1 the % PM reached 100% sooner without a magnetic field than with a magnetic field.
H. Yes; the % PM consistently reached 0% sooner with a magnetic field for all three reactions than without.
J. Yes; the % PM consistently reached 100% sooner with a magnetic field for all three reactions than without.

5. If Reaction 3 had been graphed as *percent of metal oxide* (% MO) as time increases instead of % PM:

$$\% \text{ MO} = \frac{\text{mass of metal oxide}}{\text{mass of metal oxide } + \text{ mass of pure metal}} \times 100$$

Which of the following graphs best represents how Figure 3 would have appeared?

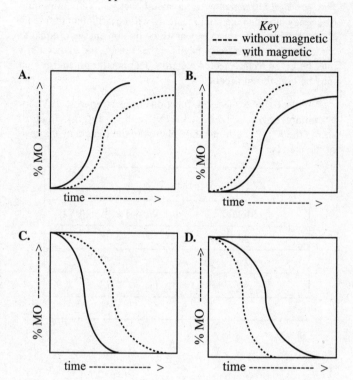

Passage II

When light strikes a metal surface, the energy of the photons is transferred to the metal surface and frees electrons from the metal in a process called the *photoelectric effect*. The energy required to free an electron differs depending on the type of metal and is called the *work function* of the metal. The energy contained within a photon can be determined by that photon's frequency. The *threshold frequency* for a metal, or f_T, is the minimum frequency at which the photon energy will be sufficient to free an electron. This is the frequency at which photon energy is equal to work function. If the frequency is higher than f_T, the extra energy may be given to the ejected electron. The maximum energy that may be transferred is called K_{max}.

Table 1 shows the work functions in electron volts (eV) for aluminum, (Al), zinc (Zn), nickel (Ni), and silver (Ag). Figure 1 shows the K_{max} of each metal in relation to the frequency for each of the metals.

Table 1	
Metal	Work function (eV)
Al	4.08
Zn	4.30
Ag	4.73
Ni	5.01

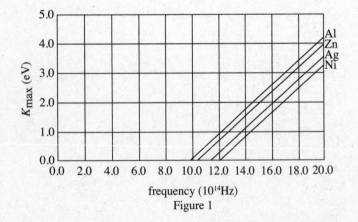

frequency (10^{14}Hz)

Figure 1

1. For a photon to free an electron from Zn, the photon's work function must be at least:

   A. 4.23 eV.
   B. 4.30 eV.
   C. 4.61 eV.
   D. 5.31 eV.

2. Based on Figure 1, which of the following correctly ranks Al, Ni, and Ag in order of increasing K_{max} at 15.0×10^{14} Hz ?

   F. Al, Ag, Ni
   G. Al, Ni, Ag
   H. Ni, Ag, Al
   J. Ni, Al, Ag

3. Based on Table 1 and Figure 1, as frequency increases, K_{max}

   A. decreases.
   B. increases.
   C. increases, then decreases.
   D. decreases, then increases.

4. Based on Figure 1, for electrons ejected from Al by photons with frequency = 26.0×10^{14} Hz, K_{max} would be:

   F. greater than 5.0 eV.
   G. between 4.5 eV and 5.0 eV.
   H. between 4.0 eV and 4.5 eV.
   J. less than 4.0 eV.

5. Photons having frequencies of 12.0×10^{14} Hz and 18.0×10^{14} Hz strike a new metal, Metal Q, resulting in freed electrons with the following K_{max}:

Photon frequency (10^{14} Hz)	K_{max} (eV)
12.0	0.5 eV
18.0	3.0 eV

Based on Table 1 and Figure 1, the work function of Metal Q is most likely closest to which of the following?

   A. 4.01 eV
   B. 4.20 eV
   C. 4.28 eV
   D. 4.51 eV

Passage III

Scientists studied the effects of Drug X on various strains of bacteria in the *Staphylococcus* genus. Table 1 shows the bacteria that were tested and the ED_{50} (the dosage necessary to achieve a therapeutic effect for 50% of the population that is given the medication) of each bacterial strain.

Table 1		
Bacterium	Species	ED_{50} of Drug X (mg/L)
A	*Staphylococcus aureus*	15.3
B	*Staphylococcus carnosus*	30.6
C	*Staphylococcus gallinarum*	22.7
D	*Staphylococcus vitulinus*	91.3
E	*Staphylococcus warneri*	62.6

Six flasks containing 500 mL of nutrient broth were prepared, each with 10,000 cells of *Staphylococcus aureus*. Drug X was then added to five of the flasks in different concentrations, and all six flasks were incubated at 37°C for 24 hours. This procedure was then repeated for the four other bacterial strains. Figure 1 shows the percentage of cells killed for each bacterial strain at each concentration of Drug X.

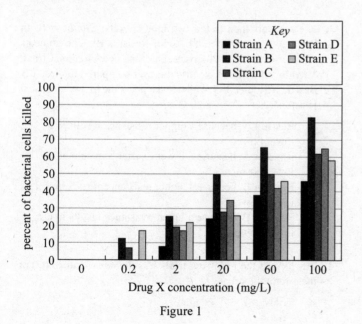

Figure 1

1. According to Figure 1, as the concentration of Drug X increased, the percent of bacterial cells killed from Strain C:

   A. increased, then remained the same.
   B. decreased, then remained the same.
   C. increased only.
   D. decreased only.

2. Based on Table 1, which strain of bacterium requires the highest concentration of Drug X to achieve a therapeutic effect for 50% of the population that is given the medication?

   F. Strain A
   G. Strain B
   H. Strain D
   J. Strain E

3. Based on Figure 1, if cells from Strain B had been treated with Drug X at a concentration of 200 mg/L, the percent of bacterial cells killed would most likely have been:

   A. less than 75%.
   B. between 75% and 80%.
   C. between 80% and 85%.
   D. greater than 85%.

4. According to Table 1, the concentration of Drug X necessary to achieve a therapeutic effect for 50% of the population from Strain E was approximately 4 times the concentration of Drug X necessary to achieve a therapeutic effect for 50% of the population from:

   F. Strain A.
   G. Strain B.
   H. Strain C.
   J. Strain D.

5. Between which of the following concentrations did Drug X most increase in effectiveness in killing bacterial cells of Strain E?

   A. Between 0 mg/L and 0.2 mg/L
   B. Between 2 mg/L and 20 mg/L
   C. Between 20 mg/L and 60 mg/L
   D. Between 60 mg/L and 100 mg/L

Passage IV

A *resistor* is an object that creates electrical resistance in a circuit.

R is the electrical resistance, in *ohms* (Ω), which describes the tendency of a resistor to oppose electric conduction. Conductance, *G*, in siemens (S), is the inverse of *R*: it describes the tendency of a resistor to allow electric conduction. When a voltage *V*, in volts (V), is run across a circuit, *R* will affect the resulting current *I*, measured in amperes (A).

Students tested several different resistors. For each trial, the students applied a series of voltages across a circuit that contained a resistor and measured the resulting current. The students then calculated the power, *P*, in watts (W), delivered through the circuit. *P* is a measure of the rate at which current flows across a circuit.

Study 1

In Trials 1–5, the circuit contained a blue resistor with *R* = 0.005 Ω. The results are shown in Table 1. Each Trial had a different voltage (*V*) across the circuit.

Table 1			
Trial	*V* (V)	*I* (A)	*P* (W)
1	0.02	4	0.08
2	0.04	8	0.32
3	0.06	12	0.72
4	0.08	16	1.28
5	0.09	18	1.62

Study 2

In Trials 6–10, the circuit contained a red resistor with *R* = 0.015. As in Study 1, each trial had a different voltage (*V*) across the circuit.

Table 2			
Trial	*V* (V)	*I* (A)	*P* (W)
6	0.02	1.3	0.03
7	0.04	2.7	0.11
8	0.06	4	0.24
9	0.08	5.3	0.43
10	0.09	6	0.54

Study 3

In Trials 11–15, the circuit contained a green resistor with *R* = 0.04 Ω. As in the prior studies, each trial had a different voltage (*V*) across the circuit.

Table 3			
Trial	*V* (V)	*I* (A)	*P* (W)
11	0.02	0.5	0.01
12	0.04	1	0.04
13	0.06	1.5	0.09
14	0.08	2	0.16
15	0.09	2.2	0.20

1. If an additional trial had been conducted in Study 1 with *V* = 0.03 V, the value of *P* for this additional trial would most likely have been:

   A. less than 0.08 watts.
   B. between 0.08 watts and 0.32 watts.
   C. between 0.32 watts and 0.72 watts.
   D. greater than 1.62 watts.

2. In each study, as the voltage across each circuit increased, the electrical power:

   F. remained the same.
   G. varied, but with no general trend.
   H. decreased only.
   J. increased only.

3. The students then tested two new circuits, Circuit A (with Resistor A) and Circuit B (with Resistor B). The students ran the same voltage across each of the new circuits. Circuit A exhibited a higher electrical power compared to circuit B. Based on Studies 1–3, which resistor has the higher electrical resistance?

   A. Resistor A, because a higher resistance results in a lower power.
   B. Resistor A, because a lower resistance results in a lower power.
   C. Resistor B, because a higher resistance results in a lower power.
   D. Resistor B, because a lower resistance results in a lower power.

4. In which of the following trials was the *conductance* (*G*) of the circuit the greatest?

   F. Trial 1
   G. Trial 6
   H. Trial 11
   J. Trials 1, 6, and 11 all have the same conductance.

5. Prior to the studies, 4 students made predictions about which of the 3 resistors, if any, would have the lowest P for a given V. Student L predicted that it would be the blue resistor. Student M predicted that it would be the red resistor. Student N predicted that it would be the green resistor, and Student O predicted that all three resistors would have the same P for a given V. Which prediction is correct?

A. Student L
B. Student M
C. Student N
D. Student O

6. A student concluded that, for a constant resistance, increasing the value of V by a factor of 3 increases the value of P by a factor of 9. Which pair of trials best supports this conclusion?

F. 1 and 8
G. 2 and 4
H. 6 and 13
J. 11 and 13

Passage V

In 3 studies, students investigated the thermal expansion of rectangular metal rods various lengths and materials (see Figure 1).

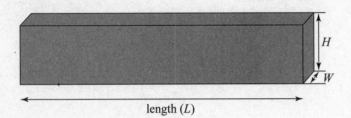

length (L)

Figure 1

Using the water bath shown in Figure 2, the students heated the rods to different temperatures.

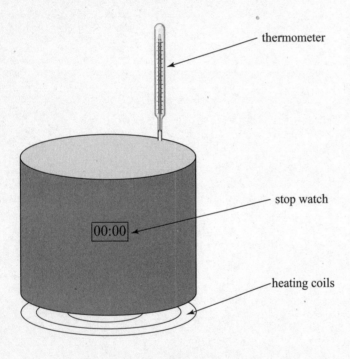

thermometer

stop watch

heating coils

Figure 2

In each trial, the rod was transferred to a water bath preheated to a particular temperature and then allowed to incubate for a set amount of time. During the incubation process, water temperature was kept constant while the metal rods underwent thermal expansion.

After completion of the incubation, the metal rod was removed, and the length, width, and height of the metal rod were promptly measured. After being measured, the metal rod returned to room temperature and reverted to its original dimensions.

The intrinsic thermal expansion of the metal rod was represented by the *volumetric expansion constant*, β.

Study 1

In Trials 1–4, students determined the change in volume, ΔV, for rods of different lengths, L (see Table 1). In every trial, the time of incubation was 30 minutes and the temperature was 80°C.

Table 1		
Trial	L (mm)	ΔV (mm³)
1	50	1.5
2	100	3.1
3	150	4.5
4	200	5.9

Study 2

In Trials 5–8, students determined ΔV for rods of the same L composed of Metals W–Z, respectively. Each metal had a different value of β (see Table 2). In every trial, $L = 100$mm, the time of incubation was 30 minutes, and the temperature was 80°C.

Table 2			
Trial	Metal	$\beta(°C^{-1})$	ΔV (mm³)
5	W	0.8	1.7
6	X	1.4	3.1
7	Y	2.2	4.9
8	Z	4.6	10.2

Study 3

In Trials 9–12, students determined ΔV for rods at different temperatures (see Table 3). In every trial, $L = 100$ mm, and the incubation time was 30 minutes.

Table 3		
Trial	Temperature (C°)	ΔV (mm³)
9	40	5.1
10	60	7.7
11	80	10.2
12	100	12.8

1. If density is defined as mass divided by volume, which of the following is true concerning the change in density of the metal beam after incubation in the water bath?

   A. Density increases because the volume increases.
   B. Density decreases because the volume decreases.
   C. Density increases because the mass increases.
   D. Density decreases because the volume increases.

2. If, in Study 3, a trial had been conducted in which the incubation temperature was 70°C, ΔV would most likely have been closest to which of the following?

   F. 6.5 mm^3
   G. 7.2 mm^3
   H. 8.9 mm^3
   J. 10.4 mm^3

3. If the thermal energy contained within the metal rod is proportional to the product of the incubation time and the initial length, in which of the following trials does the rod contain the greatest amount of thermal energy following incubation?

   A. Trial 2
   B. Trial 4
   C. Trial 10
   D. Trial 12

4. The results of Study 1 are best represented by which of the following graphs?

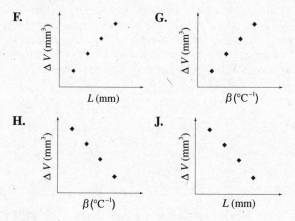

5. The beam tested in Study 3 was most likely composed of which of the metals tested in Study 2 ?

   A. Metal Z
   B. Metal Y
   C. Metal X
   D. Metal W

6. Based on the results of Studies 1 and 2, for a given temperature, which of the following combinations of L and β would yield the greatest thermal expansion?

	L (mm)	β (°C^{-1})
F.	100	4.6
G.	100	2.2
H.	200	4.6
J.	200	2.2

Passage VI

The pesticides *propargyl bromide* (PBr) and *1,3-dichloropropene* (1,3-D) are removed from the soil by a variety of factors, including uptake by plants, adsorption by soil, and breakdown by microorganisms, such as those found in manure. Also, PBr can degrade into *propargyl alcohol*.

Three pairs of pesticide-free soil samples were collected for a study: heavily manure-amended (H1, H2), slightly manure-amended (S1, S2), and unamended (U1, U2), as described in Table 1. On day 1, PBr was added to H1, S1, and U1 and 1,3-D was added to H2, S2, and U2 to produce an initial pesticide concentration of 500 mg/L in each soil sample. PBr, propargyl alcohol, and 1,3-D concentrations in the soil were measured at intervals over the next 12 weeks (see Figures 1–3).

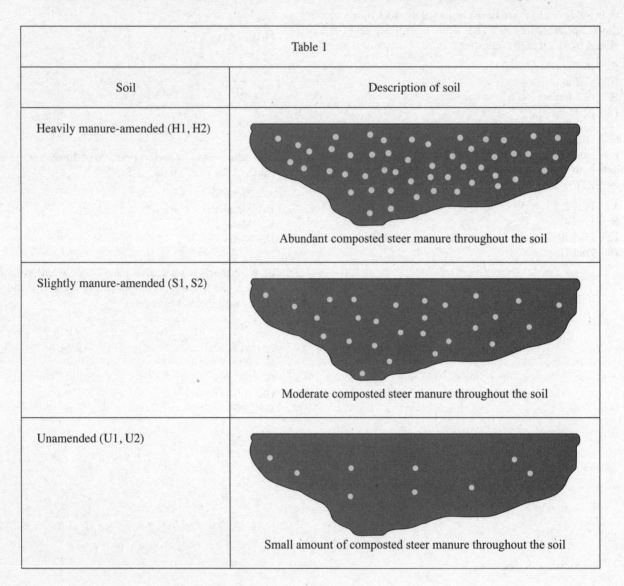

Table 1

Soil	Description of soil
Heavily manure-amended (H1, H2)	Abundant composted steer manure throughout the soil
Slightly manure-amended (S1, S2)	Moderate composted steer manure throughout the soil
Unamended (U1, U2)	Small amount of composted steer manure throughout the soil

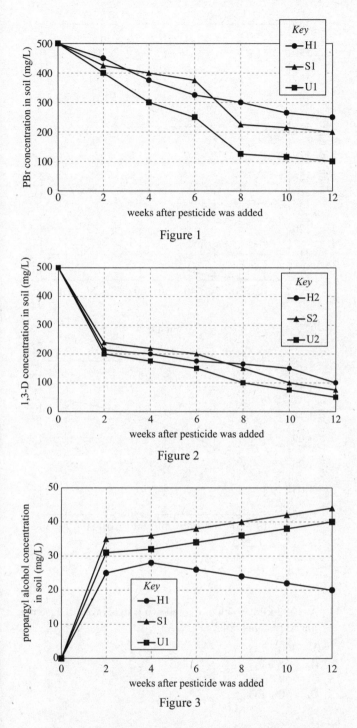

Figure 1

Figure 2

Figure 3

1. Assume that the environmental factors (ultraviolet radiation, wind drift, temperature, and moisture) for each soil sample remained constant over the 12 weeks of the study. According to Figure 2, 12 weeks after 1,3-D was added, what percent of the original 1,3-D concentration remained in the water in H2 ?

   A. Less than 10%
   B. Between 10% and 30%
   C. Between 30% and 50%
   D. Greater than 50%

2. According to Figure 1, 5 weeks after PBr was added, the concentration in the soil in S1 compared to its concentration in H1 was about:

   F. 112 mg/L lower.
   G. 112 mg/L higher.
   H. 275 mg/L lower.
   J. 275 mg/L higher.

3. According to Figures 1 and 3, as the PBr concentration in S1 decreased, the propargyl alcohol concentration:

   A. decreased only.
   B. decreased, then increased.
   C. increased only.
   D. increased, then decreased.

4. Is the statement "Over the 12 weeks of the study, PBr concentration was most reduced in the water in the unamended soil sample" supported by the data in Figure 1 ?

   F. Yes; 12 days after PBr was added, its concentration was least in the water in U1.
   G. Yes; 12 days after PBr was added, its concentration was least in the water in H1.
   H. No; 12 days after PBr was added, its concentration was least in the water in U1.
   J. No; 12 days after PBr was added, its concentration was least in the water in H1.

5. As shown in Figure 2, every time the 1,3-D concentrations in the soil in H2, S2, and U2 were measured during the study, the concentrations in S2 and H2 were found to be very similar to the concentration in U2. The most likely explanation for this is that in S2 and H2:

   A. adsorption onto soil particles and plant uptake played a more significant role in removing 1,3-D than did breakdown to form PBr.
   B. adsorption onto soil particles and plant uptake played a less significant role in removing 1,3-D than did breakdown to form PBr.
   C. bacterial decomposition played a more significant role in removing 1,3-D than did adsorption onto soil particles and plant uptake.
   D. bacterial decomposition played a less significant role in removing 1,3-D than did adsorption onto soil particles and plant uptake.

Passage VII

Ethylene glycol is the main ingredient in antifreeze and has the chemical structure shown below:

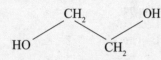

Figures 1–3 show how solutions of antifreeze vary as the concentration of ethylene glycol changes. Concentration is given as the percent ethylene glycol by volume in water (% EG) at atmospheric pressure (101.3 kPa). Figure 1 shows how the melting point (the temperature at which solid antifreeze would begin melting) of antifreeze varies with % EG. Figure 2 shows how the boiling point of antifreeze varies with % EG. Figure 3 shows how the density at 25°C varies with % EG.

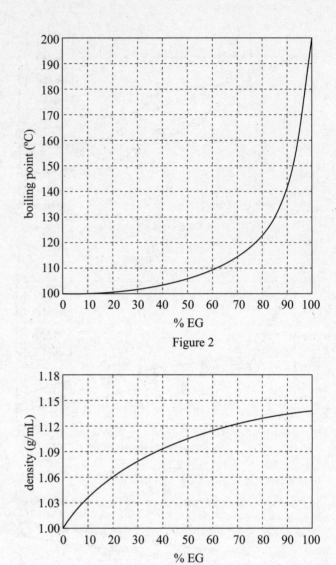

Figure 2

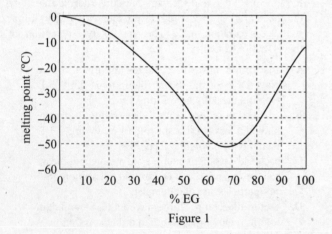

Figure 1

Figure 3

1. At 101.3 kPa, which of the following solutions will have the *lowest* freezing point?

   A.   100% EG
   B.   68% EG
   C.   50% EG
   D.   0% EG

2. According to Figure 1, the temperature at which solid anti-freeze begins to melt in a 60% EG solution at 101.3 kPa is closest to which of the following?

   F.   0°C
   G. −12°C
   H. −48°C
   J. −60°C

3. Based on Figure 2, which of the following solutions has a boiling point equal to pure water at 101.3 kPa?

   A.   0% EG
   B.   13% EG
   C.   68% EG
   D. 100% EG

4. At 25°C, as the % EG increases from 0% to 100%, the mass per unit volume:

   F. increases only.
   G. decreases only.
   H. increases, then decreases.
   J. decreases, then increases.

5. According to Figures 2 and 3, a solution of antifreeze that has a density of 1.09 g/mL at 25°C will have a boiling point closest to which of the following?

   A. 100°C
   B. 104°C
   C. 111°C
   D. 122°C

Passage VIII

A series of studies have been conducted to determine the level of harmful radiation at nuclear-waste clean-up facilities. One method of determining the level of radiation in an area is to measure the growth of certain crystals such as $Bi_4Ge_3O_{12}$ (BGO). BGO crystals come in two basic configurations that grow in environments exposed to high levels of gamma radiation. BGO (I) has a hexagonal crystalline structure and typically grows in environments that are continuously exposed to 100–200 rads of gamma radiation per day, while BGO (II) has an octagonal crystalline structure and typically grows in environments that are continuously exposed to 500–800 rads of gamma radiation per day. Scientists conducted two studies to determine which configuration of BGO crystal would be more useful in determining the amount of exposure to gamma radiation around a nuclear-waste clean-up site.

Study 1

BGO (I) and BGO (II) crystals of 4 cm³ to 8 cm³ were collected from a nuclear waste clean-up site west of Phoenix, AZ. Crystals of both types were placed into individually sealed clear-plastic containers. Ten crystals of each type were then exposed to 3 different levels of gamma radiation—150 rads per day, 450 rads per day, and 750 rads per day—for a period of 7 days. The average volume for each type of crystal and each of the 3 levels of radiation was then determined. The results are shown in Figure 1.

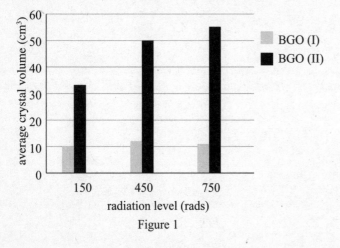

Figure 1

Study 2

The BGO (I) and BGO (II) crystals were removed from the radiation sources and weighed. The average mass of the BGO (I) was determined to be about 13 gm. The average mass of the BGO (II) crystals at each of the three levels of radiation is shown in Figure 2.

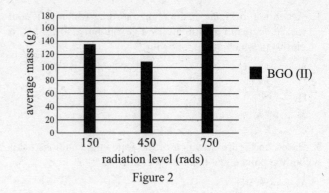

Figure 2

For each radiation level, the volume and mass of the BGO (II) crystals were plotted. The best-fit curve for each is shown in Figure 3.

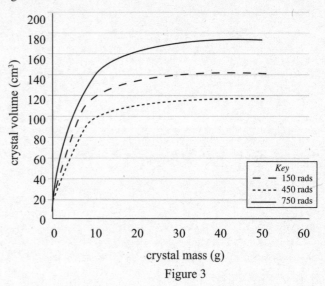

Figure 3

1. Based on Figure 3, for a radiation level of 450 rads, the size and mass of how many BGO (II) crystals were plotted?

   A. 10
   B. 12
   C. 32
   D. Cannot be determined from the given information

2. Suppose that a fourth group of BGO (II) had been exposed to radiation at a level of 300 rads. After 7 days, the average volume of each of these crystals would have been:

   F. less than 35 cm³.
   G. between 35 cm³ and 50 cm³.
   H. between 50 cm³ and 60 cm³.
   J. greater than 60 cm³.

3. Which of the following sets of data points most likely yielded the best-fit curve for BGO (II) crystals exposed to 150 rads of radiation?

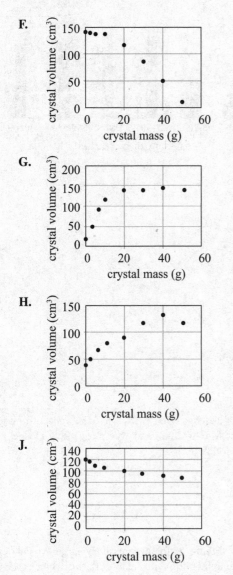

F.

G.

H.

J.

4. At the end of Study 2, a crystal of BGO (II) was found to have a mass of 10 g and a volume of 100 cm³. Based on Figure 3, this crystal most likely had been exposed to radiations of which of the following levels?

- **A.** 150 rads
- **B.** 300 rads
- **C.** 450 rads
- **D.** 750 rads

5. According to the results of Studies 1 and 2, for a given level of radiation, how did the crystals of BGO (I) compare to the crystals of BGO (II)? On average BGO (I) had:

- **A.** larger volume and greater mass.
- **B.** larger volume but lesser mass.
- **C.** smaller volume and lesser mass.
- **D.** smaller volume but greater mass.

6. Of the 10 crystals of BGO (I) that were exposed to 450 rads of radiation, 2 cracked and 8 remained whole. The total mass of all of the crystals combined can be calculated using which of the following expressions?

- **F.** 13 gm × 10
- **G.** 13 gm + 10
- **H.** 13 gm × 8
- **J.** 13 gm + 8

Passage IX

In 1789, Mt. Mantu erupted off the coast of Brunei releasing a cloud of ash that lowered global temperatures for 15 years. When a volcano erupts, it releases a cloud of ash, dust, and debris into the atmosphere thousands of times the volume of the volcano. In addition, at the time of the eruption, the volcano produces a mud and ash flow along the sides of the volcano. The ash flow around Mt. Mantu covered an area 30 times larger than the original size of the volcano. Figure 1 shows the volume of the ash clouds released by volcanoes of differing diameters during the last 200 million years.

Figure 2 shows the average amount of time elapsed between consecutive major eruptions of various volcanoes of similar sizes, for a range of volcano sizes. Figure 3 represents the percentage of land area covered by volcanic ash flows in three different mountain ranges—the Cascades, the Appalachians, and the Himalayas—for various volcanic ash flow diameters.

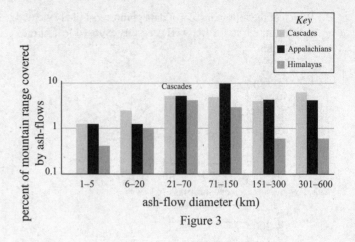

Figure 3

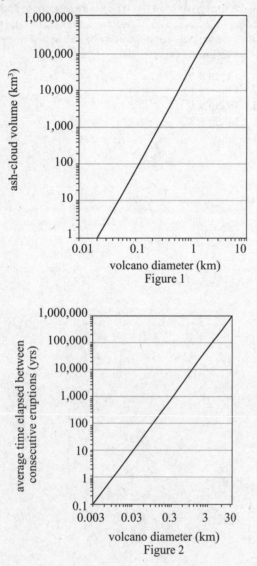

Figure 1

Figure 2

1. If 100 km³ of ash was released by Mt. Mantu, according to Figure 1, Mt. Mantu's diameter was most likely closest to which of the following?

   A. 0.02 km
   B. 0.01 km
   C. 0.1 km
   D. 1 km

2. According to Figure 2, for progressively larger volcanoes, the average amount of time that elapses between consecutive eruptions with the same diameter:

   F. increases only.
   G. decreases only.
   H. varies, but with no general trend.
   J. remains the same.

3. According to Figure 3, for any given range of volcanic ash flows, the percent of area covered in the Himalayas by ash flows is:

   A. less than the Cascades and the Appalachians.
   B. less than the Cascades but greater than the Appalachians.
   C. greater than the Cascades or than the Appalachians.
   D. greater than the Cascades but less than the Appalachians.

4. Suppose a volcano similar to Mt. Mantu created an ash flow that was 30 km in diameter. Based on Figure 1 and other information provided, that volcano would have released a volume of ash closest to which of the following?

    F.   5,000 km^3
    G.   10,000 km^3
    H.   50,000 km^3
    J.   100,000 km^3

5. Assume that a volcano with a diameter of 30 km erupted 500,000 years ago. If the time that elapses between eruptions is equal to the average amount of time given in Figure 2, the volcano should erupt approximately:

    A.   250,000 years from now.
    B.   500,000 years from now.
    C.   1,000,000 years from now.
    D.   1,500,000 years from now.

Passage X

Electromagnets are used in a variety of industrial processes and often consist of a large *solenoid*, a helical coil of wire, that produces a uniform *magnetic field strength* when a current passes through it (see Figure 1).

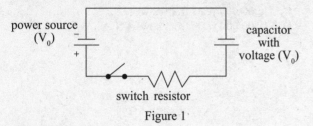

power source (V₀)

capacitor with voltage (V₀)

switch resistor

Figure 1

The magnetic field of a solenoid is a factor of its resistance to changes in current, a property called *inductance* (L). The *relative permeability*, μ, is a property of the material within the solenoid coils which may magnify the magnetic field strength.

Figure 2 shows at 25°C, for specific values of μ and L (the length of the solenoid), how the magnetic field strength varies with the current and with the number of coils (N).

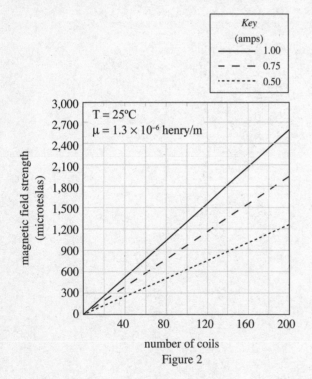

Figure 2

Figure 3 shows, for specific values of A (cross-sectional area of the solenoid) and N, how L varies with solenoid length at 25°C.

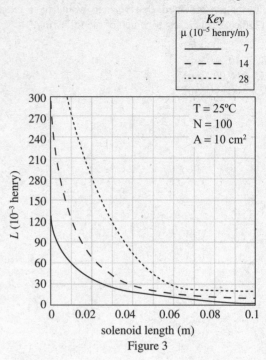

Figure 3

1. For the conditions specified in Figure 2 and I = 0.75 Amps, the solenoid will attract iron metal particles most strongly when the number of coils is closest to which of the following?

   A. 0 coils
   B. 40 coils
   C. 120 coils
   D. 200 coils

2. According to Figure 2, does magnetic field strength vary with current?

   F. Yes; as magnetic field strength increases, the current decreases.
   G. Yes; as magnetic field strength increases, the current increases.
   H. No; as magnetic field strength increases, the current decreases.
   J. Yes; as magnetic field strength increases, the current remains the same.

3. According to Figure 3, for $\mu = 14 \times 10^{-5}$ henry/m, as the length of the solenoid increases, L:

   A. increases only.
   B. decreases only.
   C. varies, but with no consistent trend.
   D. remains the same.

4. For a given solenoid length, what is the correct ranking of the values of μ in Figure 3, from the μ associated with the highest L to the μ associated with the lowest L ?

   F. 7×10^{-5} henry/m, 14×10^{-5} henry/m, 28×10^{-5} henry/m

   G. 14×10^{-5} henry/m, 28×10^{-5} henry/m, 7×10^{-5} henry/m

   H. 7×10^{-5} henry/m, 28×10^{-5} henry/m, 14×10^{-5} henry/m

   J. 28×10^{-5} henry/m, 14×10^{-5} henry/m, 7×10^{-5} henry/m

5. Based on Figure 2, a solenoid containing 100 coils with a magnetic field strength of 300 would most likely have been produced by a current:

   A. greater than 1.00 amps.

   B. between 1.00 and 0.75 amps.

   C. between 0.75 and .50 amps.

   D. less than 0.50 amps.

NOW PASSAGES: ANSWERS AND EXPLANATIONS

Passage I

1. **B**   Look at Figure 1. At time = 20 min, the % PM is between 20% and 40%. Therefore (A) and (D) can be eliminated. Since the point lies closer to 40 than 20, (B) is the correct answer.

2. **F**   The question asks you to determine what the % PM will be for Reaction 3 at time = 8 min. Eight minutes is a little more than halfway between 5 minutes and 10 minutes. At time = 8 min, the graph lies somewhere above 60%, making (F) the correct answer.

3. **A**   Compare the % PM at time = 20 min for the reaction with a magnetic field and the reaction without a magnetic field. At time = 20 min, % PM with a magnetic field was almost 100% and % PM without a magnetic field was 40%. That means that % PM without a magnetic field was 40%, or $\frac{2}{5}$ of the % PM with a magnetic field.

4. **G**   Figures 1–3 do not all express the same relationship between % PM with a magnetic field and % PM without a magnetic field. Eliminate (H) and (J). Both (F) and (G) refer to Figure 1, and since the % PM increases as time increases, eliminate (F).

5. **C**   The question asks about % MO as opposed to % PM. If % PM increases in Reaction 3, then the metal oxide is being used up as the pure metal forms. Therefore, the graphs for % MO should decrease as time increases, eliminating (A) and (B). For Reaction 3, % PM reaches 100% faster with a magnetic field than without. Therefore, the metal oxide will get used up faster for the reaction with a magnetic field, eliminating (D) and making (C) the correct answer.

Passage II

1. **B**   From Table 1, the work function for Zn is listed as 4.30 eV. Therefore, (B) is the correct answer.

2. **H**   Examine Figure 1 closely. At a frequency of 15×10^{14} Hz, Ni has the lowest K_{max} (1.25 eV), and Al has the highest K_{max} (2.1 eV). Thus, (H) is the correct answer.

3. **B**   As frequency increases, the K_{max} value increases.

4. **F** Look closely at the line plot of Al in Figure 1. At a frequency of 10.0×10^{14} Hz, the K_{max} is 0.1 eV, and at a frequency of 20.0×10^{14} Hz, the K_{max} is 4.2 eV. If this trend continues, as frequency increases by 2.0×10^{14} Hz, K_{max} increases by approximately 0.8 eV. Thus, the correct answer is (F) since at a frequency of 26×10^{14} Hz, K_{max} for Al will be considerably greater than 5.0 eV.

5. **D** We can use the given data for Metal Q and apply it to Figure 1. If Metal Q's K_{max} is 0.5 eV and 3.0 eV at frequencies of 12.0×10^{14} Hz and 18.0×10^{14} Hz, respectively, we can see that these points lie between zinc and silver. Table 1 shows the work functions of Zn and Ag as 4.30 eV and 4.73 eV, respectively. Therefore, Metal Q's work function should be between 4.30 eV and 4.73 eV, as in (D).

Passage III

1. **C** Look at Figure 1. As the concentration of Drug X increases, the percent of bacterial cells of Strain C also increases. Therefore, (C) is the correct answer.

2. **H** From Table 1, compare the values of ED_{50}. Strain D has the maximum value, so (H) is the correct answer.

3. **D** In Figure 1, the percent of bacterial cells killed increases as the concentration of Drug X increases. Thus, according to the data, a concentration of 200 mg/L would result in a greater percentage of bacterial cells killed. Since the percentage killed at a concentration of 100 mg/L is approximately 83%, the correct answer is (D).

4. **F** From the data in Table 1, Strain E has an ED_{50} of 62.6. Look for a strain with an ED_{50} that when multiplied by 4 is about 62.6. Strain A has an ED_{50} of 15.3, which when multiplied by 4 is approximately 60. Four times the ED_{50} for Strains B, C, and D are about 120, 90, and 360, respectively. Thus, the correct answer is (F).

5. **C** Examine the bars for Strain E in Figure 1. The percentages for 2 mg/L and 20 mg/L are similar, so (B) is incorrect. The greatest difference between two concentrations is an increase from approximately 25% to 45% from a concentration of 20 mg/L to 60 mg/L.

Passage IV

1. **B** Table 1 shows that as voltage increases, power increases. For $V = 0.03$ V, the voltage is between the values for Trials 1 and 2, so the expected value for P should lie between the results for Trial 1 (0.08 W) and Trial 2 (0.32W). Therefore, (B) is the correct answer.

2. **J** Tables 1, 2, and 3 all show that P increases when V increases. Choice (J) reflects this trend.

3. **C** Look at Tables 1–3 to compare trials with different resistances and the same voltage. Take Trials 2, 7, and 12, for example, which all have the same voltage. Trial 12 has the highest resistance, and Trial 2 has the lowest. Trial 12, however, has the lowest power, and Trial 2 has the highest. Therefore, as resistance increases, power decreases, and so (C) is the correct answer.

4. **F** Conductance (G) is defined in the passage as the inverse of resistance (R). The passage states that Study 1 has the lowest resistance and therefore the greatest conductance. Since the resistance differs between the three studies, eliminate (J). Choice (F) is correct because it is the only answer choice in Study 1.

5. **C** Since the different circuits had different power outputs at a given voltage, (D) is incorrect. Compare three trials, one from each study, that have the same voltage. Trials 1, 6, and 11 show that the power output is lowest for a given voltage in Study 3.

6. **J** Inspect each pair of trials to determine which has the same resistance, 3 times the value of V, and 9 times the value of P. Eliminate (F) and (H) because the trials are in different studies, so the value of R is not constant. Choice (G) is incorrect because the value of V in Trial 4 is double that in Trial 2, and the value of P is 4 times greater. Choice (J) shows the correct relationship.

Passage V

1. **D** During thermal expansion of the metal rod, the only variable that changes according to the passage is the volume. Since density is defined as mass divided by volume, when the thermal expansion causes an increase in volume, the density decreases.

2. **H** The data in Table 3 shows that ΔV for 60°C is 7.7 mm^3 and ΔV for 80°C is 10.2 mm^3. Since 70°C is between these two values, the corresponding value of ΔV should be between 7.7 mm^3 and 10.2 mm^3, so the answer is (H).

3. **B** The question states that thermal energy is proportional to the product of incubation time and initial length. In each Study, incubation time is held constant. Use POE, and look for the trial with the greatest initial length, as in (B).

4. **F** According to Table 1, the two variables are the length of the metal rod (L) and the change in volume of the metal rod (ΔV). Notice that as L increases, ΔV increases. Choices (G) and (H) display a relationship between β and ΔV, which is part of Study 2, not Study 1. Choice (J) incorrectly displays an inverse relationship between L and ΔV.

5. **A** The incubation temperature in Study 2 was held constant at 80°C. Compare the value of ΔV in Table 3 at 80°C to the values in Table 2. In Study 3, ΔV was 10.2 mm^3 at 80°C, which corresponds to Metal Z in Table 2.

6. **H** Refer to Tables 1 and 2. The greatest thermal expansion, ΔV, occurs when L is 200 mm and when β is 4.6 °C⁻¹, (H).

Passage VI

1. **B** Examine Figure 2. At the end of 12 weeks, the PBr concentration for H2 has decreased from 500 mg/L to 100 mg/L. 100 out of 500 is 20%, as in (B).

2. **G** In Figure 1, find the difference in PBr concentration between S1 and U1 after 5 weeks. Choices (H) and (J) do not reflect the actual amount of U1 after 5 weeks instead of the difference. Choice (F) reverses the relationship between U1 and S1.

3. **C** According to Figure 1, as number of weeks increases, the concentration of PBr decreases for all three soil samples. In Figure 3, as number of weeks increases, the propargyl alcohol concentration in S1 also increases. Choice (D) expresses the relationship in H1 instead of S1.

4. **F** Look at Figure 1. The unamended soil sample refers to U1, which has the lowest concentration. The statement is therefore supported, so eliminate (H) and (J). You can also safely eliminate (G) because the explanation does not match the information in Figure 1. Choice (F) is the correct answer.

5. **D** This question is asking you to explain the similarity in concentration between H2, S2, and U2 in Figure 2. Since all three soil samples differed greatly in steer manure content, according to the passage, the bacterial count should also vary. This means that bacterial decomposition does not play a significant role in the PBr concentration in the soil, which is (D). Choice (C) is the opposite of (D), and (A) and (B) incorrectly mention propargyl alcohol.

Passage VII

1. **B** "Freezing point" does not appear on any of the figures, so you'll need a bit of outside knowledge here. Think about it this way: The freezing point is the point at which a substance turns from a liquid into a solid. The melting point is the point at which a substance turns from a solid into a liquid. Therefore, freezing point and melting point are one and the same. Use Figure 1. According to the passage, all readings are taken at atmospheric pressure 101.3 kPa, so you can disregard that part of the question. The melting point of the solution seems to be lowest around 70% EG. The closest of the answers is (B), 68%.

2. **H** Use Figure 1. According to the passage, all readings are taking at atmospheric pressure 101.3 kPa, so you can disregard that part of the question. According to Figure 1, at 60% EG, the melting point is roughly −48°C, as in (H).

3. **A**   The substance that will behave most like pure water and boil at the same temperature would be pure water itself. Choice (A), 0% EG, would mean a solution of no ethylene glycol and all water. Increasing the % EG, as in (B), (C), and (D), and therefore decreasing the percentage of water, would make the solution behave less like water.

4. **F**   This question requires a bit of outside knowledge: "density" and "mass per unit length" are one in the same. Therefore, you can use Figure 3 to answer this question even though the word "density" does not appear explicitly in this question. According to the passage, all density readings are taken at a temperature of 25°C, so you can disregard that temperature and just look at the graph. According to this graph, as % EG increases, the density steadily increases as well. The best answer, therefore, comes from (F).

5. **B**   According to Figure 2, a substance with a density of 1.09 g/mL has 40% EG. Use this EG value on Figure 3. According to Figure 3, a substance with 40% EG has a boiling point of approximately 104°C. Only (B) works.

Passage VIII

1. **D**   The axes given in Figure 3 are "crystal mass (g)" and "crystal volume (cm³)." According to the key, different levels of radiation were measured. Nowhere in any of these axes or curves do we have any indication of the *number of crystals* measured. Without this information, and without any relevant information in the introduction, we can't determine how many crystals were measured, making (D) the only possible answer.

2. **G**   Although this question does not mention one specific figure, look at the variables to be compared. We'll need to make a prediction about volume based on radiation level. The only one of the three figures that compares these two variables is Figure 1. According to the information in Study 1, these readings were taken after *a period of 7 days*, so we can disregard that bit of information from the question. Now, the question asks about BGO (II), which is represented on Figure 1 by the darker of the two bars. According to the figure, as radiation level increases, crystal volume increases. Therefore, it is reasonable to assume that the volume of a crystal with a radiation level of 300 rads will be greater than that of a crystal with a radiation level of 150 rads and lesser than that of a crystal with a radiation level of 450 rads. According to Figure 1, a BGO (II) crystal with a radiation level of 150 rads has a volume of about 35 cm³, and a BGO (II) crystal with a radiation level of 450 rads has a volume of 50 cm³. Only (G) gives the appropriate range of values between these two volumes.

3. **G**   Figure 3 gives the curve for 150 rads, so find the plot in the answer choices that matches up most closely with the curve for 150 rads in Figure 3. Use POE. The curve starts at 0 cm³, heads in an upward direction, and maxes out around 140 cm³. Eliminate (F) and (J) because these curves decrease. Eliminate (H) because this curve does not start at 0 cm³. Only (G) meets all the requirements and is therefore the best answer.

4. **C**   Plot the information from the problem onto Figure 3. A crystal with a mass of 10 g and a volume of 100 cm³ matches most closely the curve appearing lowest on the figure. According to the key, this is the curve for 450 rads, as in (C).

5. **C**   Use POE. Figure 1 contains a side-by-side comparison of the volumes of the crystals at different radiation levels. The BGO (I) crystals are represented by the lighter bar, and the BGO (II) crystals are represented by the darker bar. In all cases, the BGO (I) crystals had a smaller volume, so eliminate (A) and (B). Figure 2 contains the masses of BGO (II) but not BGO (I). According to the passage, though, *The average mass of the BGO (I) crystals was determined to be about 13 gm*. Therefore, since the masses shown in Figure 2 are all well above this value, it can also be inferred that BGO (I)'s mass was smaller, eliminating (D).

6. **H**   According to the passage, *The average mass of the BGO (I) was determined to be about 13 gm*. Therefore, since there are 8 *whole* crystals left at the end of the experiment, their total mass can be found by multiplying the number of crystals by the mass of each: 13 gm × 8, as in (H).

Passage IX

1. **C**   According to Figure 1, when the volcano releases 100 km³ of ash, its diameter is approximately 0.1 km, which is (C). If you had trouble with this problem, you may have been looking at the wrong axis.

2. **F**   Figure 2 shows a direct relationship. As "average time elapsed" increases, "volcano diameter" also increases. Only (F) represents this trend.

3. **A**   Use POE. Pick any point on the graph: For 1–5% covered, for example, the bar showing the ash-flow of the Himalayas is lower than both the bars for the Cascades and the Appalachians. This same trend holds true for the other percentages as well. Only (A) accurately describes this trend.

4. **H**   The passage states that Figure 1 *shows the volume of the ash clouds released by volcanoes of differing diameters*. It also states that the *ash flow around Mt. Mantu covered an area 30 times larger than the original size of the volcano*. Therefore, if the ash flow in the question is 30 km, the original size of the volcano must be 30 times smaller, or 1 km. According to Figure 1, a volcano with a diameter of 1 km will have an ash-cloud volume of approximately 54,000 km³. Choice (H) gives the best approximation of this value.

5. **B**   According to Figure 2, a volcano with a diameter of 30 km should have approximately 1,000,000 years between eruptions. Therefore, since this volcano erupted 500,000 years ago, it will not erupt for another 1,000,000 − 500,000 = 500,000 years, as in (B).

Passage X

1. **D** The words *magnetic field strength* don't appear explicitly in the question, but they are suggested by the word *attract*. Therefore, use Figure 2 to figure out the relationship between the number of coils and the magnetic field strength. According to this Figure, the magnetic field strength increases with increasing number of coils for all three curves shown. Therefore, in order to get the strongest possible magnetic field, we will need the maximum number of coils, or 200, as in (D).

2. **G** Review the trends in Figure 2. As the number of coils increases, magnetic field strength increases, which is why all curves show a positive slope. But the key identifies the difference between each curve: The greater the current, the greater the magnetic field strength. Choice (G) provides the correct relationship.

3. **B** Find $\mu = 14 \times 10^{-5}$ in the key for Figure 3. Notice, though, that all three of these curves follow the same trend: As solenoid length increases, L decreases and then levels off at the end. Only (B) is consistent with this information.

4. **J** According to Figure 3, as solenoid length increases, L decreases. The μ curves don't follow quite so consistent a relationship. Pick a point and see how these μ values relate to one another. At a solenoid length of 0.02 m, the μ value associated with the largest L value is $\mu = 28 \times 10^{-5}$. The μ value associated with the smallest L value is $\mu = 7 \times 10^{-5}$. Therefore, the correct answer should have 28×10^{-5} as its first value and 7×10^{-5} as its last. Only (J) works.

5. **D** Find the point on Figure 2 that corresponds to 100 coils and a magnetic field strength of 300 microteslas. This point lies below all three curves. Since the magnetic field strength increases as current increases, the current should be less than 0.50 amps, as in (D).

Chapter 11
Later Passages

Passage I

In an experimental device known as a cloud chamber, energetic protons and neutrons pass through a vapor of condensed alcohol, causing the ionization (acquired charge) of some of the alcohol molecules. The ionized alcohol molecules begin as condensation nuclei around which the alcohol vapor continues to condense until a high-energy mist is formed. When the mist has acquired enough charge, energetic particles passing through the vapor form tracks visible to the naked eye. These tracks can be accelerated by the application of a magnetic force, under which positively and negatively charged ions will travel in opposite directions.

Two studies using cloud chambers were done at a research center in a temperate climate, using supercooled gaseous ethanol as a medium. The cloud chamber temperature ranged from 0°C to −150°C.

Study 1

Four types of anions (A–D) were used. Anions of each type, when released into the cloud chamber, emit groups of electrons into the chamber with a specific distribution of charges (see Table 1).

Table 1				
Anion type	Percent of groups of electrons having charges (coulombs):			
	0.1–0.5	0.6–1.0	1.1–1.5	1.6–2.0
A	70	20	8	2
B	75	10	8	7
C	80	8	7	5
D	85	7	5	3
Note: 1 coulomb is the charge of 6.24×10^{18} electrons.				

A device containing all 4 types of anions was placed next to the cloud chamber. A computer in the device determined whether or not to immediately release at least 1 anion, emitting electrons into the chamber. The computer also selected which type of anion to release, and how many anions to release to generate 10, 100, 1,000, or 10,000 condensation nuclei per cm³ within the chamber. The average number of tracks produced by each type of anion and at each concentration of condensation nuclei is shown in Figure 1.

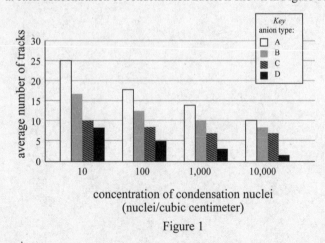

concentration of condensation nuclei
(nuclei/cubic centimeter)

Figure 1

Study 2

The magnetic force required to make each track to accelerate away from a straight line was recorded over an hour following the release of the four types of anions into two types of cloud chambers: one with ethanol vapor and one with water vapor. The averaged results for both types of cloud chambers are shown in Figure 2.

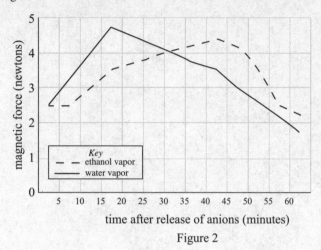

time after release of anions (minutes)

Figure 2

---

1. According to the results of Study 1, as the condensation nuclei concentration increased, the average number of tracks generated:

   A. increased for all 4 types of anions.
   B. increased for anion types A and B but decreased for anion types C and D.
   C. decreased for all 4 types of anions.
   D. decreased for anion types A and B but increased for anion types C and D.

2. Based on the passage, what is the correct order of tracks, high-energy mist, and condensation nuclei, according to the stage of development, from earliest to latest?

   F. High-energy mist, track, condensation nucleus
   G. High-energy mist, condensation nucleus, track
   H. Track, high-energy mist, condensation nucleus
   J. Track, condensation nucleus, high-energy mist

3. According to the results of Study 2, how did the magnetic force required in the cloud chamber with ethanol vapor differ from the magnetic force required in the cloud chamber with water vapor, with respect to their maximum strength?

   A. It took more time for the magnetic force in the ethanol vapor to reach a maximum strength, and it reached a greater maximum strength.
   B. It took less time for the magnetic force in the ethanol vapor to reach a maximum strength, and it reached a greater maximum strength.
   C. It took more time for the magnetic force in the ethanol vapor to reach a maximum strength, and it reached a lesser maximum strength.
   D. It took less time for the magnetic force in the ethanol vapor to reach a maximum strength, and it reached a lesser maximum strength.

4. The design of Study 1 differed from the design of Study 2 in that Study 1, the:

   F. tracks of condensation nuclei were analyzed, whereas in Study 2, the concentration of condensation nuclei was analyzed.
   G. strength of magnetic fields was measured, whereas in Study 2, the concentration of condensation nuclei was analyzed.
   H. tracks of condensation nuclei were analyzed, whereas in Study 2, the strength of magnetic fields was analyzed.
   J. strength of magnetic fields was analyzed, whereas in Study 2, tracks of condensation nuclei were analyzed.

5. Which of the following statements gives the most likely reason that data from the cloud chamber was not recorded below a temperature of –150°C? Below –150°C, there would be present:

   A. only water vapor.
   B. only alcohol vapor.
   C. ice crystals but little water vapor.
   D. solidified alcohol but little alcohol vapor.

6. Which of the following statements about the concentration of condensation nuclei in the 4 types of anions is supported by Table 1 ?

   F. For all 4 types of anions, the majority of particles belonged to the largest charge category.
   G. For all 4 types of anions, the majority of particles belong to the smallest charge category.
   H. For anion types A and B, most anions belong to the largest charge category, whereas for anion types C and D, most anions belong to the smallest charge category.
   J. For anion types A and B, most anions belong to the smallest charge category, whereas for anion types C and D, most anions belong to the largest charge category.

Passage II

Escherichia coli (E. coli) are commonly used in laboratories for the expression, replication, and purification of introduced circular pieces of DNA called *plasmids*. Engineered plasmids encode a gene of interest and often genes that confer resistances to select antibiotics. Antibiotic resistance may be analyzed using the *disk diffusion method*. During the disk diffusion method, bacteria from a single *colony*, or a cluster of genetically identical cells, are incubated in liquid growth media and spread on agar plates (see Figure 1). Small paper disks containing a known concentration of antibiotic are set on the agar plates, and the bacteria are allowed to grow at optimal temperatures. Laboratory strains of *E. coli* lacking plasmids containing genes of resistance to select antibiotics will be unable to grow near the disk containing that antibiotic. Only bacteria that have received the introduced plasmid containing an antibiotic resistance gene should be able to grow in the presence of the antibiotic-containing disk.

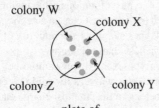

colony W

colony X

colony Z

colony Y

plate of
transformed colonies

Figure 1

Experiment 1

A biotech company has engineered new laboratory strains (A–E) of *E. coli* and is testing whether each strain could grow in the presence of a variety of common antibiotics—ampicillin (Amp), kanamycin (Kan), penicillin (Pen), and tetracycline (Tet). Each of the strains was incubated in a clear nutrient media containing either extra sugar (glucose) or an antibiotic at 37°C for 24 hours. After 24 hours, the growth media was examined for *turbidity* or cloudiness, a signal of bacterial growth (see Table 1).

Table 1					
Strain	Nutrient Media				
	Glu	Amp	Kan	Pen	Tet
A	+	−	+	−	−
B	+	−	−	+	−
C	+	−	−	+	+
D	+	+	+	−	−
E	+	−	+	+	−

Note: + indicates presence of turbidity;
− indicates no change in appearance

Experiment 2

The scientists at the biotech company tested strain A for growth after *transformation*, a process of introducing engineered plasmids with antibiotic-resistance containing plasmids. Four different transformed colonies (W, X, Y, and Z) and untransformed strain A were incubated in liquid growth media and spread on agar plates. To identify which colonies had received which resistance genes, disks containing one of each of the common antibiotics were then placed on the agar plate, and the bacteria were permitted to grow at 37°C (see Figure 2).

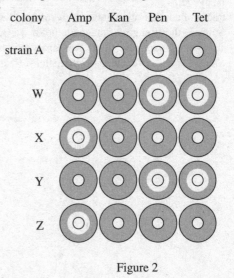

Figure 2

1. Suppose *E. coli* Strain D had been incubated on plates containing kanamycin and tetracycline (Kan⁺ Tet⁺) disks and growth near both disks was observed. Do the data in Table 1 support this observation?

   A. Yes; the results shown in Table 1 indicate that Strain D can grow in the presence of both Kan and Tet.
   B. Yes; the results shown in Table 1 indicate that Strain D cannot grow in the presence of Kan.
   C. No; the results shown in Table 1 indicate that Strain D can grow in the presence of both Kan and Tet.
   D. No; the results shown in Table 1 indicate that Strain D cannot grow in the presence of Tet.

2. Which of the labeled colonies shown in Figure 2 is most likely to have received a plasmid conferring resistance to tetracycline?

   F. Colonies W and X
   G. Colonies X and Y
   H. Colonies Y and Z
   J. Colonies X and Z

3. According to Table 1, how many strains tested in Experiment 1 were able to grow in nutrient media containing penicillin?

   A. 0
   B. 1
   C. 2
   D. 3

4. Based on Table 1 and Figure 2, which colonies, if any, likely received a plasmid with resistance genes to penicillin and tetracycline?

   F. Colony W only
   G. Colony X only
   H. Colonies X and Z
   J. Colonies W and Y

5. Before beginning the experiments, the scientists sprayed the lab area down with a disinfectant. The most likely reason that the disinfectant was used was to avoid contaminating:

   A. the nutrient growth media with strains that were lab generated.
   B. the agar plates with strains that were lab generated.
   C. both the nutrient growth media and agar plates with strains that were lab generated.
   D. both the nutrient growth media and agar plates with strains that were not lab generated.

6. Which of the colonies shown in Figure 2 did NOT grow in the presence of ampicillin?

   F. Colony W
   G. Colony X
   H. Colony Y
   J. None of the strains

Passage III

A group of students added 100 mg of Salt A to an Erlenmeyer flask containing 100 mL of water at 20°C. The mixture was heated over a Bunsen burner, and a thermometer was placed in the flask to acquire temperature readings (Figure 1).

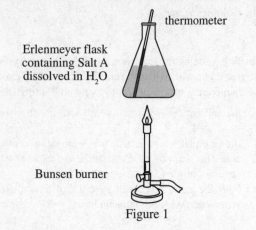

thermometer

Erlenmeyer flask containing Salt A dissolved in H_2O

Bunsen burner

Figure 1

The mixture was heated, and temperature readings were acquired every 30 sec until the solution reached a full boil and the solid had completely dissolved. The boiling temperature for the solution was measured to be 104°C. The procedure was repeated with Salt B, which resulted in a boiling temperature of 110°C.

The teacher asked 3 of the students in the group to explain why the solutions had different boiling temperatures.

Student 1

The solution containing Salt B had a higher boiling point because Salt B produces more ions in solution than Salt A. As the solid dissolves, the salt ionizes and interacts with water molecules. This causes more interactions between the ions and water thus requiring more energy for water molecules to break these interactions and become a gas (boiling). Since salts become ions in solution, salts that produce more ions will have more interactions with water than salts producing fewer ions. Thus, if two salts of equal amounts are added to water, the solution containing the salt that produces more ions will boil at the higher temperature.

Student 2

The solution containing Salt B had a higher boiling point because it had a lower *molar mass* (the mass of 6.02×10^{23} particles). Consider equal amounts of two salts with different molar masses. More mass is required of the salt with the greater molar mass to result in the same number of particles. Since more heat energy is required to boil water with more interactions, the solution with more salt particles will boil at a higher temperature. Thus, if equal amounts of two salts with different molar masses are added, the salt with the lower molar mass will result in more particles and a greater solution boiling point than a salt with a greater molar mass.

Student 3

The solution containing Salt B had a higher boiling point because Salt B releases more heat upon dissolving than Salt A. The *enthalpy change of dissolution* (ΔH°_{diss}) is a measure of the net amount of heat energy absorbed in the process of dissolving a salt. Salts that absorb more energy to dissolve will have more positive ΔH°_{diss} values and will make the solution cooler. Salts that absorb less energy than they release will have more negative ΔH°_{diss} values and will make the solution warmer. If equal amounts of two salts with different ΔH°_{diss} values are dissolved in solution, the solution containing the salt with the more negative ΔH°_{diss} value will release more heat and thus result in a greater boiling point.

The number of ions produced, molar mass, and enthalpy change dissolution (ΔH°_{diss}) of some common salts are shown in Table 1.

Table 1			
Salt	Ions produced	Molar mass (g/mol)	ΔH°_{diss} (kJ/mol)
Sodium chloride	2	58.4	+ 3.9
Calcium chloride	3	111.0	− 81.2
Ammonium nitrate	2	80.1	+ 25.7
Potassium hydroxide	2	56.11	− 57.6
Magnesium sulfate	2	120.38	− 91.0

1. Suppose that Salt A had been potassium hydroxide and Salt B had been magnesium sulfate. The results of the experiment would have supported the explanation(s) provided by which student(s)?

   A. Student 2 only
   B. Student 3 only
   C. Students 1 and 3 only
   D. Students 2 and 3 only

2. Suppose that the students also tested ammonium nitrate in the experiment and found it to have resulted in a boiling temperature in solution of 107°C. Student 2 would claim that ammonium nitrate:

   F. has a greater molar mass than Salt A, but a smaller molar mass than Salt B.
   G. has a greater molar mass than Salt B, but a smaller molar mass than Salt A.
   H. has a greater enthalpy change of dissolution than Salt A, but a smaller enthalpy change of dissolution than Salt B.
   J. has a greater enthalpy change of dissolution than Salt B, but a smaller enthalpy change of dissolution than Salt A.

3. Which of the following graphs of the relative number of particles produced is most consistent with Student 2's explanation?

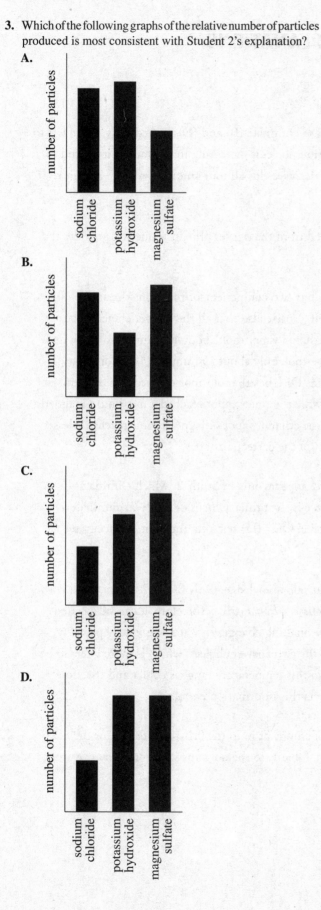

A.

B.

C.

D.

4. During the experiment, the temperature reading in the thermometer as readings were taken every 30 sec:

F. increased only.
G. decreased only.
H. increased, then decreased.
J. decreased, then increased.

5. Based on Student 3's explanation, which of the salts in Table 1 would result in the greatest solution boiling temperature?

A. Calcium chloride
B. Ammonium nitrate
C. Potassium hydroxide
D. Magnesium sulfate

6. Consider the data for cesium hydroxide shown in the table below:

Ions produced	Molar mass (g/mol)	$\Delta H°_{diss}$ (kJ/mol)
2	149.91	−71.6

Which student(s), if any, would predict that cesium hydroxide would produce a solution with a lower boiling temperature than calcium chloride?

F. Student 1 only
G. Students 2 and 3 only
H. Students 1, 2, and 3
J. None of the students

7. Is the claim "If equal amounts of salt are dissolved, sodium chloride will result in a greater boiling point than ammonium nitrate" consistent with Student 2's explanation?

A. No, because sodium chloride has a smaller molar mass than ammonium nitrate.
B. No, because sodium chloride has a more negative enthalpy change of dissolution.
C. Yes, because sodium chloride has a smaller molar mass than ammonium nitrate.
D. Yes, because sodium chloride has a more negative enthalpy change of dissolution.

LATER PASSAGES: ANSWERS AND EXPLANATIONS

Passage I

1. **C**   In Figure 1, all four anions follow the same trend, so eliminate (B) and (D) immediately. From left to right in the graph, the concentration of condensation nuclei is increasing for all four anions, and as this value increases, the average number of tracks decreases for all four anions. Only (C) accurately reflects this trend.

2. **G**   Read if and only when a question can't be answered from the figures. The introduction provides the order of development, correctly described in (G).

3. **C**   Notice from the answer choices that this question has two components: time to maximum magnetic force and maximum magnetic force itself. Notice also that all the answer choices focus on the *ethanol vapor*. According to Figure 2, the ethanol vapor took about 40 minutes to reach its maximum magnetic force, whereas the water vapor took only about 15 minutes. Therefore, the ethanol vapor took more time, eliminating (B) and (D). The ethanol vapor reached a maximum magnetic force of approximately 4.25 Newtons, while the water vapor reached a maximum magnetic force of approximately 4.75 Newtons. Therefore, the ethanol vapor's magnetic force reached a lesser maximum strength, eliminating (A) and making (C) the correct answer.

4. **H**   Note the axes on each of the graphs. *Magnetic force* appears only in Study 2, which eliminates (G) and (J) immediately. Then, since magnetic force is the primary focus of Study 2, eliminate (F) because it contains no mention of magnetic force. Only (H) remains and contains accurate information regarding both studies.

5. **D**   This requires a bit of logical thinking and some outside knowledge. Only Study 2 is concerned with *water vapor*, whereas the general introduction discusses *alcohol vapor*. Therefore, it can be inferred that the entire experiment deals with *alcohol vapor*, making changes in water vapor only partially relevant, eliminating (A) and (C). Then, between the two answer choices, which is more likely to be the case at temperatures *below* –150°C? Alcohol in this temperature range is colder and therefore more likely to be solid than vapor. Only (D) reflects this information correctly.

6. **G**   According to Table 1, 75–80% of all four types of anions fit in to the 0.1–0.5 category, or the *smallest charge category*. There are no exceptions in Table 1, so the only answer choice that can work is (G).

Passage II

1. **D**   Use POE. If you're not sure whether to answer "yes" or "no," check the reasons. According to Table 1, Strain D can grow in the presence of Glu, Amp, and Kan. Eliminate (B), which states that Strain D cannot grow in the presence of Kan. Also according to Table 1, Strain D cannot grow in the presence of Pen or Tet. Eliminate (A) and (C), which suggest that Strain D can grow in the presence of Tet. Only (D) remains.

2. **J**   The question refers to Figure 2, but the presence of Strain A at the top of the figure links back to Figure 1. According to Figure 1, Strain A can grow only when cultured in the antibiotic-free control medium (Glu) or in the presence of Kan. It cannot grow in the presence of Amp, Pen, or Tet. It can be inferred that if growth occurred in a culture, it will be pictured in Figure 2 with a smaller white region than in those colonies where growth did not occur. Therefore, the colonies that have received a *plasmid conferring resistance to tetracycline* should show a smaller white region in the Tet column. Colonies X and Z have this small white region, making (J) the best answer.

3. **D**   According to Table 1, Strains B, C, and E were able to grow in the presence of penicillin, or +Pen. Choice (D) gives the correct number.

4. **H**   According to Table 1, Strain A can grow in Glu and Kan media. It cannot grow in the presence of Amp, Pen, or Tet. It can be inferred that if growth occurred in a culture, it will be pictured in Figure 2 with a smaller white region than in those colonies where growth did not occur. Therefore, the colonies that have received a *plasmid with resistance genes to penicillin and tetracycline* should show a smaller white region in the Pen and Tet columns. Colonies X and Z have this small white region, making (H) the best answer.

5. **D**   This question requires a bit of outside knowledge about why scientists do what they do when setting up experiments. Use POE and common sense. Notice (A), (B), and (C) all contain mention of substances that are *lab generated*. Only (D) contains mention of strains that are *not lab generated*. Think about it this way: Scientists are trying to control the environment of their experiment, so they don't want things from outside (things that are *not lab generated*) to contaminate the things in the experiment. Also, notice that (C) and (D) are direct opposites, a good indication that one of them will be correct.

6. **G**   According to Table 1, Strain A can grow in Glu and Kan media. It cannot grow in the presence of Amp, Pen, or Tet. It can be inferred that if growth occurred in a culture, it will be pictured in Figure 2 with a smaller white region than in those colonies where growth did not occur. Therefore, a colony that did NOT grow in the presence of ampicillin should show a larger white region in the Amp column. Of the choices given, only colony X has a larger white region, making (G) the best answer.

Passage III

1. **B** According to Table 1, potassium hydroxide produced 2 ions, had a molar mass of 56.11 g/mol, and had a $\Delta H°_{diss}$ of –57.6 kJ/mol. Magnesium sulfate produced 2 ions, had a molar mass of 120.38 g/mol, and had a $\Delta H°_{diss}$ of –91.0 kJ/mol. Use POE. Student 1 writes, *The solution containing Salt B had a higher boiling point because Salt B produces more ions in solution than Salt A.* These findings do not agree with Table 1 for the given substances, which produced the same number of ions. Eliminate (C). Student 2 writes, *The solution containing Salt B had a higher boiling point because it had a lower molar mass (the mass of 6.02×10^{23} particles).* Salt B in this question is magnesium sulfate, which does not have a lower molar mass than potassium hydroxide, so you can eliminate (A) and (D). This leaves only (B), and the findings in the table do agree with Student 3's hypothesis.

2. **G** The passage gives the following information: *The boiling temperature for the solution of Salt A was measured to be 104°C.* The procedure was repeated with Salt B, which resulted in a boiling temperature of 110°C. According to this question, ammonium nitrate has a boiling point of 107°C, right between Salts A and B. According to Student 2, the solution containing Salt B had a higher boiling point because it had a lower molar mass. Therefore, because ammonium nitrate has a higher boiling point than Salt A, it must have a lower molar mass. Only (G) can work. Choices (H) and (J) can be eliminated because Student 2 does not discuss enthalpy change.

3. **A** According to Student 2, *the salt with the lower molar mass will result in more particles.* In other words, the lower the molar mass of a substance, the more particles it will produce. According to Table 1, sodium chloride has a molar mass of 58.4 g/mol, potassium hydroxide has a molar mass of 56.11 g/mol, and magnesium sulfate has a molar mass of 120.38 g/mol. Since potassium hydroxide has the lowest molar mass, it should produce the *most* particles. With this information alone, you can eliminate (B), (C), and (D). Only (A) remains and puts the substances in the correct relation to one another.

4. **F** The passage states, *the mixture was heated and temperature readings acquired every 30 sec until the solution reached a full boil and the solid had completely dissolved.* Since the mixture is only heated, it can be inferred that its temperature increases only. There's no indication that the substance is ever cooled, so (F) is the only answer supported by information from the passage.

5. **D** Student 3 offers the following hypothesis: *The solution containing the salt with the more negative $\Delta H°_{diss}$ value will release more heat and thus result in a greater boiling point.* According to Table 1, magnesium sulfate has the most negative $\Delta H°_{diss}$ value at –91.0 kJ/mol. Therefore, according to Student 3, this substance should have the greatest boiling point of the substances listed.

6. **H** Compare the new values given in the question to those for calcium chloride given in Table 1. Cesium hydroxide produces 2 ions, while calcium chloride produces 3. Student 1 writes, *The solution containing Salt B had a higher boiling point because Salt B produces more ions in solution than Salt A.* According to this hypothesis, calcium chloride produces more ions, so it should have a higher boiling point. The findings therefore support the hypothesis of Student 1, eliminating (G) and (J). Cesium hydroxide has a molar mass 149.91 g/mol, while calcium chloride has a molar mass of 111.0 g/mol. Student 2 writes, *The solution containing Salt B had a higher boiling point because it had a lower* molar mass *(the mass of 6.02×10^{23} particles).* According to this hypothesis, calcium chloride has a lower molar mass, so it should have a higher boiling point. The findings therefore support the hypothesis of Student 2, eliminating (F). There's no need to test the findings against Student 3's hypothesis: The only option left is (H).

7. **C** According to Student 2, the salt with the lower molar mass will result in more particles and a greater solution boiling point than a salt with a greater molar mass. Student 2 is not concerned with "enthalpy change," so you can eliminate (B) and (D) immediately. According to Table 1, sodium chloride has a molar mass of 58.4 g/mol, and ammonium nitrate has a molar mass of 80.1 g/mol. Therefore, because sodium chloride has a smaller molar mass, it should have a greater boiling point, as suggested in (C).

Chapter 12
Science Practice Test

SCIENCE TEST

35 Minutes—40 Questions

Directions: There are seven passages in this test. Each passage is followed by several questions. After reading a passage, choose the best answer to each question and fill in the corresponding oval on your answer document. You may refer to the passages as often as necessary.

You are NOT permitted to use a calculator on this test.

Passage I

Moth body coloration (see Figure 1) is a *hereditary* trait that can be passed from organisms to their offspring.

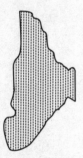 

white body coloration   black body coloration

Figure 1

Scientists studied the body coloration of 2 subspecies of moths, *Biston betularia f. typica* and *Biston betularia f. carbonaria*. Both species live in City X. Only *B. betularia f. typica* lives in City Y, while only *B. betularia f. carbonaria* lives in City Z. Both subspecies live on trees found in temperate climates, such as birch. Moths with light body coloration are camouflaged from predators while living on light-colored trees but are not hidden in heavily polluted areas where the tree bark is darkened. Moths with dark body coloration are camouflaged from predators on trees that are darkened by pollution but not on light-colored trees.

Study 1

Scientists captured 100 *B. betularia f. typica* and 100 *B. betularia f. carbonaria* in City X. They labeled each one, recorded its color, and released it. Then they calculated the percent of birds having each of the body color intensities on a scale of 1 to 10, with 1 being completely black and 10 being completely white. The researchers followed the same methods with 100 *B. betularia f. typica* moths from City Y and 100 *B. betularia f. carbonaria* moths from City Z. The results of this study are shown in Figure 2.

Study 2

After the end of Study 1, the scientists returned to City Y over the course of 10 years, from 1983 to 1992. During each visit, they captured at least 50 *B. betularia f. typica* moths and measured their body color intensities. They then calculated the average *B. betularia f. typica* body color intensity from the 1–10 scale for each of the 10 years. The scientists noted that during the 10-year period, 2 years were particularly wet, while 3 years were especially dry (see Figure 3). During wet years, pollutants tend to be washed from the surfaces of tree bark. During dry years, pollutants are more likely to concentrate on tree bark, and the tree bark itself tends to become thicker.

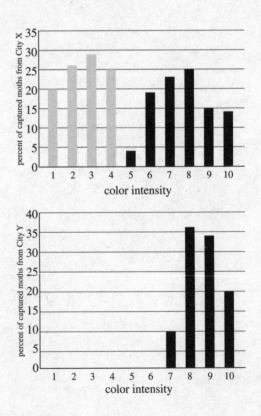

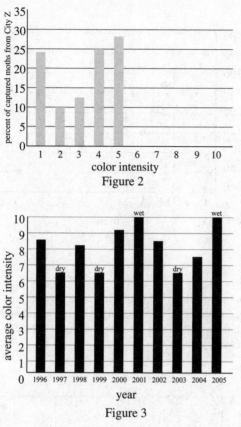

color intensity
Figure 2

average color intensity

year
Figure 3

4. The scientists most likely labeled the moths in Study 1 to:

F. determine how body coloration was affected by pollution in City X.

G. determine the average wingspan of each population of moths.

H. make sure that the body coloration of each moth was measured only once.

J. make sure that the body coloration of each moth was measured multiple times.

5. Based on the results from Study 2, would a moth with a body color intensity measuring 6.5 or a moth with a body color intensity measuring 9.5 have had a greater chance of surviving in 2005 ?

A. A moth with a body color intensity of 6.5, because pollutants concentrate more on tree bark during dry years.

B. A moth with a body color intensity of 6.5, because pollutants are removed from tree bark during dry years.

C. A moth with a body color intensity of 9.5, because pollutants concentrate more on tree bark during dry years.

D. A moth with a body color intensity of 9.5, because pollutants are removed from tree bark during dry years.

1. Based on the results from Study 1, the largest percentage of moths in City Y and City Z had a color intensity of:

	City Y	City Z
A.	8	1
B.	8	5
C.	9	4
D.	9	5

2. During which of the following years was birch bark most likely to be thickest in City Y ?

F. 2000

G. 2001

H. 2002

J. 2003

3. How was Study 1 different from Study 2 ?

A. *B. betularia f. carbonaria* moths were captured in Study 1 but not in Study 2.

B. *B. betularia f. typica* moths were captured in Study 1 but not in Study 2.

C. The moth body coloration was measured in Study 1 but not in Study 2.

D. The moth body coloration was measured in Study 2 but not in Study 1.

6. A scientist hypothesized that there would be a greater range in body coloration in the *B. betularia f. typica* moths when they are forced to coexist with another subspecies of moths. Do the results from Study 1 support this hypothesis?

F. Yes; the range of body coloration for *B. betularia f. typica* moths was greater in City X than in City Y.

G. Yes; the range of body coloration for *B. betularia f. typica* moths was greater in City Y than in City X.

H. No; the range of body coloration for *B. betularia f. typica* moths was greater in City X than in City Y.

J. No; the range of body coloration for *B. betularia f. typica* moths was greater in City Y than in City X.

Passage II

Ions in seawater, such as Cl^-, SO_4^{2-}, Na^+, and Mg^{2+}, are carried down to the ocean floor through a process known as *marine deposition*. SO_4^{2-} and Mg^{2+} primarily come from the erosion of rocks, while Cl^- and Na^+ come from both mineral erosion and underwater volcanoes and hydrothermal vents.

Study 1

A fluid motion sensor was placed on a section of the seabed in the Atlantic Ocean, and data were collected over 12 months. At 6:00 a.m. every morning, the movement of water past the sensor was recorded, and a small amount of water was sequestered. Figure 1 shows the movement of water in millions of cubic meters (m^3) per second.

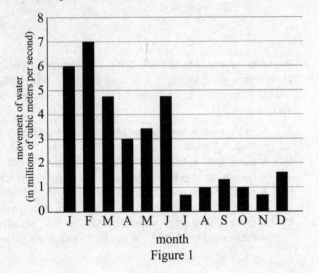

month
Figure 1

At the end of each month, the sequestered water was extracted by a science research crew, and a portion was analyzed for the concentrations of Cl^- and SO_4^{2-} ions. Using these data, the marine deposition was measured in kilograms (kg) per cubic meter (m^3) for each substance in each month (see Figure 2).

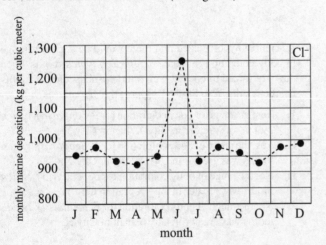

month

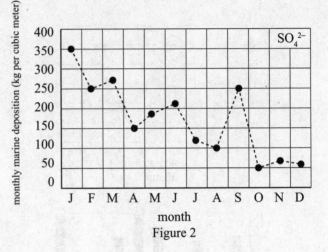

month
Figure 2

Study 2

Another portion of the monthly water sample was analyzed for concentrations of Na^+ and Mg^{2+} ions. The monthly marine deposition was calculated for each substance in equivalents (Eq) per m^3 (see Figure 3).

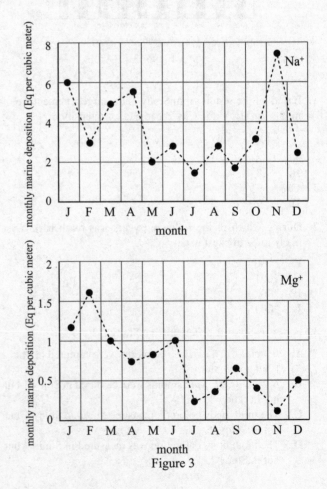

month
Figure 3

Study 3

The annual marine deposition of Cl^- and SO_4^{2-} ions over the 12-month period was calculated in kg/m³ at the test site, and also at two sites in the Arctic Ocean, located 2,000 and 4,000 miles north, respectively (see Figure 4).

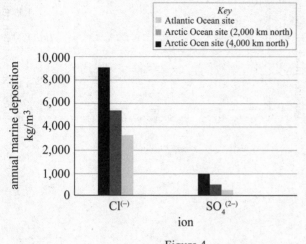

ion

Figure 4

9. A student states, "The marine deposition of Na^+ is highest in the winter and lowest in the summer, since the winter features greater activity of volcanoes and hydrothermal vents." Is this statement supported by the results of Study 2 ?

   A. No, because marine deposition of Na^+ was, on average, greater between November and January than it was between June and August.

   B. No, because marine deposition of Na^+ was, on average, less between November and January than it was between June and August.

   C. Yes, because marine deposition of Na^+ was, on average, greater between November and January than it was between June and August.

   D. Yes, because marine deposition of Na^+ was, on average, less between November and January than it was between June and August.

10. Suppose that the fluid motion sensor was placed in an underwater cave in the Atlantic Ocean where there is no net movement of water during one month of the 12-month study. The information provided indicates that during that month, there would have been:

   F. no marine deposition of any of the 4 substances.

   G. no marine deposition of Cl^- and SO_4^{2-}, but a high level of marine deposition of $Na+$ and Mg^{2+}.

   H. high marine deposition of Cl^- and SO_4^{2-}, but no marine deposition of $Na+$ and Mg^{2+}.

   J. high marine deposition of all 4 substances.

7. According to Figure 1, during the year over which data were collected, the movement of water was greatest in February and least in November. According to Figures 2 and 3, the marine deposition of which ion was also greatest in February and least in November?

   A. Cl^-
   B. Mg^{2+}
   C. Na^+
   D. SO_4^{2-}

11. According to Study 3, as the distance from the fluid motion sensor in the Atlantic Ocean decreased, the annual marine deposition:

   A. decreased for both Cl^- and SO_4^{2-}.
   B. decreased for Cl^- but increased for SO_4^{2-}.
   C. increased for Cl^- but decreased for SO_4^{2-}.
   D. increased for both Cl^- and SO_4^{2-}.

8. Based on the results from Study 1, the mean monthly marine deposition for Cl^- over the year of the study was:

   F. less than 900 kg/m³.
   G. between 900 kg/m³ and 1,000 kg/m³.
   H. between 1,000 kg/m³ and 1,200 kg/m³.
   J. over 1,200 kg/m³.

12. Which of the following variables remained constant in Study 2 ?

   F. Marine deposition of SO_4^{2-}
   G. Marine deposition of Mg^{2+}
   H. Movement of water during the month
   J. Location of the study

Passage III

Leaf area index is a unitless measure of the percent of a rainforest floor that is covered by the leaves of tall trees. Leaf area index may increase because of an increase in *precipitation* (measured as millimeters of rainfall per km^2 per year). Table 1 shows how the leaf area index formed by the *canopy layer* (30 to 45 m above the rainforest floor) varies with precipitation in a 1000 km^2 section of the Amazon Rainforest. Figures 1–3 show the relative precipitation, RP (the percent below the rainfall measured on January 1, 1985), and the monthly average leaf area index of the *emergent layer* (45 to 55 m above the rainforest floor), *canopy layer*, and *understory layer* (0 to 30 m above the rainforest floor), respectively, from January 1990 to January 2005.

Table 1

Precipitation (mm/km^2/yr)	Leaf area index
1.80	5.2
1.85	5.4
1.90	5.6
1.95	5.8
2.00	6.0

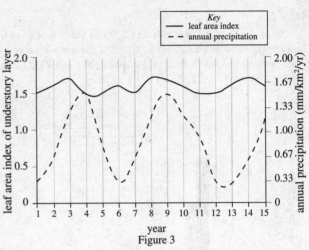

Figure 3

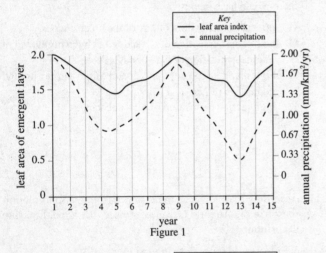

year
Figure 1

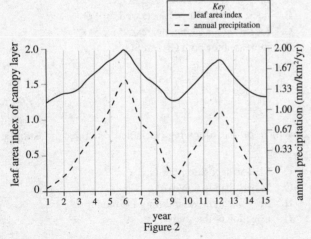

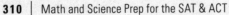

year
Figure 2

13. The leaf area index of the canopy layer covering the section of the rainforest in January of the 14th year studied was closest to which of the following?

A. 1.0
B. 1.3
C. 1.7
D. 2.0

14. Based on Table 1, a precipitation of 1.70 mm/km^2/yr would correspond to a leaf area index that is closest to which of the following?

F. 4.8
G. 5.5
H. 6.0
J. 6.5

15. A botanist states, "The leaf area index of the understory layer is more directly correlated with annual precipitation than is the leaf area index of the canopy layer." Is this statement consistent with Figures 2 and 3 ?

A. No, because the plot for the leaf area index of the canopy layer more closely resembles the plot for the annual precipitation.

B. No, because the plot for the leaf area index of the understory layer more closely resembles the plot for the annual precipitation.

C. Yes, because the plot for the leaf area index of the canopy layer more closely resembles the plot for the annual precipitation.

D. Yes, because the plot for the leaf area index of the understory layer more closely resembles the plot for the annual precipitation.

16. Which of the following figures best represents the leaf area index measured in the 7th year of the study?

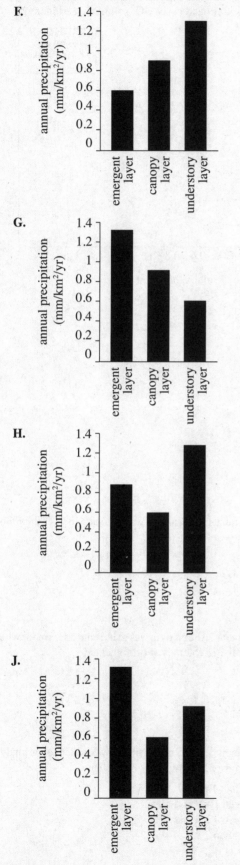

17. The emergent layer is primarily composed of small leaves that cover a wide area, while the understory layer is primarily composed of broad leaves that cover a small area. This difference is most likely because the average precipitation at heights of:

A. 0 to 30 m above the rainforest floor is above 2.00 mm/km²/yr, whereas the average precipitation at heights of 30–45 m above the rainforest floor is below 0.33 mm/km²/yr.

B. 0 to 30 m above the rainforest floor is above 2.00 mm/km²/yr, whereas the average precipitation at heights of 45–55 m above the rainforest floor is below 0.33 mm/km²/yr.

C. 0 to 30 m above the rainforest floor is below 0.33 mm/km²/yr, whereas the average precipitation at heights of 30–45 m above the rainforest floor is above 2.00 mm/km²/yr.

D. 0 to 30 m above the rainforest floor is below 2.00 mm/km²/yr, whereas the average precipitation at heights of 45–55 m above the rainforest floor is above 1.33 mm/km²/yr.

Passage IV

Oxidation-reduction titration is a method in which precise volumes of a *titrant* (an oxidizing or reducing agent) are added dropwise to a known volume of an *analyte* (a reducing or oxidizing agent, respectively). This process can be monitored by adding a *redox indicator* (a substance that changes color over a certain range of electrode potentials) to the analyte or by measuring the sample's *voltage* using a potentiometer. Voltage (measured in kilovolts, kV) is a measure of the force of an electrical current that could be transmitted by the solution.

Two titration experiments were performed at 298 K using a 0.10 M iodine (I_2) solution and either a 0.0010 M sulfur dioxide (SO_2) solution or a 0.0010 M sodium thiosulfate solution (where M is the number of moles of oxidizing or reducing agent per liter of solution). All solutions were aqueous. A redox indicator solution of *starch* was also used. Starch and I_2 form a complex with a deep blue color, but when I_2 is reduced to 2 iodide (I^-) ions, the complex dissipates and the solution becomes colorless.

Experiment 1

A drop of starch solution was added to an Erlenmeyer flask containing 100.0 mL of the SO_2 solution. A potentiometer, which acts as a control input for electronic circuits, was placed in the solution. The I_2 solution was incrementally added to the SO_2 solution. After each addition, the SO_2 solution was stirred and the solution's color and voltage were recorded (see Figure 1).

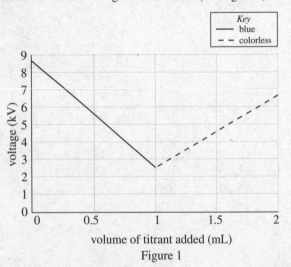

Figure 1

Experiment 2

Experiment 1 was repeated, except that the sodium thiosulfate solution was used instead of the SO_2 solution (see Figure 2).

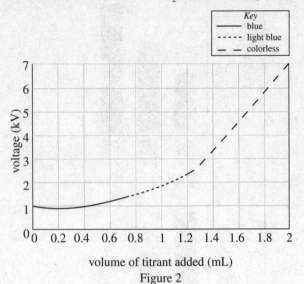

volume of titrant added (mL)

Figure 2

18. In Experiment 1, the analyte was blue at which of the following volumes of titrant added?

   F. 0.7 mL
   G. 1.1 mL
   H. 1.5 mL
   J. 1.9 mL

19. In Experiment 2, the analyte was in its reduced form for which of the following volumes of titrant added?

   A. 0.3 mL
   B. 0.6 mL
   C. 0.9 mL
   D. 1.2 mL

20. In Experiment 1, if 2.5 mL of titrant was added to the analyte, the voltage would most likely have been:

   F. less than 1 kV.
   G. between 1 kV and 4 kV.
   H. between 4 kV and 7 kV.
   J. more than 7 kV.

21. In Experiment 2, which solution was the analyte and which solution was the titrant?

titrant	sample solution
A. Sodium thiosulfate	I
B. SO_2	I_2
C. I_2	Sodium thiosulfate
D. I_2	SO_2

22. In Experiments 1 and 2, the potentiometer that was placed in the analyte most likely did which of the following?

F. Detected the concentration of starch in the solution

G. Conducted an electric current initiated by ions in the solution

H. Heated the solution to its boiling point

J. Cooled to solution to its freezing point

23. A chemist states that in Experiment 2, the analyte was fully reduced with 0.2 mL of titrant added, but not with 1.8 mL of titrant added. Do the results of Experiment 2 support this claim?

A. Yes; at a value of 0.2 mL of titrant added, the analyte was blue, while at a value of 1.8 mL of titrant added, the analyte was colorless.

B. Yes; at a value of 0.2 mL of titrant added, the analyte was colorless, while at a value of 1.8 mL of titrant added, the analyte was blue.

C. No; at a value of 0.2 mL of titrant added, the analyte was blue, while at a value of 1.8 mL of titrant added, the analyte was colorless.

D. No; at a value of 0.2 mL of titrant added, the analyte was colorless, while at a value of 1.8 mL of titrant added, the analyte was blue.

Passage V

An astrophysics class is given the following facts about the burning out of stars.

1. The burning out of a star can be divided into 3 stages: *helium fusion*, *planetary nebula formation*, and *white dwarf development*.

2. Mid-sized stars fuse hydrogen nuclei (composed of protons) into helium nuclei at their centers, in a process known as helium fusion. These include yellow dwarves, like our Sun, and the slightly smaller orange dwarves. Helium fusion releases a significant amount of kinetic energy.

3. As kinetic energy continues to be released, a planetary nebula may form, in which colorful, ionized gas spreads out from the star's center.

4. The remaining material at the center of the planetary nebula condenses into a white dwarf, which is relatively cool and small in size.

5. Red dwarves are smaller stars that can also carry out helium fusion. These stars can develop into white dwarves sooner than yellow and orange dwarves, and they do not form planetary nebulas.

Two students discuss the eventual fate of three stars in the Alpha Centauri system. Alpha Centauri A, a 1.10-solar-mass yellow dwarf star, where one *solar mass* unit is equivalent to the mass of the Sun; Alpha Centauri B, a 0.91-solar-mass orange dwarf star; and Alpha Centauri C, a 0.12-solar-mass red dwarf star. Alpha Centauri A and B comprise a binary star system that revolves around a common center of mass, while Alpha Centauri C revolves around a nearby center of mass.

Student 1

The 3 stars of the Alpha Centauri system all formed at the same time from the same collection of matter. Alpha Centauri C was initially the most massive of the three stars, and Alpha Centauri A and Alpha Centauri B had the same size. The large Alpha Centauri C had more helium fusion than the other two stars, so it quickly became the smallest of the stars. More of its matter flowed to Alpha Centauri A than to Alpha Centauri B, making Alpha Centauri A slightly larger than Alpha Centauri B.

Student 2

Alpha Centauri A and Alpha Centauri B formed at a different time than Alpha Centauri C. Alpha Centauri A and Alpha Centauri B formed at the same time from a common collection of matter, and Alpha Centauri A was initially more massive than Alpha Centauri B. Alpha Centauri C formed later from a different, smaller collection of matter and never became bigger than a red dwarf. At some point, the small Alpha Centauri C was attracted to the other two stars, resulting in a triple star system.

24. Based on Student 2's discussion, Alpha Centauri C is part of the Alpha Centauri system because of which of the following forces exerted on Alpha Centauri C by the original binary star system?

F. Electromagnetism
G. Gravitation
H. Strong nuclear interaction
J. Weak nuclear interaction

25. Based on Student 1's discussion and Fact 2, while matter flowed between Alpha Centauri C and Alpha Centauri A, Alpha Centauri C released most of its energy by fusing:

A. helium nuclei into hydrogen nuclei at its core.
B. hydrogen nuclei into helium nuclei at its core.
C. helium nuclei into hydrogen nuclei at its periphery.
D. hydrogen nuclei into helium nuclei at its periphery.

26. Suppose that stars that form from the same collection of matter have similar chemical composition, but stars that form from different collections of matter have different chemical compositions. Student 2 would most likely agree with which of the following statements comparing chemical compositions of the stars in the current Alpha Centauri system at the time that they were formed?

F. Alpha Centauri A and Alpha Centauri B had the most similar compositions.
G. Alpha Centauri A and Alpha Centauri C had the most similar compositions.
H. Alpha Centauri B and Alpha Centauri C had the most similar compositions.
J. Alpha Centauri A, Alpha Centauri B, and Alpha Centauri C all had the same compositions.

27. If the mass of the Sun is 2.0×10^{30} g, what is the mass of Alpha Centauri A ?

A. 1.8×10^{30} g
B. 2.0×10^{30} g
C. 2.2×10^{30} g
D. 2.4×10^{32} g

28. Which of the following statements best explains why the process described in Fact 2 requires a high initial temperature and pressure?

F. All electrons are negatively charged, and like charges attract each other.
G. All electrons are negatively charged, and like charges repel each other.
H. All protons are positively charged, and like charges attract each other.
J. All protons are positively charged, and like charges repel each other.

29. Based on Fact 5 and Student 1's discussion, which of the 3 stars in the Alpha Centauri system, if any, is most likely to develop into a white dwarf?

   A. Alpha Centauri A
   B. Alpha Centauri B
   C. Alpha Centauri C
   D. The three stars will likely develop into white dwarves at the same time.

30. Based on Fact 5, would Student 2 agree that by the time Alpha Centauri B develops into a white dwarf, it will have spent as much time as a mid-sized star as Alpha Centauri A ?

   F. Yes, because according to Student 2, Alpha Centauri A has always been less massive than Alpha Centauri B.
   G. Yes, because according to Student 2, Alpha Centauri A has always been more massive than Alpha Centauri B.
   H. No, because according to Student 2, Alpha Centauri A has always been less massive than Alpha Centauri B.
   J. No, because according to Student 2, Alpha Centauri A has always been more massive than Alpha Centauri B.

Passage VI

Three experiments were conducted using the gases nitrogen (N_2), nitrogen dioxide (NO_2), and xenon (Xe). For each gas:

1. A cap was placed on a 2 L metal chamber, containing sensors to measure temperature and pressure and a vale to allow gas to enter.

2. Air was pumped out of the chamber until the pressure inside was measured to be 0.00 mmHg.

3. The chamber was placed on an analytical balance, which was then reset to 0.00 g.

4. Some of the gas was added to the chamber.

5. When the gas in the vessel reached room temperature (298 K), the mass and pressure inside were recorded.

6. Steps 4 and 5 were repeated for different masses.

The experiments were repeated using a 4 L metal chamber (see Figures 1 and 2).

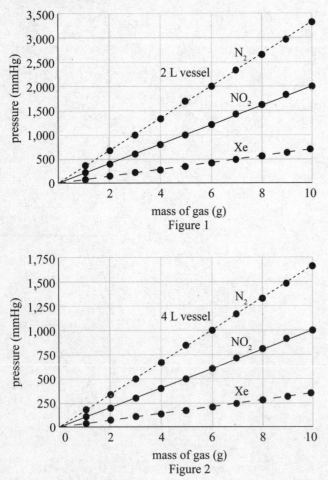

Figure 1

Figure 2

31. Based on Figure 2, if 12 g of Xe had been added to the 4 L vessel, the pressure would have been:

A. less than 300 mmHg.
B. between 300 and 600 mmHg.
C. between 600 mmHg and 900 mmHg.
D. greater than 1,200 mmHg.

32. Suppose the experiments had been repeated, except with a 3 L vessel. Based on Figures 1 and 2, the pressure exerted by 10 g of NO_2 would most likely have been:

F. less than 1,000 mmHg.
G. between 1,000 and 2,000 mmHg.
H. between 2,000 and 2,500 mmHg.
J. greater than 2,500 mmHg.

33. Based on Figures 1 and 2, for a given mass of N_2 at 298 K, how does the pressure exerted by the N_2 in a 4 L vessel compare to the pressure exerted by the N_2 in a 2 L vessel? In the 4 L vessel, the N_2 pressure will be:

A. half as great as in the 2 L vessel.
B. the same as in the 2 L vessel.
C. twice as great as in the 2 L vessel.
D. 4 times as great as in the 2 L vessel.

34. Which of the following best explains why equal masses of N_2 and NO_2 at the same temperature and in vessels of similar sizes had different pressures? The pressure exerted by the N_2 was:

   F. greater, because there were fewer N_2 molecules per gram than there were NO_2 molecules per gram.

   G. greater, because there were more N_2 molecules per gram than there were NO_2 molecules per gram.

   H. less, because there were fewer N_2 molecules per gram than there were NO_2 molecules per gram.

   J. less, because there were more N_2 molecules per gram than there were NO_2 molecules per gram.

35. Suppose the experiment involving N_2 and the 4 L vessel had been repeated, except at a temperature of 287 K. For a given mass of N_2, compared to the pressure measured in the original experiment, the pressure measured at 287 K would have been:

   A. greater, because pressure is directly proportional to temperature.

   B. greater, because pressure is inversely proportional to temperature.

   C. less, because pressure is directly proportional to temperature.

   D. less, because pressure is inversely proportional to temperature.

Passage VII

The *absolute threshold pressure for hearing* is the minimum air pressure at each audio frequency that can produce a sound that is detectable by the human ear. The *pain threshold pressure for hearing* is the maximum air pressure at each frequency that the human ear can withstand without sensing pain.

Figure 1 below displays the absolute and pain threshold pressures for hearing in two media: air and water. The figure also shows P, the percentage increase in compression of the air or water with increasing sound pressure. Audio frequency is given in cycles per second (cyc/sec), and sound pressure level is given in decibels (db).

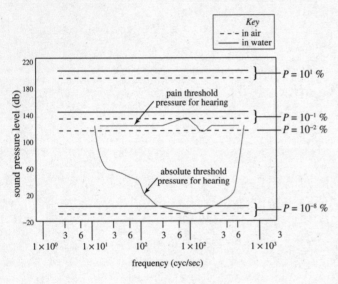

Figure 1

36. According to Figure 1, which of the following is the closest to the highest frequency that can be heard by a human being?

F.   1 cyc/sec
G.   10 cyc/sec
H.   100 cyc/sec
J.   1,000 cyc/sec

37. Based on Figure 1, a sound of a given frequency will have the highest sound level pressure for which of the following sets of conditions?

	Sound in	P
A.	Air	$10^{-8}\%$
B.	Air	$10^{-1}\%$
C.	Water	$10^{-8}\%$
D.	Water	$10^{-1}\%$

38. As humans grow older, there is often a loss in the ability to hear sounds at high frequencies. Which of the following figures best illustrates this?

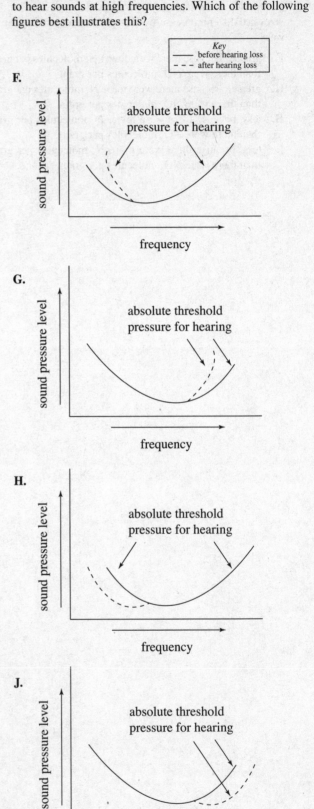

39. A scientist developed a hypothesis that sounds with any sound pressure level would be painful to humans if the frequency were 10^4 cyc/sec. Does the data from Figure 1 support this hypothesis?

    A. No, because humans are unable to hear sounds over 10^4 cyc/sec.

    B. No, because the absolute threshold of pain for hearing is relatively constant with changes in frequency.

    C. Yes, because the absolute threshold of pain for hearing is relatively constant with changes in frequency.

    D. Yes, because as frequency increases above 10^4 cyc/sec, the absolute threshold of pain for hearing also increases.

40. Based on Figure 1, does P depend on the frequency of sound at a given sound pressure level?

    F. No, because as frequency increases, P increases.

    G. No, because as frequency increases, P remains constant.

    H. Yes, because as frequency increases, P increases.

    J. Yes, because as frequency increases, P remains constant.

Chapter 13
Science Practice
Test: Answers and
Explanations

SCIENCE PRACTICE TEST ANSWER KEY

1. B
2. J
3. A
4. H
5. C
6. F
7. B
8. G
9. C
10. F
11. A
12. J
13. B
14. F
15. A
16. G
17. D
18. F
19. D
20. J

21. C
22. G
23. C
24. G
25. B
26. F
27. C
28. J
29. C
30. J
31. B
32. G
33. A
34. G
35. C
36. J
37. D
38. G
39. A
40. G

SCORE YOUR PRACTICE TEST

Step A
Count the number of correct answers: _____. This is your *raw score*.

Step B
Use the score conversion table below to look up your raw score. The number to the left is your *scale score*: _____.

Science Scale Conversion Table

Scale Score	Raw Score	Scale Score	Raw Score	Scale Score	Raw Score
36	40	27	32	18	16–17
35	39	26	30–31	17	15
34	--	25	28–29	16	14
33	38	24	26–27	15	13
32	37	23	25	14	12
31	--	22	23–24	13	11
30	36	21	21–22	12	10
29	35	20	19–20	11	9
28	33–34	19	18	10	7–8

SCIENCE PRACTICE TEST EXPLANATIONS

Passage I

1. **B** This question asks about Study 1, so we'll need to look at Figure 2. The color intensity for the moths in City Y is shown on the right side of the second graph in black, and the highest percentage of these moths had a color intensity of 8. Eliminate (C) and (D). The color intensity for the moths in City X is shown on the left side of the third graph in gray, and the highest percentage of these moths had a color intensity of 5. Eliminate (A), and the only remaining answer is (B).

2. **J** The blurb in Study 2 contains the following information: *During dry years, pollutants are more likely to concentrate on tree bark, and the tree bark itself tends to become thicker.* Therefore, bark is thickest during dry years, and of the years listed on Figure 3, only 2003 is listed as a "dry" year, so (J) is the best answer from the given choices.

3. **A** Study 1 contains the following information: *Scientists captured 100 B. betularia f. typica and 100 B. betularia f. carbonaria in City X.* Study 2 contains the following information: *During each visit* [from 1983 to 1992], *they captured at least 50 B. betularia f. typica moths and measured their body color intensities.* Therefore, it can be assumed that they *did not* catch *B. bethularia f. carbonaria* in Study 2, making (A) the best answer. For color intensity, note the axes of each of the graphs. Color intensity is a variable plotted along the *x*-axis in Figure 2 and along the *y*-axis in Figure 3, meaning that it was measured in both studies.

4. **H** Choices (H) and (J) are direct opposites, which means that one of them is likely to be true. You'll need to use a bit of science common sense here to choose between these two. In Study 1, the scientists are trying to count the number of moths in these various cities; therefore, in order to make this count accurate, they will need to make sure that each moth is only counted once, as in (H). Choice (F) is incorrect because *pollution* is measured in Study 2, and (G) is incorrect because *wingspan* is not measured in either study.

5. **C** Figure 3 shows that 2005 was a wet year, and the average color intensity was 10. First, it is clear that moths with higher color intensities are more likely to survive in the wet years than the dry years, so the moth with a color intensity of 9.5 is more likely to survive than the moth with a color intensity of 6.5. Eliminate (A) and (B). Then, notice that Study 2 contains the following information: *During wet years, pollutants tend to be washed from the surfaces of tree bark.* This information agrees with (C).

6. **F** This question is difficult to answer yes or "No" immediately, so work with the reasons given in each of the answer choices. In City X, the coloration of *B. betularia f. typica* ranges from 5 to 10. In City Y, the coloration of *B. betularia f. typica* ranges from only 7 to 10. Eliminate (G) and (J). The hypothesis that a greater range in body coloration is produced by a diversity in the subspecies is therefore

supported by this information because City X contains two subspecies and City Y contains only one. This question is tricky: You don't need to use the *y*-axis at all because nothing in the question asks about the percent of captured moths. The only variable at play is body coloration.

Passage II

7. **B**   According to Figure 3, the marine deposition of Mg^{2+} is highest in February and lowest in November, making (B) the correct answer. The marine deposition of Cl^- is highest in June and lowest in October, eliminating (A). The marine deposition of Na^+ is highest in November and lowest in July, eliminating (C). The marine deposition of SO_4^{2-} is highest in January and lowest in October, eliminating (D).

8. **G**   Look carefully at Figure 2. The marine deposition of Cl^- is around 950 kg/m³ except in June, at which point it is much higher. Because it has only this single outlier, we can reasonably expect that the *mean*, or *average*, monthly deposition will be closer to 950, as (G) suggests.

9. **C**   This question is difficult to answer Yes or No immediately, so work with the reasons given in each of the answer choices. Use Figure 3 to check these reasons. According to Figure 3, the monthly deposition of Na^+ is highest in the winter months and lowest in the summer months. We can therefore eliminate (B) and (D), which give information that contradicts Figure 3. This information then *supports* the statement in the problem that the *marine deposition of Na⁺ is highest in the winter and lowest in the summer*, thus making (C) the correct answer.

10. **F**   The introduction to the passage gives the following information: *Ions in seawater, such as Cl^-, SO_4^{2-}, Na^+, and Mg_2^+, are carried down to the ocean floor through a process known as* marine deposition. Therefore, in order for there to be *marine deposition*, ions must be *carried down* somewhere. If the water does not move during an entire month, then the ions will not move and no marine deposition will occur during this month.

11. **A**   Make sure you pay careful attention to the key in Figure 4. According to Figure 4, the annual marine depositions of both ions were highest in the Arctic Ocean, the site farthest from the Atlantic Ocean. The annual marine depositions of both ions decrease as the sensor gets closer to the Atlantic Ocean site.

12. **J**   According to Figure 3, the marine deposition of SO_4^{2-} was not studied, eliminating (F). The marine deposition of Mg^{2+} changed during the study, eliminate (G). According to Figure 1, the movement of water during the month changed every month during the twelve-month period, eliminating (H). Only the location of the study, the Atlantic Ocean, was held constant, making (J) the correct answer. The location of the study was not changed until Study 3.

Passage III

13. **B**   We're dealing with Figure 2, which shows the data for the canopy layer. The question asks about the leaf area index, so we need the solid line and the *y*-axis shown on the left side of the figure. Once all those elements are in place, you find that the leaf area index in Year 14 was closest to 1.3. Make sure you are dealing with the correct figure and the correct axes given on that figure.

14. **F**   Table 1 shows a direct relationship: As precipitation goes up, leaf-area index goes up. Therefore, we can expect the leaf-area index at 1.70 mm/km²/yr of precipitation to be below the leaf-area index at 1.80 mm/km²/yr. The leaf-area index at 1.80 mm/km²/yr is 5.2, and the only answer choice that gives a value in between is (F).

15. **A**   This problem asks about the *canopy* layer and the *understory* layer, so we will need to use Figures 2 and 3. Take a look at these two graphs: The two curves in the *canopy*-layer graph seem to go up and down at roughly the same rate, whereas the two curves in the *understory*-layer graph don't seem to have a consistent relationship. Because the *canopy*-layer graph shows a more consistent relationship, we can eliminate (B) and (D). A more consistent *canopy*-layer graph also *disagrees* with the botanist's statement from the problem, eliminating (C). Only (A) contains the correct answer to the question and the correct reason for that answer.

16. **G**   Use Figures 1, 2, and 3 to determine each of the annual precipitation values in Year 7. This is the dotted curve, and the values are on the *y*-axis on the right side of each figure. For the *emergent* layer shown in Figure 1, the annual precipitation was roughly 1.33. For the *canopy* layer shown in Figure 2, the annual precipitation was roughly 1.0. For the *understory* layer shown in Figure 3, the annual precipitation was roughly 0.67. You don't need to worry about exact figures: *emergent* should be the largest and *understory* should be the smallest. Only (G) works.

17. **D**   Use POE. All the answers use values of meters above the rainforest, but meters is not a variable on any figure. A quick scan of the introduction for those values identifies "0–30" as the understory layer, "30–45" as the canopy layer, and "45–55" as the emergent layer. Eliminate (A) and (C) since each addresses the canopy layer and the question is about the other two. Choice (B) is disproven by Figure 3, and (D) is proven by Figures 1 and 3.

Passage IV

18. **F**   Use Figure 1. The key in the corner of the graph says that the anything graphed with a solid line is *blue,* and anything graphed with a dotted line is *colorless.* The curve shown in this graph changes from solid to dotted at 1 mL of titrant added, meaning that all the solution at all values less than 1 mL will be blue, and the solution at all values greater than 1 mL will be colorless. The only one of the answer choices that gives a value less than 1 mL is (F).

19. **D** The blurb contains the following sentence: Starch and I_2 form a complex with a deep blue color, but when I_2 is reduced to 2 iodide (I^-) ions, the complex dissipates and the solution becomes colorless. In other words, when the solution is reduced, it becomes colorless. According to Figure 2, the solution is colorless (and therefore reduced) above 1 mL of titrant added. Only (D) gives a value greater than 1 mL.

20. **J** Figure 2 does not show the voltage at 2.5 mL of titrant added, but the curve follows a clear trend. As the volume of titrant added increases, the voltage increases as well. At 2 mL of titrant added, the voltage is equivalent to 7 kV. Therefore, at 2.5 mL of titrant added, the voltage will most likely be greater than 7 kV, as in (J).

21. **C** The experiment detailed in this passage is described in the first line as follows: *Oxidation-reduction titration is a method in which precise volumes of a titrant (an oxidizing or reducing agent) are added dropwise to a known volume of an analyte (a reducing or oxidizing agent, respectively).* In other words, one substance (the titrant) is added gradually to a certain amount of another substance (the analyte). Therefore, when Experiment 1 says that the I_2 solution was incrementally added to the SO_2 solution, it can be inferred that the I_2 is the titrant, and the SO_2 is the analyte. In Experiment 2, the sodium thiosulfate solution was used instead of the SO_2 solution; therefore, in Experiment 2, the I_2 is still the titrant, and the sodium thiosulfate solution is the analyte, as in (C). If you picked (D), be careful—you may not have noticed the change from Experiment 1 to Experiment 2.

22. **G** Use POE. Experiment 1 contains the following information: *A potentiometer, which acts as a control input for electronic circuits, was placed in the solution.* The key word here is *electric currents*. There's nothing to suggest that the potentiometer has anything to do with *concentration*, eliminating (F), or *freezing* or *boiling point*, eliminating (H) and (J). Only (G) contains any reference to *electric currents* and is therefore the best answer.

23. **C** Use POE. If you're not sure how to answer "Yes" or "No," have a look at the reasons. According to the blurb, starch and I_2 form a complex with a deep blue color, but when I_2 is reduced to 2 iodide (I^-) ions, the complex dissipates and the solution becomes colorless. In other words, when the solution is reduced, it becomes colorless. At 0.2 mL of titrant added, the solution is blue, and at 1.8 mL of titrant added, the solution is colorless. Eliminate (B) and (D), whose reasons contradict this information. Then answer the question: Do these findings agree with the scientist's hypothesis? They don't because the titrant is not reduced at values below 1 mL, so the answer must be no, eliminating (A). Only (C) remains.

Passage V

24. **G** This question requires a bit of outside knowledge. Student 2 concludes with the following sentence: *At some point, the small Alpha Centauri C was attracted to the other two stars, resulting in a triple star system.* Gravity is the attraction between two objects with mass, so attracted matches up most closely with (G), *gravitation*.

25. **B** Student 1's hypothesis contains the following sentence: *The large Alpha Centauri C had more helium fusion than the other two stars, so it quickly became the smallest of the stars. More of its matter flowed to Alpha Centauri A than to Alpha Centauri B.* In other words, Alpha Centauri C released most of its matter by helium fusion. According to Fact 2, mid-sized stars fuse hydrogen nuclei (composed of protons) into helium nuclei at their centers, in a process known as helium fusion. It can therefore be inferred that Alpha Centauri C, in undergoing this process of helium fusion, was fusing hydrogen nuclei into helium nuclei at its center. Only (B) contains information consistent with Student 1 and Fact 2.

26. **F** Student 2's hypothesis contains the following sentence: *Alpha Centauri A and Alpha Centauri B formed at the same time from a common collection of matter.* As the question suggests, stars that form from the same collection of matter have similar chemical compositions. Therefore, Student 2 would likely suggest that Alpha Centauri A and Alpha Centauri B have similar chemical compositions because they formed *from a common collection of matter.* Alpha Centauri C formed from a different collection of matter, eliminating (G), (H), and (J). Only (F) remains.

27. **C** The introduction to this passage contains the following information: *Alpha Centauri A, a 1.10-solar-mass yellow dwarf star, where one* solar mass *unit is equivalent to the mass of the Sun.* The question states that the mass of the Sun is 2.0×10^{30} g. Therefore, the mass of Alpha Centauri A must be 1.10 times this value, given the definition of solar mass. Don't worry about calculating the exact value: You know that this value must be slightly greater than the mass of the sun, and only (C) gives a value slightly greater than 2.0×10^{30} g.

28. **J** Use POE. This question requires a bit of outside knowledge, but it can be solved easily with a bit of common sense. First of all, Fact 2 states that the nuclei being fused are *composed of protons.* It is therefore not likely that the answer to this question will have anything to do with *electrons,* eliminating (F) and (G). *Helium fusion* describes the process by which these protons are *fused,* or put together. Think about it this way: If these protons are attracted to each other to begin with, do you think it would take a bunch of extra energy to put them together? Not likely! Eliminate (H), and only (J) remains.

29. **C** Fact 5 contains the following information: Red dwarves are smaller stars that can also carry out helium fusion. These stars can develop into white dwarves sooner than yellow and orange dwarves. Student 1 states, *The large Alpha Centauri C had more helium fusion than the other two stars, so it quickly became the smallest of the stars.* Therefore, according to this information, Alpha Centauri C is one of those smaller stars that can develop into white dwarves sooner. Choice (C) is our best answer. Also, Scientist 1 doesn't ever really talk about any differences between Alpha Centauri A and Alpha Centauri B, so it's unlikely that one would be correct and the other incorrect.

30. **J** Use POE. If you're not sure how to answer "Yes" or "No," look at the reasons. Student 2's hypothesis contains the following information: *Alpha Centauri A was initially more massive than Alpha Centauri B.* This eliminates (F) and (H) immediately. Fact 5 contains the following information: *Red dwarves*

are smaller stars that can also carry out helium fusion. These stars can develop into white dwarves sooner than yellow and orange dwarves. Therefore, since Alpha Centauri B is smaller, it is one of the smaller stars that can develop into white dwarves sooner. Therefore, it is not likely that it will spend the same amount of time as a white dwarf. Think about it this way: Fact 5 suggests that the main qualification for a white dwarf is its size. If Student 2 is correct about Alpha Centauri A and Alpha Centauri B having different sizes, their white dwarf qualifications can't be the same, so eliminate (G).

Passage VI

31. **B** Figure 2 only gives the information up to 10 g of gas added, but fortunately, all these curves have a very consistent relationship: As mass of gas goes up, the pressure goes up. In the 4 L vessel, when 10 g of Xe is added, the pressure is approximately 300 mmHg. At 12 g of Xe, the pressure should be slightly higher, somewhere around 450 mmHg. Only (B) gives a range that contains this value.

32. **G** As you compare Figures 1 and 2, notice how much higher the pressure values are in Figure 1. It can therefore be assumed that the 2 L vessel has higher pressure values than the 4 L vessel, shown in Figure 2. The pressure values in a 3 L vessel should therefore be greater than those of the 4 L vessel but less than those of the 2 L vessel. In the 2 L vessel, 10 g of NO_2 gives a pressure of approximately 2,000 mmHg. In the 4 L vessel, 10 g of NO_2 gives a pressure of approximately 1,000 mmHg. Therefore, in a 3 L vessel, 10 g of NO_2 should give a pressure between 1,000 and 2,000 mmHg, as in (G).

33. **A** Temperature is not mentioned in either figure, but the passage indicates that the experiments were conducted at 298 K, so we can use Figures 1 and 2. Since we need to compare the N_2 values from Figures 1 and 2, it's best to find values as exact as possible. Notice that at mass 6 g, the 2 L vessel has a pressure of 2,000 mmHg, and the 4 L vessel has a pressure of 1,000 mmHg. Therefore, the pressure in the 4 L vessel is *half as great as* the pressure in the 2 L vessel. Only (A) works.

34. **G** Use POE. In Figures 1 and 2, the pressure when N_2 is used is consistently greater than the pressure when the NO_2 is used. Eliminate (H) and (J). Then you'll need a bit of outside knowledge to complete the question. Simply stated, an N_2 molecule has fewer components than an NO_2 molecule, so it has a smaller mass. Therefore, in order to get the same mass of both molecules, you will need more N_2 molecules per gram, eliminating (F).

35. **C** This question requires a bit of outside knowledge. You need to know the relationship between pressure and temperature: As pressure increases, so does temperature. This is a *direct* relationship, eliminating (B) and (D). Because of this relationship, as the temperature decreases from 298 K to 287 K, the pressure will decrease also, as in (C).

Passage VII

36. **J**   The first line of the passage states the following: *The absolute threshold pressure for hearing is the minimum air pressure at each audio frequency that can produce a sound that is detectable by the human ear.* In other words, the absolute threshold pressure for hearing gives the highest pressure and frequency at which humans can hear. In order to answer this question, we'll need to use Figure 1 and the curve labeled "*Absolute pressure threshold for hearing,*" and we will need to find its maximum frequency, listed on the *x*-axis. According to Figure 1, this curve maxes out right around 1×10^3 cyc/sec, or 1,000 cyc/sec, as in (J). If you selected (H) be careful, this is the point of minimum sound pressure level, not the maximum frequency.

37. **D**   Use POE. Note the key at the bottom of Figure 1. According to this key, *Water* is shown on the graph with a solid line, and *Air* is shown on the graph with a dotted line. The solid line is consistently higher than the dotted, suggesting that *Water* can withstand higher frequencies, eliminating (A) and (B). Then note the *P*-values on the right side of the graph. According to the graph, these *P*-values increase with increasing sound pressure level, so in order to increase the sound pressure level, we will want the highest possible *P*-value, which in the list of remaining answer choices is 10^{-1} %, as in (D).

38. **G**   Use POE. According to this question, some change happens at high frequencies. Accordingly, whichever graph we choose will need to show a change at high frequency, rather than low frequency. Based on this information alone, we can eliminate (F) and (H). The dotted curve ("*after hearing loss*") should indicate some kind of hearing loss at high frequencies, so it should show a curve that does not quite reach the highest frequencies, as only (G) does. If you selected (J), you may have reversed the two curves.

39. **A**   The frequency of 10^4 cyc/sec doesn't appear on the graph, but according to Figure 1, the absolute threshold of hearing is around 10^3 cyc/sec. The pain threshold of hearing is within the absolute threshold, so if 10^4 cyc/sec isn't within the absolute threshold, it won't be within the pain threshold either. Think of it this way: In order for something to hurt when you hear it, you need to be able to hear it first. Therefore, only (A) can work because it is the only answer choice with a reason consistent with the information in Figure 1.

40. **G**   Use POE. If you're unsure whether to answer yes or no, check the reasons. Use Figure 1. Frequency appears on the *x*-axis, and Pressure appears on the *y*-axis. According to the lines showing the pressure in *Air* and in *Water*, the increasing frequency has no effect on the pressure values. Eliminate (F) and (H). Therefore, the pressure does *not* depend on the frequency, making (G) the correct answer.

Part III
Math on the
ACT

ALL ABOUT THE MATH TEST

In some ways, the Math test of the ACT is the content-heaviest of all the tests: In other words, there are many problems on the Math that test concepts similar to those you've learned in your Math classes. In fact, ACT makes a big deal about how "curricular" the exam is, claiming that the Math test is "designed to assess the mathematical skills students have typically acquired in courses taken up to the beginning of grade 12." They even go so far as to offer a list of how the topics will break down in any given administration.

Topic	Number of Questions
Pre-algebra	14
Elementary Algebra	10
Intermediate Algebra	9
Plane Geometry	14
Coordinate Geometry	9
Trigonometry	4

But as with all things ACT, these distinctions may not mean a ton to you, the test taker. Nor should they. At best, this chart should help to drive home one main point:

> The Math test of the ACT is roughly half Algebra and half Geometry.

While there's really no substitute for a solid and complete knowledge of Math fundamentals (and not-so-fundamentals), there are a number of ways you can still get a really great Math score by being a smart test taker. You've already seen in Chapter 2 some of the pacing strategies that can help you maximize your scores.

Test Tip
The ACT Math test is in Order of Difficulty. Keep an eye on the question numbers!

Let's have a look in the next two chapters at some of the specific ways you can improve your scores in Algebra and Geometry. As we move through the next two chapters in this book, keep an eye on the problem number. ACT Math is the one section that is in Order of Difficulty, so the problem numbers offer a nice gauge of how difficult ACT considers certain concepts and types of Word Problems.

Chapter 14
Algebra

So you've got roughly 33 algebra questions to tackle on any given Math test. It's probably a good idea to comb the test looking for those 14 pre-algebra questions first, and then to track down the 10 elementary-algebra questions, and then to go back and look for the intermediate-algebra questions, right? No way! That would be a tremendous waste of time, and even a nearly impossible task—what are the distinctions among these three categories anyway?

For our money, it's best to think of Algebra problems (and really all Math problems) as broken down into two categories: *Plug-and-Chug* and *Word Problems*. Plug and Chug questions are short, testing basic rules, formulas, or terms. Word problems are longer and place the math content in the context of a real-life setting. Many of the Math skills you use in these problems will be the same, but each will require a slightly different approach, for the obvious reason that Word Problems require that you deal with, well, words.

But let's start with a nice, straightforward, "Plug and Chug" problem:

MADSPM
(Multiply/Add, Divide/Subtract, Power/Multiply)

When you *multiply* two like bases, you *add* their exponents.

$$\text{e.g., } x^2 \times x^3 = x^5$$

When you *divide* two like bases, you *subtract* their exponents.

$$\text{e.g., } \frac{x^5}{x^3} = x^2$$

When you raise a base to a *power*, you *multiply* the exponents.

$$\text{e.g., } \left(x^2\right)^3 = x^6$$

25. The expression $-4y^2\left(9y^7 - 3y^5\right)$ is equivalent to:

    A. $-36y^9 + 12y^7$

    B. $-36y^9 - 12y^7$

    C. $-36y^{14} + 12y^{10}$

    D. $-36y^{14} - 12y^{10}$

    E. $-24y^4$

Here's How to Crack It

Sure, there are words in this problem, but all it's really asking you to do is to match up the expression in the question with one of the expressions in the answer choices. Remember to distribute and use MADSPM.

Let's see how this works with the equation given in question 25.

$$-4y^2(9y^7 - 3y^5) = y^2(-36y^7 + 12y^5)$$
$$= -36y^9 + 12y^7$$

This matches up with (A). If you worked through this problem and got one of the other answer choices, think about what you may have done wrong. If you chose (B), you may have forgotten to distribute the negative sign when you multiplied the −4. If you chose (C), you may have multiplied the exponents rather than adding them together. If you chose (D), you may have multiplied the exponents and forgotten to distribute the negative. If you chose (E), you may have forgotten that when you add or subtract like bases, do nothing to the exponents.

Whatever the case may be, don't sell these problems short. Even though they don't take as long, they're worth just as much as the "harder" problems. Recall from the introduction how few questions you really need to pull up your math score. Make sure you work carefully on all your Now and Later questions. There is no partial credit on the ACT, so a careless error leaves you with an answer just as wrong as a random guess.

> Fixing a few careless math errors can improve your ACT Math
> score significantly by ensuring that you get all the points on
> questions you know how to do.

Let's take a look at the next question.

43. $4x^2 + 20x + 24$ is equivalent to:

   A. $(4x + 4)(x + 6)$
   B. $(4x − 4)(x − 6)$
   C. $(4x + 24)(x − 1)$
   D. $2(2x − 4)(x − 3)$
   E. $2(2x + 4)(x + 3)$

This one looks a lot like question 25, but the math is a good deal more difficult. In fact, even if you're pretty good at factoring quadratic equations, you might still find this one to be a bit of an issue. If you can do the factoring quickly and accurately, great, but if not, help is on the way!

PLUGGING IN

When you look at topic breakdown for the ACT, what is it about "Pre-algebra" that sounds so much easier than "Intermediate" or even "Elementary Algebra"? Well, for one thing, with Algebra inevitably come *variables*. You probably remember first hearing about these things in sixth or seventh grade and thinking to yourself how much easier life was when math was just plain numbers.

Here's the good news. Many of the algebra problems on the ACT, even the most complex, can be solved with what we like to call *Plugging In*. What Plugging In enables you to do is to solve difficult variable problems using basic arithmetic.

First, you'll need to identify whether you can Plug In.

Plug It In
A content-based approach to math questions isn't always necessary! Simply "Plug In" to find the correct answer.

Plug In when

- there are variables in the answer choices

- there are variables in the question

- the question is dealing with fractions, percents, or other relational numbers

Here's How to Crack It

Plugging In works with both Word Problems and Plug and Chug questions. Question 43 may look like it requires a "content-based" approach, but let's see how much easier it is if we Plug In.

First, let's Plug In a number for the variable. The best numbers to Plug In are usually small and easy to deal with: numbers such as 2, 5, and 10. Let's try 2 in this problem. If $x = 2$,

$$4(2)^2 + 20(2) + 24 = 4(4) + 20(2) + 24$$
$$= 16 + 40 + 24$$
$$= 56 + 24$$
$$= 80$$

So if we Plug In 2 everywhere there's an x, the expression gives us 80. Now, since the question is merely asking for an equivalent expression, we will want the same result as we plug our value into the answer choices. In this case, 80 is our *target answer*. Let's go to the answer choices and see which one matches up:

43. $4(2)^2 + 20(2) + 24$ is equivalent to $\boxed{80}$.

    A. $(4(2) + 4)((2) + 6) = (12)(8) = 96$
    B. $(4(2) - 4)((2) - 6) = (4)(-4) = -16$
    C. $(4(2) - 24)((2) - 1) = (-16)(1) = -16$
    D. $2(2(2) - 4)((2) - 3) = 2(0)(-1) = 0$
    E. $2(2(2) + 4)((2) + 3) = 2(8)(5) = 80$

The only one that matches up is (E), the correct answer. No quadratic formula or difficult factoring required!

Let's review the steps:

Once you've determined that you can Plug In, follow these steps.

1. Plug In an easy-to-use value for your variable or variables.

2. Work the information in the question using the numbers you've Plugged In to find a *target answer*.

3. Plug the variables into the answer choices to find the one that matches up with the target.

4. Make sure you check all the answer choices. If more than one answer choice works, Plug In a new set of numbers and try again.

Let's try another one.

28. As part of an analysis to determine how summer vacations affect students' retention of school materials, scientists conducted an experiment. As shown in the chart below, they showed the time, d days, since the student had finished and the number of facts, f, that the student remembered from the previous year.

d	1	3	5	7	9
f	96	72	48	24	0

Which of the following equations represents all the data found in this study?

F. $f = 9 - d$

G. $f = 3(9 - d)$

H. $f = 3d + 3$

J. $f = 3(36 - 4d)$

K. $f = 96d$

Here's How to Crack It

This problem looks very different from our last two, but notice that it has some important features in common with them. Most important for our purposes are the variables in the answer choices. With these we know that we can Plug In on this question.

This problem is much bulkier than the last two, though, and in many ways more intimidating. This is because it's a *Word Problem*. As we mentioned earlier in this chapter, even though Word Problems often use the same mathematical concepts, they ask about them in much more convoluted ways. Here's a simple Basic Approach for dealing with Word Problems.

When dealing with Word Problems on the ACT Math test

1. **Know the question**. Read the whole problem before calculating anything, and underline the actual question.

2. **Let the answers help.** Look for clues on how to solve and ways to use POE (Process of Elimination).

3. **Break the problem into bite-sized pieces.** Watch out for tricky phrasing.

Let's use these steps to solve this problem.

1. **Know the question.** We need to find an equation that can accommodate all of the information in the table for d and f. The question in this problem is below the chart. How much of the other stuff do we need? Not much.
2. **Let the answers help.** Remember how important the answers have been in what we've done so far in this chapter. If there are variables in those answer choices, we can usually Plug In. We have variables in these answer choices, so we'll plan to Plug In here.
3. **Break the problem into bite-sized pieces.** We know we need an equation that will work for all the points in this chart. Let's pick one set of points that will be easy to test, and then a second set to confirm our answers. Go easy on yourself! There's no reason to pick the biggest numbers. Let's try first the point to the far right of the chart: $d = 9$, $f = 0$. We want an equation that will work for these points, so let's try the answers:

F. $0 = 9 - 9$ ✔

G. $0 = 3(9 - 9)$ ✔

H. $0 = 3(9) + 3$ ✗

J. $0 = 3(36 - 4(9))$ ✔

K. $0 = 96(9)$ ✔

Okay, we've eliminated two of the answer choices. Now let's try another set of points: $d = 7, f = 24$.

F. $24 = 9 - 7$ ✗
G. $24 = 3(9 - 7)$ ✗
H. $f = 3d + 3$
J. $24 = 3(36 - 4(7))$ ✔
K. $f = 96d$

Only one remains, and our best answer is (J). All using basic arithmetic in the formulas provided.

_____○_____

PLUGGING IN THE ANSWERS

Now, what happens when we don't have the hallmarks of easy Plugging In problems: variables in the answer choices or in the problem? Like question 45:

_____○_____

45. A high-school basketball player has shot 170 free throws and has made 100 of those free throws. Starting now, if she makes each free throw she attempts, what is the least number of free throws she must attempt in order to raise her free-throw percentage to at least 70% ?

A. 19
B. 20
C. 63
D. 64
E. 70

In this problem, there are no variables anywhere to be seen. Still, we're going to need to put together some kind of equation or something that will enable us to answer the question. For this one, we can *Plug in the Answers* (PITA).

PITA when

- the question asks for a specific amount. Look for "How many?" or "How much?" or "What is the value of?"

- there are no variables in the answer choices

Care for Some PITA?
Note that the PITA strategy is slightly different from just Plugging In. With PITA, you're specifically using the answer choices.

Question 45 is a Word Problem, so let's go through the steps:

1. **Know the question.** We need to figure out how many additional free throws this player will need to have a free-throw percentage of 70%. Also, when ACT italicizes or capitalizes a word, pay special attention. In this case, they've italicized the word *least*. Keep this in mind, it tells you that a number of the answer choices may work, but the correct will be the *least* of these. The phrase "What is the least number?" is the kind of very specific question that usually makes for a good PITA problem.
2. **Let the answers help.** There are no variables in these answer choices, and that coupled with the fact that it asks for a specific value is a good indication that we'll be using these answer choices to PITA. Notice the answer choices are listed in ascending order, which means it might be smart to start with the middle choice. That way we can eliminate answers that are too high or too low.
3. **Break the problem into bite-sized pieces.** With many PITA problems, it can help to create columns, building on the information given in the answer choices and the problem. Start with the question that's being asked: You've already got five possible answers to that question.

45. A high-school basketball player has shot 170 free throws and has made 100 of those free throws. Starting now, if she makes each free throw she attempts, <u>what is the least number of free throws she must attempt in order to raise her free-throw percentage to at least 70% ?</u>

Free-throws	Total free-throws	Total completed	Percentage free-throws
A. 19			
B. 20			
C. 63	233	163	69.9%
D. 64			
E. 70			

Here's How to Crack It

As (C) has shown, 63 additional free throws only raises the percentage to 69.9%. We know this is wrong because we want to raise it to 70%. Therefore, since (C) gives a value that is too small, (A) and (B) must be too small as well. Let's try (D).

Our best answer here is (D) because it produces a free-throw percentage of 70.1%. Choice (E) will produce a percentage greater than 70% as well, but remember, this question is asking for the *least*.

45. A high-school basketball player has shot 170 free throws and has made 100 of those free throws. Starting now, if she makes each free throw she attempts, <u>what is the least number of free throws she must attempt in order to raise her free-throw percentage to at least 70%</u> ?

Free-throws	Total free-throws	Total completed	Percentage free-throws
~~A. 19~~	189	89	47.1
~~B. 20~~	190	90	47.4%
~~C. 63~~	233	163	69.9%
D. 64	234	164	70.1%
E. 70			

Let's review what we've learned about this type of question so far.

When you've identified a problem as a PITA problem, do the following:

- Start with the middle answer choice. This can help with POE (Process of Elimination).

- Label your answer choices—they answer the question you underlined in the problem.

- When you find the correct answer, stop! But make sure you're answering the right question.

- Make sure you account for all the relevant information. PITA is most effective in simplifying difficult Word Problems, but make sure you've got everything you need!

Let's try another problem.

18. The product of two distinct integers is 192. If the sum of those same two integers is 28, what is the value of the larger of the two integers?

F. 18
G. 16
H. 12
J. 10
K. 8

Here's How to Crack It

Let's go through the steps.

1. **Know the question.** "What is the value of the larger of the two integers?" The key word here is *larger*. The numbers in the answer choices will be possibilities for this *larger* value. Notice this is asking for a specific value, which means we can PITA.

2. **Let the answers help.** We've got a list of non-variable answers in ascending order. Each one offers a possible answer to the specific question posed in the problem. Let's PITA, and use the answers to work backwards through the problem.

3. **Break the problem into bite-sized pieces.** Even though this is a short problem, there's a lot of information here, so we should use columns to help us keep all the information straight. The problem says that the *sum* of the two integers is 28, so let's start there. Begin with (C) to help with Process of Elimination.

18. The product of two distinct integers is 192. If the sum of those same two integers is 28, <u>what is the value of the larger of the two integers?</u>

Larger integer	Smaller integer	(Larger × Smaller) = 192?
F. 18		
G. 16		
H. 12	16	CAN'T WORK
J. 10		
K. 8		

We can eliminate (H) right off the bat. Just from what we've found, 12 can't be the *larger* integer if 16 is the *smaller* integer. We will therefore need a number larger than 12, so we can eliminate (J) and (K) as well. Let's try (G).

18. The product of two distinct integers is 192. If the sum of those same two integers is 28, <u>what is the value of the larger of the two integers?</u>

Larger integer	Smaller integer	(Larger × Smaller) = 192?
F. 18		
G. 16	12	16 × 12 = 192 Yes!
~~**H.** 12~~	~~16~~	~~CAN'T WORK~~
~~**J.** 10~~		
~~**K.** 8~~		

Choice (G) works, so we can stop there. Notice how PITA and Plugging In have enabled us to do these problems quickly and accurately without getting bogged down in generating difficult algebraic formulas.

A NOTE ON PLUGGING IN AND PITA

Plugging In and PITA are not the only ways to solve these problems, and it may feel weird using these methods instead of trying to do these problems "the real way." You may have even found that you knew how to work with the variables in Plugging In problems or how to write the appropriate equations for the PITA problems. If you can do either of those things, you're already on your way to a great Math score.

But think about it this way. We've already said that ACT doesn't give any partial credit. So do you think doing it "the real way" gets you any extra points? It doesn't: On the ACT, a right answer is a right answer, no matter how you get it. "The real way" is great, but unfortunately, it's often a lot more complex and offers a lot more opportunities to make careless errors.

The biggest problem with doing things the real way, though, is that it essentially requires that you invent a new approach for every problem. Instead, notice what we've given you here: two strategies that will work toward getting you the right answer on any number of questions. You may have heard the saying, "Give a man a fish and you've fed him for a day, but teach a man to fish and you've fed him for a lifetime." Now, don't worry, our delusions of grandeur are not quite so extreme, but Plugging In and PITA are useful in a similar way. Rather than giving you a detailed description of how to create formulas and work through them for these problems that won't themselves ever appear on an ACT again, we're giving you a strategy that will help you to work through any number of similar problems in future ACTs.

Try these strategies on your own in the drill that concludes this chapter.

2. If $\dfrac{3n}{4} - 7 = 2$, then $n =$

   F. -9

   G. $-\dfrac{7}{3}$

   H. $\dfrac{7}{3}$

   J. 9

   K. 12

9. Which of the following expressions is equivalent to

   $(3x^2 - 2x + 4) + (2x - 1) - (x^2 - 3x + 2)$?

   A. $x^2 - 2x + 3$
   B. $x^2 + 2x - 1$
   C. $2x^2 - 3x - 5$
   D. $2x^2 - 3x - 1$
   E. $2x^2 + 3x + 1$

11. If b is a positive integer greater than 1, what is the smallest integer value of a for which there exists a value of b such that $\sqrt{a} - b^2 > 0$?

   A. 5
   B. 16
   C. 25
   D. 36
   E. 49

16. Which of the following expressions is equivalent to $\dfrac{p^2 - 3p}{2p} + \dfrac{1}{p^2}$?

   F. $\dfrac{p^2 - 3p + 1}{2p^3}$

   G. $\dfrac{2p^2}{p^3 - 3p^2 + 2}$

   H. $\dfrac{p^3 - 3p^2 + 2}{2p^2}$

   J. $\dfrac{p - 3p^2}{p^3 + 4}$

   K. $\dfrac{2 - p^2}{p^2 + p - 2}$

18. Amethyst's route to work is 48 miles long. Along the way, she stops for coffee and notices that the ratio of the number of miles she's driven so far to the number of miles left to go is 3:1. How many miles does she have left to drive?

   F. 6
   G. 12
   H. 24
   J. 30
   K. 36

23. If $\dfrac{w - 1}{2} = z$ and $\dfrac{w + z}{2} = 11$, then which of the following is equivalent to z ?

   A. 5
   B. 7
   C. 11
   D. 13
   E. 15

24. A salesman earns \$600 per week in base salary. For each successful sale, he receives \$125 in commission. Which of the following represents the amount of money, in dollars, the salesman earns in a given week in which he makes s successful sales?

   F. $725s$
   G. $125s - 600$
   H. $600s + 125$
   J. $600 - 125s$
   K. $600 + 125s$

27. The expression $(n^2 - 6n + 5)(n + 4)$ is equivalent to:

   A. $n^3 - 2n^2 - 19n + 20$
   B. $n^3 - n^2 + 9n + 20$
   C. $n^3 - 2n^2 - 7n + 20$
   D. $n^3 + 2n^2 - 24n + 20$
   E. $n^3 - 2n^2 - 29n + 20$

30. If $|2n + 6| = |3n + 4|$, then what are the possible values of n ?

   F. 0 and 2
   G. 0 and -2
   H. -2 and 2
   J. 2 only
   K. -2 only

32. If $f(a) = a^2 + 3$ and $g(a) = 3a - 1$, which of the following is an expression for $g(f(a))$?

F. $a^2 + 3a + 2$
G. $3a^2 - 3$
H. $-a^2 + 3a - 2$
J. $3a^2 + 9a - 3$
K. $3a^2 + 8$

40. In a professional sports league consisting of x teams, y represents the number of teams that qualify for the playoffs in a given season. Which of the following could be used to determine the fraction of teams that does NOT make the playoffs in a given season?

F. $\dfrac{x - y}{x}$

G. $\dfrac{y - x}{x}$

H. $\dfrac{y}{x}$

J. $\dfrac{x - y}{y}$

K. $\dfrac{x + y}{x}$

41. For positive real numbers x, y, and z such that $3x = 4y$ and $\dfrac{2}{3}y = \dfrac{1}{3}z$, which of the following inequalities is true?

A. $x < y < z$
B. $x < z < y$
C. $y < x < z$
D. $y < z < x$
E. $z < y < x$

45. Which of the following gives the solution set for $\sqrt[3]{(n^2 - 6n)} = 3$?

A. $\{3\}$
B. $\{2 \pm \sqrt{3}\}$
C. $\{-3, 9\}$
D. $\{3, -9\}$
E. $\{27\}$

46. If $x > y$, then $-|y - x|$ is equivalent to which of the following?

F. $\sqrt{y - x}$
G. $x - y$
H. $|y - x|$
J. $-(x - y)$
K. $|x - y|$

48. If $-1 < x < 0$, then which of the following must be true?

F. $0^x > 0$

G. $-\dfrac{1}{x} > 1$

H. $x + \dfrac{1}{x} = 0$

J. $\dfrac{1}{x} > 0$

K. $x^0 < 0$

49. If n is a real number, then what is the solution to the equation $27^{2n} = 81^{(n+1)}$?

A. $n = 0$
B. $n = 1$
C. $n = 2$
D. $n = 3$
E. $n = 4$

55. Which of the following is an irrational value of n that is a solution to the equation $|n^2 - 30| - 6 = 0$?

A. $\sqrt{6}$
B. 6
C. $2\sqrt{6}$
D. $3\sqrt{6}$
E. $4\sqrt{6}$

59. Consider all pairs of positive integers a and b whose sum is 6. For how many values of a does $a^b = b^a$?

A. None
B. 1
C. 2
D. 3
E. 6

PLUGGING IN AND PITA DRILL 1 ANSWER KEY

2. K
9. E
11. C
16. H
18. G
23. B
24. K
27. A
30. H
32. K
40. F
41. C
45. C
46. J
48. G
49. C
55. C
59. D

PLUGGING IN AND PITA DRILL 1 EXPLANATIONS

2. **K** Plug In the Answers on this one. No harm in starting with the middle answer choice, but if you want this problem to be as easy as possible (and it is question 2, so it should be relatively easy), you might try the whole numbers in the answers first. With (J), it means that $\frac{3(9)}{4} - 2 = 7$. Since $\frac{3(9)}{4} = 6.75$, you can eliminate it. Try (K): $\frac{3(12)}{4} - 2 = 7$. $\frac{3(12)}{4} = 9$, and $9 - 2 = 7$, so you've found your answer.

9. **E** If the expressions confuse you, just plug in an easy number, such as $x = 2$. Substitute it into the equation: $(3(2)^2 - 2(2) + 4) + (2(2) - 1) - ((2)^2 - 3(2) + 2)$. Do the exponents and multiplication first: $(12 - 4 + 4) + (4 - 1) - (4 - 6 + 2)$. Now do the addition and subtraction: $12 + 3 - 0 = 15$. The target is 15. Now plug 2 into each of the answers, and pick the one that equals 15. It's (E). Don't forget to check all five answers.

11. **C** This is a tricky and confusing problem made simple by Plugging In the Answers. Since the problem asks for the smallest possible value of a, start with the smallest answer choice. Work your way up to 25, and the problem reads $\sqrt{25} - b^2 > 0$. The question becomes, "Is there a value of b (remember, b must be an integer greater than 1) that makes that equation true?" Sure there is: If $b = 2$, then $5 - 4 > 0$.

16. **H** The algebra is fairly complicated here, so the best approach is to plug in a relatively small and simple number. If you say, for example, that $p = 3$, then the original expression comes out to $\frac{1}{9}$; this is your target answer. Now plug $p = 3$ into the expressions in the answer choices in order to determine which one matches your target answer. Choice (F) becomes $\frac{1}{54}$; (G) becomes 9; (H) becomes $\frac{1}{9}$; (J) becomes $-\frac{24}{31}$; and (K) becomes $-\frac{7}{10}$. Choice (H) is therefore the only one that matches your target, and thus is correct.

18. **G** Note that the problem is asking for the number of miles left to go. Plug In the Answers starting with (H). If she has 24 miles left, then she's halfway there—that's not far enough along, so eliminate (H) and any answer with higher mileage. Plug in (G). If she's got 12 miles left to go, that means $48 - 12 = 36$, meaning she's driven 36 miles so far. Since the ratio of 36:12 is 3:1, (G) is your answer.

23. **B** This question is best approached through PITA. Since all of the answer choices are integers, start with the one in the middle, (C). If $z = 11$, then $\dfrac{w-1}{2} = 11$. Multiply both sides by 2 and solve to determine that $w = 23$. If you put these two values into the left-hand side of the second equation provided in the question stem, you get $\dfrac{23+11}{2} = \dfrac{34}{2} = 17$. This is too big, so eliminate (C) and test (B). If $z = 7$, then $\dfrac{w-1}{2} = 7$. Multiply both sides by 2 and solve to determine that $w = 15$. If you put these two values into the left-hand side of the second equation provided in the question stem, you get $\dfrac{15+7}{2} = \dfrac{22}{2} = 11$. This matches the information in the question stem, and thus (B) is correct.

24. **K** Plug In a small number for the number of sales he's completed so the math is as easy as possible. If he completed 2 sales, then he's made $250 commission to go with his $600 base salary, for total earnings of $850. Choice (K) gets you the same value.

27. **A** Play it safe and Plug In 2. $(2^2 - 6(2) + 5)(2 + 4)$ means $(4 - 12 + 5)(6)$, which gives you -18 as a target answer. Choice (A) will read $2^3 - 2(2)^2 - 19(2) + 20$. Simplified, $8 - 8 - 38 + 20 = -18$.

30. **H** This question is best approached through PITA. The answer choices are all different combinations of three numbers: 2, –2, and 0. So these numbers need to be plugged in. If $n = -2$, then the left-hand side of the equation is $|2(-2) + 6| = |-4 + 6| = |2| = 2$. If $n = -2$, then the right-hand side of the equation is $|3(-2) + 4| = |-6 + 4| = |-2| = 2$. This works, so any answer choice that does not have $n = -2$ as a solution can be eliminated; cross off (F) and (J). Now try the other solution from (H): if $n = 2$, then the left-hand side of the equation is $|2(2) + 6| = |4 + 6| = |10| = 10$. If $n = 2$, then the right-hand side of the equation is $|3(2) + 4| = |6 + 4| = |10| = 10$. This also works, so (H) is the correct answer.

32. **K** When you have one function inside another, start with the one on the inside and work your way out. And of course, you should Plug In! So plug in 2, and start with $f(2) = 2^2 + 3$. That means $f(2) = 7$. That's now the value you can plug in to the other function: $g(7) = 3(7) - 1$, so your target answer is 20. Plug 2 into the answer choices, and (K) will read $3(2)^2 + 8$, which is 20.

40. **F** Plug In values for the number of teams in the league and the number of teams that qualify for the playoffs. Say there are 15 teams in the league (represented by x) and 8 of them qualify (represented by y). That leaves 7 for the number of teams that do not qualify, which means that your target answer is $\dfrac{7}{15}$. Choice (F) becomes $\dfrac{15-8}{15}$, or $\dfrac{7}{15}$.

41. **C** Plugging In is the easiest way to solve this problem, but we need to choose numbers that work with the given equations. Start with the first equation, $3x = 4y$. The easy thing to do here is choose $x = 4$ and $y = 3$ because $(3)(4) = (4)(3)$. Now we can solve the second equation: $\frac{2}{3}(3) = \frac{1}{3}z$, so $2 = \frac{1}{3}z$ and $z = 6$. Now it's a simple matter to put them in order: $3 < 4 < 6$, so $y < x < z$.

45. **C** To make things a little easier, you can cube both sides to get rid of the radical. The right side of the equation is now 27. Now, Plug In the Answers and see which one works. In (C), $(-3)^2 - 6(-3) = 9 - (-18) = 27$, and $(9)^2 - 6(9) = 81 - 54 = 27$.

46. **J** Plug In anything you want as long as $x > y$, such as $x = 3$ and $y = 2$. In the original problem, $-|2 - 3| = -|-1|$, so the target answer is -1. Try this out in the answer choices. Choice (J) works: $-(3 - 2) = -1$.

48. **G** This question can be approached by thinking about abstract number properties, but it is easier to plug in a simple number for x and check whether the answer choices are true. Try an easy number, such as $x = -\frac{1}{2}$. Choice (F) becomes $0^{-\frac{1}{2}} = 0$, which is not greater than 0; eliminate (F). Choice (G) becomes $-\frac{1}{-\frac{1}{2}} = \frac{1}{\frac{1}{2}} = 2$, which is greater than 1, so keep (G) for now. Choice (H) becomes $-\frac{1}{2} + \frac{1}{-\frac{1}{2}} = -\frac{1}{2} + (-2) = -2\frac{1}{2}$, which is not equal to 0; eliminate (H). Choice (J) becomes $\frac{1}{-\frac{1}{2}} = -2$, which is not greater than 0; eliminate (J). Choice (K) becomes $\left(-\frac{1}{2}\right)^0 = 1$, which is not less than 0; eliminate (K) and choose (G).

49. **C** This question is best approached by Plugging In the Answers. Start with (C): if $n = 2$, then the equation becomes $27^{2(2)} = 81^{2+1}$ or $27^4 = 81^3$. Put these numbers into your calculator to determine whether they are, in fact, equal. Both 27^4 and 81^3 are equal to 531,441, so (C) is correct.

55. **C** The problem asks for an irrational solution, so while (B) would work, it is rational, so cross it off. Then Plug In the Answers. When you Plug In the value in (C), the equation reads $|(2\sqrt{6})^2 - 30| - 6 = 0$. When you square $2\sqrt{6}$, you get 24, so it's $|24 - 30| - 6 = 0$. The value inside the absolute value symbol becomes -6, the absolute value of which is 6. The final equation is now much simpler: $6 - 6 = 0$.

59. **D**   First, figure out all the pairs of positive integers which add up to 6 and Plug In. 1^5 and 5^1 aren't equal, so try 2 and 4: $2^4 = 4^2$. Be sure to keep track of what the problem asks: How many values of *a* satisfy the equation? Consider that *a* could occupy the place of either the 2 or the 4, so those are 2 possible values for *a*. The last pair of numbers is 3 and 3. Since $3^3 = 3^3$, 3 is the third value for *a*.

PLUGGING IN AND PITA DRILL 2

3. Which of the following expressions is equivalent to $a^2 - 8a + 16$?

   A. $(a-4)(a-4)$
   B. $(a-4)(a+4)$
   C. $(a-2)(a-8)$
   D. $(a-2)(a+8)$
   E. $(2a-4)(2a-4)$

6. A 62-centimeter-long string is cut into 4 pieces such that the first piece is twice as long as the second piece, the second piece is three times as long as the third piece, and the third piece is three times as long as the fourth piece. How many centimeters in length is the longest of the 4 pieces?

   F. 2
   G. 8
   H. 18
   J. 26
   K. 36

7. The expression $-w\left[x-(y+z)\right]$ is equivalent to:

   A. $-wx - wy - wz$
   B. $-wx + wy - wz$
   C. $-wx + wy + wz$
   D. $-wx - y + z$
   E. $wx - y + z$

9. Jenna is swimming laps in a pool on 5 consecutive days. If the numbers below represent the number of laps she swims each day, what 3 numbers should be placed in the blanks below so that the difference between the laps Jenna swims on consecutive days remains the same?

   5, ____, ____, ____, 53

   A. 12, 24, 36
   B. 16, 32, 48
   C. 17, 29, 41
   D. 20, 30, 40
   E. 21, 29, 37

18. Teddy, Harry, and Obie are buying baseball cards. Teddy always buys cards in packs of 15, Harry always buys cards in packs of 10, and Obie always buys cards in packs of 25. What is the smallest number of cards all three could buy such that they all have the same number of cards?

    F. 25
    G. 150
    H. 250
    J. 750
    K. 3,750

19. Which of the following variable expressions would represent the area of a parallelogram if its base is represented by $a+3$ and its height is represented by $a-5$?

    A. $2a-2$
    B. $a^2 - 15$
    C. $a^2 - 8a - 15$
    D. $a^2 - 2a - 15$
    E. $a^2 - 2a + 15$

20. The expression $(2x+5y)-(3x-2y)$ is equivalent to:

    F. $-x-3y$
    G. $-x+7y$
    H. $x-3y$
    J. $x+7y$
    K. $5x-3y$

21. For all positive integers a, b, and c, which of the following expressions is equivalent to $\dfrac{a-b}{b}$?

    A. $\dfrac{a+b+c}{b+c}$
    B. $\dfrac{a \cdot c - b \cdot c}{b \cdot c}$
    C. $\dfrac{a - b \cdot c}{b \cdot c}$
    D. $\dfrac{a \cdot c + b \cdot c}{b \cdot c}$
    E. $\dfrac{-a - b \cdot c}{-b \cdot c}$

22. Sheldon has 30 comic books. Some of the comic books were originally 10¢, and the others were originally 45¢. The original value of all 30 comic books is $9.65. How many 45¢ comic books does Sheldon have?

- **F.** 11
- **G.** 13
- **H.** 15
- **J.** 19
- **K.** 21

23. Let a be a real number. Which of the following is a value of a such that $a^2 + 9a = 0$?

- **A.** 18
- **B.** 6
- **C.** 3
- **D.** −3
- **E.** −9

26. Given $7a - b = 2a + 3b$, which of the following is an expression for b ?

- **F.** $-\left(\dfrac{2a + 3b}{7a}\right)$
- **G.** $-\dfrac{5a}{4}$
- **H.** $\dfrac{5a}{4}$
- **J.** $\dfrac{5a}{2}$
- **K.** $\dfrac{2a + 3b}{7a}$

27. The height of a parallelogram is 7 inches shorter than the base from which the height is measured. If the area of the parallelogram is 60 square inches, what is the height, in inches?

- **A.** 5
- **B.** 9
- **C.** 12
- **D.** 24
- **E.** 53

33. For all real values y, $\dfrac{\left[4(y - 3)\right]^2}{8} = ?$

- **A.** $\dfrac{1}{2}y^2 - 3y + \dfrac{9}{2}$
- **B.** $y^2 - 9$
- **C.** $2y^2 - 18$
- **D.** $2y^2 - 12y - 18$
- **E.** $2y^2 - 12y + 18$

35. Brian and Miguel decide to have a race. Miguel decides to give Brian a 20-meter lead at the beginning of the race. Brian runs at a speed of $2\dfrac{1}{2}$ meters per second. Miguel runs at a speed of 5 meters per second. If they start running at the same time, in how many seconds will it take for Miguel to catch Brian?

- **A.** $2\dfrac{1}{2}$
- **B.** 4
- **C.** 8
- **D.** $12\dfrac{1}{2}$
- **E.** 20

47. If b is an integer, then the difference of $3b$ and $7b$ is *always* divisible by which of the following?

- **A.** 3
- **B.** 4
- **C.** 7
- **D.** 10
- **E.** 21

49. Luree is measuring a quilt that is in the shape of a parallelogram. She discovers that the area of the quilt is A feet squared, and the base is b feet. The height of the parallelogram is y feet longer than its base. Which of the following equations would give Luree the length y in terms of A and b ?

- **A.** $y = A - 2b$
- **B.** $y = \dfrac{A}{2} - b$
- **C.** $y = \dfrac{A}{b}$
- **D.** $y = \dfrac{A}{b} - b$
- **E.** $y = \dfrac{A}{b} - 2b$

50. Party Hats X and Y are both right circular cones. The radius of the base of Hat X is 6 times the radius of the base of Hat Y, and the height of Hat X is 3 times the height of Hat Y. The volume of Hat X is how many times the volume of Hat Y ?

(Note: $V_{cone} = \dfrac{1}{3}\pi r^2 h$)

- **F.** 9
- **G.** 18
- **H.** 36
- **J.** 54
- **K.** 108

51. What real value of x satisfies the equation $27^{x+2} = \dfrac{3^2}{9^{x-3}}$?

A. -1

B. $\dfrac{2}{5}$

C. $\dfrac{3}{2}$

D. 2

E. 3

53. Let x and y be real numbers. If $(x-y)^2 = -2xy$, it *must* be true that:

A. both x and y are zero.

B. both x and y are negative.

C. both x and y are fractions.

D. either x or y is zero.

E. x is positive and y is negative.

PLUGGING IN AND PITA DRILL 2 ANSWER KEY

3. A
6. K
7. C
9. C
18. G
19. D
20. G
21. B
22. J
23. E
26. H
27. A
33. E
35. C
47. B
49. D
50. K
51. B
53. A

PLUGGING IN AND PITA DRILL 2 EXPLANATIONS

3. **A**   If you're not sure how to factor this expression, choose a value for a and find the value of the expression. Then substitute the same value for a to see which of the answer choices has the same value. Try an easy number to avoid complicated calculations, such as $a = 2$. In the original expression, $a^2 - 8a + 16 = (2)^2 - 8(2) + 16 = 4 - 16 + 16 = 4$. When you plug $a = 2$ into each of the answer choices, only (A) gives a value of 4: $(2-4)(2-4) = (-2)(-2) = 4$.

6. **K**   The question asks for the length of the longest piece of string, so use the provided answers as a guideline. Start in the middle with (H), so the longest piece of string would be 18 centimeters. The second piece of string would be half that length, or 9 centimeters. The third piece of string is one-third the length, or 3 centimeters, and the fourth piece is one-third of that, or 1 centimeter. The sum of these lengths would be 18 + 9 + 3 + 1 = 31, which does not agree with the 62 centimeters given in the question. Eliminate (F) and (G), which will also be too low. With (K), the longest piece of string would have a length of 36 centimeters, the second piece would be 18 centimeters, the third would be 6 centimeters, and the fourth would be 2 centimeters. The total length of all four pieces would be 36 + 18 + 6 + 2 = 62, which agrees with the total given in the question.

7. **C**   Because the distributing in this problem can be difficult, try picking a few values. Keep them simple: let's say $w = 2$, $x = 3$, $y = 4$, and $z = 3$. In the given expression, this will mean $-2[3 - (4 + 5)] = -2[3 - 9] = -2[-6] = 12$. Plug these numbers in to the answer choices to see which gives a value of 12. Only (C) works, so it is the correct answer.

9. **C**   You can use the answer choices to help solve this question. If you start with (C), the sequence of numbers would be 5, 17, 29, 41, 53. According to the question, the difference between consecutive numbers should remain the same. So, since 17 − 5 = 12, all the other differences between consecutive numbers should also be 12: 29 − 17 = 12, 41 − 29 = 12, and 53 − 41 = 12, so this is the correct answer. The other choices each have the same difference between the three numbers in the choices themselves, but none of them carries that difference to the 5 and 53 given in the problem. Make sure that you check every pair of consecutive numbers when trying each answer choice, and don't forget the numbers from the problem!

18. **G**   To find the smallest number of cards that all three can buy, use the answer choices. The correct answer will need to be divisible by 10, 15, and 25. Remember, though, that even if an answer choice works, you need to find the *smallest* number, so start with (F). Since 25 is not divisible by either 10 or 15, (F) is not correct. Choice (G) is divisible by 10, 15, and 25, so it is the answer. Choices (H), (J), and (K) are larger than (G), so it is irrelevant whether they are divisible by our numbers or not.

19. **D**   Assign a number to represent the value of a. When choosing a value for a, make sure that the number you choose does not cause either dimension of the parallelogram to be negative. Try $a = 10$, which

means that the base would be 13, and the height would be 5. The formula for area of a parallelogram is $A = bh$, so $A = 13 \times 5 = 65$. When you substitute $a = 10$ into each of the answer choices, only (D) gives a value of 65.

20. **G**   Since the distributing and subtraction can be complex, try picking values for x and y. If $x = 2$ and $y = 3$, then $(2(2) + 5(3)) - (3(2) - 2(3)) = (4 + 15) - (6 - 6) = 19 - 0 = 19$. Plug these x and y values in to the answer choices to find that only (G) yields a value of 19. If you chose (J), be careful: You may have forgotten to distribute the negative sign.

21. **B**   Choose values for a, b, and c, and substitute those values into the given equation. Then substitute the same values into the answer choices and figure out which choice has the same value. Try $a = 2$, $b = 3$, and $c = 4$. This makes the original expression $\frac{a-b}{b} = \frac{2-3}{3} = -\frac{1}{3}$. Only (B) has the same value: $\frac{a \cdot c - b \cdot c}{b \cdot c} = \frac{2 \cdot 4 - 3 \cdot 4}{3 \cdot 4} = \frac{8-12}{12} = -\frac{1}{3}$. If you chose (C) be careful: The c will not divide out of the equation equally if it is not multiplied by the a as well as the b.

22. **J**   Use the provided answer choices to determine the correct number of 45¢ comic books. Start in the middle: this will help with POE. With (H), the total value of the 45¢ comic books would be $0.45 \times 15 = \$6.75$. Since 15 of the comic books are 45¢, the other 15 would be 10¢ comics. So, the total value of the 10¢ comic books would be $0.10 \times 15 = \$1.50$, and the total value for all 30 comic books would be $\$6.75 \times \$1.50 = \$8.25$, which is less than \$9.65, the value given in the problem. Therefore, there must be more comic books at 45¢. For (J), the total value would be $0.45 \times 19 + \$0.10 \times 11 = \$6.65$. If you chose (F), be careful: This is the number of 10¢ comics.

23. **E**   If you're not sure how to factor this problem, try the numbers from the answer choices. Start in the middle to help with POE. If $a = 3$, then $(3)^2 + 9(3) = 36 \neq 0$, so eliminate (C). You can also eliminate (A) and (B) because those values will be too large. Try (E). If $a = -9$, then $(-9)^2 + 9(-9) = 0$, which works. Choice (E) is therefore the only possible answer.

26. **H**   You can isolate b in the given equation, but you can also plug in a value for a and find the corresponding value for b. Try $a = 4$. If $a = 4$, then $7(4) - b = 2(4) + 3b$, $28 - b = 8 + 3b$, $-4b = -20$, and $b = 5$. Now, plug in 4 for a in each answer choice. Choices (F) and (K) are incorrect because if you want to solve for b, you cannot have b in your expression. Choice (G) forgets to divide by a negative, and (J) results from incorrectly combining the b terms. Only (H) correctly yields the target value of 5.

27. **A**   Use the formula for area of a parallelogram, $A = bh$. Since the answer choices are all possible values for the height of the parallelogram, substitute each choice to figure out which value yields an area of 60 in.^{2}. With (C), the height would be 12 in., which means that the base is 19 in. because the height is 7 in. shorter than the base. Use the formula for area of a parallelogram to find $A = b \cdot h = 19 \cdot 12 = 228$ in.^{2}, which is greater than the target area of 60. Eliminate (C), (D), and (E), because you'll need a shorter

height. Choice (A) gives a height of 5, which results in a base of 12 and an area of $12 \cdot 5 = 60$. If you chose (C), be careful: This is the base of the parallelogram, and the problem is asking for the height.

33. **E** If you substitute a value for y, you can avoid some of the common algebraic errors. Let $y = 2$.

Substitute this into the given expression to get $\dfrac{[4(2-3)]^2}{8} = \dfrac{[4(-1)]^2}{8} = \dfrac{[-4]^2}{8} = \dfrac{16}{8} = 2$. When

you substitute $y = 2$ into each of the answer choices, only (E) has a value of 2. If you got one

of the other answers, make sure you applied the square to the 4 in the numerator.

35. **C** To figure out when Miguel will catch Brian, you need to know the time at which their total distances

will be the same. Use the numbers in the answer choices to figure out how far each of them traveled

and see whether the totals are equivalent. If you try (C), they both have run for 8 seconds. In that

time, traveling at 5 meters per second, Miguel will have traveled $8 \times 5 = 40$ meters. Brian,

given a 20–meter lead and running at a speed of $2\dfrac{1}{2}$ meters per second, will have traveled

$20 + \left(8 \times 2\dfrac{1}{2}\right) = 20 + 20 = 40$ meters as well. Since their total distances are equal, Miguel needs

8 seconds to catch Brian. If you chose (B), you may have found only the time it takes Miguel to

run 20 m, but remember, Brian is moving also.

47. **B** Since the question only tells you that b has to be an integer, choose any integer for b and then solve

the problem. Try $b = 2$. The two values are then $3(2) = 6$ and $7(2) = 14$, which have a difference

of $14 - 6 = 8$. The correct answer must divide evenly into 8, so the answer is (B). If you're not

convinced, try another value for b. You'll find that it yields the same final answer.

49. **D** First, to make the question easier to understand, replace the values for the base and height with

actual numbers. Set $b = 3$ and $y = 2$. This means that the base of the parallelogram is 3 feet, and the

height of the parallelogram is $b + y = 2 + 3 = 5$ feet. Using the formula for the area of a parallelogram,

the resulting area should be $A = b \quad h = 3 \quad 5 = 15$ square feet. Substitute the values into the answer

choices, and the only equation that is true is the one given in (D).

50. **K** You can solve this question by choosing values for the dimensions of each hat. Make sure to obey the

relationships given in the question. Since Hat Y is the smaller hat, choose the radius and height for

Hat Y first. For Hat Y, let $r_Y = 3$ and $h_Y = 2$. Using the given formula for volume of a cone,

$V_Y = \dfrac{1}{3}\pi(3)^2 \cdot 2 = \dfrac{1}{3}\pi \cdot 9 \cdot 2 = 6\pi$. The problem states that the base of Hat X is 6 times the radius of

the base of Hat Y, so $r_X = 18$. The problem then states that the height of Hat X is 3 times the height of

Hat Y, so $h_X = 6$. With these values, $V_Y = \frac{1}{3}\pi(18)^2 \cdot 6 = \frac{1}{3}\pi \cdot 324 \cdot 6 = 648\pi$. To compare V_X to V_Y, divide the two volumes: $\frac{648\pi}{6\pi} = 108$. Choice (F) is the total of the two numbers given in the question, and (G) is their product. If you picked (J), you may have squared the height instead of the radius.

51. **B** You can use the answer choices and your calculator to help you find the value of x. When using your calculator, remember to use parentheses correctly! Start in the middle with (C). Substitute $x = \frac{3}{2}$ into the equation to find $27^{\frac{3}{2}+2} = \frac{3^2}{9^{\frac{3}{2}-3}}$. You'll notice that this gives a *huge* number on the left side of the equation, so let's eliminate (C), (D), and (E), and try something smaller. In (B), if $x = \frac{2}{5}$, then the equation will read $27^{\frac{2}{5}+2} = \frac{3^2}{9^{\frac{2}{5}-3}}$. Calculate these values to find that the two sides are equal, and the correct answer is (B).

53. **A** Find values for x and y that work in the given equation. Let the answers help if you're not sure where to start. If $x = 0$ and $y = 0$, the equation works: $(0 - 0)^2 = -2(0)(0)$ and $0 = 0$. Because these two values work, we can keep (A) and eliminate (B), (C), and (E). Test (D) by plugging in a few values, and you'll find that no other values can work. Only (A) gives the values that *must* be true.

Chapter 15
Geometry

We've seen in the Algebra chapter that a smart test-taking strategy, in and of itself, can improve your Math score. That is no less true for Geometry problems, but for these you typically have to bring a bit more to the table. ACT doesn't give you the formulas like SAT does, so you need to have them stored in your brain (or your calculator) when test day rolls around. Remember, counting Trigonometry, Geometry makes up about half of any given ACT Math test.

THE BASIC APPROACH
Let's try a straightforward geometry problem.

22. In right triangle $\triangle STU$ shown below, V is the midpoint of $\overline{TU}$. In inches, what is the length of $\overline{UV}$?

F. 6
G. 9
H. 12
J. 72
K. 144

Step 1: Ballpark
First, ACT has actually done us a big favor on this problem. While they claim that "illustrative figures are NOT necessarily drawn to scale," it's usually safe to assume that they are at least close. Remember what we're looking for here, the length of $\overline{UV}$. Look closely at this figure: You can tell just by looking at it that the longest side is $\overline{SU}$, which has a length of 13, so it's not likely that any smaller part of the triangle will have a longer length, eliminating (J) and (K). We can probably eliminate (H) as well because $\overline{SU}$ is so much longer than $\overline{UV}$. This way, if we were running short on time and had to guess, we have improved our chances of guessing from 20% to 50%. Not bad for no work, huh?

Step 2: Write on the Figure
Now, let's dig in to get our final answer. Rather than trying to keep everything in your mind, make sure you are writing all over your figure. The problem says that V is the midpoint of $\overline{TU}$, so make sure you mark that on your figure. It's probably worth emphasizing the portion, $\overline{UV}$, that you are looking for as well.

Step 3: Write Down Formulas

As for the formulas, get those down before you begin working the problem as well. For this problem, you are dealing with the sides of a right triangle, so it is likely that you will need the Pythagorean theorem: $a^2 + b^2 = c^2$, where c is the longest side. Plug in the information you have, and write anything new that you find on the figure:

$$a^2 + b^2 = c^2$$
$$(5)^2 + \left(\overline{TU}\right)^2 = (13)^2$$
$$\left(\overline{TU}\right)^2 = (13)^2 - (5)^2$$
$$\left(\overline{TU}\right)^2 = 169 - 25$$
$$\left(\overline{TU}\right)^2 = 144$$
$$\overline{TU} = 12$$

Don't make your brain work any harder than it needs to! Make sure you're writing everything down. Hopefully by now your scratch paper looks something like this:

$$a^2 + b^2 = c^2$$
$$(5)^2 + \left(\overline{TU}\right)^2 = (13)^2$$
$$\left(\overline{TU}\right)^2 = (13)^2 - (5)^2$$
$$\left(\overline{TU}\right)^2 = 169 - 25$$
$$\left(\overline{TU}\right)^2 = 144$$
$$\overline{TU} = 12$$

Now, once you've got all the information on the figure, it's probably very clear that the answer is (F) because $\overline{TU}$ is 12, and $\overline{UV}$ is one-half of this value. If you know your Pythagorean triples, you may have found $\overline{TU}$ even more quickly, but make sure you're reading the question carefully. If you don't read all the way, you might fall into the trap and pick (H).

> **Know Your Pythagorean Triples**
> Pythagorean triples are easy-to-remember, commonly tested ratios for the sides of a right triangle. Memorizing them can save you a lot of time by enabling you to bypass the Pythagorean theorem. The most common Pythagorean triples are 3:4:5, 6:8:10, and 5:12:13, each listed from the shortest to the longest side. Which one does question 22 use?

So let's review the basic approach for Geometry problems.

> **The Basic Approach for Geometry**
>
> 1. Use ballparking to eliminate wrong answers on questions in which a figure is given.
>
> 2. Write any information given by the question on the provided figure.
>
> 3. Write down any formulas you need and Plug In any information you have.
>
> 4. If the question doesn't provide a figure, draw your own.

THE FORMULAS

Here are some of the formulas you may find useful on Geometry questions.

Circles

Think CArd! (Circumference, Area, radius, diameter)

If you have one of these, you can always find the other three.

$$d = 2r \qquad C = \pi d = 2\pi r \qquad A = \pi r^2$$

When dealing with the parts of a circle, set up a ratio.

$$\frac{part}{whole} = \frac{central\ angle}{360°} = \frac{arc}{2\pi r} = \frac{sector\ area}{\pi r^2}$$

For Coordinate Geometry, be able to recognize the equation of a circle:

$$(x - h)^2 + (y - k)^2 = r^2$$

where (h,k) is the center of the circle, and (x,y) is any point on the circle.

Triangles

$$\text{Area} = A = \frac{1}{2}bh$$

Perimeter: P = sum of the sides

Sum of all angles: 180°

Similar triangles have congruent angles and proportional sides.

Right Triangles

The Triangle rules apply, but there are some special rules for right triangles.

Pythagorean theorem, where a, b, and c are the sides of the triangle, and c is the hypotenuse:

$$a^2 + b^2 = c^2$$

SOHCAHTOA (ratios between sides and angles of right triangles)

$$\sin\theta = \frac{\text{Opposite}}{\text{Hypotenuse}} \qquad \cos\theta = \frac{\text{Adjacent}}{\text{Hypotenuse}} \qquad \tan\theta = \frac{\text{Opposite}}{\text{Adjacent}}$$

Special Right Triangles

When you've determined the angles of your right triangle, use the following ratios to bypass the Pythagorean theorem:

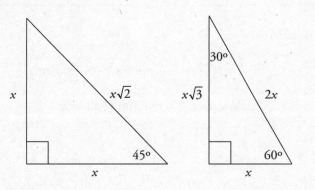

If a triangle problem contains a $\sqrt{2}$ or a $\sqrt{3}$, you can most likely use one of these special triangles.

If you don't know the angles, you can often bypass the Pythagorean theorem with the Pythagorean triples:

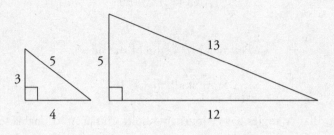

These Pythagorean triples are basic ratios, so they can be multiplied to be used with larger numbers.

6:8:10 is commonly cited as a Pythagorean triple, but it is just the 3:4:5 multiplied by 2.

Four-Sided Figures (Quadrilaterals)

Parallelogram: Opposite sides are parallel, opposite sides and angles are equal

Rhombus: Opposite sides parallel, ALL sides equal, opposite angles equal.
A rhombus is a *parallelogram* in which all four sides are equal.

Rectangle: Opposite sides parallel, opposite sides equal, ALL angles 90°
A rectangle is a *parallelogram* with four right angles.

Square: Opposite sides parallel, ALL sides equal, ALL angles 90°
A square is a type of *parallelogram*, *rhombus*, and *rectangle*.

For any of these four shapes:

Area: $A = bh$, where b and h are perpendicular

Perimeter: $P =$ the sum of all sides

Coordinate Geometry Formulas

All points are written (x,y), where x gives the x-coordinate and y gives the y-coordinate.

Two lines *intersect* when they meet at a single point.

$$\text{Slope: } \frac{\text{rise}}{\text{run}} = \frac{y_2 - y_1}{x_2 - x_1}$$

where (x_1, y_1) and (x_2, y_2) are two points on a line.

$$\text{Slope-intercept formula: } y = mx + b$$

where (x,y) is a point on the line, m is the slope, and b is the y-intercept, or the point at which the line crosses the y-axis.

Use the slope-intercept form when a question asks for the slope of a *perpendicular* line. The slope of a line perpendicular to it will be the opposite reciprocal or $-\frac{1}{m}$. That is, if slope of a line is 2, the slope of a perpendicular will be $-\frac{1}{2}$.

Parallel lines have equal slopes.

THE PROBLEMS

Plane Geometry

Let's use these formulas and the Basic Approach to solve some problems.

---

44. A circle has a diameter of 8 inches. What is the area of the circle, to the nearest 0.1 square inch?

    F. 12.6
    G. 25.1
    H. 50.3
    J. 64.0
    K. 201.1

Here's How to Crack It
Remember the Basic Approach. There's no figure, so draw your own. Once you've done that, mark it up with information from the problem, and get all your formulas down. Think CArd!

Your paper should look something like this:

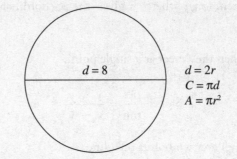

$d = 8$

$d = 2r$
$C = \pi d$
$A = \pi r^2$

Write It Down!
If there's no figure given to you, draw your own. This will allow you to better grasp what the question is asking and make sense of the provided information. See the figure to the right for an example.

Now work the formulas to get the answer. We know that the diameter of this circle is 8, which means its radius is 4. Use the radius in the Area formula, and use your calculator to find this Area:

$$A = \pi r^2$$
$$A = \pi(4)^2$$
$$A = 16\pi$$
$$A \approx 50.3$$

This matches up nicely with (H). If you don't have a calculator, or you're not especially handy with it, no problem. Use ballparking. You know that π is roughly equivalent to 3, so your answer will need to be close to 16×3 or 48. Only (H) is close enough.

○

Coordinate Geometry

Let's try a Coordinate Geometry problem. ACT likes to make a big deal about the distinction between Plane and Coordinate Geometry, but as we'll see, your approach won't really differ at all.

○

23. In the standard (x,y) coordinate plane, point G lies at $(-3,-4)$, and point H lies at $(2,5)$. What is the length of $\overline{GH}$ in coordinate units?

A. 7

B. 4

C. $\sqrt{14}$

D. $\sqrt{45}$

E. $\sqrt{106}$

Here's How to Crack It

Your first impulse here will probably be to whip out the distance formula and complete this problem in lightning-fast time. The only problem is that the distance formula looks like this:

$$d = \sqrt{(x_2 - x_1)^2 + (y_2 - y_1)^2}$$

Yikes. If you've got this formula stored away in the RAM of your brain, great. Unfortunately, for most of us, this is a really easy formula to forget, or worse, to remember incorrectly. What you'll find about ACT Geometry is that for 90% of the problems, you're best off just dealing with the basics. For weird shapes in Plane Geometry, this will mean carving things up into recognizable shapes and working from there. On Coordinate Geometry, you will find that simple formulas and the Basic Approach can get you plenty of points.

Let's use the Basic Approach. First and foremost, this is a Geometry problem, and they haven't given you a figure. Draw your own. It should look something like this:

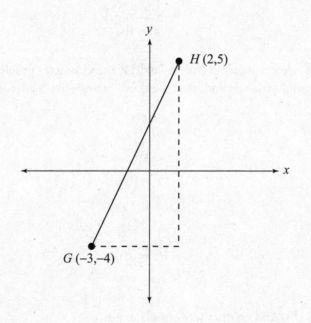

Now, look carefully at the line you've drawn for $\overline{GH}$. Remind you of anything? How about the hypotenuse of a right triangle? Remember, you want to work with the basics, and you know your triangles, so let's turn this thing into a right triangle.

Draw in the sides and find the lengths of those sides. To find the base of the triangle, figure out how much you're moving from one *x*-coordinate to the other. The points are (–3,–4) and (2,5), so the *x*-coordinate will go from –3 to 2, or 5 units. The *y*-coordinate will go from –4 to 5, or 9 units. After you've drawn all this in and marked up your figure, you should have something like this:

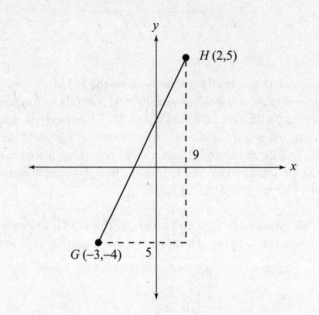

And now this is just a plain old ("plane" old?) Plane Geometry problem. You know two sides of a right triangle and need the third. Sounds like a job for the Pythagorean theorem.

$$a^2 + b^2 = c^2$$
$$(5)^2 + (9)^2 = \left(\overline{GH}\right)^2$$
$$\left(\overline{GH}\right)^2 = 25 + 81$$
$$\left(\overline{GH}\right)^2 = 106$$
$$\overline{GH} = \sqrt{106}$$

The answer is (E). And no distance formula required.

Trigonometry

There's a common misconception about the ACT regarding Trigonometry. Many believe that if you don't have a solid foundation in Trigonometry, you can't get a good score on the ACT Math test. However, let's think back to the chart from the beginning of this lesson. Remember, there are only 4 trig questions on any given ACT.

What's more, two of these questions will deal with basic SOHCAHTOA, which you clearly don't need a whole semester or year of trig to learn. The other two questions may deal with radians, or the unit circle, or some of the trig identities, but you shouldn't worry about these until you've solidified a math score of at least 28.

So let's have a look at one of these basic SOHCAHTOA questions.

Trig Tip

Don't worry about Advanced Trigonometry concepts unless you are consistently scoring a 28 or higher on the ACT Math test. It's way too much to learn for only two questions!

42. According to the measurements given in the figure below, which of the following expressions gives the distance, in meters, from the house to the garage?

    F. 40 tan 38°

    G. 40 cos 38°

    H. 40 sin 38°

    J. $\dfrac{40}{\cos 38°}$

    K. $\dfrac{40}{\sin 38°}$

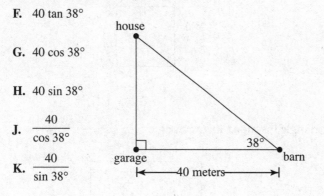

Here's How to Crack It

They've already written most of the information you'll need on the figure, but it can be worth noting the side that you are looking for: the side that shows the distance from the house to the garage.

Let the answer choices help. These choices tell you a lot more than you may think: First of all, they offer the main indication that this will be a SOHCAHTOA problem by showing that you will need to choose sine, cosine, or tangent. Next, they tell you that you'll only be dealing with one angle, the 38° one. Finally, they tell you that you won't need to do any weird rounding with decimals because they just want the sine, cosine, or tangent expression.

Have a close look at the sides you're dealing with. Where are they relative to the 38° angle? The base of the triangle is touching the 38° angle, so it's *adjacent*, and the side you're looking for is *opposite* the 38° angle. It looks like we won't be dealing with the *hypotenuse* at all. So which trig function deals with the *opposite* and *adjacent* sides? Remember SOHCAHTOA. The function we'll need is tangent. And don't do more work than you need to. Only (F) offers an expression featuring the tangent function, so it must be the correct answer.

Shapes Within Shapes: What's the Link?

ACT's favorite way to ask hard Geometry questions is to put shapes within shapes. You know the drill: Some shape inscribed in some other shape, or two shapes share a common side. They've got all kinds of ways to ask these questions. But when you see a shape drawn within another shape, there's usually one question that will blow the question wide open: *What's the link between the two shapes?* Let's try a few.

1. A square inscribed in a circle

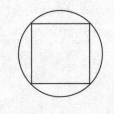

2. A triangle inscribed in a rectangle

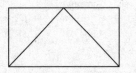

3. A square overlapping with a circle

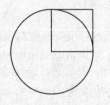

So, what's the link?

1. What's the link? The diagonal of the square is the diameter of the circle.

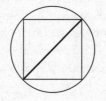

2. What's the link? The base of the triangle is the long side of the rect-angle, and the height of the triangle is the short side of the rectangle.

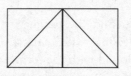

3. What's the link? The side of the square is equivalent to the radius of the circle.

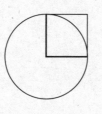

Let's try a problem that deals with these concepts.

37. In the square shown below, points E and F are the midpoints of sides $\overline{AB}$ and $\overline{CD}$, respectively. Two semicircles are drawn with centers E and F. What is the perimeter, in feet, of the shaded region?

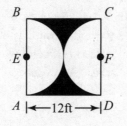

A. $12 + 12\pi$
B. $24 + 12\pi$
C. $24 + 24\pi$
D. $48 + 12\pi$
E. $48 + 24\pi$

Here's How to Crack It

Make sure you write everything you need on the figure, including the relevant square and circle formulas. Since you are dealing with shapes within shapes, now is also a good time to figure out what the link is, what these two (or three, in this case) shapes have in common. Don't worry about digging up a formula for the perimeter of that hourglass-shaped thing. Stick with the shapes you know.

For this problem, the links occur on the right and left sides of the figure: The left and right sides of the square are the same as the diameters of each of the semi-circles. We can therefore say that if all sides of a square are equal, each of these sides is 12. Since the diameter of each semicircle is equivalent to a side of the square, then the diameters of both semicircles must also be 12.

Let's use this information to find the perimeters of each of these semicircles. Remember, when you're dealing with circles, the perimeter is called the *circumference*, which can be found with the formula $C = \pi d$. Since you're dealing with a semi-circle here, you'll need to divide its circumference in half. Let's find the circumference of the semicircle with center E.

$$\frac{C_E}{2} = \frac{\pi d}{2}$$
$$= \frac{\pi(12)}{2}$$
$$= 6\pi$$

The semicircle with center F will have the same circumference because it has the same diameter. Now all we need to do is add up our perimeters to find our answer. You know the sides of the square will each be 12 and the circumference of each semicircle will be 6π, so the total perimeter of the shaded region will be $12 + 12 + 6\pi + 6\pi = 24 + 12\pi$, as in (B).

So let's hear it once more:

> Don't do more work than you have to on Geometry problems by trying to remember every weird formula you've ever learned. Stick to the formulas you know, and work with the Basic Approach.

Now go ahead and give some of these concepts a try in the following drills.

GEOMETRY DRILL 1

Plane Geometry

8. In the figure below, $\overline{AB} \parallel \overline{CD}$. What is the value of y?

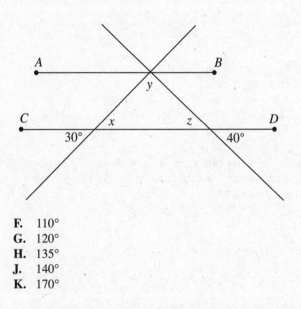

F. 110°
G. 120°
H. 135°
J. 140°
K. 170°

14. The 8-sided figure below is divided into 6 congruent squares. The total area of the 6 squares is 96 square centimeters. What is the perimeter, in centimeters, of the figure?

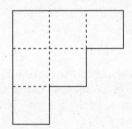

F. 16
G. 28
H. 48
J. 56
K. 96

22. The base of triangle M is four times the base of triangle N, while the height of triangle N is half the height of triangle M. The area of triangle M is how many times that of triangle N?

F. 2
G. 4
H. 8
J. 10
K. 16

26. A rectangular horse corral is built along one side of a square barn whose area is 5,776 square feet. The length of the corral is the same as the length of the side of the barn, while the width of the corral is one-fourth the length of the side of the barn. What is the area of the horse corral, in square feet?

F. 76
G. 1,016
H. 1,284
J. 1,444
K. 5,776

27. In right triangle $\triangle FHK$ below, $\overline{GJ}$ is parallel to $\overline{FK}$, and $\overline{GJ}$ is perpendicular to $\overline{HK}$ at J. The length of $\overline{HK}$ is 12 inches, the length of $\overline{GJ}$ is 6 inches, and the length of $\overline{GH}$ is 10 inches. What is the length, in inches, of $\overline{FK}$?

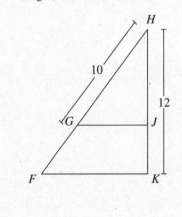

A. 7
B. 8
C. 9
D. 10
E. 11

30. The diameter of circle *A* is twice that of circle *B*. If the area of circle *A* is 36π, then what is the circumference of circle *B* ?

F.   π
G.   3π
H.   6π
J.   9π
K.   18π

36. In the figure below, the distance from *A* to *B* is $\frac{1}{3}$ the distance from *B* to *C*. The area of △*BDE* is what fraction of the area of rectangle *ACDE* ?

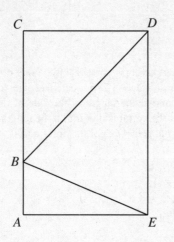

F. $\frac{1}{6}$

G. $\frac{1}{3}$

H. $\frac{1}{2}$

J. $\frac{3}{5}$

K. $\frac{2}{3}$

39. The circle with center *E* is inscribed in square *ABCD* as shown in the figure below. If line $\overline{AC}$ (not shown) has a length of $8\sqrt{2}$, then what is the area of the circle?

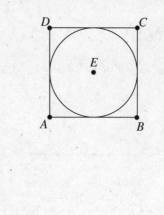

A.   π
B.   4π
C.   8π
D.   12π
E.   16π

48. In the figure below, the circle with center *X* has a radius of 8 centimeters, and the measure of ∠*SRX* is 70°. What is the measure of $\overline{RS}$?

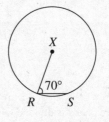

F.   20°
G.   40°
H.   50°
J.   55°
K.   70°

54. The side of an equilateral triangle is *s* inches longer than the side of a second equilateral triangle. How many inches longer is the altitude of the first triangle than the altitude of the second triangle?

F. $\frac{\sqrt{3}}{2}s$

G. $\sqrt{2}s$

H.   2*s*

J.   3*s*

K.   *s*³

55. In the figure below, the circles' centers at N and O intersect at X and Y, and points $N, X, Y,$ and O are collinear. The lengths of $\overline{MN}, \overline{OP},$ and $\overline{XY}$ are 10, 8, and 3 inches, respectively. What is the length, in inches, of $\overline{NO}$?

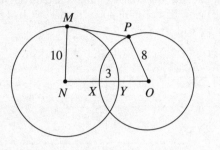

- **A.** 10
- **B.** 11
- **C.** 12
- **D.** 15
- **E.** 18

57. The five semicircles in the figure below touch only at their corners. If the distance from A to F along the diameters of the semicircles is 60 inches, what is the distance, in inches, from F to A along the arcs of these semicircles?

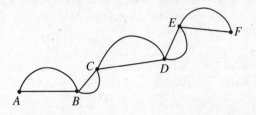

- **A.** 30π
- **B.** 40π
- **C.** 60π
- **D.** 72π
- **E.** 90π

Coordinate Geometry

3. A point at (5,–4) in the standard (*x*,*y*) coordinate plane is shifted left 3 units and up 6 units. What are the new coordinates of the point?

   A. (11, 7)
   B. (8, 2)
   C. (8,10)
   D. (2, 2)
   E. (2,10)

13. The points $A(-6,8)$ and $B(10,2)$ lie in the standard (*x*,*y*) coordinate plane. What is the midpoint of $\overline{AB}$?

   A. (–3, 4)
   B. (2, 5)
   C. (4,10)
   D. (5, 1)
   E. (8,–3)

19. What is the *x*-intercept of the line $y = 5x + 2$?

   A. $\left(0, -\dfrac{2}{5}\right)$

   B. $\left(0, \dfrac{2}{5}\right)$

   C. $(2, \ \ 0)$

   D. $\left(\dfrac{2}{5}, \ 0\right)$

   E. $\left(-\dfrac{2}{5}, 0\right)$

24. Points $O(5,3)$ and $P(-3,8)$ lie in the standard (*x*,*y*) coordinate plane. What is the slope of a line that is perpendicular to line of $\overline{OP}$?

   F. $-\dfrac{8}{5}$

   G. $-\dfrac{5}{8}$

   H. $\dfrac{5}{8}$

   J. 1

   K. $\dfrac{8}{5}$

33. What are the quadrants of the standard (*x*,*y*) coordinate plane below that contain points on the graph of the equation $8x + 4y = 12$?

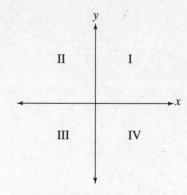

Quadrants of the standard
(*x*,*y*) coordinate plane

   A. II and IV only
   B. I, II, and III only
   C. I, II, and IV only
   D. I, III, and IV only
   E. II, III, and IV only

39. On a map in the standard (*x*,*y*) coordinate plane, the cities of Everton and Springfield are represented by the points (–3,–5) and (–6,–8), respectively. Each unit on the map represents an actual distance of 20 kilometers. Which of the following is closest to the distance, in kilometers, between these 2 cities?

   A. 316
   B. 120
   C. 85
   D. 60
   E. 49

41. The figure below shows the graph in the standard (x,y) coordinate plane of one of the following functions. Which function is shown?

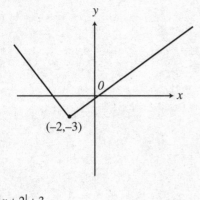

A. $y = |x+2| + 3$

B. $y = |x-2| - 3$

C. $y = |x+2| - 3$

D. $y = |x+3| - 2$

E. $y = |x-3| + 2$

47. The figure below shows the graph of line ℓ in the standard (x,y) coordinate plane. Which of the following could be the equation of line ℓ ?

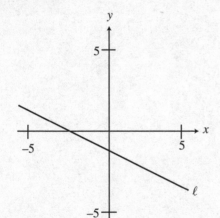

A. $y = -\dfrac{5}{2}x - 1$

B. $y = \dfrac{5}{2}x + 1$

C. $y = -\dfrac{2}{5}x - 1$

D. $y = -\dfrac{2}{5}x + 1$

E. $y = \dfrac{2}{5}x - 1$

48. The graph of $f(x) = x^3$ is shown in the standard (x,y) coordinate plane below. For which of the following equations is the graph of the cubic function shifted 4 units to the left and 3 units up?

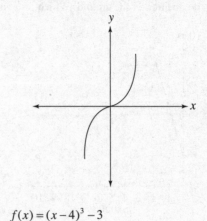

F. $f(x) = (x-4)^3 - 3$

G. $f(x) = (x-4)^3 + 3$

H. $f(x) = (x+3)^3 - 4$

J. $f(x) = (x+4)^3 + 3$

K. $f(x) = (x+4)^3 - 3$

50. If a circle in the standard (x,y) coordinate plane has the equation $(x+3)^2 + (y-5)^2 = 16$, then which of the following points represents the center of the circle?

F. $(-5,\ 3)$

G. $(-3,-5)$

H. $(\ 3,\ 5)$

J. $(-5,-3)$

K. $(-3,\ 5)$

56. The graph below shows the distance a hot-air balloon is from the ground for a period of 10 minutes. A certain order of 3 of the following 5 actions describes the balloon's movement in relation to the position of the ground. Which order is it?

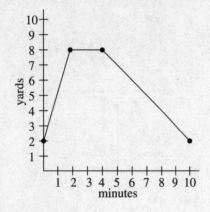

I.   Remains stationary for 2 minutes
II. Moves away at 3 yards per minute
III. Moves toward at 3 yards per minute
IV. Moves away at 1 yard per minute
V.   Moves toward at 1 yard per minute

F. I, II, II
G. II, I, V
H. III, I, IV
J. IV, I, III
K. V, I, II

Trigonometry

21. In right triangle $\triangle LMN$ below, $\sin L = \dfrac{3}{8}$. Which of the following expressions is equal to $\sin M$?

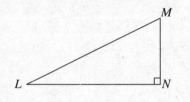

A. $\dfrac{8}{3}$

B. $\dfrac{\sqrt{73}}{3}$

C. $\dfrac{\sqrt{55}}{3}$

D. $\dfrac{\sqrt{73}}{8}$

E. $\dfrac{\sqrt{55}}{8}$

23. In isosceles right triangle ABC (not shown), $\overline{AB} = \overline{AC} = 3$. Which of the following represents the value of $\cos \angle ABC$?

A. $\dfrac{\sqrt{2}}{2}$

B. $\dfrac{\sqrt{3}}{2}$

C. $\sqrt{2}$

D. $\sqrt{3}$

E. 2

25. A painter leans a 10-foot ladder against a wall at an angle of $65°$ relative to the ground. How far away from the wall is the base of the ladder?

A. $10 \tan 65°$

B. $10 \sin 65°$

C. $10 \cos 65°$

D. $\dfrac{10}{\sin 65°}$

E. $\dfrac{10}{\cos 65°}$

29. For the polygon below, which of the following represents the length, in inches, of $\overline{FK}$?

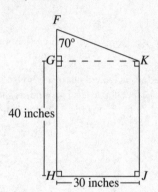

A. 10

B. 30

C. $\dfrac{10}{\sin 70°}$

D. $\dfrac{30}{\sin 70°}$

E. $\sin 70°$

35. A right triangle is shown in the figure below. Which of the following expressions gives θ ?

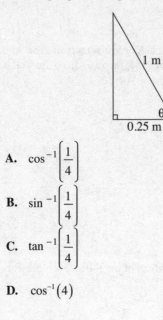

A. $\cos^{-1}\left(\dfrac{1}{4}\right)$

B. $\sin^{-1}\left(\dfrac{1}{4}\right)$

C. $\tan^{-1}\left(\dfrac{1}{4}\right)$

D. $\cos^{-1}(4)$

E. $\tan^{-1}(4)$

37. A straight ladder is leaned against a house so that the top of the ladder is 12 feet above level ground, as shown in the figure below. Which of the following gives the length, in feet, of the ladder?

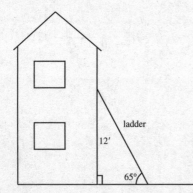

A. $x = 12\cos 65°$

B. $x = 12\sin 65°$

C. $x = \dfrac{12}{\cos 65°}$

D. $x = \dfrac{12}{\sin 65°}$

E. $x = \dfrac{12}{\tan 65°}$

53. In $\triangle XYZ$, the measure of $\angle X$ is 57°, the measure of $\angle Y$ is 72°, and the length of $\overline{XZ}$ is 12 inches. Which of the following is an expression for the length, in inches, of $\overline{YZ}$?

(Note: The law of sines states that for any triangle, the ratios of the lengths of the sides to the sines of the angles opposite those sides are equal.)

A. $\dfrac{\sin 57°}{12\sin 72°}$

B. $\dfrac{\sin 72°}{12\sin 57°}$

C. $\dfrac{12\sin 72°}{\sin 57°}$

D. $\dfrac{12\sin 57°}{\sin 72°}$

E. $\dfrac{(\sin 57°)\,(\sin 72°)}{12}$

56. If $\cos\theta = \dfrac{3}{4}$ and $0 < \theta < \dfrac{\pi}{2}$, which of the following is equal to $\sin\theta\tan\theta$?

F. $\dfrac{7}{12}$

G. $\dfrac{4}{3\sqrt{7}}$

H. $\dfrac{4}{3}$

J. $\dfrac{4\sqrt{7}}{3}$

K. $\dfrac{12}{7}$

58. The angle in the standard (x,y) coordinate plane shown below has its vertex at the origin. One side of this angle includes the positive x-axis, and the other side with measure θ passes through $(-12,5)$. What is the sine of θ ?

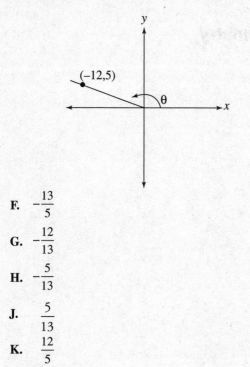

F. $-\dfrac{13}{5}$

G. $-\dfrac{12}{13}$

H. $-\dfrac{5}{13}$

J. $\dfrac{5}{13}$

K. $\dfrac{12}{5}$

59. The domain of the function $f(x) = 4\sin(3x - 1) + 2$ is all real numbers. Which of the following is the range of the function $f(x)$?

A. $-4 \le f(x) \le 4$

B. $-6 \le f(x) \le 2$

C. $-5 \le f(x) \le 3$

D. $-2 \le f(x) \le 6$

E. All real numbers

GEOMETRY DRILL 1 ANSWER KEY

Plane Geometry

8. F
14. H
22. H
26. J
27. C
30. H
36. H
39. E
48. G
54. F
55. D
57. A

Coordinate Geometry

3. D
13. B
19. E
24. K
33. C
39. C
41. C
47. C
48. J
50. K
56. G

Trigonometry

21. E
23. A
25. C
29. D
35. A
37. D
53. D
56. F
58. J
59. D

GEOMETRY DRILL 1 EXPLANATIONS

Plane Geometry

8. **F** According to the figure, the angle opposite x is 30°, so $x = 30$. Similarly, the angle across from z is 40°, so $z = 40$. Since x, y, and z form a triangle, the sum of these three angles must be 180°. The value of y is therefore $180 - 30 - 40 = 110°$, which is (F).

14. **H** Since the area of the six congruent squares is 96, the area of each square is $\frac{96}{6} = 16$. It might be tempting to select (F) here, but remember you're looking for the perimeter of the entire figure, not the area of each square. The area of a square is equal to s^2, so the length of the side of each square is $\sqrt{16} = 4$. The perimeter of the figure consists of 12 sides of congruent squares, so the perimeter is $12 \times 4 = 48$. Choice (G) confuses the sides of the square with the sides of the figure. Choice (J) misuses the fact that the figure is 8-sided; (K) finds the perimeter if all 4 sides of the 6 squares were exposed.

22. **H** This question can be approached algebraically or by plugging in your own numbers. If you plug in some small numbers for the base and height of triangle N, such as 2 and 3, respectively, the base and height of triangle M would then be four times as big and twice as big, or 8 and 6, respectively. The area of triangle M would be $\frac{1}{2}bh = \frac{1}{2}(8)(6) = 24$, while the area of triangle N would be $\frac{1}{2}bh = \frac{1}{2}(2)(3) = 3$. Triangle M is therefore 8 times larger than triangle N, which is (H).

26. **J** If the area of the barn is 5,776 square feet, you can take the square root of that number on your calculator to determine that the sides of the barn have a length of 76 feet. This is also the length of the corral. The width of the corral is one-fourth its length, so $\frac{76}{4} = 19$ feet. The area of the corral is thus $76 \times 19 = 1,444$ square feet, so (J) is the answer.

27. **C** Given $\overline{GJ}$ is parallel to $\overline{FK}$, $\triangle FHK$ and $\triangle GHJ$ are similar triangles, so they have proportional sides. $\triangle GHJ$ is a right triangle, so you can either use the Pythagorean theorem or identify the sides as the Pythagorean triplet 6:8:10 to determine $\overline{HJ}$ is 10. Then set up the proportion $\frac{\overline{FK}}{\overline{GJ}} = \frac{\overline{HK}}{\overline{HJ}}$ to determine $\overline{FK}$: $\frac{\overline{FK}}{6} = \frac{12}{8}$, so $\overline{FK}$ is 9 inches.

30. **H**   If the area of circle A is 36π, and the area of any circle is πr^2, then the radius of circle A must be 6. The diameter of circle A is therefore 12, and the diameter of circle B is half that, or 6. The circumference of any circle is $2\pi r$ or πd, so the circumference of circle B is 6π. Choice (H) is correct.

36. **H**   Plug in some numbers for the sides of the rectangle. Let's say $AB = 2$. Since AB is $\frac{1}{3}$ of BC, $BC = 6$, and $AC = DE = 8$. There are no restrictions on AE, so let's say $AE = CD = 3$. The area of $ACDE =$ $(8)(3) = 24$. To find the area of $\triangle BCD$, subtract the areas of triangles ABE and CBD. The area of $ABE = \frac{1}{2}(3)(2) = 3$, and the area of $CBD = \frac{1}{2}(3)(6) = 9$, so the area of $BDE = 24 - (3 + 9) = 12$. Therefore, BDE is $\frac{1}{2}$ the area of $ACDE$.

39. **E**   If the length of $\overline{AC}$ is $8\sqrt{2}$, then the sides of the square must be 8 (splitting a square in half gives you two 45-45-90 triangles with ratios $1{:}1{:}\sqrt{2}$). The radius of the circle is half the length of the side of the square, so the radius is 4. The area of the circle is $\pi r^2 = \pi(4^2) = 16\pi$. Therefore, the answer is (E).

48. **G**   Both $\overline{RX}$ and $\overline{SX}$ are radii of the circle, making them congruent. The triangle $\triangle RSX$, therefore, is isosceles, and $\angle SRX$ and $\angle RSX$ are congruent, each measuring 70°. The third angle $\angle RSX$ $= 180° - 2(70°) = 40°$ and is equal to the measure of $\overparen{RS}$. Choices (J) and (K) make the incorrect pair of angles congruent.

54. **F**   Plug in values for the sides of the triangles: Triangle 1 can have a side length of 8 and triangle 2 can have a side length of 6, making $s = 2$. Equilateral triangles can be split into two 30-60-90 triangles, thus their altitudes are $\frac{1}{2}$(side length)$\times\sqrt{3}$. Triangle 1's altitude is $4\sqrt{3}$, and triangle 2's altitude is $3\sqrt{3}$, making the answer $4\sqrt{3} - 3\sqrt{3} = \sqrt{3}$. Choice (G) confuses 30-60-90 with 45-45-90, and (H), (J), and (K) do not have a $\sqrt{3}$.

55. **D** $\overline{MN}$ and $\overline{OP}$ are the radii of their respective circles, so the radius $\overline{NY}$ of circle N is 10 inches, and radius $\overline{OP}$ of circle O is 8 inches. Given $\overline{XY}$ is 3 inches long, $\overline{NX}$ is $10 - 3 = 7$ inches and $\overline{OY}$ is $8 - 3 = 5$ inches. Adding the three segments $\overline{NX}$, $\overline{XY}$, and $\overline{OY}$, the length of $\overline{NO}$ is $7 + 3 + 5 = 15$ inches. Choices (A) and (B) are too small, (C) calculates the length with $\overline{XY}$, and (E) doesn't consider the radii overlapping in $\overline{XY}$.

57. **A**   The problem gives us no information about the relative lengths of the different diameters, so it must not matter, and the easiest thing to do is to make them all the same. There are five diameters, so $\frac{60}{5} = 12$. A circle with diameter 12 has a circumference of 12π, so a semicircle with diameter 12 will have a length of $\frac{1}{2}(12\pi) = 6\pi$. There are 5 semicircles, so the total distance from F to A along the semicircles is $(5)(6\pi) = 30\pi$.

Coordinate Geometry

3. **D**   To shift left, subtract from the x-coordinate: $5 - 3 = 2$; to shift up, add to the y-coordinate: $-4 + 6 = 2$. Choice (A) confuses the x- and y-coordinates, and (B), (C), and (E) confuse the addition and subtraction.

13. **B**   The coordinates for midpoint are the averages of the endpoints: $\left(\dfrac{x_1 + x_2}{2}, \dfrac{y_1 + y_2}{2}\right)$. For segment $\overline{AB}$, the midpoint is at $\dfrac{-6 + 10}{2} = 2, \dfrac{8 + 2}{2} = 5$. Choices (A) and (D) incorrectly take half the coordinate of one of the endpoints. Choice (C) adds, rather than averages, the endpoints. Choice (E) subtracts, rather than adds, the endpoint coordinates.

19. **E**   The x-intercept is the point at which a line crosses the x-axis, so the y-value of that point will always be 0. Plug in 0 for the y in the equation, and solve for x: $0 = 5x + 2 \rightarrow -2 = 5x \rightarrow -\dfrac{2}{5} = x$. The x-intercept is thus $\left(-\dfrac{2}{5}, 0\right)$, which is (E).

24. **K**   Use the point-slope formula to determine the slope of line $\overline{OP}$: $\dfrac{y_2 - y_1}{x_2 - x_1} = \dfrac{8 - 3}{-3 - 5} = -\dfrac{5}{8}$. The slope of a line perpendicular to this one will have a negative reciprocal slope: $\dfrac{8}{5}$, so (K) is correct.

33. **C**   To determine the graph of the equation, you must isolate the y by subtracting $8x$ and dividing by 4. The resulting equation is $y = -2x + 3$, which is a line with a slope of -2 and a y-intercept of 3. Because the y-intercept is positive, the line crosses the y-axis from Quadrant II to Quadrant I and extends into Quadrant IV. The line never passes through Quadrant III, eliminating (B), (D), and (E). Choice (A) is a partial answer and does not include Quadrant I. Alternatively, once the equation is in slope-intercept form, just plug it into your graphing calculator and look at the graph.

39. **C**   Find the distance between the points using the distance formula: $d = \sqrt{(x_1 - x_2)^2 + (y_1 - y_2)^2} = \sqrt{[(-3) - (-6)]^2 + [(-5) - (-8)]^2} = \sqrt{(3)^2 + (3^2)} = \sqrt{18} = 3\sqrt{2}$. Multiply the coordinate distance by 20 to get the distance in kilometers. Choices (A) and (E) incorrectly calculate the distance by adding the coordinates and forgetting to square the differences, respectively. Choices (B) and (D) result when the distance formula is not used. If you have trouble remembering the distance formula, sketch a figure, and use the Pythagorean theorem as detailed in the introductory chapter.

41. **C**   The correct answer is (C). There are two good ways to solve this question. Even if you don't know anything about absolute value questions, you can still get this right by plugging the given point into the answer choices. Here's what you get:

A. $-3 = |-2+2| + 3$, which simplifies to $-3 = 3$. Incorrect.

B. $-3 = |-2-2| - 3$, which simplifies to $-3 = 1$. Incorrect.

C. $-3 = |-2+2| - 3$, which simplifies to $-3 = -3$. **Correct.**

D. $-3 = |-2+3| - 2$, which simplifies to $-3 = -1$. Incorrect.

E. $-3 = |-2-3| + 2$, which simplifies to $-3 = 7$. Incorrect.

A slightly faster way to do this question is to memorize the basic form of an absolute value equation. For the equation $y = |x - a| + b$, the vertex is (a, b). Plugging the vertex $(-2, -3)$ into this formula gives us $y = |x - (-2)| - 3$, which simplifies to $y = |x + 2| - 3$.

47. **C**   This question is best done with POE and a little bit of ballparking. First, deal with the y-intercept. Since the line crosses the y-axis below the origin, the y-intercept must be negative, so eliminate (B) and (D). Next, deal with the sign of the slope. A line that slopes down from left to right has a negative slope, so eliminate (E). Finally, decide whether the numerator is more or less than the denominator. Remember, slope is rise over run. The total run of this line (distance from left to right) is 10, but the rise is considerably less than that, so the numerator must be less than the denominator. Eliminate (A), leaving only (C).

48. **J**   For any function $f(x + h) + k$, h indicates horizontal shifts, and k indicates vertical shifts. Because the horizontal shift is 4, not 3, you can eliminate (H). A negative h indicates a shift right, not left, eliminating (F) and (G). A negative k indicates a shift down, not up, eliminating (K).

50. **K**   The standard equation for a circle is $(x - h)^2 + (y - k)^2 = r^2$, where the center of the circle is the point (h, k). Therefore, the center of this circle is at the point $(-3, 5)$, which makes (K) the correct answer.

56. **G**   The balloon remains stationary in the middle stage, so action (I) should be second in the order of events, eliminating (F). In the first stage, the graph is increasing, which means the distance between the balloon and the ground increases, so the balloon is moving away, eliminating (H) and (K). The rate of increase is greater than the rate of decrease in the third stage, so (J) is incorrect. Only (G) gives the correct actions in the correct order.

Trigonometry

21. **E** Draw a triangle and use SOHCAHTOA to label the known sides: leg $\overline{MN}$ is 3, and hypotenuse $\overline{LM}$ is 8. Use the Pythagorean theorem to determine the third side: $\overline{LN}^2 + 3^2 = 8^2$, so $\overline{LN} = \sqrt{55}$, eliminating (B) and (D). Since $\sin = \dfrac{\text{opposite}}{\text{adjacent}}$, $\sin M = \dfrac{\overline{LN}}{\overline{LM}} = \dfrac{\sqrt{55}}{8}$. Choice (A) gives cos M, and (C) gives tan M.

23. **A** Since no diagram is provided, make your own. The triangle will look something like this:

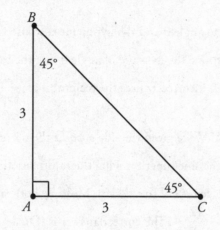

You can solve this question on your calculator, but that will give you a decimal. Based on the formatting of the answer choices, it is easier to figure out the length of $\overline{BC}$. Because this is a 45-45-90 triangle with ratios $1:1:\sqrt{2}$, $\overline{BC}$ is $3\sqrt{2}$. Since cosine is defined as $\dfrac{\text{adjacent}}{\text{hypotenuse}}$, $\cos \angle ABC = \dfrac{3}{3\sqrt{2}}$, which simplifies to $\dfrac{\sqrt{2}}{2}$. Therefore, (A) is correct.

25. **C** Since no diagram is provided, make your own. The figure will look something like this:

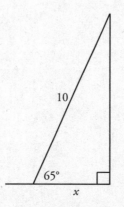

Since you are looking for the distance between the base of the ladder and the wall, represented by x, you are dealing with the side that is adjacent to the 65° angle as well as the hypotenuse. Since cosine is defined as $\frac{\text{adjacent}}{\text{hypotenuse}}$, $\cos 65 = \frac{x}{10}$. Multiply both sides by 10 to get $x = 10 \cos 65$, which is (C).

29. **D** Because quadrilateral *GHJK* has four right angles, it is a rectangle, and $\overline{GK}$ measures 30 inches. We must use SOHCAHTOA to determine the side lengths of right triangle *FGK*, eliminating (A) and (B). Since we know the measure of $\angle F$, use SOH: $\sin 70° = \frac{30}{FK}$, which rearranges to give $\overline{FK} = \frac{30}{\sin 70°}$.

35. **A** We know the side adjacent to angle θ and the hypotenuse, so use CAH to set up the problem: $\cos \theta = \frac{0.25}{1} = \frac{1}{4}$. To determine the measure of angle θ, use the inverse function $\cos^{-1}$, eliminating (B), (C), and (E). Choice (D) incorrectly uses the reciprocal of $\frac{\text{adjacent}}{\text{hypotenuse}}$.

37. **D** Remember SOHCAHTOA! We're given the side *opposite* the 65° angle, and we want to find the *hypotenuse*, so we need the sine function. Plug the information you have into the function: $\sin 65° = \frac{12}{x}$ (where x is the length of the ladder). Multiply both sides by x to get $x \sin 65° = 12$. Then divide by $\sin 65°$ to get $x = \frac{12}{\sin 65°}$. The correct answer is (D).

53. **D** Draw the triangle to determine that side $\overline{YZ}$ is opposite $\angle X$, and side $\overline{XZ}$ is opposite $\angle Y$. Using the law of sines, set up the proportion: $\frac{12 \text{ inches}}{\sin 72°} = \frac{\overline{YZ}}{\sin 57°}$. Multiply both sides by $\sin 57°$ to get $\overline{YZ} = \frac{12 \sin 57°}{\sin 72°}$. Choice (C) does not use the correct angle-side pairs, and (A), (B), and (E) use the incorrect proportions.

56. F The correct answer is (F). We can use SOHCAHTOA and a right triangle to defeat this seemingly hard problem. Draw a right triangle and mark in angle θ. If $\cos\theta = \dfrac{3}{4}$, that means the adjacent side is 3, and the hypotenuse is 4. Now use the Pythagorean theorem to find the third side: $3^2 + b^2 = 4^2$, so $9 + b^2 = 16$, which simplifies to $b^2 = 7$ and finally to $b = \sqrt{7}$. Your sketch should look something like this:

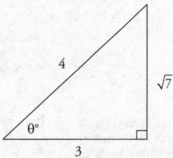

Now just plug your dimensions into the functions: $\sin\theta\tan\theta = \dfrac{\sqrt{7}}{4} \cdot \dfrac{\sqrt{7}}{4} = \dfrac{7}{12}$.

58. J In the standard (x,y) coordinate plane, the sine of an angle in Quadrant II is always positive, eliminating (F), (G), and (H). Make a right triangle with the x-axis, which gives you a 5-12-13 triangle. The angle θ is at the origin, so the leg opposite the angle is 5 and the hypotenuse is 13. Sine is defined as "opposite over hypotenuse," which in this case gives $\dfrac{5}{13}$, so the answer is (J).

59. D The range of $\sin x$ is normally between -1 to 1, inclusive; however, the range can change depending on the graph's amplitude and vertical shift. In the general form $A\sin(Bx + C) + D$, amplitude is indicated by A, vertical shift is indicated by D, and the range is between $-A + D$ and $A + D$. The range for this function, therefore, is $-4 + 2 \leq f(x) \leq 4 + 2$. Choice (A) neglects the vertical shift of the graph; (B) subtracts rather than adding the vertical shift of $+D$; (C) uses the horizontal rather than vertical shift value; and (E) gives the domain, not the range of the function.

GEOMETRY DRILL 2

Plane Geometry

7. What is the perimeter, in meters, of a parallelogram with side lengths of 12 m and 10 m ?

   A. 22
   B. 44
   C. 48
   D. 60
   E. 120

15. Kayla is mowing her lawn and the lawn of her neighbor. She discovers that the two lawns have the same area. Her lawn is a triangle with a base of 90 feet, and the height of the triangle is 80 feet. If her neighbor's lawn is a square, what is the length, in feet, of a side of the square?

   A. $\sqrt{170}$
   B. 30
   C. 60
   D. 170
   E. 240

17. In the figure below, parallel lines M_1 and M_2 intersect transversal l. What is the value of $x + y$?

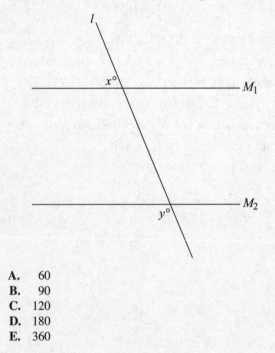

   A. 60
   B. 90
   C. 120
   D. 180
   E. 360

18. Brandie bought a few cans of paint, and each can contains enough paint to cover 300 square meters. She is painting a triangular mural on a wall that is 6 meters tall. She opens 1 can of paint and starts painting. Before Brandie needs to open another can of paint, she can paint a triangle that is the height of the wall and is how many meters long?

   F. 6
   G. 50
   H. 100
   J. 294
   K. 1,800

27. The ratio of the lengths of corresponding sides of 2 similar isosceles triangles is 3:5. One of the equal sides in the larger isosceles triangle is 30 centimeters long. How many centimeters long is one of the equal sides in the smaller isosceles triangle?

   A. 18
   B. 38
   C. 45
   D. 50
   E. 90

32. The radius of a circle is 12 inches. What is the area of the circle, in square inches?

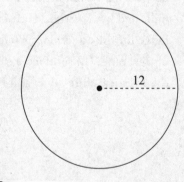

   F. 12π
   G. 24π
   H. 48π
   J. 144π
   K. 576π

35. The perimeter of an isosceles triangle is 57 centimeters, and one side measures 22 centimeters. If it can be determined, what is one possibility for the lengths, in centimeters, of the other two sides?

A. 13, 22
B. 13, 44
C. 19, 22
D. 22, 35
E. Cannot be determined from the given information

37. Triangle *XYZ* below has an area of 72 square inches. Circle *O* is tangent to the triangle at *W*, and the height of the triangle is equal in length to the base. If the line *WY* is a diameter of circle *O*, what is the area, in square inches, of the circle?

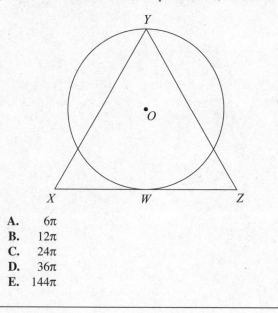

A. 6π
B. 12π
C. 24π
D. 36π
E. 144π

Use the following information to answer questions 38–40.

Shown below is a rectangular pool with a ramp leading up to one side. A water pump fills the pool at an average rate of 70 cubic yards per hour as it fills the pool. The pool is a rectangular box of length of 20 yards, width of 10 yards, and height of 3 yards. Also shown below is a ramp that leads to the top of the pool. The ramp is attached to the top of the pool and has an angle of elevation of 48°.

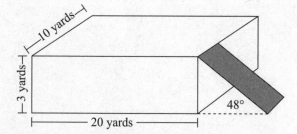

38. Which of the following is closest to the length of the ramp, to the nearest 0.1 yards?

(Note: $\sin 48° \approx 0.74$; $\cos 48° \approx 0.67$; $\tan 48° \approx 1.11$)

F. 2.7
G. 3.3
H. 3.0
J. 4.1
K. 4.5

39. The water pump starts to fill a completely empty pool and continues until the pool is completely filled. To the nearest 0.1 hours, for how many hours does the pump fill the pool with water?

A. 8.5
B. 8.6
C. 14.3
D. 103.0
E. 114.3

40. Rosie wants to build a pool that is geometrically similar to the pool shown in the figure. The new pool will have a height of $4\frac{1}{2}$ yards. What will be the length, in yards, of the longest side of the new pool?

F. 10
G. $13\frac{1}{3}$
H. 15
J. $21\frac{1}{2}$
K. 30

---

41. Triangle *ABC* shown below is isosceles, and line segment *DE* is parallel to *AC*. What is the perimeter, in inches, of the quadrilateral *ADEC* ?

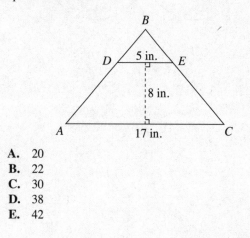

A. 20
B. 22
C. 30
D. 38
E. 42

42. A rectangular box is 20 inches high, 14 inches long, and 8 inches wide. What is the surface area, in square inches, of the rectangular box?

   F.   552
   G.   672
   H. 1,104
   J.   1,680
   K. 2,240

43. Jackie decides to draw shapes using chalk on the sidewalk. The first shape Jackie decides to draw is a rectangle. Her rectangle has a perimeter of 32 inches, and the length of the rectangle is three times its width. What is the area, in square inches, of the rectangle?

   A.   32
   B.   36
   C.   48
   D.   64
   E. 144

50. In the figure below, a table in the shape of an equilateral triangle is placed on top of 3 circular stands. The length of each side of the table is 20 inches. The stands are congruent, and each stand is tangent to the other 2 stands. Each vertex of the table lies on the center of a circle. The region that is interior to the table and exterior to all 3 stands is shaded. What is the area, to the nearest square inch, of the shaded region?

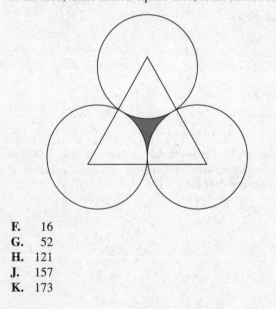

   F.   16
   G.   52
   H. 121
   J. 157
   K. 173

60. In a regular octagon, all 8 interior angles are congruent. What is the measure of each interior angle of a regular octagon?

   F.   45°
   G.   90°
   H. 108°
   J. 135°
   K. 180°

Coordinate Geometry

12. What is the slope–intercept form of $-3x - y + 7 = 0$?

   F. $y = -3x - 7$
   G. $y = -3x + 7$
   H. $y = 3x - 7$
   J. $y = 3x + 7$
   K. $y = 7x + 3$

21. What is the slope–intercept form of $6x + 2y - 4 = 12$?

   A. $y = 3x + 8$
   B. $y = 3x - 8$
   C. $y = -3x + 8$
   D. $y = -3x - 8$
   E. $y = -8x + 3$

22. What is the slope of any line perpendicular to the line $2x + 5y = -10$?

   F. $-\dfrac{5}{2}$

   G. $-\dfrac{2}{5}$

   H. $\dfrac{2}{5}$

   J. $\dfrac{1}{2}$

   K. $\dfrac{5}{2}$

23. A line in the standard (x,y) coordinate plane has equation $-5x + 3y = -9$. What is the slope of this line?

   A. -3

   B. $-\dfrac{5}{3}$

   C. $\dfrac{3}{5}$

   D. $\dfrac{5}{3}$

   E. 3

31. What is the y-coordinate of the point in the standard (x,y) coordinate plane at which the lines $y = 4x + 7$ and $y = 6x - 3$ intersect?

   A.   5
   B.   6
   C.   7
   D.   10
   E.   27

36. What is the slope of the line that passes through both of the points $(3,7)$ and $(9,11)$ in the standard (x,y) coordinate plane?

   F. $-\dfrac{3}{2}$

   G. $-\dfrac{2}{3}$

   H. $\dfrac{2}{3}$

   J. $\dfrac{3}{2}$

   K.   10

41. Which of the following equations, when graphed in the standard (x,y) coordinate plane, would cross the x-axis at $x = -3$ and $x = 5$?

   A. $y = -3(x-3)(x+5)$
   B. $y = -3(x+3)(x-5)$
   C. $y = 3(x+3)(x+5)$
   D. $y = 5(x-3)(x-5)$
   E. $y = 5(x-3)(x+5)$

Use the following information to answer questions 44–45.

The points $P(-5,6)$, $Q(-3,4)$, $R(-3,12)$, and $S(4,4)$ are shown in the standard (x,y) coordinate plane below.

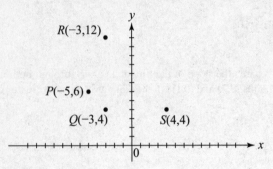

59. Which of the following equations describes a line that is parallel to a line with equation $-4x + 3y = 24$?

A. $-8x + 6y = 36$

B. $-4x - 3y = 12$

C. $-3x + 4y = 18$

D. $4x + 3y = 9$

E. $8x + 6y = 21$

44. What is the slope of $\overleftrightarrow{PR}$?

F. 3

G. $-\dfrac{2}{9}$

H. -1

J. $-\dfrac{9}{4}$

K. -4

45. What is the tangent of the smallest angle in right triangle QRS ?

A. $\dfrac{7}{15}$

B. $\dfrac{7}{\sqrt{105}}$

C. $\dfrac{8}{\sqrt{105}}$

D. $\dfrac{7}{8}$

E. $\dfrac{8}{7}$

Trigonometry

24. The right triangle shown below has a hypotenuse of 9 centimeters. The measure of the angle indicated is 78°. Which of the following is closest to the length, in centimeters, of the side opposite the 78° angle?

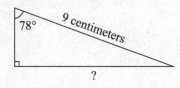

(Note: $\sin 12° \approx 0.2079$ $\sin 78° \approx 0.9781$

$\cos 12° \approx 0.9781$ $\cos 78° \approx 0.2079$

$\tan 12° \approx 0.2126$ $\tan 78° \approx 4.7046$)

- **F.** 0.978
- **G.** 1.871
- **H.** 8.800
- **J.** 8.803
- **K.** 42.342

28. Mario is standing on the ground and looking at the top of a flagpole. He knows that the flagpole is exactly 18 feet high and that $\sin \theta = \dfrac{5}{13}$, where θ is the angle indicated in the figure below. About how many feet long is the indicated distance from Mario on the ground to the top of the flagpole?

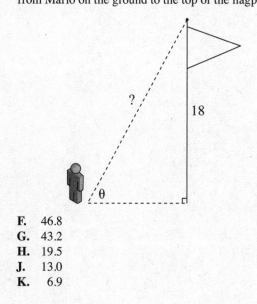

- **F.** 46.8
- **G.** 43.2
- **H.** 19.5
- **J.** 13.0
- **K.** 6.9

35. A right triangle is given in the figure below. Which of the following expressions gives θ ?

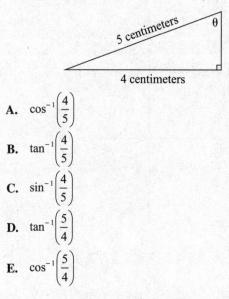

- **A.** $\cos^{-1}\left(\dfrac{4}{5}\right)$
- **B.** $\tan^{-1}\left(\dfrac{4}{5}\right)$
- **C.** $\sin^{-1}\left(\dfrac{4}{5}\right)$
- **D.** $\tan^{-1}\left(\dfrac{5}{4}\right)$
- **E.** $\cos^{-1}\left(\dfrac{5}{4}\right)$

48. Tommy lives on the edge of a lake and wants to travel by boat to his friend Sherrie's house. Tommy travels the 550 yards from his house to Sherrie's house along a straight line in a direction (shown below) that is 33° clockwise from due east. To the nearest yard, Sherrie's house is how many yards due south and how many miles due east from Tommy's house?

(Note: $\sin 33° \approx 0.545$, $\cos 33° \approx 0.839$)

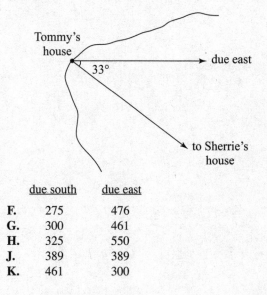

	due south	due east
F.	275	476
G.	300	461
H.	325	550
J.	389	389
K.	461	300

52. An angle with measure θ such that $\cos\theta = \dfrac{24}{25}$ is in standard position with its terminal side extending into Quadrant IV, as shown in the standard (x,y) coordinate plane below. What is the value of $\tan\theta$?

F. $\dfrac{24}{7}$

G. $\dfrac{24}{25}$

H. $-\dfrac{7}{25}$

J. $-\dfrac{7}{24}$

K. $-\dfrac{24}{25}$

GEOMETRY DRILL 2 ANSWER KEY

Plane Geometry

7. B
15. C
17. D
18. H
27. A
32. J
35. A
37. D
38. J
39. B
40. K
41. E
42. H
43. C
50. F
60. J

Coordinate Geometry

12. G
21. C
22. K
23. D
31. E
36. H
41. B
44. F
45. D
59. A

Trigonometry

24. J
28. F
35. C
48. G
52. J

GEOMETRY DRILL 2 EXPLANATIONS

Plane Geometry

7. **B**   To solve for the perimeter of a parallelogram, recall that the opposite sides of a parallelogram are equal in length. The lengths of the four sides of this parallelogram are therefore 12 m, 10 m, 12 m, and 10 m. The perimeter of the parallelogram is the sum of these four values, 44 m. If you picked (A), you may have found the sum of the given two sides.

15. **C**   Since you know that the two lawns have equal areas, you can use the area of Kayla's lawn to find the length of the sides of her neighbor's lawn. The formula for area of a triangle is $A = \frac{1}{2}bh$, which means that the area of Kayla's triangular lawn is $A = \frac{1}{2}(90)(80) = \frac{1}{2}(7,200) = 3,600$ ft^2. Using that as the total area of the square lawn, use the formula for the area of a square to solve for each side. The formula for the area of a square is $A = s^2$, where s is the length of each side of the square. Use the area of Kayla's lawn to find $s^2 = 3,600$, and $s = 60$. If you chose (E), be careful: this is the perimeter of the square, not its side length.

17. **D**   When two parallel lines are intersected by a transversal, it forms small angles and big angles. Any small angle is equal to any other small angle, and any big angle is equal to any other big angle. Lastly, any small angle and any big angle are supplementary, and their measures sum to 180°. In the figure, the angle measuring $x°$ is a small angle, and the angle measuring $y°$ is a big angle, so their sum equals 180°. The other choices make specific assumptions about the angles, which can't be supported by the information given in the problem.

18. **H**   The question gives the height and total area of Brandi's triangular wall. To find the length of the base, use the formula for area of a triangle, which is $A = \frac{1}{2}bh$. Substitute the given information to find $300 = \frac{1}{2}b(6)$, 300 = 3b, and b = 100 meters, or (H). If you picked (G), you may have forgotten the fraction $\frac{1}{2}$ in the area formula.

27. **A**   Similar triangles have corresponding sides that are proportional to one another. In this question, you are given that the corresponding sides in two similar triangles are in a ratio of 3:5, or $\frac{3}{5}$. Since the length of one of the equal sides in the larger isosceles triangle is 30 centimeters, set up a proportion to find the length of one of the equal sides in the smaller triangle. If x is the length of the side in the smaller triangle, then $\frac{3}{5} = \frac{x}{30}$. Cross-multiplying gives 5x = 90, and x = 18, as in (A). If you chose (D), you may have reversed the numbers in the proportion and treated 30 cm as a side of the *smaller* triangle.

32. **J**   To find the area of a circle, use the area formula $A = \pi r^2$. Given that the radius of the circle is 12 inches, you can substitute 12 into the formula to find that $A = \pi(12)^2 = 144\pi$. Choice (F) multiplies the radius by π. Choice (G) is the diameter of the circle, and (H) is twice that. Choice (K) finds the diameter of 24 inches and uses that as the radius in the area formula.

35. **A**   Since two sides of an isosceles triangle have equal lengths, the given side, 22 centimeters, could be one of the equal sides, or it could be the third side of the triangle. If it were the third side of the isosceles triangle, the lengths of the other two sides would be equal. Using the perimeter, we know that the last two sides must total $57 - 22 = 35$ cm in length. So each side would measure $\frac{35}{2} = 17.5$ cm, which is not in the answer choices. Therefore, you can conclude that the side of 22 centimeters must be one of the two equal sides, and the third side is $57 - 22 - 22 = 13$ cm, as in (A). Choice (E) is rarely correct on the ACT, and in this case, we were able to solve directly for our answer.

37. **D**   Given that triangle XYZ has the same base and height, you can solve for the height and base by using the area formula for a triangle, which is $A = \frac{1}{2}bh$. Since base and height are the same, the equation then becomes $A = \frac{1}{2}h \cdot h$, or $A = \frac{1}{2}h^2$. Therefore, since the area of the triangle is 72 square inches, $\frac{1}{2}h^2 = 72$, and $h = 12$. Since the circle is tangent to the triangle at point W, the line WY is both the height of the triangle and the diameter of circle O. Therefore, the radius of the circle is 6, and you can plug this radius in to the formula for area of a circle, which is $A = \pi r^2$. So, $A = \pi(6)^2$, and $A = 36\pi$. If you chose (B), be careful: this is the circumference of the circle. If you chose (E), you may have forgotten to halve the diameter before finding the area of the circle.

38. **J**   The length of the ramp is the hypotenuse of the right triangle formed by the height of the ramp, the height of the pool, and the ground. The only length you are given is the height of the pool, which is 3 yards. The length of the ramp will be the hypotenuse of this triangle, so use SOHCAHTOA. In this case, $\sin 48° = \dfrac{3}{\text{ramp}}$. Substitute the approximation $\sin 48° \approx 0.74$ into your equation to get $0.74 = \dfrac{3}{\text{ramp}}$, or $\text{ramp} = \dfrac{3}{0.74} \approx 4.1$ yards when rounded to the nearest 0.1 yards.

39. **B**   First, find the volume of the pool to figure out how much water needs to be pumped into the pool. The formula for volume of a rectangular box is $V = l \cdot w \cdot h$, so $V_{Pool} = 20 \cdot 10 \cdot 3 = 600$ cubic yards. In the explanation above the figure, you are given that the water pump fills the pool at an average rate of 70 cubic yards per hour. So, to find the amount of time it takes to fully fill the pool, divide the entire volume by the rate given, which is $\dfrac{600}{70} \approx 8.6$ hours, which is (B). If you selected (A), you may not have rounded correctly.

40. **K** Shapes that are geometrically similar to one another have sides that are proportional in length. Since you know that the height of the original pool is 3 yards, and the length of the longest side is 20 yards, you can set up the proportion $\frac{3}{4.5} = \frac{20}{x}$, where x is the length of the longest side in the new pool. Cross-multiplying gives you $3x = 90$, and $x = 30$ yards for the length of the longest side of the new pool. If you chose (G), be careful: you may have reversed the terms in the proportion, and if you chose (H), you may have found the new length of the wrong side.

41. **E** To find the perimeter of the quadrilateral $ADEC$, find the lengths of sides AD and EC. Since DE is parallel to AC, draw a line from point D perpendicular to AC and a line from point E also perpendicular to AC. The lengths of each of these segments is 8 inches because parallel lines are always the same distance apart from each other. Therefore, this rectangle has length 8 inches and width 5 inches with two smaller right triangles on either side. Since triangle ABC is isosceles, the base of each of the right triangles is exactly half of the remaining length of the base of triangle ABC, or $\frac{17-5}{2} = \frac{12}{2} = 6$. Given two sides of each smaller right triangle, you can use the Pythagorean theorem, $a^2 + b^2 = c^2$, to find the length of the third side. In this case, that third side is the hypotenuse, c, and plugging the given values into the equation gives $(6)^2 + (8)^2 = c^2$, or $c^2 = 100$, which means that the hypotenuse is exactly 10 inches. The perimeter is the sum $AD + DE + EC + AC = 5 + 10 + 17 + 10 = 42$ inches, or (E).

42. **H** Draw a figure to help you visualize this problem. To find the surface area of a rectangular box, add the areas of all the faces of the box. In a rectangular box, faces that are opposite one another are equal, so you can find the area of the front, top, and side of the box and multiply that result by 2. The area of the front face is $14 \times 20 = 280$. The area of the top face is $14 \times 8 = 112$, and the area of the right side of the box is $8 \times 20 = 160$. The total of those three sides is $280 + 112 + 160 = 552$, which is (F). However, this value gives only three of the faces of the box, so multiply 552 by 2 to get 1,104 square inches, which is (H). If you picked (K), you may have found the volume of the box rather than its surface area.

43. **C** The formula for perimeter of a rectangle is $P = 2l + 2w$. For this rectangle, the length is three times the width, or $l = 3w$. Substituting $3w$ for l and 32 for P into the formula for perimeter gives $32 = 2(3w) + 2w$, or $32 = 6w + 2w$, $8w = 32$, and $w = 4$. So since the width of the rectangle is 4 inches, using the relationship $l = 3w$, the length is 12 inches. To find the area, use the formula for area of a rectangle: $A = l \ w = 12 \ 4 = 48$ square inches, or (C).

50. **F** Since you're looking for the area of the shaded region of the triangular table, you first need to find the area of the table and then subtract the areas of the circular stands on the inside of the

table. The area of the triangle is $A = \frac{1}{2}bh$, so you first need to find the height. Draw a line from one vertex perpendicular to the opposite side, to form two 30-60-90 triangles. Since the sides of this triangle have a ratio of $x : x\sqrt{3} : 2x$, and the value of x for this triangle is 10, the height of the equilateral triangle is $x\sqrt{3}$, or $10\sqrt{3}$ inches. Substitute the base and height into the formula to get $A = \frac{1}{2}bh = \frac{1}{2}(20)(10\sqrt{3}) = (10)(10\sqrt{3}) = 100\sqrt{3}$ square inches. Now find the areas of the three circle sectors, which are all equal because the circles all have the same radius. Each of the angles of an equilateral triangle is 60°, so the three sectors have central angles of 60°. The radius of each circle is exactly half of the side length of the equilateral triangle, or $\frac{1}{2}(20) = 10$ inches. The area of one sector of the circle is $\frac{60°}{360°} = \frac{1}{6}$ of the entire circle, so the area of a sector is $A = \frac{1}{6}\pi r^2 = \frac{1}{6}\pi(10)^2 = \frac{1}{6}(100\pi) = \frac{50}{3}\pi$ square inches. Therefore, the total area of the three sectors is $3\left(\frac{50}{3}\pi\right) = 50\pi$ square inches. Now subtract the area of the sectors from the area of the triangle: $100\sqrt{3} - 50\pi \approx 16$, or (F). If you picked (H), you may have subtracted the area of only one of the sectors.

60. **J**   The total degrees in any *n*-sided polygon is given by the equation $(n-2)\cdot 180°$. You use this equation to figure out that for an octagon, the total number of degrees is $(8-2)\cdot 180° = 6\cdot 180° = 1{,}080°$. Divide the total number of degrees by 8 to find the measure of each interior angle: $\frac{1.080°}{8} = 135°$. If you picked any of the other answers, you may have been using an incorrect value for the total degrees in the octagon.

Coordinate Geometry

12. **G**   The slope-intercept form of a line is $y = mx + b$. To put an equation in this form, isolate *y* on the left-hand side of the equation. First, add $3x$ to each side to get $-y = 3x - 7$, and then subtract 7 from each side to get $-y = 3x - 7$. Now, you just need to multiply (or divide) both sides by –1 to get $7 = -3x + 7$, so the answer is (G). Choices (F), (H), and (J) are similar versions of the correct answer that each make an error involving a negative sign, either when adding or subtracting terms from the left side or when multiplying the final equation by –1.

21. **C**   To find the slope-intercept form of a line, rewrite the equation in the form $y = mx + b$. Begin by subtracting $6x$ from each side of the equation to get $2y - 4 = -6x + 12$. Next, add 4 to each side to get $2y = -6x + 16$. Finally, divide each side by 2 to get $y = -3x + 8$. Choices (A), (B), and (D) all make mistakes involving negative signs, and (E) switches the coefficient of x with the constant on the right side of the equation.

22. **K**   First, find the slope of the line by writing it in slope-intercept form. Subtract $2x$ from each side and then divide each side by 5 to get $y = -\frac{2}{5}x - 2$. Perpendicular lines have opposite reciprocal slopes. Since the slope of the original line is $-\frac{2}{5}$, the negative reciprocal would be $\frac{5}{2}$, as in (K). Choice (F) forgets to take the *negative* reciprocal. Choice (G) is the slope of a parallel line, and (H) gives the negative of the original slope, but not the negative reciprocal.

23. **D**   When finding the slope of a line given in the standard (x,y) coordinate plane, rewrite the equation in slope-intercept form, which is $y = mx + b$. In this case, start by adding $5x$ to each side of the equation to isolate y, which results in $3y = 5x - 9$. Now divide both sides by 3, giving $y = \frac{5}{3}x - 3$. In this case, the slope is the coefficient of x, which is $\frac{5}{3}$. If you chose (B), be careful: You may have switched some negative signs.

31. **E**   To find the y-coordinate of the point of intersection of two lines, you need to find values for x and y that satisfy both equations. Both equations are equal to y, so set the right side of the first equation equal to the right side of the second equation: $4x + 7 = 6x - 3$. Then solve for x to get $-2x = -10$, and $x = 5$. To find the value of y, substitute $x = 5$ into either of the original equations. If you use the first equation, for example, $y = 4(5) + 7 = 20 + 7 = 27$. If you chose (A) be careful: this is the x-coordinate!

36. **H**   To find the slope of a line given two points in the standard (x,y) coordinate plane, use the slope formula: $\text{slope} = \frac{\text{rise}}{\text{run}} = \frac{y_2 - y_1}{x_2 - x_1}$. Using the points $(3,7)$ and $(9,11)$, $\text{slope} = \frac{11 - 7}{9 - 3} = \frac{4}{6} = \frac{2}{3}$, or (H). If you chose (F) or (G), be careful: You may have forgotten one of the negatives in the slope formula. If you chose (J), you might have found $\frac{\text{run}}{\text{rise}}$ rather than $\frac{\text{rise}}{\text{run}}$.

41. **B**   In the standard (x,y) coordinate plane, when a function crosses the x-axis, y will be equal to 0. So, you are looking for an equation in which, when $x = -3$ and when $x = 5$, $y = 0$. When you plug in $x = -3$ to all the equations, only (B) and (C) result in $y = 0$. When you plug in $x = 5$ to those two remaining answer choices, only (B) still gives you $y = 0$. Choices (A) and (E) give equations that, when graphed, cross the x-axis at $x = 3$ and $x = -5$, and (D) gives an equation that, when graphed, crosses the x-axis when $x = -3$ and $x = -5$.

44. **F** To find the slope of a line given two points on the standard (x, y) coordinate plane, use the formula for slope: $\text{slope} = \dfrac{\text{rise}}{\text{run}} = \dfrac{y_2 - y_1}{x_2 - x_1}$. Plug in the given coordinate points into the equation to get $\dfrac{12 - 6}{-3 - (-5)} = \dfrac{6}{2} = 3$, as in (F). If you chose (H) or (J), you may have found the slope of a different line. Choice (H) is the slope of $\overleftrightarrow{PQ}$, and (G) is the slope of $\overleftrightarrow{PS}$.

45. **D** Start by drawing the three sides of the right triangle QRS and find the lengths of its legs. Since QR is a vertical segment, the length of QR is the difference between the y-coordinates, or 8 units. Since QS is a horizontal segment, the length of QS is the difference between the x-coordinates, or 7 units. In all triangles, the shortest side is always opposite the smallest angle. Therefore, $\angle R$ is the smallest angle because it is opposite the shortest side. To find the tangent of $\angle R$, use SOHCAHTOA, which tells you that $\tan \theta = \dfrac{\text{opposite}}{\text{adjacent}}$. So $\tan R = \dfrac{7}{8}$, which is (D). If you chose one of the other answers, make sure you are solving for the correct function. Choice (E) is the tangent of $\angle S$. Choice (B) is the sine of $\angle R$, and (C) is the cosine of $\angle R$.

59. **A** To find which line is parallel to the given line, begin by writing the original equation in slope-intercept form, or $y = mx + b$. Start by adding $4x$ to each side of the equation, giving you $3y = 4x + 24$, and then divide each side by 3 to get $y = \dfrac{4}{3}x + 6$. The slope of this equation is $\dfrac{4}{3}$, and any line parallel to this line must also have a slope of $\dfrac{4}{3}$. Convert each answer choice to slope-intercept form to find the equation that also has a slope of $\dfrac{4}{3}$. Choice (A) is the answer because the equation in slope-intercept form is $y = \dfrac{4}{3}x + 6$. Choices (B), (C), and (E) all have slopes of $-\dfrac{4}{3}$, and (C) has a slope of $-\dfrac{3}{4}$, which is the slope of a line perpendicular to the original equation.

Trigonometry

24. **J** Since you are asked to find the *opposite* side of a particular angle, and you are given the *hypotenuse*, use the first part of SOHCAHTOA, which indicates that $\sin \theta = \dfrac{\text{opposite}}{\text{hypotenuse}}$. Substitute the given information to find $78° = \dfrac{x}{9}$. Multiply each side of the equation by 9, so $x = 9 \cdot \sin 78°$. Using the provided approximation for $\sin 78°$, $x = 9 \times 0.9781 = 8.8029$, which rounds to 8.803. Choice (H) is close, but it isn't the closest approximation. If you picked (K), you may have found the tangent instead of the sine.

28. **F** First, since the hypotenuse of the triangle must be its longest side, eliminate (H), (J), and (K). Given that $\sin\theta = \dfrac{5}{13}$, use SOHCAHTOA. This means that $\sin\theta = \dfrac{opposite}{hypotenuse}$, so you can set up a proportion to find the length of the hypotenuse. Let x be the length of the hypotenuse, and $\sin\theta = \dfrac{18}{x}$. Set the two values for $\sin\theta$ equal to each other to get $\dfrac{5}{13} = \dfrac{18}{x}$. Solve the equation by multiplying each side by $13x$ to $5x = 234$, or $x = 46.8$ feet. If you picked (G), be careful: This is the horizontal distance between Mario and the flagpole.

35. **C** In the figure, you are given the hypotenuse of the right triangle, as well as the side that is opposite the indicated angle θ. Therefore, use SOHCAHTOA, specifically the relationship of $\sin\theta = \dfrac{opposite}{hypotenuse}$. Substitute the information given in the question to find $\sin\theta = \dfrac{4}{5}$. To solve for the value of θ, take the inverse sine of each side of the equation, which would give $\sin^{-1}\left(\sin\theta\right) = \sin^{-1}\left(\dfrac{4}{5}\right)$. The inverse sine function and sine function cancel each other out, leaving you with $\theta = \sin^{-1}\left(\dfrac{4}{5}\right)$.

48. **G** Redraw the right triangle with a 33° angle and a hypotenuse of length 550 yards. The length of the leg adjacent to the 33° angle is the distance due east, and the length of the leg opposite the 33° angle is the distance due south. To figure out the lengths of those legs, choose one and use SOHCAHTOA. To find the distance due south, or the distance *opposite* the given angle, use $\sin\theta = \dfrac{opposite}{hypotenuse}$, so $\sin 33° = \dfrac{south}{550}$. Using the provided information, $\dfrac{south}{550} = 0.545$, and $south = 0.545 \cdot 550 \approx 300$. Choice (G) is the only answer choice with the correct due south distance, so you can stop there. If you prefer to start by finding the distance due east, use $\sin\theta = \dfrac{adjacent}{hypotenuse}$, so $\sin 33° = \dfrac{east}{550}$. Using the provided information, $\dfrac{east}{550} = 0.839$, and $east = 0.839 \cdot 550 \approx 461$. If you picked (K), be careful: The sides are reversed in this answer choice.

52. **J** This is a difficult problem, but it is easy to solve if you know a few basic trig facts. First, remember "All Students Take Calculus." This is a helpful reminder of which quadrants have positive functions. In Quadrant I, *all* trig functions are positive. In Quadrant II, *sine* is positive. In Quadrant III, *tangent* is positive. In Quadrant IV, *cosine* is positive. This is helpful because it tells us that a tangent value in Quadrant IV must be negative, eliminating (F) and (G). Then, because $\tan\theta = \dfrac{opposite}{adjacent}$, our final value cannot include the hypotenuse 25, eliminating (H) and (K) and leaving only (J).

Chapter 16
Math Practice Test 1

ACT MATHEMATICS TEST
60 Minutes—60 Questions

DIRECTIONS: Solve each problem, choose the correct answer, and then darken the corresponding oval on your answer document.

Do not linger over problems that take too much time. Solve as many as you can; then return to the others in the time you have left for this test.

You are permitted to use a calculator on this test. You may use your calculator for any problems you choose, but some of the problems may best be done without using a calculator.

Note: Unless otherwise stated, all of the following should be assumed:

1. Illustrative figures are NOT necessarily drawn to scale.
2. Geometric figures lie in a plane.
3. The word *line* indicates a straight line.
4. The word *average* indicates arithmetic mean.

---

1. Bob's Burgers charges $8 dollars for a hamburger and $5 for an order of French fries. Last month, h hamburgers and f orders of fries were purchased. Which of the following expressions gives the total amount of money, in dollars, Bob's Burgers earned on hamburgers and fries last month?

   A. $5h + 8f$
   B. $8h + 5f$
   C. $13(h + f)$
   D. $40(h + f)$
   E. $8(h + f) + 5f$

2. If $a = 8, b = -2$, and $c = 3$, what does $(a - b + c)(b + c)$ equal?

   F. -65
   G. -13
   H. 9
   J. 13
   K. 65

3. An artist at the State Fair paints 40 portraits per day. A second artist paints 50 portraits per day. The second artist opens for business three days after the first. Both remain open until the Fair closes, which is 11 days after the first artist began. Together, the two artists have painted how many portraits?

   A. 400
   B. 440
   C. 720
   D. 840
   E. 900

4. Josh has been a professional baseball player for four years. His home run totals each year have been 30, 39, 51, and 44, respectively. In order to maintain his current average number of home runs per season, how many home runs must Josh hit next year?

   F. 31
   G. 39
   H. 41
   J. 44
   H. 51

DO YOUR FIGURING HERE.

GO ON TO THE NEXT PAGE.

5. A craftswoman is paid $9.00 per necklace for making up to 30 necklaces per week. For each necklace over 30 that she is asked to make in a week, she is paid 1.5 times her regular pay. How much does she earn in a week in which she is asked to make 34 necklaces?

A. $162
B. $270
C. $306
D. $324
E. $459

6. Which of the following mathematical expressions is equivalent to the verbal expression "The square root of a number, n, is 19 less than the value of 5 divided by n" ?

F. $n^2 = \dfrac{5}{n} - 19$

G. $n^2 = \dfrac{n}{5} - 19$

H. $\sqrt{n} = 19 - \dfrac{n}{5}$

J. $\sqrt{n} = \dfrac{y}{n} - 19$

K. $\sqrt{n} = \dfrac{5}{n} - 19$

7. If $12(y - 3) = -7$, then $y = ?$

A. $-\dfrac{43}{12}$

B. $-\dfrac{10}{12}$

C. $-\dfrac{7}{12}$

D. $\dfrac{29}{12}$

E. $\dfrac{43}{12}$

8. At a department store, purses sell for $12 each during a one-day sale. Rita spent $84 on purses during the sale, $38.50 less than if she had bought the purses at the regular price. How much do purses cost at the regular price?

F. $ 5.50
G. $15.50
H. $16.00
J. $17.50
K. $20.00

GO ON TO THE NEXT PAGE.

9. $(2a - 5b^2)(2a + 5b^2) =$

   A. $4a^2 - 25b^4$
   B. $4a^2 - 10b^4$
   C. $4a^2 + 25b^4$
   D. $2a^2 - 25b^4$
   E. $2a^2 - 10b^4$

10. A rectangle's perimeter is 18 feet, and its area is 18 square feet. What is the length of the longest side of the rectangle?

   F. 10
   G. 8
   H. 6
   J. 3
   K. 2

11. In $\triangle XYZ$, $\angle X$ is 64°. What is the sum of $\angle Y$ and $\angle Z$?

   A. 26°
   B. 64°
   C. 116°
   D. 126°
   E. 128°

12. Each morning, a glee club member chooses her outfit among 4 plaid skirts, 5 pairs of argyle socks, 3 sweaters, and 4 headbands. How many different outfits are possible for her to put together on any given morning consisting of one skirt, one pair of socks, one sweater, and one headband?

   F. 4
   G. 15
   H. 16
   J. 120
   K. 240

13. Positive integers x, y, and z are consecutive such that $x < y < z$. The sum of x, $2y$, and $\frac{z}{2}$ is 59. What are the values of x, y, and z, respectively?

   A. 10, 11, 12
   B. 11, 12, 13
   C. 14, 15, 16
   D. 16, 17, 18
   E. 18, 19, 20

14. A function $h(x)$ is defined as $h(x) = -5x^3$. What is $h(-2)$?

   F. $-1{,}000$
   G. -40
   H. 30
   J. 40
   K. $1{,}000$

GO ON TO THE NEXT PAGE.

15. If $z = \sqrt[4]{97}$, then which of the following must be true?

- **A.** $2 < z < 3$
- **B.** $3 < z < 4$
- **C.** $4 < z < 5$
- **D.** $5 < z < 6$
- **E.** $6 < z$

16. What is the greatest common factor of 96, 108, and 144 ?

- **F.** 12
- **G.** 18
- **H.** 24
- **J.** 36
- **K.** 48

17. Cowan Cola is holding a contest to develop a new, more environmentally efficient can for its soft drink. The winning can is a cylinder ten inches tall, with a volume of 40π in³. What is the radius, in inches, of the can?

- **A.** 1
- **B.** 2
- **C.** 4
- **D.** 5
- **E.** 8

18. A clock has 12 numbered points. Four points W, X, Y, Z lie on the clock representing certain numbers. W represents 3:00. X is 4 units clockwise from W. Y is 9 units counterclockwise from W. Z is 5 units counterclockwise from W and 7 units clockwise from W. What is the order of points, starting with W and working clockwise around the circle?

- **F.** W, X, Y, Z
- **G.** W, X, Z, Y
- **H.** W, Y, X, Z
- **J.** W, Y, Z, X
- **K.** W, Z, Y, X

19. Tribbles reproduce at a rate described by the function $f(a) = 12(3)^a$, where a represents the number of days and $f(a)$ represents the number of tribbles. At this rate, how many tribbles will there be at the end of Day Four?

- **A.** 48
- **B.** 96
- **C.** 240
- **D.** 972
- **E.** 1,296

GO ON TO THE NEXT PAGE.

20. The height of a triangle is half the height of a larger triangle. The two triangles have the same base. The area of the larger triangle is Y square feet. The area of the smaller triangle is xY square units. Which of the following is the value of x ?

F. $\dfrac{1}{4}$

G. $\dfrac{1}{2}$

H. 1

J. 2

K. 4

DO YOUR FIGURING HERE.

21. $(2x+3y+4z)-(6x-7y+8z)$ is equivalent to:

A. $-4x+10y-4z$

B. $-4x+10y+12z$

C. $-4x-4y-4z$

D. $-8x+10y+12z$

E. $-8x-4y+12z$

22. The right triangle shown below has lengths measured in inches. What is $\cos\theta$?

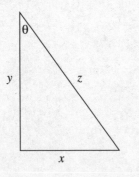

F. $\dfrac{x}{y}$

G. $\dfrac{x}{z}$

H. $\dfrac{y}{x}$

J. $\dfrac{y}{z}$

K. $\dfrac{z}{y}$

GO ON TO THE NEXT PAGE.

23. On a dead-end street, 8 houses are evenly spaced around a circular cul-de-sac. A newspaper delivery person bikes around the cul-de-sac and tosses the newspapers onto the driveway of each house. The delivery person bikes rapidly enough that the person can only toss to every third house. On which lap around the cul-de-sac will the delivery person have delivered newspapers to all 8 houses on the street?

   A. 2nd
   B. 3rd
   C. 4th
   D. 8th
   E. 11th

DO YOUR FIGURING HERE.

24. Lines q and m are in the standard (x,y) coordinate plane. The equation for line q is $y = 23x + 500$. The y-intercept of line m is 10 less than the y-intercept of line q. What is the y-intercept of line m ?

   F. 2.3
   G. 13
   H. 50
   J. 490
   K. 510

25. The expression $-9a^5(8a^7 - 4a^3)$ is equivalent to:

   A. $-36a^9$
   B. $-72a^{12} + 36a^8$
   C. $-72a^{12} - 36a^8$
   D. $-72a^{35} + 36a^{15}$
   E. $-72a^{35} - 36a^{15}$

26. $-4|-9 + 2| =$

   F. -44
   G. -28
   H. 3
   J. 28
   K. 44

GO ON TO THE NEXT PAGE.

27. In right triangle △WYZ shown below, $\overline{XV}$ is perpendicular to $\overline{WZ}$ at point V and is parallel to $\overline{YZ}$. Line segments $\overline{WY}$, $\overline{XV}$, and $\overline{WV}$ measure 30 inches, 6 inches, and 8 inches, respectively. What is the measurement, in inches, of $\overline{YZ}$?

DO YOUR FIGURING HERE.

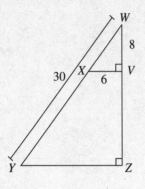

A. 15
B. 18
C. 20
D. 24
E. 27

28. As an experiment in botany class, students tracked a plant growing at a constant rate upward, perpendicular to the ground. As shown in the table below, they measured the height, h inches, of the plant at 1-week intervals from $w = 0$ weeks to $w = 4$ weeks.

w	0	1	2	3	4
h	7	10	13	16	19

Which of the following equations expresses this data?

F. $h = w + 7$
G. $h = 3w + 4$
H. $h = 3w + 7$
J. $h = 7w + 3$
K. $h = 10w$

29. The inequality $4(n-3) < 5(n+2)$ is equivalent to which of the following inequalities?

A. $n > -22$
B. $n > -14$
C. $n > -13$
D. $n > -2$
E. $n > 2$

GO ON TO THE NEXT PAGE.

2 △ △ △ △ △ △ △ △ △ **2**

30. The sides of an equilateral triangle are 4 inches long. One vertex of the triangle is at (1,1) on a coordinate graph labeled in inch units. Which of the following could give the coordinates of another vertex of the triangle?

   F. (−4, 1)
   G. (0, 1)
   H. (2, 3)
   J. (1,−3)
   K. (5,−3)

31. For △LMN, shown below, which of the following expresses the value of m in terms of n ?

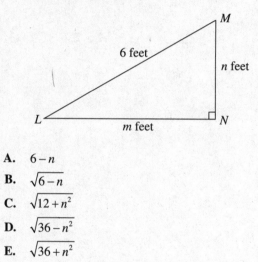

   A. $6-n$
   B. $\sqrt{6-n}$
   C. $\sqrt{12+n^2}$
   D. $\sqrt{36-n^2}$
   E. $\sqrt{36+n^2}$

32. A jar holds 10 pear jellybeans, 16 cherry jellybeans, and 19 watermelon jellybeans. How many extra pear jellybeans must be added to the 45 jellybeans currently in the jar so that the probability of randomly selecting a pear jellybean is $\frac{3}{8}$?

   F. 9
   G. 11
   H. 21
   J. 35
   K. 45

GO ON TO THE NEXT PAGE.

33. The graph of the equation $6x + 3y = 12$ is found in which quadrants of the standard (x,y) coordinate plane below?

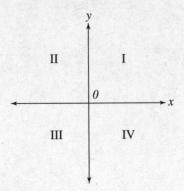

A. II and IV only
B. I, II, and III only
C. I, II, and IV only
D. I, III, and IV only
E. II, III, and IV only

34. The graph of $y = -2x^2 + 10$ contains the point $(3, 4n)$ in the standard (x,y) coordinate plane. What is the value of n ?

F.   7
G.   1
H.   −2
J.   −4
K.   −8

35. Jennifer, Kelly, and Meredith split their apartment rent. Jennifer paid $\frac{2}{3}$ of the rent, Kelly paid $\frac{1}{4}$ of the rent, and Meredith paid the rest. What is the ratio of Jennifer's contribution to Kelly's contribution to Meredith's contribution?

A.   1:3:8
B.   3:8:1
C.   3:1:8
D.   8:3:1
E.   8:1:3

GO ON TO THE NEXT PAGE.

36. In the standard (x,y) coordinate plane, a circle has an equation of $x^2 + (y+4)^2 = 28$. Which of the following gives the center and radius of the circle, in coordinate units?

	center	radius
F.	$(0,-4)$	$\sqrt{28}$
G.	$(0,-4)$	14
H.	$(0,-4)$	28
J.	$(0, 4)$	$\sqrt{28}$
K.	$(0, 4)$	14

DO YOUR FIGURING HERE.

37. An equilateral triangle and 2 semicircles have dimensions as shown in the figure below. What is the perimeter, in inches, of the figure?

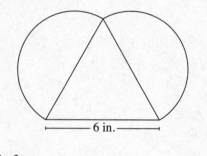

— 6 in. —

- **A.** $3 + 3\pi$
- **B.** $6 + 6\pi$
- **C.** $6 + 12\pi$
- **D.** $18 + 6\pi$
- **E.** $18 + 12\pi$

38. In the figure below, points H, J, K, and L bisect the sides of rhombus $DEFG$, and point M is the intersection of $\overline{HK}$ and $\overline{JL}$. The area enclosed by $DEFG$ except the area enclosed by $HEFM$ is shaded. What is the ratio of the area of $HEFM$ to the area of the shaded area?

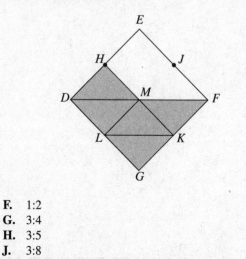

- **F.** 1:2
- **G.** 3:4
- **H.** 3:5
- **J.** 3:8
- **K.** Cannot be determined from the given information

GO ON TO THE NEXT PAGE.

39. In the standard (x,y) coordinate plane, the endpoints of $\overline{FG}$ lie on the coordinates $(-6,10)$ and $(8,-2)$. What is the y-coordinate of the midpoint of $\overline{FG}$?

A. 1
B. 2
C. 4
D. 6
E. 8

DO YOUR FIGURING HERE.

40. What is the volume, in cubic feet, of a cube with a side of length 9 feet?

F. 729
G. 486
J. 243
H. 81
K. 27

41. The system below has linear equations, in which r, s, t, and v are positive integers.

$$rx + sy = t$$
$$rx + sy = v$$

Which of the following best describes a possible graph of such a system of equations in the standard (x,y) coordinate plane?

   I.   2 lines intersecting at only 1 point
  II.   1 single line
 III.   2 parallel lines

A. I only
B. III only
C. I and II only
D. II and III only
E. I and III only

GO ON TO THE NEXT PAGE.

42. Given the dimensions in the figure below, which of the following expresses the distance, in feet, from the tree to the house?

DO YOUR FIGURING HERE.

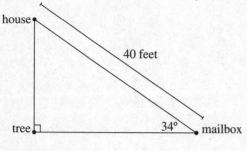

F. 40 sin 34°

G. 40 cos 34°

H. 40 tan 34°

J. $\dfrac{40}{\sin 34°}$

K. $\dfrac{40}{\cos 34°}$

43. The chart below shows the percentage of students, by grade, enrolled in a school. A student is picked randomly in a lottery to win a new graphing calculator. What are the odds (in the grade:not in the grade) that the winning student is in Grade 6 ?

Grade	5	6	7	8	9
Percentage of total number of students	12	22	25	27	14

A.   1:4
B.   1:5
C.   7:25
D.   11:39
E.   11:50

GO ON TO THE NEXT PAGE.

Use the following information to answer questions 44–46.

The figure below shows the pattern of a square tile mosaic to decorate the wall of Chelsea's Mexican Café. Grout fills the small spaces between individual tile pieces. All white triangular tiles are equilateral and share a vertex with each adjacent triangular piece. A green square piece is at the center of the mosaic. The length of the mosaic is 3 meters.

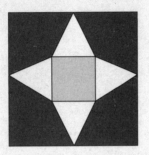

44. How many lines of symmetry in the plane does the pattern of the tile mosaic have?

F. 2
G. 3
H. 4
J. 8
K. Infinitely many

45. What is the length of the diagonal of the mosaic, to the nearest 0.1 meters?

A. 2.4
B. 3.0
C. 3.4
D. 4.2
E. 5.7

46. Joe wants to put a tile mosaic on the wall of his office. The pattern of the mosaic will be identical to that in the restaurant. The length of the office wall is 20% shorter than the length of the mosaic. The office wall is how many meters long?

F. 0.6
G. 2.4
H. 2.8
J. 3.6
K. 6.0

GO ON TO THE NEXT PAGE.

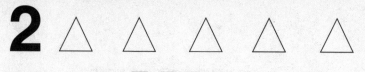

DO YOUR FIGURING HERE.

47. In the figure below, $\overline{DE} \parallel \overline{FG}$, $\overline{DG}$ bisects $\angle HDE$, and $\overline{HG}$ bisects $\angle FGD$. If the measure of $\angle EDG$ is 68°, what is the measure of $\angle DHG$?

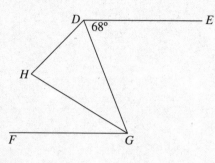

A. 68°
B. 78°
C. 80°
D. 82°
E. Cannot be determined from the given information

48. In the figure shown below, points A, B, and C lie on the circle with an area of 16π square meters and center O (not shown). $\overline{AC}$ is the longest chord in the circle, and the measure of $\overline{AB}$ is 4 meters. What is the degree measure of minor arc BC ?

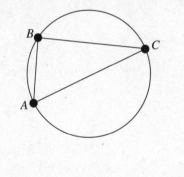

F. 60°
G. 90°
H. 120°
J. 145°
K. Cannot be determined from the given information

49. For which of the following values of b would the system of equations below have no solutions?

$$12x + 8y = 16$$

$$3x + by = 2$$

A. 2
B. 4
C. 8
D. 16
E. 32

GO ON TO THE NEXT PAGE.

Use the following information to answer
questions 50–52.

Rebecca and Scott make and sell pies and cookies for school bake
sales. It takes them 1 hour to make a dozen cookies and 3 hours
to make a pie. The shaded triangular region shown below is the
graph of a system of inequalities representing weekly constraints
Rebecca and Scott have on their baking. For making and selling d
dozen cookies and p pies, they make a profit of $12d + 25p$ dollars.
They sell all the goods they bake.

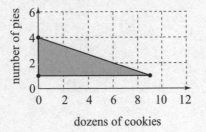

50. The constraint represented by the horizontal line segment
    containing (9,1) means that each school-week, Rebecca and
    Scott make a minimum of:

    F.   1 pie
    G.   9 pies
    H.   1 dozen cookies
    J.   9 dozen cookies
    K.   10 dozen cookies

51. What is the maximum profit Rebecca and Scott can earn from
    the baking they do in 1 school-week?

    A. $100
    B. $109
    C. $122
    D. $133
    E. $237

52. During the third week of October each year, school is closed
    for Fall Break, and Rebecca and Scott have more time than
    usual to bake. During that week, for every hour that they spend
    baking, they donate $2 to the school's fund for after-school
    reading programs. This year, they baked 5 pies and 3 dozen
    cookies during Fall Break. Which of the following is closest
    to the percent of that week's profit they donated to the reading
    program fund?

    F.   5%
    G.   9%
    H.   15%
    J.   18%
    K.   22%

GO ON TO THE NEXT PAGE.

DO YOUR FIGURING HERE.

53. The *determinant* of a matrix $\begin{bmatrix} a & c \\ b & d \end{bmatrix}$ equals $ad - bc$. What must be the value of w for the matrix $\begin{bmatrix} w & w \\ w & 10 \end{bmatrix}$ to have a determinant of 25 ?

A. 5

B. $\dfrac{10}{3}$

C. $\dfrac{5}{2}$

D. $-\dfrac{5}{3}$

E. -5

54. Henry discovers that the population of the bacterial colony in his lab can be calculated using the equation $x = B(1 + .2g)^n$, where x is the current population, B is the original number of bacteria, g is a growth rate constant for that species, and n is the number of days elapsed. Which of the following is an expression for B in terms of g, n, and x ?

F. $x \cdot .2g^n$

G. $x + .2g^n$

H. $\left[\dfrac{x}{1 + .2g}\right]^n$

J. $\dfrac{x}{(1 - .2g)^n}$

K. $\dfrac{x}{(1 + .2g)^n}$

55. If m and n are real numbers such that $m < -1$ and $n > 1$, then which of the following inequalities *must* be true?

A. $\dfrac{n}{m} > 1$

B. $|n|^2 > |m|$

C. $\dfrac{n}{7} + 2 > \dfrac{m}{7} + 2$

D. $n^2 + 1 > m^2 + 1$

E. $n^{-2} > m^{-2}$

GO ON TO THE NEXT PAGE.

56. Triangles *TVW* and *XYZ* are shown below. The given side lengths are in inches. The area of $\triangle TVW$ is 45 square inches. What is the area of $\triangle XYZ$ in square inches?

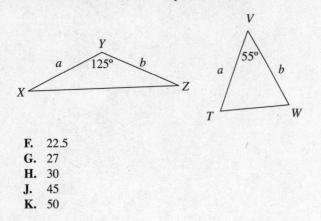

- **F.** 22.5
- **G.** 27
- **H.** 30
- **J.** 45
- **K.** 50

57. Triangle *JKL* is shown in the figure below. The measure of $\angle K$ is $50°$, $JK = 9$ cm, and $KL = 6$ cm. Which of the following is the lengths, in centimeters, of *LJ* ?

(Note: For a triangle with sides of length a, b, and c opposite

angles $\angle A$, $\angle B$, and $\angle C$, respectively, the law of sines states

$\dfrac{\sin \angle A}{a} = \dfrac{\sin \angle B}{b} = \dfrac{\sin \angle C}{c}$, and the law of cosines states $c^2 = a^2 + b^2 - 2ab\cos \angle C$.)

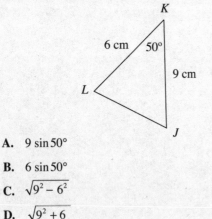

- **A.** $9 \sin 50°$
- **B.** $6 \sin 50°$
- **C.** $\sqrt{9^2 - 6^2}$
- **D.** $\sqrt{9^2 + 6}$
- **E.** $\sqrt{9^2 + 6^2 - 2(9)(6)\cos 50°}$

58. What is the sum of the first 3 terms of the arithmetic sequence in which the 7th term is 13.5, and the 11th term is 18.3 ?

- **F.** 15.9
- **G.** 22.5
- **H.** 25.5
- **J.** 32.4
- **K.** 43.5

59. In the equation $w^2 - pw + q = 0$, p and q are integers. The *only* possible value for w is 8. What is the value of p?

   A. −16
   B. −8
   C. 8
   D. 16
   E. 64

DO YOUR FIGURING HERE.

60. The solution set of which of the following equations is the set of real numbers that are 4 units from −1?

   F. $|x + 1| = 4$

   G. $|x - 1| = 4$

   H. $|x + 4| = 1$

   J. $|x - 4| = 1$

   K. $|x + 4| = -1$

END OF TEST.
STOP! DO NOT TURN THE PAGE UNTIL TOLD TO DO SO.

Chapter 17
Math Practice Test 1:
Answers and
Explanations

MATH SCORING DIRECTIONS

Score Your Practice Test

Step A

Count the number of correct answers: _____. This is your *raw score*.

Step B

Use the score conversion table below to look up your raw score. The number to the left is your *scale score*: _____.

Math Scale Conversion Table

Scale Score	Raw Score	Scale Score	Raw Score	Scale Score	Raw Score
36	60	27	45–47	18	24–25
35	59	26	42–44	17	21–23
34	58	25	40–41	16	17–20
33	56–57	24	37–39	15	14–16
32	55	23	35–36	14	11–13
31	54	22	33–34	13	9–10
30	52–53	21	31–32	12	7–8
29	50–51	20	29–30	11	6
28	48–49	19	26–28	10	5

MATH PRACTICE TEST 1 ANSWER KEY

1. B
2. J
3. D
4. H
5. D
6. K
7. D
8. J
9. A
10. H
11. C
12. K
13. D
14. J
15. B
16. F
17. B
18. H
19. D
20. G
21. A
22. J
23. B
24. J
25. B
26. G
27. B
28. H
29. A
30. J

31. D
32. G
33. C
34. H
35. D
36. F
37. B
38. H
39. C
40. F
41. D
42. F
43. D
44. H
45. D
46. G
47. B
48. H
49. A
50. F
51. D
52. K
53. A
54. K
55. C
56. J
57. E
58. G
59. D
60. F

MATH PRACTICE TEST 1 EXPLANATIONS

1. **B** Since h represents the number of hamburgers, multiply it by $8 to get the total amount of money paid for burgers; since f represents the number of orders of fries, multiply it by $5 to get the total amount of money paid for fries. You want the total amount of money earned, so you need to add the two expressions together: $8h + 5f$. You can also just plug in values for h and f and see which answer choice matches the target answer you get for those values—only (B) will work for all values of h and f.

2. **J** Plug in the values given in the question. The problem should then read $(8 -[-2] + 3)(-2 + 3)$. Follow the order of operations and do the arithmetic within each parenthesis individually before multiplying: $(13)(1) = 13$.

3. **D** Figure out the two artists separately, and then combine. The first one paints 40 portraits a day for 11 days, so 440 total. The second paints 50 per day for 8 days, so 400 total. Add them up, and there are 840 portraits.

4. **H** If you add together all the home runs, you get 164. Divide that by four seasons, and his average number of home runs per season is 41. The question is simply asking you how to keep a 41 home run average going after a fifth year. Simple: Hit 41 home runs exactly in year five.

5. **D** The trick here is that you must calculate the first 30 necklaces at the regular rate of $9.00 each: She makes $270 for the first 30. Then figure out what 1.5 times her usual rate is (it's $13.50), and multiply that by the extra four necklaces. She gets $54 for the extras; add that to the $270, and she makes a total of $324 for the week.

6. **K** This question is about translating English into math. The trickiest part is remembering to subtract 19 from $\dfrac{5}{n}$ instead of the other way around. Read closely and make sure you take the square root and not the square of n.

7. **D** Those answer choices are ugly, but if you have a good calculator and are comfortable with all the fractions and parentheses, you can PITA. Otherwise, just solve for the variable. First, distribute the 12 on the left side, and you get $12y - 36 = -7$. Add 36 to both sides and you get $12y = 29$. Divide both sides by 12, and you're done.

8. **J** First, calculate how many $12 purses you get for $84—you can buy seven of them. The difference between the prices is $38.50, so divide this by 7, and you get the value of the discount per purse, which turns out to be $5.50. Now add that to the sale price of a single purse, and you get $17.50 as the non-discount price.

9. **A**   You can Plug In, though the numbers will get fairly large once you start taking things to the 4th power. Or you can solve it as a quadratic, using FOIL. You may recognize it as a twist on $(x + y)(x - y)$. You know that when one binomial is a sum and the other a difference, their product will be the difference of two squares, so eliminate (C). After that, just make sure everything gets squared, coefficients as well as variables, and you wind up with (A).

10. **H**   The formula for a rectangle's area is base × height. PITA to find which answer choice fits the parameters in the question. Remember to start with the middle value! If we use 6 for the longer side of the rectangle, that means the short side will be 3 because we need an area of 18. Adding all four sides together gives us $6 + 6 + 3 + 3 = 18$, the perimeter given in the question, so (H) is the correct answer.

11. **C**   The sum of all the angles in any triangle is 180. Since $\angle X$ is 64°, the sum of $\angle Y$ and $\angle Z$ is calculated by subtracting 64° from 180°, leaving 116°.

12. **K**   Every possibility must be accounted for. For each of the four skirts, there are five sock options. $4 \times 5 = 20$, so there are 20 skirt/sock combinations. For each of those 20 combinations, there are three sweater options: $20 \times 3 = 60$, so there are 60 skirt/sock/sweater combinations. Finally, for each of these 60 combinations, there are 4 headband options: $60 \times 4 = 240$ total outfit combinations.

13. **D**   Use PITA. Start with the middle answer, (C), and you'll get $14 + 2(15) + \dfrac{16}{2} = 52$, so you know you need a higher set of numbers. Go to (D), and you'll get $16 + 2(17) + \dfrac{18}{2} = 59$.

14. **J**   When ACT gives you a function and then identifies a number inside the parentheses, it means to plug that number in for x every time it appears in the question. In this case, $x = -2$, so the function will end up reading $h(x) = -5(-2)^3$. Then you get $h(x) = -5(-2)^3$. $(-2)^3 = -8$, and when you multiply that by -5, you get 40. Watch out for the traps in (F) and (K), which involve cubing the -5 along with the x.

15. **B**   Don't overcomplicate here. Grab your calculator to see what the 4th root of 97 is (it's in the "Math" menu of your graphing calculator). Another approach would be to recognize that $z = \sqrt[4]{97}$ could be altered to read $z^4 = 97$. This way, you can PITA. Since $3^4 = 81$, and $4^4 = 256$, the value of z must be between 3 and 4.

16. **F**   The simplest approach is to PITA. Grab your calculator and divide each of the numbers in the question by each answer choice, starting with the highest answer choice because the question asks for

the greatest. 24 and 48 are factors of 96 and 144, but not of 108, so (H) and (K) must be eliminated. 18 and 36 are factors of 108 and 144, but not of 96, so (G) and (J) must be eliminated. That leaves (F) as the correct answer because 12 divides evenly into all three numbers.

17. **B** You'll need to know the formula for volume of a cylinder: $V = \pi r^2 h$. So plug the known height (10") into the formula, and set it equal to the known volume: $40\pi = \pi r^2 (10)$. $6\pi = \pi r^2(4)$. Solve from here, and you will find that $r = 2$. You can also PITA because the answer choices represent the radius in that formula.

18. **H** This problem is very difficult to visualize, so make sure you draw a figure. Since W represents 3:00, count the hours in the directions indicated in the problem, and mark the points that you reach. X will be 7:00; Y will be 6:00, and Z will be 10:00. So the order, clockwise, will be W, Y, X, Z.

19. **D** The trouble with this problem is that it looks more complicated than it is. Since a represents the number of days and the problem asks you about Day Four, plug 4 in for a, and solve the equation. 3^4 is 81 and 81(12) is 972 tribbles.

20. **G** The best approach is to Plug In. You need the formula for area of a triangle: $\frac{1}{2}bh$. The two triangles have the same base, so start there—plug in 5, for instance. Then Plug In for the heights; try 4 for the larger and 2 for the smaller. Now you can compute the respective areas. For the larger, $\frac{1}{2}(5)(4) = 10$ square feet (the problem calls this y), and for the smaller, $\frac{1}{2}(5)(2) = 5$ square feet. So the final step is to re-read the problem and confirm what you're being asked for. $Y = 10$, and $xY = 5$, so $x = \frac{1}{2}$.

21. **A** To simplify the expression, distribute the negative to every term in the second set of variables and drop the parentheses: $2x + 3y + 4z - 6x + 7y - 8z$. Combine like terms to get $-4x + 10y - 4z$. Choices (B), (C), (D), and (E) forget to distribute the negative to at least one of the terms.

22. **J** Use SOHCAHTOA for right triangles: CAH means $\cos\theta = \dfrac{adjacent}{hypotenuse}$, which is $\dfrac{y}{z}$. Remember to identify the adjacent and opposite legs of the triangle relative to angle θ. Choice (G) incorrectly gives the adjacent leg as x rather than y; (F) gives tan θ; (H) gives cot θ; and (K) gives sec θ.

23. **B** Draw a diagram with numbers 1–8 evenly spaced around a circle. On the first run, the paper is delivered to houses 1, 4, and 7; on the second run, the paper is delivered to houses 2, 5, and 8; and on the third run, the paper is delivered to houses 3 and 6. Therefore, by the third lap, the paper has been delivered to all the houses.

24. **J** In the equation of a line, $y = mx + b$, the y-intercept is given by constant b, thus line q has a y-intercept of 500. The y-intercept of line m is 10 less than line q, so subtract 10 from 500 to get 490. Choice (K) incorrectly adds 10; (H) calculates the y-intercept as 10 *times* less, rather than 10 less than that of line m. Choices (F) and (G) use the slope rather than the y-intercept.

25. **B** Simplify the expression by multiplying $-9a^5$ to each term in the parentheses. Remember MADSPM. When bases are multiplied, exponents are added. Therefore, the equation should look like this: $-9a^5(8a^7 - 4a^3) = -72a^{(5+7)} + 36a^{(5+3)} = -72a^{(12)} + 36a^8$. Choices (D) and (E) incorrectly multiply the exponents. Choice (C) doesn't distribute the negative sign to the second term. Choice (A) incorrectly subtracts non-combinable terms inside the parentheses and then multiplies $-9a^5$.

26. **G** Consider PEMDAS and first combine the terms inside the absolute value: $-4|-9 + 2| = -4|-7|$. Then take the absolute value of -7, which is $+7$, and multiply by -4 to get -28. Choices (F) and (K) incorrectly take the absolute value of -9 and 2 first and then combine. Choice (H) adds rather than multiplies -4 and $+7$. Choice (J) neglects to take the absolute value of -7.

27. **B** Given YZ is parallel to XV, $\triangle WXV$ and $\triangle WYZ$ are similar triangles, thus they have proportional sides. First, use the Pythagorean theorem ($WX^2 = 6^2 + 8^2$) to find that WX is 10, or remember that this is one of the special right triangles. Then set up the proportion $\dfrac{WX}{WY} = \dfrac{XV}{YZ}$ to find YZ: $\dfrac{10}{30} = \dfrac{6}{YZ}$, and YZ is 18 inches. Choices (A), (C), and (E) do not use the correct proportions; (D) is the length of WZ, not YZ.

28. **H** Plug in a w value from the table, and eliminate equations that do not give the corresponding h value. When you plug in $w = 0$, (G), (J), and (K) do not give $h = 7$. When you plug in $w = 1$, (F) gives $h = 8$, not 10, so it can also be eliminated.

29. **A** Simplify the expression by distributing the coefficients on both sides of the inequality: $4(n - 3) < 5(n + 2)$ becomes $4n - 12 < 5n + 10$. Combine like terms to get $-4n < 22$ and divide by -1, remembering to flip the inequality sign. Choices (B), (C), (D), and (E) all result from either neglecting to distribute the coefficient completely through the parentheses or mixing up the positive and negative signs.

30. **J** The other vertices of the triangle must be 4 inches from $(1,1)$. Use POE. Choice (F) is 5 units to the left, and (G) is only 1 unit to the left. Using either right triangles or the distance formula, you can determine (H) is not long enough, and (K) is too long. Choice (J) is 4 units due south from $(1,1)$. If you have trouble remembering the distance formula, just sketch and ballpark!

31. **D** Use the Pythagorean theorem: $m^2 + n^2 = 6^2$. Isolate m by subtracting n^2 and square rooting both sides. Choices (A), (B), and (C) do not correctly square each side length before isolating m. Choice (E) treats side m as the hypotenuse rather than one of the legs of the right triangle. If you get stuck with the algebra, plug in a value for n, and use your calculator.

32. **G** Probability is the fraction of what you want (pear jellybeans) over total number of possibilities (all jellybeans). Use PITA. There are currently $10 + 16 + 19 = 45$ jellybeans in the jar. Start with (H). If 21 pear jellybeans are added, then there will be a total of 66 jellybeans in the jar. The probability of selecting a pear jellybean will be $\dfrac{21}{66}$, which is too low. Go to (G). If 11 jellybeans are added, there will be a total of 56 jellybeans in the jar. The probability of selecting a pear jellybeans will be $\dfrac{21}{56}$, which simplifies to $\dfrac{3}{8}$, making (G) the correct answer.

33. **C** To determine the graph of the equation, you must isolate the y by subtracting $6x$ *and* dividing by 3. The resulting equation is $y = -2x + 4$, which is a line with a slope of -2 and a y-intercept of $+4$. Because the y-intercept is positive, the line crosses y-axis from Quadrant II to Quadrant I and extends into Quadrant IV. The line never passes through Quadrant II, eliminating (B), (D), and (E). Choice (A) is a partial answer and does not include Quadrant I. Remember, in order to avoid doing any figuring, once you've got the equation in slope-intercept form, you can just plug it in to your graphing calculator.

34. **H** Substitute the values $(3, 4n)$ in for (x, y) in the equation to get $4n = -2(3)^2 + 10$. Remember PEMDAS: $4n = -2(9) + 10$, so $4n = -8$, and $n = -2$. Choice (F) results when you mix up the positive and negative signs. Choices (G) and (J) result when you do not use PEMDAS correctly. Choice (K) is a partial answer and gives the value of $4n$, not n.

35. **D** Plug In! Make sure you choose a value for the rent that divides evenly by 3 and 4. Let's say the rent is $24. In that case, Jennifer pays $16, Kelly pays $6, and Meredith pays the remainder, or $2. The ratio of Jennifer's contribution to Kelly's contribution to Meredith's contribution is then 16:6:2, which simplifies to 8:3:1, or (D).

36. **F** The general equation of a circle is $(x - h)^2 + (y - k)^2 = r^2$, for which (h, k) are the coordinates for the center of the circle, and r gives the radius length. For the given equation, the $h = 0$ and $k = -4$; (J) and (K) confuse the sign in front of k. Since $r^2 = 28$, the radius of the circle is $\sqrt{28}$. Choice (G) divides by 2 rather than square rooting 28. Choice (H) gives the value of r^2, not r.

37. **B** The perimeter of the figure consists of one side of the equilateral triangle and the arc length of two semicircles. You can immediately eliminate (A), (D), and (E) because the length of one side of the equilateral triangle is 6 inches. Both semicircles have a diameter of 6, and given $C = d\pi = 6\pi$, each

semicircle has an arc length of 3π. With the exposed side of the triangle, the perimeter of the figure should be $P = 6 + 3\pi + 3\pi = 6 + 6\pi$. If you selected (C), you may have found the circumferences of two full circles rather than two semicircles.

38. **H** Because *DEFG* is a rhombus, which has equal sides and equal angles, all 8 triangles formed by drawing the diagonals in the figure are equivalent. *HEFM* encloses the area of 3 triangles and the shaded region the area of 5 triangles, thus the ratio is 3:5. Choice (J) is the ratio of the unshaded area to the total area.

39. **C** The midpoint is the average of the endpoints, so the *y*-coordinate of the midpoint is $\frac{y_1 + y_2}{2} = \frac{10 + (-2)}{2} = 4$. Choice (A) is the *x*-coordinate of the midpoint. Choices (B) and (E) only find the sum of the endpoint coordinates. Choice (D) confuses the negative sign and finds the average of 10 and 2.

40. **F** The volume of a cube is s^3, so this cube is $9^3 = 729$ cubic feet. Choice (G) gives the surface area of the cube. Choice (J) the area of 3 faces of the cube, (H) gives the area of 1 face, and (J) confuses the side as 3 feet rather than 9.

41. **D** Rearrange both equations into $y = mx + b$ form to compare their slopes and *y*-intercepts. The first equation, $rx + sy = t$, becomes $y = -\frac{r}{s}x + \frac{t}{s}$. The second equation, $rx + sy = v$, becomes $y = -\frac{r}{s}x + \frac{v}{s}$. Both functions have the slope of $-\frac{r}{s}$, so they cannot intersect at only 1 point, eliminating (I), and thus (A), (C), and (E). A system of two linear functions can give a single line graph if the equations have the same slope and *y*-intercept, which occurs if $t = v$. Lines with same slope and different *y*-intercepts are parallel and never intersect, so when *t* and *v* are not equal, you'll get two parallel lines, so the answer must be (D).

42. **F** Because you are finding the side opposite the 34° angle and are given the hypotenuse, use SOHCAHTOA or the *sine* function, eliminating (G), (H), and (K). Since $\sin 34° = \frac{\text{opposite}}{40}$, you solve for the distance by multiplying 40, not dividing and thus eliminating (J).

43. **D** Because 6th graders comprise 22% of the total number of students, $100 - 22 = 78\%$ of the students are not in 6th grade. The odds is the ratio of 22:78, which reduces to 11:39. Choice (E) incorrectly calculates the ratio of 6th graders to the total number of students. Choices (A), (B), and (C) are approximations of 22%; however, not as accurate as (D).

44. **H** Lines of symmetry cut the figure into two mirror images.

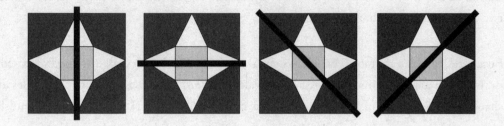

Since each of the divisions above creates two mirror images, the figure has four lines of symmetry.

45. **D** Because a square has right angles, you can determine the diagonal length using the Pythagorean theorem: $3^2 + 3^2 = d^2$. The diagonal is $3\sqrt{2}$ meters ≈ 4.2 meters. Choices (A) and (C) take the square root of 6 and 12, rather than 18. Choices (B) and (E) incorrectly calculate the diagonal without the Pythagorean theorem.

46. **G** Because the office wall is shorter, you can eliminate (J) and (K) immediately. Calculate 20% of the length of the current mosaic: 0.20×3 meters $= 0.6$ meters. Since the length is 20% shorter, subtract 0.6 meters from the original 3 meters. Choice (F) is a partial answer, but it does not give the actual length of the office wall. Choice (H) subtracts 0.2 rather than 20%.

47. **B** Because $\overline{DG}$ bisects $\angle HDE$, $\angle HDG = \angle EDG = 68°$. Since $\overline{DE} \parallel \overline{FG}$, $\angle FGD = \angle EDG = 68°$. Since $\overline{HG}$ bisects $\angle FGD$, $\angle DGH = 34°$ and $\angle DHG + \angle HDG + \angle DGH = 180°$, thus $\angle DHG = 78°$.

48. **H** Given the area of the circle is 16π square meters, the radius is 4 meters. $\overline{AC}$ is the longest chord in the circle, which is the diameter of the circle, so O can be labeled as the midpoint. $\overline{OA}$ and $\overline{OB}$ are each 4 meters, so ΔOAB is an equilateral triangle whose angles measure 60°. $\angle AOB + \angle BOC = 180°$, so $\angle BOC$ measures 120°, making the arc degree also 120°. Choice (F) gives the measure of arc AB rather than BC. Choices (G) and (J) use an incorrect triangle.

49. **A** A system of equations has no solutions if the equations have the same slope and different y-intercepts. Two linear equations have the same slope if they have the same ratio of coefficients for x and y. Set up a proportion of the coefficients: $\dfrac{12}{8} = \dfrac{3}{b}$. $12b = 24$, so $b = 2$. Choices (B), (C), (D), and (E) do not give slopes equal to that of the first equation.

50. **F** The shading above the horizontal line segment means that the *y*-values, which represent the number of pies Rebecca and Scott make, are never less than 1. In other words, they always make at least 1 pie, which is (F).

51. **D** The best way to approach this question, since it asks about the *maximum*, is check the endpoints or extremes of the graph: (9,1) and (0,4). Using the provided expression for weekly profit, $12(9) + 25(1)$ = \$133, which is (B). Check the other extreme to see that $12(0) + 25(4) = \$100$, which is less than \$133.

52. **K** If Rebecca and Scott made 5 pies at 3 hours each and 3 dozen cookies at 1 hour each, then they spent 18 hours baking that week. They donated \$2 for every hour they spent baking, so they donated \$36. The question asks what percent of that week's profit they donated, so calculate that week's profit. According to the provided expression for weekly profit, $12(3) + 25(5) = \$161$. The \$36 donated, out of \$161 earned, is approximately 22%, which is (K).

53. **A** Following the formula provided, $(w)(10) - (w)(w) = 25$. Rearranging, $10w - w^2 = 25$ becomes $w^2 - 10w + 25 = 0$. Factoring the quadratic into $(w - 5)(w - 5) = 0$, the only possible value for w is 5, so the answer is (A).

54. **K** This formula may look complicated, but if you're careful with the pieces, this will be basic golden-rule algebra. If $x = B(1 + .2g)^n$, then divide both sides by $(1 + .2g)^n$ to get $\dfrac{x}{\left(1 + .2g\right)^n} = B$, which is (K). If you find the algebra daunting, you can also plug in simple numbers and find a target value for B.

55. **C** The main things you know for sure about m and n are that m is negative, and n is positive. The least complicated option is to plug in values for m and n that adhere to the rules you're given, making m negative and n positive. Testing each answer choice using those values allows you to eliminate any that don't work out to be true. Even if you have several answer choices remaining after crossing out the ones that don't work with those numbers, picking a second set of numbers—still playing by the rules!—and testing each of your *remaining* answer choices with your new values should help you narrow it down to one. Alternatively, consider your answer choices. For (A), a positive number divided by a negative number will produce a negative number, not something greater than 1. Cross this answer out. For (B), remember that absolute value makes the inside result positive, and this will happen to both n and m. Then $|n|$ is squared, which will still be positive. A positive number, $|n|^2$, may or may not be bigger than another positive number, $|m|$, so cross this answer out. In (C), subtract

2 from both sides, and then multiply both sides by 7, so the expression becomes simply $n > m$, which you know to be true. Keep this answer. In (D), squaring both m and n make both values positive, without any sense of how large or small these newly positive numbers are. Thus, even after adding 1, there's still no way to say for sure which side is larger or smaller. As for (E), n^{-2} and m^{-2}, which are $\frac{1}{n^2}$ and $\frac{1}{m^2}$, are both positive numbers, but again you're given no sense of which is larger or smaller. The only answer that *must* be true is (C).

56. **J**

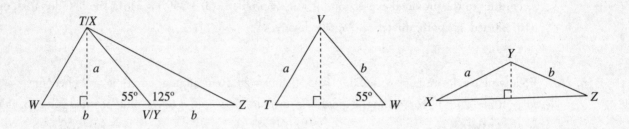

There are several ways to think about this question. There's not a lot of information to go on, so it becomes really important to pay very careful attention to what you do know and, since you're being asked to compare two things, any relationships you can discern. Noticing that the 55° angle and the 125° angle were supplementary might lead you to match up the a-sides to make the big triangle pictured above on the left. If Area $= \frac{1}{2} bh$, then for $\triangle TVW$, $\frac{1}{2} bh = 45$, so $bh = 90$. Looking at $\triangle TZW$, Area $= \frac{1}{2}(2b)(h) = bh = 90$. If the area of $\triangle TZW$ is 90, and the area of $\triangle TVW$ is 45, then $90 - 45 = 45$, so the area of $\triangle XYZ$ is also 45, so the answer is (J). Alternatively, consider the two triangles side by side, as pictured above on the right. Given that a and b are the legs of both triangles, to go from the 55° angle to the 125° angle requires dropping the height and lengthening the base proportionally. Because the base and height are inversely related this way, the area will stay constant even as the height and base shift.

57. **E**   The first decision you have to make is which one (or both) of these laws is useful to you. You're trying to solve for a side where you have the opposite angle, but you don't have angles to match up with either of the other two sides you know. The sides are not equivalent, so you can't assume that the angles are

equivalent. Consequently, you may not have enough information to use the law of sines. The law of cosines, on the other hand, would let you solve for the missing side, c, knowing only the other sides and the opposite angle. Line up each piece of the formula to find that $LJ^2 = 9^2 + 6^2 - 2(9)(6) \cos 50°$. Before you start calculating this value, glance at your answer choices—they aren't asking you to solve completely, just to match up the filled-in formula. Take the square root of both sides to find $LJ = \sqrt{9^2 + 6^2 - 2(9)(6)\cos 50°}$, or (E).

58. **G**   Break this problem up into little pieces. An arithmetic sequence has a common difference between terms, so the same number is being added to get from one term to the next. If the 7th term is 13.5 and the 11th term is 18.3, the 9th term must be exactly halfway between them at 15.9. Halfway between the 7th term and the 9th term is the 8th term, which would be at 14.7. If the 7th term is 13.5 and the 8th term is 14.7, then the common difference between terms is 1.2. Working backward from the 7th term, the 6th term is 12.3, the 5th term is 11.1, the 4th term is 9.9, the 3rd term is 8.7, the 2nd term is 7.5, and the 1st term is 6.3. Adding up the first three terms, $6.3 + 7.5 + 8.7 = 22.5$, which is (G). There is a formula for arithmetic sequences, but when you're dealing with relatively small numbers in relatively small quantities, sometimes the most reliable thing to do is simply write it out.

59. **D**   If the *only* possible value for w is 8, then the quadratic in factored form is $(w - 8)(w - 8) = 0$. Expanding this by FOILing gives you $w^2 - 16w + 64 = 0$. Line this up with the original equation to find that p must be 16, and q must be 64. With your answer choices, make sure you know what you're looking for—if you picked (E), you may have solved for q instead of p.

60. **F**   The simplest thing to do is to start by determining which values the problem is describing. Since it wants the numbers that are 4 units from −1, only two points satisfy that: −5 and 3. If you're having trouble thinking about that, simply draw a number line and count it out.

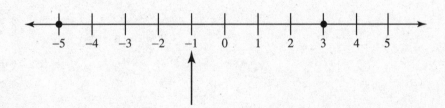

If the answer choices describe the solution set of −5 and 3, then you can test these values in each of the answer choices to eliminate ones that don't work. In (F), $|3 + 1| = 4$, and $|-5 + 1| = 4$. Both values work, so this will be your answer. In (G), $|3 - 1| \neq 4$, so eliminate that. In (H), $|3 + 4| \neq 1$, so eliminate that. In (J), $|-5 - 4| \neq 1$, so eliminate that, too. In (K), $|3 + 4| \neq 1$, so eliminate that.

Chapter 18
Math Practice Test 2

ACT MATHEMATICS TEST

60 Minutes—60 Questions

DIRECTIONS: Solve each problem, choose the correct answer, and then darken the corresponding oval on your answer document.

Do not linger over problems that take too much time. Solve as many as you can; then return to the others in the time you have left for this test.

You are permitted to use a calculator on this test. You may use your calculator for any problems you choose, but some of the problems may best be done without using a calculator.

Note: Unless otherwise stated, all of the following should be assumed:

1. Illustrative figures are NOT necessarily drawn to scale.

2. Geometric figures lie in a plane.

3. The word *line* indicates a straight line.

4. The word *average* indicates arithmetic mean.

---

1. Four railroad lines, A, B, C, and D, are pictured below, such that the pair of lines A and B and C and D run parallel to each other, respectively. If the obtuse angle created by the intersection of line A and C measures 110°, what is the measure of the obtuse angle at which line B intersects line D ?

DO YOUR FIGURING HERE.

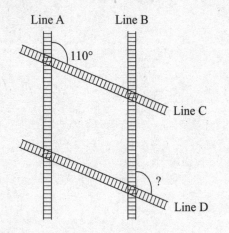

- **A.** 110°
- **B.** 120°
- **C.** 170°
- **D.** 210°
- **E.** 250°

2. Which of the following is the simplified form of the expression $5(x-3)-3x+10$?

- **F.** $2x-5$
- **G.** $5x+7$
- **H.** $8x-5$
- **J.** $12x+10$
- **K.** $22x$

GO ON TO THE NEXT PAGE.

3. In the standard (x,y) coordinate plane, a point lies at $(4,-7)$. If the point is shifted up 4 units and left 10 units, what are the new coordinates of the point?

   A. $(-14,-9)$
   B. $(-3,-9)$
   C. $(-6,-9)$
   D. $(-6,-3)$
   E. $(0, 3)$

DO YOUR FIGURING HERE.

4. At a certain golf club, participants in a tournament must pay $13 if they belong to the club and $15 if they do not belong to the club. What is the total cost, in dollars, for x participants who belong to the club and 30 members who do not belong to the club?

   F. $13x + 15(30)$

   G. $(13 + 15)x$

   H. $13(x + 15)$

   J. $13(x + 30)$

   K. $x + 30$

5. If a new computer has its price increased from $500 to $650, by what percent did the computer's price increase?

   A. 5%
   B. 15%
   C. 23%
   D. 28%
   E. 30%

6. In the parallelogram $WXYZ$, $\angle W$ and $\angle Y$ are congruent, the measure of $\angle X$ is $112°$. What is the measure of $\angle Y$?

   F. $56°$
   G. $68°$
   H. $90°$
   J. $112°$
   K. $136°$

GO ON TO THE NEXT PAGE.

DO YOUR FIGURING HERE.

7. Nathan will choose one marble randomly from a sack containing 32 marbles that are in the colors and quantities shown in the table below. Each of the marbles is one color only.

Color	Quantity
White	5
Purple	1
Indigo	2
Cyan	8
Maroon	6
Tan	10

What is the probability that Nathan will choose a tan or maroon marble?

A. $\dfrac{3}{16}$

B. $\dfrac{5}{16}$

C. $\dfrac{7}{16}$

D. $\dfrac{1}{2}$

E. $\dfrac{1}{3}$

8. If a speedboat is travelling 100 miles in the span of $1\dfrac{1}{3}$ hours, what is the speedboat's average speed, in miles per hour?

F. 25
G. 33
H. 75
J. 100
K. 133

9. In order to calculate an employee's overall performance review value, Mr. Donovan removes the lowest value and then averages the remaining values. Shawna was evaluated 6 times with the following results: 22, 23, 26, 31, 35, and 43. What was Shawna's overall performance review value as determined by Mr. Donovan?

A. 27.4
B. 30.0
C. 31.0
D. 31.4
E. 31.6

GO ON TO THE NEXT PAGE.

10. Which of the following gives x in terms of P and q, given the equation $\dfrac{3x}{p} = q$?

    F. $\dfrac{q}{3p}$

    G. $\dfrac{p}{3q}$

    H. $\dfrac{pq}{3}$

    J. $pq - 3$

    K. $q + p - 3$

11. What is the value of $5x$ if $3x - 16 = 5$?

    A. 7
    B. 21
    C. 35
    D. 56
    E. 72

12. If the area of a square is 25 square feet, what is the perimeter of the square, in feet?

    F. 5
    G. 10
    H. 20
    J. 25
    K. 100

13. What is 11% of 3.22×10^4 ?

    A. 354,200
    B. 3,542
    C. 35.42
    D. 1.123
    E. 0.1123

14. Of the following expressions, which is a factor of the expression $x^2 + 3x - 18$?

    F. $x - 6$
    G. $x + 3$
    H. $x + 6$
    J. $x + 9$
    K. $x + 15$

15. Of the following real numbers, $v, w, x, y,$ and z such that $v < w$, $y > x, y < v,$ and $z > w$, which of the numbers if the smallest?

    A. v
    B. w
    C. x
    D. y
    E. z

DO YOUR FIGURING HERE.

GO ON TO THE NEXT PAGE.

16. A new operation, ♣, is defined as follows: (w,x) ♣ $(y,z) =$ $(wz - yx)(wx - yz)$. What is the value of $(3,2)$ ♣ $(5,0)$?

F. −120
G. −60
H. 0
J. 6
K. 60

DO YOUR FIGURING HERE.

17. A team of artists requires 2 types of structures—spheres and pyramids—for a collaborative art piece. The 2 types of structures are created by overlapping 5-inch squares made of 3 different materials. The team will consist of three artists. The requirements for each structure type are provided in the tables below. The table with material types indicates how many squares are required for each type of structure, and the table with the artists indicates how many of each structure type each artist is to create.

	Wood	Iron	Plastic
Sphere	10	5	12
Pyramid	5	14	10

	Sphere	Pyramid
Suzuki	5	5
Mona	5	15
Jamilica	10	5

How many 5-inch squares of wood does Jamilica need to create her structures?

A. 150
B. 125
C. 52
D. 39
E. 29

18. Which of the following represents the least common multiple of 100, 60, and 20 ?

F. 80
G. 120
H. 300
J. 1,200
K. 120,000

GO ON TO THE NEXT PAGE.

19. The right triangle below represents three stores—Teddy's, ValuTime, and Burger Burger—as its vertices. The distances given on the triangle represent the numbers of miles required to travel between the stores on a road. Two customers leave Teddy's to shop at ValuTime. If the first customer travels from Teddy's to ValuTime on Coles St., while the second customer travels from Teddy's to Burger Burger on Monmouth St. before taking Brunswick Ave. to ValuTime, how many miles shorter is the first customer's trip than the second's?

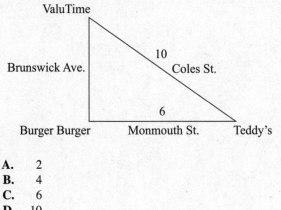

A. 2
B. 4
C. 6
D. 10
E. 14

20. Which of the following expressions is equivalent to $\left(y^6\right)^{12}$?

F. $72y$
G. $12y^6$
H. $6y^{12}$
J. y^{72}
K. y^{216}

21. Given the function $f(x) = 2x^3 + x^2$, which of the following represents the value of $f(-2)$?

A. -24
B. -20
C. -16
D. -13
E. -12

22. The Merry Mechanics Shop has just ended its discount program, raising the price of all repairs by 20%. Which of the following gives the price, in dollars, of any repair with price r ?

F. $0.2r$
G. $r + 0.2r$
H. $r - 0.2r$
J. $r + 0.2$
K. $r + 20r$

GO ON TO THE NEXT PAGE.

23. A local television advertisement offers 3 pairs of shoes for $30.97. Given the price of the shoes, how much would it cost to purchase 5 pairs of shoes?

   A. $10.32
   B. $10.33
   C. $20.65
   D. $51.61
   E. $51.62

DO YOUR FIGURING HERE.

24. Terra is opening a store. Her monthly earnings are calculated by subtracting her monthly expenses from the total amount she earns each day. If her monthly expenses are $500, and she earns $100 per day on a particular month, which of the following graphs represents her earnings as a function of the number of days of business.

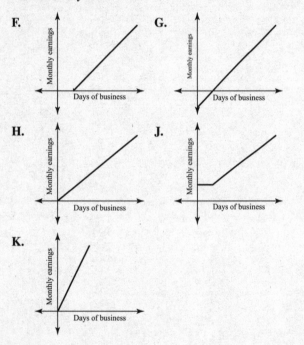

25. The positive integer $x!$ is defined as the product of all the positive integers less than or equal to x. For example, $4! = 1(2)(3)(4) = 24$. What is the value of the expression $\dfrac{6!4!}{5!}$?

   A.   1
   B.   2
   C.   4
   D.   72
   E.   144

GO ON TO THE NEXT PAGE.

26. Alfred spent $25 to purchase 65 stamps. If each stamp costs either $0.20 or $0.45, how many of the more expensive stamps did he purchase?

    F. 17
    G. 48
    H. 56
    J. 65
    K. 125

DO YOUR FIGURING HERE.

27. A square with a side length of 2 feet is circumscribed, as shown below.

    What is the area of the shaded region, in square feet?

    A. π
    B. $\pi - 4$
    C. $2\pi - 1$
    D. $2\pi - 2$
    E. $2\pi - 4$

28. Two similar triangles have sides that are in the ratio 3:4. The length of one of the sides of the larger triangle is 12 feet long. What is the length, in feet, of the corresponding side of the smaller triangle?

    F. 6
    G. 7
    H. 9
    J. 11
    K. 16

29. For the polygon below points V, Z, and Y are collinear. Which of the following represents the length, in inches, of $\overline{VZ}$?

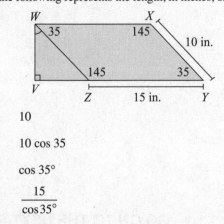

    A. 10

    B. $10 \cos 35$

    C. $\cos 35°$

    D. $\dfrac{15}{\cos 35°}$

    E. $\dfrac{10}{\cos 35°}$

GO ON TO THE NEXT PAGE.

30. The perimeter of a rectangle is 144 feet, and one side measures 32 feet. If it can be determined, what are the lengths, in feet, of the other three sides?

- **F.** 32, 40, 40
- **G.** 32, 32, 46
- **H.** 32, 48, 48
- **J.** 32, 66, 66
- **K.** Cannot be determined from the given information

31. If $9 + 4x < 2x - 7$, which of the following represents the solution?

- **A.** $x > -12$
- **B.** $x > -8$
- **C.** $x < -8$
- **D.** $x < -2$
- **E.** $x < 8$

32. The drama team wants to post a triangular advertisement for its next play. The base of the advertisement will be 2.25 feet, and the height will be 3.5 feet. Which of the following is closest to the area, in square feet, of the advertisement?

- **F.** 3.0
- **G.** 3.9
- **H.** 6.0
- **J.** 7.9
- **K.** 9.0

33. $-8|-2-7| = ?$

- **A.** −112
- **B.** −92
- **C.** −72
- **D.** 40
- **E.** 72

34. In a local deli, some sandwiches have only one kind of meat, and other sandwiches have more than one kind of meat. Using the information given in the table below about the kinds of meat in the sandwiches, how many sandwiches have roast beef only?

Number of sandwiches	Meat
8	at least roast beef
10	at least chicken
12	at least turkey
4	both chicken and turkey, but no roast beef
1	both roast beef and turkey, but no chicken
3	chicken only
2	roast beef, chicken, and turkey

- **F.** 9
- **G.** 7
- **H.** 5
- **J.** 4
- **K.** 2

DO YOUR FIGURING HERE.

GO ON TO THE NEXT PAGE.

Use the following information to answer questions 35–37.

The 4-H club at Arlington High School cares for various animals in the school's stockyards. The members of the clubs sell the animals in order to raise funds for the club, and Marcus and Jae are taking inventory of the animals. The table below gives the numbers of groups of animals. For example, there are 5 groups of pigs with 1 pig per group, 20 groups of chickens with 5 chickens per group, and 20 groups of rabbits with 10 rabbits per group. All of the animal groups have been counted except for the 5-animal groups of rabbits.

Animals	Number of 1-animal groups	Number of 5-animal groups	Number of 10-animal groups
Chickens	0	20	30
Rabbits	5	?	20
Pigs	5	10	0
Goats	22	10	0

35. Marcus finishes the inventory and afterward tells Jae that the number of rabbits is equal to the number of chickens. How many 5-animal groups of rabbits are in the stockyards?

    A. 15
    B. 25
    C. 35
    D. 39
    E. 195

36. Mrs. Bradshaw purchased $\frac{1}{5}$ of the chickens for $1,200.00. What was the price of 1 chicken?

    F. $10.00
    G. $15.00
    H. $20.00
    J. $60.00
    K. $120.00

37. Bethany takes all of the goats in the 1-animal groups and combines them to create as many 5-animal groups as possible. How many complete 5-animal groups of goats can Bethany create?

    A. 22
    B. 14
    C. 10
    D. 5
    E. 4

GO ON TO THE NEXT PAGE.

Use the following information to answer questions 38–40.

Isosceles triangle *DEF* is shown in the standard (*x,y*) coordinate plane below. The coordinates for two of its vertices are *D*(0,0) and *E(c,d)*.

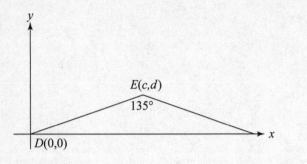

38. What are the coordinates of *F* ?

    F. (0,   2*d*)
    G. (2*c*,   0)
    H. (*c* + *d*, 0)
    J. (2*c*, 2*d*)
    K. (*c* + *d*,2*d*)

39. What is the measure of the angle formed by *DE* and the *y*-axis?

    A. 22.5°
    B. 30.0°
    C. 45.0°
    D. 60.0°
    E. 67.5°

40. Isosceles triangle *DEF* is rotated clockwise (↵) by 180° about the origin. At what ordered pair is the image of *E* located?

    F. (−*c*, *d*)
    G. (*c*,−*d*)
    H. (−*d*,−*c*)
    J. (−*c*,−*d*)
    K. (*d*, *c*)

GO ON TO THE NEXT PAGE.

41. A gallon is 231 cubic inches. Which of the following is closest to the area of the base, in square inches, of a pyramid shaped container, shown below, with height 15 inches and volume 2 gallons?

(Note: The volume of a pyramid with base area b and height h is $\frac{1}{3}bh$.)

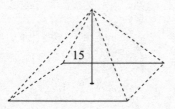

- **A.** 92
- **B.** 132
- **C.** 276
- **D.** 432
- **E.** 1,296

42. For law school, Nathan must read a book of legal cases in 6 months. He reads $\frac{1}{8}$ each of the first 2 months. For the remaining 4 months, what portion of the book, on average, must Nathan read per month?

- **F.** $\frac{3}{16}$
- **G.** $\frac{3}{32}$
- **H.** $\frac{1}{16}$
- **J.** $\frac{1}{32}$
- **K.** $\frac{1}{64}$

43. Which of the following equations indicates the correct application of the quadratic formula to the equation $2x^2 + 3x - 10 = 0$?

- **A.** $\dfrac{3 \pm \sqrt{9 - 4(2)(-10)}}{2(2)}$
- **B.** $\dfrac{3 \pm \sqrt{9 + 4(2)(-10)}}{2(2)}$
- **C.** $\dfrac{-3 \pm \sqrt{9 + 4(2)(-10)}}{2(2)}$
- **D.** $\dfrac{-3 \pm \sqrt{9 - 4(2)(-10)}}{2(2)}$
- **E.** $\dfrac{-3 \pm \sqrt{9 - 4(2)(10)}}{2(2)}$

GO ON TO THE NEXT PAGE.

44. In the standard (x,y) coordinate plane, the point $(-2,5)$ is the midpoint of the line segment with endpoints $(-7,3)$ and (c,d). What is (c,d) ?

    F. $(-19,8)$
    G. $(-12,1)$
    H. $(-12,7)$
    J. $(3,1)$
    K. $(3,7)$

45. A straight 4-meter-tall lamppost casts a shadow at an angle of 55°, as shown in the figure below. Which of the following expressions gives the length, in meters, of the shadow along the level ground?

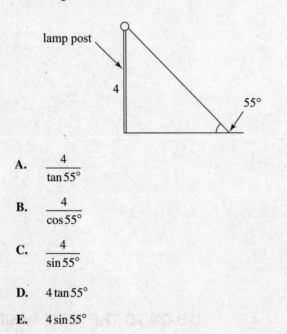

    A. $\dfrac{4}{\tan 55°}$

    B. $\dfrac{4}{\cos 55°}$

    C. $\dfrac{4}{\sin 55°}$

    D. $4\tan 55°$

    E. $4\sin 55°$

GO ON TO THE NEXT PAGE.

46. One of the following equations is graphed in the standard (x,y) coordinate plane below. Which one?

DO YOUR FIGURING HERE.

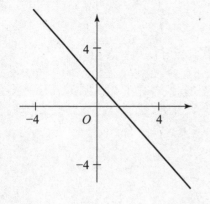

F. $y = 2x + 2$

G. $y = \dfrac{1}{2}x + 4$

H. $y = -\dfrac{1}{2}x + 2$

J. $y = -2x + 2$

K. $y = -2x - 4$

47. The vertices of $ABCD$ have the (x,y) coordinates indicated in the figure below. What is the area, in square coordinate units, of $ABCD$?

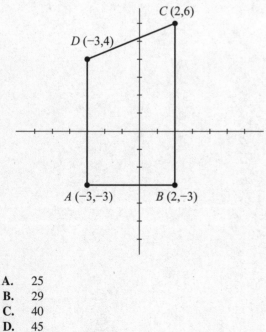

A. 25
B. 29
C. 40
D. 45
E. 81

GO ON TO THE NEXT PAGE.

48. Ms. Parker's economics class is reviewing slopes of lines. The class is tasked to graph the total expenditures, E, required for p products that cost 45¢ each. Ms. Parker instructs the class to characterize the slope between any 2 points (p,E) on the graph. Francine gives a correct answer that the slope between any 2 points on this graph must be:

F. two.
G. multiple positive values.
H. multiple negative values.
J. one positive value.
K. one negative value.

49. If the first four terms of a geometric sequence are 10, 15, 22.5, and 33.75, what is the fifth term in the sequence?

A. 35
B. 50.625
C. 56.25
D. 70.625
E. 75

50. The total surface area of a cube is 54 square inches. What is the volume, in cubic inches, of the cube?

F. 9
G. 18
H. 27
J. 81
K. 729

51. In the figure below, a region of a circle with a radius of 5 is shown shaded. The area of the shaded region is 15π. What is the measure of the central angle of the shaded region?

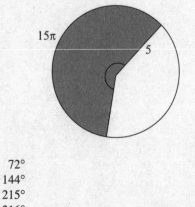

A. 72°
B. 144°
C. 215°
D. 216°
E. 315°

DO YOUR FIGURING HERE.

GO ON TO THE NEXT PAGE.

52. Which of the following equations represents the graph of a circle with center (2,–6) and radius 4 coordinate units in the standard (*x*,*y*) coordinate plane?

F. $(x-2)^2 + (y+6)^2 = 4$

G. $(x+2)^2 + (y-6)^2 = 4$

H. $(x-2)^2 + (y-6)^2 = 16$

J. $(x-2)^2 + (y+6)^2 = 16$

K. $(x+2)^2 + (y-6)^2 = 16$

53. In $\triangle XYZ$, the value of $\angle X$ is 53°, the value of $\angle Y$ is 88°, and the length of $\overline{YZ}$ is 11 inches. Which of the following is an expression for the length, in inches, of $\overline{XZ}$?

(Note: The law of sines states that for any triangle, the ratios of the lengths of the sides to the sines of the angles opposite those sides are equal.)

A. $\dfrac{(\sin 88°)(\sin 53°)}{11}$

B. $\dfrac{\sin 88°}{11 \sin 53°}$

C. $\dfrac{\sin 53°}{11 \sin 88°}$

D. $\dfrac{11 \sin 53°}{\sin 88°}$

E. $\dfrac{11 \sin 88°}{\sin 53°}$

54. The radius of a circle is *p* feet shorter than the radius of a second circle. How many feet shorter is the circumference of the first circle than the circumference of the second circle?

F. $\sqrt{p}$

G. p^2

H. πp

J. p

K. $2\pi p$

55. If $y \le -3$, then $|y+3| = ?$

A. $y-3$

B. $y+3$

C. $-y-3$

D. $-y+3$

E. 0

GO ON TO THE NEXT PAGE.

56. There are 18 countries in the trade union. Of these 18 countries, 7 have fewer than 20 cities, 7 have more than 21 cities, and 2 have more than 22 cities. What is the total number of countries in the trade union that have 20, 21, or 22 cities?

F.   15
G.   11
H.   9
J.   7
K.   4

57. If $\sin x = -\dfrac{3}{4}$, what is the value of $\cos 2x$?

(Note: $\left(\sin x\right)^2 = \dfrac{1-\cos 2x}{2}$)

A. $-\dfrac{3}{4}$

B. $-\dfrac{1}{4}$

C. $-\dfrac{1}{8}$

D. $\dfrac{1}{8}$

E. $\dfrac{13}{4}$

58. Let $f(x) = x^3$ and $g(x) = \dfrac{x}{2} - k$. In the standard (x,y) coordinate plane, $y = f\left(g(x)\right)$ passes through $(-2,8)$. What is the value of k?

F.   2
G.   1
H.   −3
J.   −8
K.   −9

59. A plane contains 7 vertical lines and 7 horizontal lines. These lines partition the plane into disjoint regions. How many of these disjoint regions have a finite, nonzero area?

A.   12
B.   14
C.   25
D.   36
E.   49

60. Which of the following must be less than 0, if x, y, and z are real numbers and $x^3y^4z^6 < 0$?

F. xy
G. xy^2
H. yz
J. xyz
K. $x^2y^2z^3$

END OF TEST.
STOP! DO NOT TURN THE PAGE UNTIL TOLD TO DO SO.

Chapter 19
Math Practice Test 2:
Answers and
Explanations

SCORE YOUR PRACTICE TEST

Step A

Count the number of correct answers: _____. This is your *raw score*.

Step B

Use the score conversion table below to look up your raw score. The number to the left is your *scale score*: _____.

Math Scale Conversion Table

Scale Score	Raw Score	Scale Score	Raw Score	Scale Score	Raw Score
36	60	27	45–47	18	24–25
35	59	26	42–44	17	21–23
34	58	25	40–41	16	17–20
33	56–57	24	37–39	15	14–16
32	55	23	35–36	14	11–13
31	54	22	33–34	13	9–10
30	52–53	21	31–32	12	7–8
29	50–51	20	29–30	11	6
28	48–49	19	26–28	10	5

MATH PRACTICE TEST 2 ANSWER KEY

1. A
2. F
3. D
4. F
5. E
6. G
7. D
8. H
9. E
10. H
11. C
12. H
13. B
14. H
15. C
16. G
17. B
18. H
19. B
20. J
21. E
22. G
23. E
24. G
25. E
26. G
27. E
28. H
29. B
30. F

31. C
32. G
33. C
34. H
35. D
36. G
37. E
38. G
39. E
40. J
41. A
42. F
43. D
44. K
45. A
46. J
47. C
48. J
49. B
50. H
51. D
52. J
53. E
54. K
55. C
56. H
57. C
58. H
59. D
60. G

MATH PRACTICE TEST 2 EXPLANATIONS

1. **A** In a figure where two parallel lines are intersected by a third line, all small angles have the same measurement, and all large angles have the same measurement. In this figure, since lines C and D are parallel to each other, the same is true about the angles they make with lines A and B. Because the angle in question is a large angle, it has the same measurement as the marked large angle, 110°.

2. **F** Begin by distributing the 5, $5x - 15 - 3x + 10$. Then combine the x terms, $2x - 15 + 10$. Finally, combine the -15 and 10 to get the correct answer, $2x - 5$.

3. **D** To shift a point up four units, add 4 to the y-value: $-7 + 4 = -3$. To shift the point to the left 10 units, subtract 10 from the x-value: $4 - 10 = -6$. The new coordinates of the point are $(-6, -3)$. Choice (E) incorrectly shifts the original point down 4 units and to the left 10 units.

4. **F** Multiply the number of club members by the member price to get $13x$, and the number of non-members by the non-member price to get $15(30)$. Add the two together to get the total cost, $13x + 15(30)$.

5. **E** The formula for percent change is as follows: % change $= \dfrac{\text{difference}}{\text{original}} \times 100\%$. Start by finding the difference between the old price and the new price: $\$650 - \$500 = 150$. To find the percent increase, divide the difference by the original price and multiply by 100%, $\dfrac{150}{500} \times 100\% = 30\%$. Be careful of (C); to get this answer, you'd be incorrectly dividing 150 by the new price, $650.

6. **G** A parallelogram has parallel sides, and its opposite angles are equivalent. Therefore, if $\angle W$ and $\angle Y$ are congruent, this must mean that $\angle X$ and $\angle Z$ are congruent, and $\angle Z = 112°$. Subtract the measures of $\angle X$ and $\angle Z$ from 360° for a difference of 136°. Then, because $\angle W$ and $\angle Y$ are congruent, $\angle Y$ must be half of this remainder, 68°.

7. **D** Take the number of maroon marbles plus the number of tan marbles, $6 + 10 = 16$, and divide by the total number of marbles to get $\dfrac{16}{32} = \dfrac{1}{2}$. Choice (A) gives the probability of picking only a maroon marble. Choice (B) gives the probability of picking only a tan marble.

8. **H** The distance formula is $d = r \times t$. Plug in the information you have to get $100 = r \times 1\frac{1}{3}$. Divide both sides by $1\frac{1}{3}$ to solve, $r = 75$. Choice (G) incorrectly multiplies 100 by $\frac{1}{3}$ only. Choice (K) incorrectly multiplies 100 by $1\frac{1}{3}$.

9. **E**   Begin by discarding the lowest performance review value, 22. Add the others, $26 + 35 + 43 + 23 + 31 = 158$, then divide by the number of values, 5, to get the average, $158 \div 5 = 31.6$. Choice (A) discards the highest value. Choice (B) averages all 6 performance review values without discarding any. Choice (C) is the median of the five remaining numbers, not the average. Choice (D) discards 23 instead of the lowest 22.

10. **H**   Multiply both sides of the equation by p to get $3x = pq$, then divide both sides by 3 to get $x = \dfrac{pq}{3}$.

11. **C**   Start by solving for x. Add 16 to both sides to get $3x = 21$, then divide both sides by 3 to get $x = 7$. Plug 7 in for x in the expression $5x$ to get $5 \times 7 = 35$. Choice (A) gives the value of x, but the problem asks for the value of $5x$.

12. **H**   The formula for the area of a square is $A = s^2$. Plug 25 in for A to get $25 = s^2$. Take the square root of each side to get $s = 5$. The perimeter of a square is $P = 4s$, so plug 5 in for s to get $4 \times 5 = 20$. Choice (F) is the length of one side. Choice (G) is $s \times 2$. Choice (J) is the area.

13. **B**   Start by expanding out the expression 3.22×10^4 to get 32,220. Since "of" means "times," multiply 32,220 by 11%, or .11, to find $.11 \times 32,220 = 3,542$. Choice (A) takes 322×10^4, leaving out the decimal point. Choice (C) multiplies 322 by .11.

14. **H**   To factor $x^2 + 3x - 18$, find two numbers that multiply to -18 and add to 3. Those numbers are 6 and -3. The factored expression is $(x + 6)(x - 3)$. If you chose (F) or (G), you may have reversed the negative signs.

15. **C**   In order to make this problem easier to handle, start by making all the inequalities "less than" signs. You have $v < w$, $x < y$, $y < v$, and $w < z$. Then order the expressions to get $x < y$, $y < v$, $v < w$, $w < z$, where x is the smallest, so (C) is the correct answer.

16. **G**   Plug the numbers given into the definition of the function, $w = 3$, $x = 2$, $y = 5$, and $z = 0$. $(3 \times 0 - 5 \times 2)(3 \times 2 + 5 \times 0) = (0 - 10) (6 + 0) = (-10)(6) = -60$. Choice (K) misses the negative sign. Choice (J) is the value of the second set of parentheses only. Note: This problem may seem intimidating if you don't know what the ♣ sign means, but remember, the problem gives you its definition!

17. **B** Start with the bottom chart to find that Jamilica is making 10 spheres and 5 pyramids. Each sphere requires 10 wood squares, and each pyramid requires 5 wood squares. Multiply the number of spheres by 10 and the number of pyramids by 5. Then add them together to get the total: $(10 \times 10 + 5 \times 5) = 125$. Choice (A) incorrectly accounts for 10 wood squares for both pyramids and spheres. Choice (E) adds the number of squares of each material required to make one pyramid.

18. **H** Try each answer choice, starting with the smallest one since the question asks for the least common multiple. Choice (F) is a multiple of 20 but not of 100 or 60. Choice (G) is a multiple of 60 and 20 but not of 100. Choice (H) is a multiple of 100, 60, and 20, so it is the correct answer. Even if (J) and (K) give multiples of the three numbers, this problem is asking for the *least* common multiple.

19. **B** Begin by finding the distance between ValuTime and Burger Burger along Brunswick Ave. The side lengths given fit the Pythagorean triplet ratio of 3:4:5, multiplied by 2 to create a 6:8:10, so the missing side length is 8. The distance the first customer travels is 10, while the distance the second customer travels is $6 + 8 = 14$. The difference between the two trips is $14 - 10 = 4$. If you chose (D) or (E), you haven't found the *difference* between the two trips.

20. **J** When raising an exponent to a power, multiply the exponents: $(y^6)^{12} = y^{6 \times 12} = y^{72}$.

21. **E** Plug In −2 in for x in the $f(x)$ expression: $f(-2) = 2(-2)^3 + (-2)^2 = 2(-8) + 4 = -16 + 4 = -12$.

22. **G** Plug in $100 for the original price of a repair, r. To increase the price 20%, multiply $100 by 1.2, $100 \times 1.2 = $120. Plug $r = $100 into the answer choices and find the one that equals $120. Choice (F) gives 20% of $100 only. Choice (H) subtracts the 20% instead of adding it. Choice (J) adds .2 to $100 instead of adding .2 × 100. Choice (K) multiplies $100 by 20 instead of by .2.

23. **E** If 3 pairs cost $30.97, divide that price by 3 to find the price of one pair: $30.97 ÷ 3 = 10.32\overline{3}$. Then multiply the single pair price by 5: 10.32\overline{3}$ × 5 = 51.61\overline{6}$. Round the decimal up to get the correct answer, $51.62. Choice (D) incorrectly rounds the decimal down. Choices (A) and (B) are possible prices for one pair of shoes, and (C) is the price of two pairs of shoes.

24. **G** Plug in a number of days to find a point on the graph. If Terra's store is open on no days, she earns no money. Subtracting her expenses then gives $0 - (500) = -500$. Choice (G) is the only one that has the point $(0, -500)$ on it.

25. **E** Expand out the 6! and the 5! in the original expression to get $\dfrac{6 \times 5 \times 4 \times 3 \times 2 \times 1 \times 4!}{5 \times 4 \times 3 \times 2 \times 1}$. Cancel out all the numbers in the denominator, and you're left with $6 \times 4!$. Since the problem tells you that $4! = 24$, multiply 6 by 24: $6 \times 24 = 144$.

26. **G**   Try PITA for this one. Since they're in order, start with (H). If Alfred buys 56 stamps for $0.45 each, he spends 56 × $0.45 = $25.20 on the more expensive stamps. Since the total he spends on all stamps is $25, (H) is too large, and you can also eliminate (J) and (K). Try (G): if Alfred buys 48 stamps for $0.45 each, he spends 48 × $0.45 = $21.60 on the more expensive stamps. Because he bought 65 stamps total, subtract the number of $0.45 stamps to find the number of $0.20 stamps: 65 − 48 = 17. Multiply 17 by $0.20 to find the amount Alfred spent on the less expensive stamps: 17 × $0.20 = $3.40. Add the amount he spend on the more expensive stamps to the amount he spent on the less expensive stamps: $21.60 + $3.40 = $25. This total matches what you're given in the problem, so (G) is correct.

27. **E**   To find the area of the shaded region, find the area of the larger figure and subtract the area of the smaller figure. If the square has a side of length 2, its area is $A = s^2 = 2^2 = 4$. To find the area of the circle, draw a diagonal in the square, which is also the diameter of the circle. Dividing the square in half diagonally gives you two 45-45-90 triangles. Since the ratio of sides of a 45-45-90 triangle is $x : x : x\sqrt{2}$ and here $x = 2$, the length of the diagonal is $2\sqrt{2}$. The radius of the circle is half the diameter, so divide the length of the diagonal by 2 to find the radius: $2\sqrt{2} \div 2 = \sqrt{2}$. The area of the circle is $A = \pi r^2 = \pi(\sqrt{2})^2 = 2\pi$. Subtract the area of the square from the area of the circle to find the area of the shaded region, $2\pi - 4$.

28. **H**   Set up a proportion using the ratio given for the triangles, and the one side length given, $\dfrac{3}{4} = \dfrac{x}{12}$, then solve for x. Cross-multiply to get $36 = 4x$, then divide both sides by 4 to get $x = 9$. Choice (K) sets up the proportion as $\dfrac{3}{4} = \dfrac{12}{x}$, which incorrectly matches the length of 12 to the smaller triangle in the proportion.

29. **B**   Start by finding the measure of $\angle VZW$. Since $\angle WZY$ and $\angle VZW$ make a straight line, $\angle VZW = 180° − 145° = 35°$. As figure $WXYZ$ is a parallelogram, you know the measure of $\overline{WZ}$ is equal to 10, the length of $\overline{XY}$. You can now solve for $\overline{VZ}$. Use this information to find out that cos 35°= $\dfrac{\text{adjacent side}}{\text{hypotenuse}}$, and so cos 35°= $\dfrac{\overline{VZ}}{10}$. Multiply both sides by 10 to find that $\overline{VZ}$ = 10 cos 35°. You may notice that (D) incorrectly uses the measure of side $\overline{ZY}$; (C) ignores the side of the triangle adjacent to $\angle VZW$; and (A) incorrectly assumes that $\overline{VZ}$ has the same measure as $\overline{WZ}$. If the measure of $\angle VZW$ is 35°, the measure of $\angle WVZ$ must be 55°, so the measures of the opposite sides cannot be equivalent.

30. **F**   Try PITA. Since a rectangle must have 2 sides of one length and 2 sides of another length, (G) is incorrect. All four sides added together, the 32 given in the problem plus the 3 sides in the answer choice, should add up to 144. For (F), 32 + 32 + 40 + 40 = 144, the correct answer. Choice (H) adds up to 160, and (J) adds up to 196.

31. **C**   Start by subtracting 9 from both sides of the inequality, $4x < 2x - 16$. Next, subtract $2x$ from both sides: $2x < -16$. Finally, divide both sides by 2: $x < -8$. If you chose (B), you may have flipped the inequality unnecessarily.

32. **G**   The formula for the area of a triangle is $A = \dfrac{bh}{2}$. Fill in the dimensions you're given: $A = \dfrac{(2.25)(3.5)}{2} \approx 3.9$. Choice (J) is (2.25)(3.5) without dividing by 2.

33. **C**   Begin with the expression inside the absolute value: $|-2 - 7| = |-9| = 9$. Then multiply by -8: $-8(9) = -72$. Choice (E) misses the negative sign. Choice (A) incorrectly multiplies the 7 and 2 inside the absolute value. Choice (D) incorrectly adds +2 to −7 inside the absolute value.

34. **H**   Start with the number of sandwiches that have at least roast beef, which is 8. Eliminate (F) because only 8 sandwiches have roast beef. One sandwich has both roast beef and turkey, but no chicken, so subtract that from 8: 8 − 1 = 7. Two sandwiches have roast beef, chicken, and turkey, so subtract that from 7: 7 − 2 = 5, to get the number of sandwiches with roast beef only. This eliminates (G), and because there is no indication that any of the remaining sandwiches contain roast beef with any other meet, the answer must be (H).

35. **D**   Find the total number of chickens by multiplying the number of groups of each kind by the number of animals in the group and adding them together: (0)(1) + (20)(5) + (30)(10) = 400. The counted rabbits include 5 1-animal groups and 20 10-animal groups for a total of (5)(1) + (20)(10) = 205. To find the number of uncounted rabbits, subtract the counted number from the total: 400 − 205 = 195. To find the number of 5-animal groups, divide the uncounted rabbits by 5: 195 ÷ 5 = 39. Choice (E) gives the number of uncounted rabbits instead of the number of 5-animal groups. Choice (C) incorrectly counts the 5 1-animal groups as 5-animal groups. Choice (B) makes the number of groups of rabbits equal to the number of groups of chickens, but yields different total numbers of each animal. Choice (A) subtracts the number of 1-animal groups from the number of 10-animal groups of rabbits.

36. **G**   Find the total number of chickens by multiplying the number of groups of each kind by the number of animals in the group and adding them together: (0)(1) + (20)(5) + (30)(10) = 400. Find $\dfrac{1}{5}$ of the

total: $\frac{1}{5}(400) = 80$. To find the price per chicken, divide the total price by the number of chickens purchased: $\$1,200 \div 80 = \$15$.

37. **E** There are 22 goats in 1-animal groups. To find the number of 5-animal groups that could be created, divide 22 by 5: $22 \div 5 = 4.4$, or 4 with a remainder of 2, so 4 complete groups can be created. Choice (D) incorrectly rounds 4.4 up to 5. Choice (B) adds the correct answer, 4, to the existing number of 5-animal groups of goats, 10. Choice (A) gives the number of goats.

38. **G** Since point F is on the x-axis, the y-coordinate must be 0, which means that (F), (J), and (K) can be eliminated. You know triangle DEF is isoceles, so DE must be equal to EF since $\angle DEF$ is obtuse. Point E then comes halfway between points D and F, meaning the x-coordinate of point F is twice the x-coordinate of point E, or $2c$.

39. **E** $\angle EDF$ and $\angle EFD$ add up to $180° - 135° = 45°$. Since triangle DEF is isoceles, each angle is $45° \div 2 = 22.5°$. To find the measure of the angle formed by DE and the y-axis, subtract $\angle EDF$ from $90°$: $90° - 22.5° = 67.5°$. Choice (A) gives the measure of DE and the x-axis. Choice (C) gives the measure of $\angle EDF$ and $\angle EFD$ together.

40. **J** When the triangle is rotated $180°$, point E will lie in Quadrant III. In Quadrant III, both coordinates will be negative, which means (F), (G), and (K) can be eliminated. Point E will be the same distance from the origin on both the x- and y-axes, but in the opposite direction, so both coordinates should be the opposite of the original values, or $(-c, -d)$ as in (J).

41. **A** The total volume of the pyramid is 2 gallons, or $2 \times 231 = 462$ in.^{3}. Plug the values you know into the given equation to get $462 = \frac{1}{3}b(15)$. To solve for b, multiply both sides by 3, $1,386 = b(15)$, then divide both sides by 15, $b = 92.4$. Round down to get (A).

42. **F** Nathan read $2\left(\frac{1}{8}\right) = \frac{1}{4}$ of his book in the first month. That leaves him $\frac{3}{4}$ to read in the remaining 4 months. To find how much he must read in each of the remaining 4 months, divide the amount left by the number of months, $\frac{3}{4} \div 4 = \frac{3}{4} \times \frac{1}{4} = \frac{3}{16}$.

43. **D** The quadratic equation is $x = \frac{-b \pm \sqrt{b^2 - 4ac}}{2a}$. In this equation, $a = 2$, $b = 3$, and $c = -10$. Start by looking at the $-b$. Since $b = 3$, (A) and (B) can be eliminated. Choice (E) can be eliminated because it incorrectly suggests that $c = 10$. Of the remaining choices, only (D) correctly puts a subtraction sign in the middle of the radical.

44. **K**   The midpoint formula is $\left(\dfrac{x_1 + x_2}{2}, \dfrac{y_1 + y_2}{2}\right)$. Start with the x-coordinate, $-2 = \dfrac{-7 + x_2}{2}$, and solve

for x_2. Multiply both sides by 2: $-4 = -7 + x_2$, then add -7 to both sides to get $x_2 = 3$. Eliminate

(F), (G), and (H), all of which have the incorrect x-coordinate. Do the same with the y-coordinate:

$5 = \dfrac{3 + y_2}{2}$. Multiply by 2, $10 = 3 + y_2$, then subtract 3, $y_2 = 7$. Choice (K), (3,7), is correct.

45. **A**   Since the unknown side is adjacent to the 55° angle, and the height of the lamppost is known, use

$\tan 55° = \dfrac{\text{opposite side}}{\text{adjacent side}}$ to get $\tan 55° = \dfrac{4}{x}$. Multiply both sides by x, $x \tan 55° = 4$, then divide both

sides by $\tan 55°$, $x = \dfrac{4}{\tan 55°}$.

46. **J**   Because the line shown crosses the y-axis above the origin, the y-intercept, or b in the slope-intercept

equation $y = mx + b$ must be positive. Choice (K) can be eliminated because it gives a negative value

for b. Because the line shown slopes down, the slope, or m, must be negative. Choices (F) and (G)

can be eliminated because they have positive values for m. Because $m = \dfrac{y_2 - y_1}{x_2 - x_1}$ and the line crosses

the x-axis at about 1, a slope of -2 is appropriate, and (J) is correct.

47. **C**   Divide the quadrilateral into a rectangle and a triangle by drawing a horizontal line from point

D across to the point (2,4). To find the dimensions of the rectangle, count the number of units

from point A to point B, which is 5, and the number of units from point A to point D, which is

7. The area of the rectangle is $A = l \times w = 5 \times 7 = 35$. Add to that the area of the triangle on top,

$A = \dfrac{bh}{2} = \dfrac{(5)(2)}{2} = 5$ for a total area of $35 + 5 = 40$.

48. **J**   An increased number of products will mean increased expenditures, so the slope of the line will be

positive, and (H) and (K) can be eliminated. Choice (F) can be eliminated because you don't have

any information about what the expenditure per product is, so you can't assign a specific value to it.

A line passing between two points can't have more than one slope, so (J) is correct.

49. **B**   A geometric sequence has a constant ratio between terms. To figure out what the ratio in this

sequence is, divide the second term by the first term: $15 \div 10 = 1.5$. To find the fifth term, multiply

the fourth term by the ratio of 1.5: $33.75 \times 1.5 = 50.625$.

50. **H**   The surface area of a cube is $SA = 6(s^2)$. Plug in the given surface area, and solve for the length of a side, s, $54 = 6(s^2)$. Divide both sides by 6, $9 = s^2$, then take the square root of both sides, $s = 3$. The volume of a cube is $V = s^3$, so $V = 3^3 = 27$. Choice (F) gives the area of one face of the cube. Choice (G) multiples the area of one face of the cube by 2 instead of by 3. Choice (J) squares the area of one face of the cube. Choice (K) uses 9, the area of one face, instead of 3 for s. Note: If you can't remember the formula for surface area, draw a figure.

51. **D**   The area of the shaded region has the same proportion to the area of the entire circle that the central angle of the shaded region has to 360°. Begin by finding the area of the entire circle: $A = \pi r^2 = \pi(5)^2 = 25\pi$. Then set up the proportion, and solve for x: $\dfrac{15\pi}{25\pi} = \dfrac{x}{360°}$. Cancel the π on the left side, and then multiply both sides by 360°: $\dfrac{(15)(360°)}{25} = x$, or $x = 216°$. Choice (B) gives the central angle of the unshaded region.

52. **J**   The circle formula is $(x - h)^2 + (y - k)^2 = r^2$, where (h,k) is the center of the circle, and r is the radius. Use Process of Elimination. Choices (F) and (G) can be eliminated because they do not square the radius. Choice (K) can also be eliminated because the x-coordinate of the center is $+2$, so the first part of the equation should be $(x - 2)^2$, not $(x + 2)^2$. Choice (H) can be eliminated because the y-coordinate is -6, so the second part should be $(y + 6)^2$ not $(y - 6)^2$. Only (J) remains.

53. **E** $\overline{YZ}$ is the side opposite $\angle X$, and $\overline{XZ}$ is opposite $\angle Y$. Set up a proportion according to the law of sines given in the note, $\dfrac{\sin 53°}{11} = \dfrac{\sin 88°}{\overline{XZ}}$, then solve for $\overline{XZ}$. Cross-multiply first, $(\overline{XZ}) \sin 53° = 11 \sin 88°$, then divide by $\sin 53°$: $\overline{XZ} = \dfrac{11 \sin 88°}{\sin 53°}$.

54. **K**   Plug in a value for the radius of the circle, $r_1 = 3$, then pick a value for p: $p = 2$. Since the radius of the first circle is p feet shorter than the radius of the second circle, $r_2 = 3 + 2 = 5$. The circumference of the first circle is $C_1 = 2\pi r = 2\pi(3) = 6\pi$, and the circumference of the second circle is $C_2 = 2\pi r = 2\pi(5) = 10\pi$. To find the difference in circumference, subtract C_1 from C_2: $10\pi - 6\pi = 4\pi$. Plug $p = 2$ into the answer choices to find the one that gives you the correct difference of 4π, which is (K).

55. **C**   Plug in some values for y to solve this problem. If $y = -4$, then $|y + 3| = |-4 + 3| = 1$. Plug $y = -4$ into the answer choices to see which ones match. Choice (A) can be eliminated because it gives you $-4 - 3 = -7$. When you plug in for (B), you get $-4 + 3 = -1$; eliminate this choice. Plugging in for (C), you find that $-(-4) - 3 = 1$; keep this choice. Choice (D) can be eliminated because $-(-4) + 3 = 7$. Eliminate (E) because 0 does not match the target. Therefore, the correct answer is (C).

56. **H** The first piece of information given is the countries that have fewer than 20 cities. Since these cities do not have 20, 21, or 22 cities, subtract them from the total: $18 - 7 = 11$. The next piece of information, the countries that have more than 21 cities, doesn't affect the total because some of those will have 22 cities. The third piece of information, countries that have more than 22 cities, does need to be subtracted from the new total, $11 - 2 = 9$, which gives the number of countries with 20, 21, or 22 cities.

57. **C** Plug the information given into the identity given in the note: $\left(-\dfrac{3}{4}\right)^2 = \dfrac{1 - \cos 2x}{2}$. Apply the exponent to get $\dfrac{9}{16} = \dfrac{1 - \cos 2x}{2}$, then multiply both sides by 2 to get $\dfrac{9}{8} = 1 - \cos 2x$. Subtract 1 from both sides, $\dfrac{9}{8} - 1 = \dfrac{1}{8} = -\cos 2x$, then divide both sides by -1 to get $-\dfrac{1}{8} = \cos 2x$.

58. **H** The point $(-2, 8)$ gives the x and y values for the functions given, so that $8 - f(g(-2))$. Substitute x^3 for $f(x)$ to get $f(g(-2)) = [g(-2)]^3 = 8$. Solve for $g(-2)$ by taking the cube root of both sides: $g(-2) = 2$. Then substitute $\dfrac{x}{2} - k$ for $g(x)$ and -2 for x to get $g(-2) = \dfrac{-2}{2} - k = 2$, or $-1 - k = 2$. Add 1 to both sides, $-k = 3$, then divide both sides by -1 to get $k = -3$. Choice (K) solves for k using only $g(x)$.

59. **D** Disjoint regions are non-overlapping regions. 7 vertical lines and 7 horizontal lines overlapping each other create a grid with a 6×6 section of enclosed rectangles, which each have a finite, nonzero area. There are also 2- or 3-sided areas around the outside that are open on 1 or 2 sides, which would have an infinite area. So the number of disjoint regions is $6 \times 6 = 36$. Choice (E) incorrectly counts 7×7 disjoint regions, and (C) incorrectly counts 5×5 disjoint regions.

60. **G** Because any number raised to an even power will always be positive, in order for $x^3 y^4 z^6 < 0$ to be true, x^3 must be less than 0, which means that x must be less than 0. Since y and z can be either positive or negative, start by plugging in negative numbers for all three. Plug $x = -2$, $y = -3$, and $z = -4$, into the answer choices. Choice (F) is incorrect because $(-2)(-3) = 6$. Choice (H) is incorrect because $(-3)(-4) = 12$. Next try changing the y value to positive, so that $x = -2$, $y = 3$, and $z = -4$. Choice (J) is incorrect because $(-2)(3)(-4) = 24$. Then change the z value to positive also, so that $x = -2$, $y = 3$, and $z = 4$. Choice (K) is incorrect because $(-2)^2(3)^2(4)^3 = (4)(9)(64) = 2,304$. Only (G) is less than 0 with any combination of values.

NOTES

NOTES

NOTES

Are you an international student looking to study in the U.S.A.?

Visit us at
https://www.princetonreview.com/global